A Kayaker's Guide to
Lake George
the Saratoga Region &
Great Sacandaga Lake

Critical Praise for Russell Dunn's Guidebooks

A Kayaker's Guide to New York's Capital Region

"Russell Dunn has created a paddling guidebook like no other, a brilliant idea appropriately executed." **Fred LeBrun,** *Times Union* columnist

Adirondack Trails with Tales: History Hikes through the Adirondack Park, and the Lake George, Lake Champlain & Mohawk Valley Regions

(coauthored with Barbara Delaney)

"There are lots of Adirondack trail guides. And there are lots of Adirondack history books. But there aren't many books that do both equally well. Licensed guides Russell Dunn and Barbara Delaney have successfully achieved this merger with Adirondack Trails with Tales. **Neal Burdick,** *Adirondack Explorer*

Trails with Tales: History Hikes through the Capital Region, Saratoga, Berkshires, Catskills & Hudson Valley

(coauthored with Barbara Delaney)

"To find such a wide and eclectic variety between the covers of one book, and also within an easy drive of home, is a wonderful gift." **Karl Beard,** New York Projects Director of the Rivers, Trails & Conservation Assistance Program of the **National Park Service**

Adirondack Waterfall Guide

"Many of the falls are well known, but this is an especially good guide to cataracts that hikers might otherwise miss." *Adirondack Life*

"This book is indeed a joy to read." *Trailwalker*

Catskill Region Waterfall Guide

"A must-own tool." **Arthur Adams**

Hudson Valley Waterfall Guide

"Will very likely open eyes to a world of the outdoors that would have passed us by otherwise." **Fred LeBrun,** *Times Union*

Mohawk Region Waterfall Guide

"This is the latest in a series of waterfall guides written by Russell Dunn that I recommend to anyone interested in gems which are often overlooked by the public." **Fred Schroeder,** *The Long Path North News*

Berkshire Region Waterfall Guide

"It's a totable package that unveils some hard-to-find springs in the area. Illustrated with historic postcard photos and Dunn's anecdotes, the book is both practical and enjoyable." *Berkshire Living*

blackdomepress.com
1-800-513-9013

A Kayaker's Guide to
Lake George
the Saratoga Region &
Great Sacandaga Lake

Russell Dunn

BLACK·DOME

Published by Black Dome Press Corp.
649 Delaware Ave., Delmar, N.Y. 12054
blackdomepress.com
(518) 439-6512

First Edition Paperback 2012
Copyright © 2012 by C. Russell Dunn

ISBN-13: 978-1-883789-69-5
ISBN-10: 1-883789-69-9

Library of Congress Cataloging-in-Publication Data:

Dunn, Russell.

 A kayaker's guide to Lake George, the Saratoga region & Great Sacandaga lake / Russell Dunn.
    p. cm.
  Includes bibliographical references and index.
  ISBN 978-1-883789-69-5 (trade paper : alk. paper)
  1. Kayaking--New York (State)—George, Lake, Region (Lake)—Guidebooks. 2. Kayaking--New York (State)--Saratoga Region—Guidebooks. 3. Kayaking—New York (State)—Great Sacandaga Lake Region—Guidebooks. 4. George, Lake, Region (N.Y. : Lake)—Guidebooks. 5. Saratoga Region (N.Y.)—Guidebooks. 6. Great Sacandaga Lake Region (N.Y.)—Guidebooks. I. Title.

 GV776.N72G44 2012

 797.122′409747—dc23

                              2012010030

CAUTION: Outdoor recreational activities are by their very nature potentially hazardous and contain risk. See "Caution: Safety Tips" beginning on page xxi.

Front cover photograph: John Flynn of the Lake George Kayak Co. paddling on Lake George. Photograph by Danny Mongno of Werner Paddles.

Maps created using TOPO! software © National Geographic Maps. To learn more visit: http://www.natgeomaps.com.

Design: Ron Toelke Associates, www.toelkeassociates.com

Printed in the USA

10 9 8 7 6 5 4 3 2 1

Dedication

To seven wonderful Canavan grandchildren—
Matthew, Julian, Andrew, Shannon,
Olivia, Aidan, and Elizabeth

Contents

Foreword

The most prominent natural feature of the Capital Region of eastern New York is its rich array of waters. Included are great rivers, the myriad of tributaries that feed them, and the beautiful lakes that the glaciers left behind. The best way to explore and appreciate these waters, to my mind, is from the seat of a small human-powered boat. With *A Kayaker's Guide to Lake George, the Saratoga Region & Great Sacandaga Lake*, Russell Dunn opens wide the door to these watery wonders, giving us a great tool to help enrich our souls as we wet a paddle.

A couple of winters ago, I received as a gift one of Russell's earlier books, *Adirondack Trails with Tails*, which he coauthored with Barbara Delaney. I loved the idea of a trail guide with stories of the natural history and human history of the area woven in. The very next day, out of the blue, an email arrived from Russell, introducing himself and asking if I would be willing to review some manuscript chapters of his first paddler's guidebook, *A Kayaker's Guide to New York's Capital Region*.

As a voracious student of nature and of human history, Russell writes more than the standard "launch here, paddle here" sort of guidebook. Do you ever wonder about the paddlers who have dipped their blades into the same waters you are kayaking? He gives the reader some clues, telling for instance about the 1,300 Iroquois warriors in birch bark canoes that passed through Saratoga County via Fish Creek on their way to a confrontation with enemies along the St. Lawrence River.

As a long-time paddler, I often wonder what story lies behind the name of an island or the remains of an old building or dock along my favorite waterways. Each January 1, I put on lots of fleece and a dry suit, and go with the Adirondack Pirate Paddlers on their traditional New Year's paddle trip on Lake George. We usually set our course up the western shore from Lake George Village and circle the tiny Tea Island. As we round the island and float through the narrow passage that separates it from the lakeshore, I would wonder where the name of the island came from. In his new book Russell answers this and many other questions of the like. Now I know about the tea house that operated on the island starting around 1828, and about the legend of treasure buried there by a British general.

During my long career as an environmental educator and nature interpreter with the New York State Department of Environmental Conservation, I learned to give my audience a sense of the whole story, rather than just isolated facts. This is not to say that you should tell people all you know about a subject—that is often overwhelming. There is an art to telling the story, what to put in and what to leave out. Russell captures that art in these pages. His tales of the waters, their geologic origins and the human saga of what happened along their banks combine to make a rich tapestry for the paddler. He also gives you the references where you can learn more, if you like.

Over the past decade, there has been a tremendous upswing in the sales of kayaks and canoes. Even in a down economy, interest in paddle sports continues to grow. I believe that paddling has a huge positive influence on our world. Time spent on the water often leads people to an interest and concern for all things that make up our water environments. Russell Dunn is doing us a great service, making it easier to get out paddling and to see the stories behind the scenery, giving us reasons to care.

Alan Mapes
Delmar, New York
May 2011

Alan Mapes is retired from the New York State Department of Environmental Conservation, having served as Director of Five Rivers Environmental Education Center in Delmar and as Chief of the Bureau of Environmental Education. Currently he works part-time as a kayak guide and instructor with Atlantic Kayak Tours, usually at their Norrie Point Paddlesport Center in Staatsburg, New York.

Acknowledgments

I t is impossible to give enough credit to my editor and publisher, who make up an unbeatable duo. Steve Hoare's hard work often goes unnoticed and therefore unsung, but his deft editorial touch is on every page of this book. I thank Steve for making me look good. Debbie Allen, my former publisher, has been equally as involved in polishing this book to make it shine like gold. Without fail she always manages to come up with significant ways to improve both content and structure, ensuring that the book achieves the highest quality possible. Her continued push for excellence has been manifested by the awards Black Dome Press has received for its outstanding work.

I am eternally grateful to Ron and Barbara of Toelke Associates for providing their graphic arts expertise in making the book so irresistible that readers will automatically reach into their wallets to buy it.

My wife, Barbara Delaney, remains my faithful paddling partner (she has been on many of the paddles listed in this book) and tackles computer problems for me when they come up, as they always do. She has coauthored several hiking guidebooks with me, and probably would have written this book had I not beaten her to the punch while she was engrossed in writing her first work of literary fiction.

I am very pleased that Alan Mapes, environmentalist, retired Chief of the Bureau of Environmental Education (NYS DEC), and instructor and guide for Atlantic Kayak Tours at Norrie Point Paddlesport Center, has agreed to set the tone for this book by writing a highly informative and insightful foreword.

If errors are found in any of the chapters, it is not the fault of the reviewers who so generously gave of their time and expertise.

Special thanks go to Sharon Jones Witbeck who, in addition to reviewing several chapters including Kayaderosseras Creek, Lake Lonely, Saratoga Lake, and Fish Creek, acted as a "central clearinghouse," organizing other paddlers with their particular areas of expertise and familiarity to review additional chapters for content and accuracy.

I remain deeply indebted to: Andrew Alberti, manager, Lakes to Locks Passage, for reviewing the chapters on Halfway Creek, Rogers Island, Champlain Canal Lock #C-5, and Fort Edward Public Dock; Deborah Dennis for reviewing the chapter on Cossayuna Lake; Joe Dinapoli, president of the Bolton Landing Chamber of Commerce, for helpful information provided on Bolton Landing; John Duncan, owner/operator of the Sacandaga Outdoor Center, for reviewing the chapter on the Sacandaga River; Adam Dunn, whitewater tuber, for reviewing the chapter on the Sacandaga River; John Flynn, manager of the Lake George Kayak Company, for reviewing the chapters on Huddle Beach, Green Island, and Northwest Bay; Bruce Goodale, president of the Saratoga Lake Association, for reviewing the chapter on Saratoga Lake and for the many suggestions he made; Wendy Hord for reviewing the chapter on Cossayuna Lake; Joy C. Houle, executive director at the Brookside Museum/Saratoga County Historical Society, for reviewing the chapters on Round Lake, Ballston Lake, and Saratoga Lake; Pete and Sara Juliano, who graciously introduced me and my wife to the Thurman Station/Thousand Acres Ranch Resort section of the Hudson River; Michael Kalin for reviewing chapters on Lake Avenue Park, Hague Town Beach, Champlain Canal Lock C-4, and Schuylerville Boat Launch; Scott Keller, Trails and Special Projects Director, Hudson River Valley Greenway, for reviewing the entire manuscript, making valuable comments, and suggesting corrections and additions; Sharon Leighton, director of community relations, New York State Canal Corporation, for reviewing the introductory chapter to the Champlain Canal section; Aaron Miller, proprietor of Tinney's Tavern, for reviewing the chapter on Lake Desolation; Patty Pensel, marina manager, Boats By George, for suggestions made regarding the Lake George section; Howard Raymond, president of the board of trustees for the Feeder Canal Alliance, for reviewing the chapters on the Glens Falls Feeder Canal; Don Seauvageau for reviewing the chapters on Saratoga Lake and Fish Creek; Larry Seney, chief, Lock C-7, for consultation on accessing the Hudson River and the Batten Kill; John Sherman, mayor, Village of Stillwater, for reviewing the chapters related to the Stillwater area; Curtis Truax for providing input on the Hearthstone Point Campground; Tom Wakely for reviewing the chapters on Kayaderosseras Creek and Fish Creek; Susan Weber, Kattskill Bay resident, for reviewing the chapters on Warner Bay, Dunham Bay, the introduction to the Lake George section, and for her valuable suggestions on streamlining the format of the book; Jeanne Williams, executive director, Feeder Canal Alliance, for reviewing the chapters on the Glens Falls Feeder Canal; and Tom Wright for reviewing the chapters on Kayaderosseras Creek and Lake Lonely.

One of the most difficult and least rewarding tasks in the final preparation of a book for publication is proofreading it. For this I am forever indebted to Barbara Delaney, Richard Delaney, Scott Keller, Alan Mapes, and Natalie Mortensen for the time they gave to improve the quality of the text.

I am pleased to have on the cover Danny Mongno's photograph of a kayaker on Lake George framed by dusky mountains in the background.

Thanks also go to: Faith Bouchard for information regarding the Big Boom; Judy Dean, owner of the Schuyler Yacht Basin, who provided historical information on Schuyler Island and Schuylerville; Jaime Deluca, GISP, GIS Manager, New York State Canal Corporation, and John M. Dimura, trails director, New York State Canal Corporation, for materials provided on New York State's system of canals; Lil Julian, Monday Paddlers organizer; Christine Molella, Lake George

Chamber of Commerce; Mona Seeger, Lake George Association; Tonya Thompson, town clerk of Ticonderoga, for help with information on Tiroga Beach; and Larry Woolbright, president of the Friends of Kayaderosseras.

All postcard images in the book are from the private collection of Russell Dunn or from Bob Drew, whose collection continues to grow beyond 200,000 cards and may soon collapse his house as it pushes out against the side walls.

Photographic images are by Russell Dunn and Barbara Delaney.

Preface

When the last ice age in the Northeast came to an end, it left behind thousands of lakes and ponds. Some, like Lake George and Lake Champlain, are of significant size. In places without lakes and ponds, streams were dammed by early settlers and industrialists, and artificial lakes and ponds were created. The reshaping of the landscape by mankind has continued to the present day. Twenty-nine-mile-long Great Sacandaga Lake was created in 1930 when a portion of the Sacandaga River was dammed. Today, through the foresightedness of many conservationists, a high percentage of these lakes and ponds, both natural and man-made, are publicly accessible—particularly to nonmotorized watercraft—which means that conditions for kayaking and canoeing in the Lake George–Saratoga–Sacandaga region couldn't be better.

How does one distinguish between a lake and a pond? Generally speaking, lakes are larger than ponds, but some ponds are quite large and some lakes are quite small. The answer lies not in size, but in biology. Lakes have an aphotic zone, meaning that they are deep enough that sunlight is unable to penetrate all the way to the bottom to stimulate plant growth. Ponds are photic, meaning that they are able to sustain plant life across their bottoms.

There are also a number of impressive secondary rivers—tributaries of either the Hudson or Mohawk rivers—that can be paddled for appreciable distances. These streams provide further opportunities for exploring the region by kayak or canoe.

The first volume in my series of paddling guidebooks, A Kayaker's Guide to New York's Capital Region (Black Dome Press, 2010), explored the Hudson River from Hudson and Catskill to Mechanicville. This second volume picks up where that book left off and continues the exploration of the Hudson north from Stillwater to Thurman Station. This is an entirely different river from the one below the Federal Dam at Troy and is characterized by a succession of large dams that transforms sections of the river into mini-lakes. In addition, the Hudson River from Stillwater to Fort Edward is a section of the Champlain Canal.

The Lake George/Saratoga Region is defined by the numerous mountain ranges that surround it. To the north are the Adirondacks (New York State's highest peaks); to the south are the Catskills (New York State's second-highest peaks); to the southeast can be found the Rensselaer Plateau and, farther east yet, the Taconics; to the southwest are the Helderbergs; and to the west are numerous hills that rise up on each side of the Mohawk River, the northern slope of which constitutes the foothills of the southern Adirondacks. During the winter these high elevations collect snow and then release it as snowmelt during the warming days of spring and early summer. These naturally timed discharges are what keep the waterways animated until summer's desiccation sets in.

Although Lake George and Great Sacandaga Lake can become very rough in windy conditions, and boat traffic is a concern, few of the outings described in this book require more than basic paddling skills. Typically the excursions take place on the flat water of lakes and ponds or, as in the case of the upper Hudson River and a number of secondary rivers, on waters that are fast-moving in early spring but change to moderate-to-slow-moving currents in the summer, allowing paddlers to choose the conditions that best match their abilities. All of the Hudson River paddles described herein take place upriver from the Federal Dam in Troy, so none are affected by the tides that are such a major factor in paddling the river below the dam.

This is not a guidebook for hardcore kayakers whose concept of adventure is to paddle twenty miles through formidable terrain, traverse across a series of lakes interspersed by mile-long portages, or plummet down Class IV and V waters (see "Categories of River Difficulty"). The most challenging paddle in this book is the 3.5-mile-long journey down the Sacandaga River at Hadley—a Class III paddle. This should not pose a problem for an intermediate-level paddler; in fact, many of the commercial water sports businesses encourage tourists to descend this section of the river in rafts, kayaks, and inner tubes.

Paddles involving long portages have been excluded. The goal is to get readers onto the water as quickly as possible, not to lead them across endless terrain.

One should always be prepared, however, to make unexpected portages when paddling on tributary streams. A creek can be clear of blowdown and debris one year, only to become blocked the next year by a fallen tree or beaver-created dam. Always be ready for the unexpected and be willing to turn around and go back if the way ahead becomes too difficult.

When traveling on streams noted for good fishing—and especially when launching or taking out at a fishing access site—be considerate of other users of the river and only paddle between the hours of 9:30 AM to 5:30 PM, when anglers are least likely to be out fishing. Keep an eye out for fishing lines in the water when passing anglers so you don't become entangled.

Many of the paddles described take place in areas where history abounds. For this reason most of the chapters contain fairly extensive material on history—material that can be expanded upon if you wish to consult the sources listed in the notes and bibliography to further enrich your experience.

No two paddles are alike. As a regional kayaker's guide this book is intended to help the user find numerous access points along the lake shorelines and riverbanks, all within the context of the multilayered history that the region contains. The adventure begins when you push out onto the water.

While the theme of urban kayaking was presented in *A Kayaker's Guide to New York's Capital Region*, this book takes us on paddles that are more suburban and rural, yet still close enough to the region's population centers to be reached easily by anyone with a car and a desire to explore the great outdoors. Despite the Lake George and Saratoga region being fairly heavily populated with numerous villages and sprawling suburbs, and crisscrossed by an endless parade of highways, the sights and sounds of civilization often melt into the background or vanish completely once you set out on a stream or lake and begin to paddle. This is the beauty of exploring the area by water, returning you to a different era when streams and lakes were the principal highways.

The Lake George–Saratoga region contains more lakes and ponds than may at first be apparent. Unlike in the North Country, with its thousands of natural lakes and ponds, many of these bodies of water are artificially created. In nearly all instances these impoundments were built to provide hydropower for numerous downstream industries or, as in the case of Great Sacandaga Lake, built for flood control. Some of the natural ponds and lakes also were dammed in order to increase their height and size to satisfy power-hungry industries downstream.

Today very little of this past industry is evident. Virtually all of the mills and factories are gone, essentially reduced to rubble by the actions of wind, rain, snow, ice, and the erosive effects of vegetation. In modern times, camps and primary residences have taken over along streams where industries once thrived.

Why Kayak?

Within the last decade interest in kayaking has taken a quantum leap forward and shows no signs of slowing down. No longer is it unusual to see a passing car with one or two kayaks mounted on its roof racks, or to walk along the bank of a river or lake and watch a myriad of colorful kayaks gliding along gracefully through the waters. Suddenly, kayaks seem to be everywhere.

What happened?

Kayaks used to be clunky affairs, made out of fiberglass and generally fancied by white-water enthusiasts. Back then kayaks were more thrill-sports-oriented and much less family friendly. Today, kayaks are sleek and elegant. Many have storage compartments that allow essentials to be stowed away inside, or elastic cords across the upper surface where extra paddles and miscellaneous gear can be secured and easily accessed. The newer models also tend to be slightly lighter, thereby increasing their attractiveness and accessibility to a wider range of the public. Some of the newer kayaks have rudders that can be lowered or raised to provide greater tracking and control. Some kayaks even allow you to rig a sail to take advantage of the wind, or to increase your speed by pedaling to drive a set of underwater flippers. These are truly hybrid kayaks—part sailboat or part bicycle. All of these design factors have led to kayaks becoming more attractive to a greater number of people.

There have also been societal changes. Today many people are more conscious of the benefits of physical exercise and are seeking new and varied experiences in the outdoors. They are looking for adventure and challenge and for opportunities to stretch themselves further both physically and mentally. Kayaking provides just such challenges and opportunities and does so in abundance.

Kayaking is a way of returning to bygone days when life was simpler and quieter, to a time before boom boxes and the internal combustion engine, to an age when rivers and streams were used as highways by Native Americans and frontiersmen to guide them through forests that were often lacking in distinguishable landmarks and sometimes were impenetrable. Those who traveled by land in the early days had to contend with the ever-present dangers of becoming lost in dense woods or of falling victim to a human adversary or a large predator waiting behind a tree. In contrast, waterways provided fixed and clearly defined points of reference that made navigating the wilderness easier. Wide rivers kept travelers at a safer distance from attack. Water travel also allowed the transporting of cargo and possessions with ease, sparing backbreaking overland carries.

Today the woods do not pose the same degree of hardship and danger that they once did, but the waterways have changed little. For the most part they are just as inviting today as they were four hundred years ago. Waterways still hold the promise of taking you on adventures into the unknown.

When you push off in your kayak or canoe, imagine that you are an eighteenth-century explorer heading out onto uncharted waters, seeking adventure. You can let go of all traces of civilization as you leave the shoreline behind you. This is the magic and wonder of kayaking. There are thousands of nooks and crannies, bays and coves, inlets and outlets, tributaries and outlet streams waiting to be explored. All that's needed is to drive up to a launch site and push off.

Kayaks have a number of practical features that many find irresistible. They displace little water compared to motorized vessels, thereby allowing you to paddle into shallow areas that would be inaccessible by foot or by motorized crafts. What's more, it is in these shallow areas where the flora and fauna often prove to be the most interesting (and the least encroached upon).

Then there's the adrenalin rush. Few things are more thrilling than paddling through waters on a fine day in natural surroundings with the wind in your face and the water rushing under your kayak—all the while safely ensconced in your watercraft. It is at times like these when you realize just how good life is.

Another plus for kayaking is that the sport doesn't require additional expenses once such upfront costs as the purchase of a kayak, paddle, gear, and carrying rack have been incurred. Once these initial costs have been reckoned with, you are basically set. This is not true for powerboat enthusiasts, who not only have the initial start-up expenses, but the ongoing costs of maintaining, storing, and fueling their vessels.

Kayaking also provides an excellent way to exercise your upper body, which is great news to anyone who bikes, swims, jogs, or skis and is interested in new ways of cross-training.

The reasons for kayaking are numerous, but why bother to list any more? When you get right down to it, one reason stands out head and shoulders above the rest—it's simply a lot of fun.

Layout of Each Chapter

Launch Sites: Most of the launch sites demand little if any effort to reach and, once there, only the slightest nudge to set a watercraft afloat. In the few instances where these generalities don't apply, a canoe/kayak carrier can prove to be very helpful. At a few locations, access may prove challenging because of a steep riverbank or large rocks along the shoreline.

Most launch sites may be accessed from sunrise to sunset. Exceptions are noted. The majority of the access sites are free. Parking fees are charged at some New York State Park launches, usually on a seasonal basis, but not at DEC launch sites, which are fishing access points. The DEC launch sites are financed in part by Wallop-Breaux Funds, an excise tax on fishing gear. Fees are charged at most private marinas.

Some of the chapters offer additional launch sites so that paddlers have a variety of possibilities from which to choose.

Delorme: Delorme's *New York State Atlas & Gazetteer: Fifth Edition* is an invaluable tool for plotting out driving routes, particularly if you are going from one launch site to the next. The coordinates listed in each chapter start with the page number, followed by the row, and end with the column. Thus, "p. 10, C6" tells you to turn to page 10, look across row C (horizontal axis), and then down column 6 (vertical axis) to find the intersection of these coordinates.

GPS Coordinates: The coordinates given are *reasonably* accurate, many having been generated by computer software rather than an on-site read (these are indicated as "approximate"). There may be minor discrepancies as a result.

Destinations and Mileages: This section enumerates the areas to which you will be paddling. Unless otherwise indicated, all paddling mileages are one-way.

Comments: Different waters contain different hazards, and these are addressed in the "Comments" section of each paddle, in addition to other pertinent information that may apply. This supports but in no way supplants the "Caution: Safety Tips" section or the introductions to the five chapters in this book, with which readers are strongly advised to thoroughly acquaint themselves before setting out.

Directions: Knowing where to go and how to get there is the most crucial element of any guidebook. If you can't get to the water, then the value of the rest of the book becomes academic. For this reason every effort has been made to ensure that the directions are clear and free of ambiguity. Highway mileages have been derived from odometer readings and numbers generated by computer topographic software, and should be accurate to within 0.1 mile.

The Paddles: The "bare bones" of the paddle are described here, the focus being on mileages and points of interest.

In the section on the upper Hudson River, various paddles can be extended by using the NYS Barge Canal system of locks to go from one section of the river to the next.

The Hike: Several chapters contain a short, supplemental hike or walk.

Maps: The maps accompanying the paddles provide overviews of the routes taken; they are not intended for navigational purposes. For navigation, consult nautical charts where applicable.

Discovery awaits at every turn of the river. Photograph 2010.

CAUTION

Outdoor recreational activities are by their very nature potentially hazardous and contain risk. All participants in such activities must assume responsibility for their own actions and safety. No book can be a substitute for good judgment. The outdoors is forever changing. The author and the publisher cannot be held responsible for inaccuracies, errors, or omissions, or for any changes in the details of this publication, or for the consequences of any reliance on the information contained herein, or for the safety of people in the outdoors.

This book is intended for experienced paddlers who are comfortable being on the water, well versed in self-rescue procedures, and can handle sudden changes in weather, strong currents, and heavy boat traffic.

Wind, current, and waves on lakes and rivers can change abruptly, often with little warning and in spite of the weather forecast. Always check the forecast and weather before setting out. Generally wind and waves are quietest in the early morning and early evening. Do not leave shore if storms and/or high winds are predicted or if the weather forecast is at all questionable.

Remain close to the shoreline except when paddling to an island or crossing to the opposite shore. When you move away from the shoreline, look both ways to make sure no powerboats are approaching; then cross as quickly as possible. Be prepared for increased wind when you move away from the shoreline. Pay particular attention to the shoreline's appearance as you leave so that you can return to the same starting point without hesitation. Turn back quickly if the weather begins to deteriorate.

Many of the waterways experience heavy boat traffic. Operators of small watercraft like kayaks and canoes must be ever-vigilant on these waters. Don't assume boats can see you. Wear bright colors. If you must cross a boat channel, cross in a group and keep the group together. If you see an oncoming boat in the distance, wait for it to pass. Make sure that you do not cross its path. Some large boats move surprisingly fast, and distance can be hard to judge.

Users of this guidebook should acquaint themselves with all of the advice and cautions that follow:

Before You Take the Plunge

Take a water safety course and learn self-rescue techniques. Study navigation charts for the section of water you plan to paddle, familiarizing yourself with shipping lanes (if applicable) and underwater hazards. The maps in this book provide overviews of the routes taken; they are not intended for navigational purposes.

Choosing the Right Craft for Paddling

There is a dizzying array of types of canoes and kayaks from which to choose. A craft that is perfect for white-water kayaking may not be suited for paddling on a quiet pond or riding in the wake of a supertanker on a tidal river.

Recreational kayaks are generally 9.5–14 feet in length. They are noticeably wider, easier to handle, and less expensive than touring kayaks, and they are the best choice for paddlers who want to get out onto smaller lakes or follow along the protected shorelines of larger lakes.

Touring kayaks are longer than recreational kayaks and are generally 14–16 feet in length (sea kayaks can be even longer). Touring kayaks are narrower than recreational kayaks and track better, which pays dividends when paddling great distances or when heading into heavy winds or waves.

Kayaks are made out of different materials, which can affect weight, resistance, and overall durability. One can choose from polyethylene (PE), thermoplastics, and composites (combinations of fiberglass, Kevlar, and graphite).

Your local canoe/kayak dealer can help you select a craft that will best meet your particular needs. See Appendix C for dealers in the Lake George/Saratoga area and the greater Capital Region.

Wind and Waves

Turn back and return on another day if the current looks too strong or the water too choppy. This applies especially following episodes of prolonged, intensive rainfall, or in the early spring when the rivers' currents, fed by winter's snowmelt, are unusually strong. Fast-moving currents increase the potential for trouble. Strainers (downed trees with branches raking the water) can become more than obstacles on fast-moving rivers if the current pushes you against one. Your canoe or kayak could capsize, exposing you to the possibility of getting caught underwater and pinned. Remember that water in motion can exert tremendous force—thousands of pounds of pressure per square inch—that can easily snap a canoe or kayak in half. Violently moving waters can even roll large boulders along a riverbed.

Always be mindful of wind when you are out on the water. Long, fingerlike lakes and wide rivers unbroken by islands can produce significant waves, even on days with mild to moderate winds. Wind speed over water can be as much as 50 percent greater than it is over land.[1]

Hypothermia

Most paddlers should restrict their excursions to the late spring, summer, and early fall. True, there is more boat traffic in the summer, but should you capsize—and sooner or later you will—warm-weather water is infinitely more comfortable and less exacting on the body than early spring or late fall water.

If you unexpectedly become immersed and feel chilled, abort the rest of your planned adventure and return to your car at once. Hypothermia (a lowering of one's core body temperature) can kill, and the water and air temperatures don't have to be below 32 degrees Fahrenheit for hypothermia to occur. Shivering occurs when the body's core temperature begins to drop below 97°. By 93° you have lost much of your manual dexterity and mental capacity. By 86° you are most likely unconscious, and by 80°, lifeless.[3]

Cold water chills the body four times faster than air at comparable temperatures. Agitated water (which is encountered in white-water kayaking) cools the body even faster.

The Effects of Hypothermia in Cold Water

Water Temperature (F)	Exhaustion or Unconsciousness	Expected time of survival
32.5	Under 15 min.	Under 15–45 min.
32.5–40	15–30 min	30–90 min.
40–50	30–60 min.	1–3 hrs.
50–60	1–2 hrs.	1–6 hrs.
60–70	2–7 hrs.	2–40 hrs.
70–80	2–12 hrs.	3 hrs–indefinite
Lake Champlain Paddlers' Trail, 2008 Guidebook & Stewardship Manual, 10th edition (Lake Champlain Committee), p.16.		

Before hypothermia reaches a life-threatening stage, however, your body has begun to fail in other ways. Sudden cold-water immersion can induce a powerful gasping reflex which, if you are momentarily thrown underwater, can cause you to inhale a lungful of water, increasing the risk of immediate drowning.

Elevated heart rate and elevated blood pressure induced by abrupt and severe cold to the head and chest can cause cardiac arrest. Hyperventilation (uncontrolled rapid breathing), if unchecked, can result in unconsciousness. All of these can lead to death long before the final stages of hypothermia have set in.

But worse yet is the immediate effect of cold-water immersion on your extremities. Within minutes your arms, legs, and hands can become useless, unable to keep you afloat or even to help you pull yourself up on an overturned kayak. For this reason wearing a flotation device (PFD) is imperative even if you are a world-class swimmer.

Kayakers need to be mindful of these risks and take precautions when the water is cold—even when the air temperature is warm or hot. Dress for immersion. Wearing a neoprene wetsuit and spray skirt are prudent choices. Some paddlers even wear drysuits if conditions are severe enough to warrant it.

For more information regarding hypothermia, visit www.hypothermia.org.

Other Boats
Always be mindful of powerboats when you are out on the water. Don't assume that boats can see you. Wear bright colors. You will not be the winner if you and a fast-moving boat cross paths. Cross in a group and keep the group together. If you see a boat in the distance, let it pass before you set out. Some large boats

move surprisingly fast, and distance can be hard to judge. When it is necessary to cross shipping lanes to reach your objective, cross as quickly as possible and continually check for traffic in both directions. Bear in mind that a canoe or kayak is not considered a vessel on New York State waters that are not regulated by the Coast Guard, and therefore does not legally have the right of way on those waters.

Watch out for incoming waves that have the potential to flip your watercraft over; turn into heavy waves to meet them head-on. Waves are produced by winds and boats. The size of the wave is affected by the force produced by the wind or boat, the water depth, and the fetch (the uninterrupted distance over water that the wind has blown). The longer the fetch, the greater the power of the wave. Watch out for rebounding waves that come at you for a second time after bouncing off bluffs along the shoreline. Remember that boat traffic increases significantly during the summer season. You can't always rely on boaters to remember to slow down when they pass by a paddler. Don't stay too close to the shore when a large boat passes by. The ship's large hull displacement causes water to rush in quickly behind it, pulling water momentarily away from the shoreline and then slamming it back.

Boat Channels (Shipping Lanes)

Boats heading upriver on the Hudson River keep the red buoys to their right (starboard) and the green buoys to their left (port), and the reverse when going downriver. One way to remember this is, "red, right, returning from the sea." This information could prove helpful if you need to know on which side of a buoy a speeding boat heading toward you will pass. In most instances, it will be on the side farthest from the shoreline.

Now, Where Did I Put In?

When leaving the launch site, take a moment to look back at the shoreline to familiarize yourself with the surroundings as seen from the water. This will save you time and aggravation later, on your return trip, when an otherwise featureless shoreline could make finding your starting point difficult.

So Obvious We Shouldn't Need To Mention, But …

If you don't know how to swim, now is the time to learn, before you get into a canoe or kayak.

Do not consume alcohol before embarking or while on the water. Most water-based accidents involve alcohol, so be advised—alcohol and water, like oil and water, don't mix.

(Often) No Rest for the Weary

Catherine Frank and Margaret Holden had it right about the availability of restrooms and rest stops for kayakers when they wrote, "We found restrooms at launch sites, public beaches, marinas, and food purveyors. The remaining 99 percent of the [Lake Champlain] lakeshore does not have these conveniences." (*A Kayaker's Guide to Lake Champlain: Exploring the New York, Vermont & Quebec Shores*, Black Dome Press, 2009)

Paddlers should be aware before they put in at nearly all of the sites listed in this book that the probability is high that there will be no convenient places to stop and rest. This is particularly important to remember if you are paddling with children.

There are a number of things paddlers can do, however, to help make a longer paddle as comfortable as possible. First of all—it should go without saying—use a restroom before you start the trip. Paddling is not like hiking. There are no convenient bushes or trees to hide behind, and most of the shoreline is privately owned.

Keep food and beverage within reach so that you don't have to get out of the kayak to access it.

Most of the paddles described in this book are two-way treks, which means that your return trip nearly duplicates the outbound trek. If at any time you feel that you are becoming overextended, simply turn around and head back to the launch. Don't feel compelled to complete the entire outbound paddle before reversing direction and returning to the launch. Only you know your own limits.

If you need to rest for a short period of time, it is best to do so near the shoreline, ideally in a cove away from wind and boats.

To rest your upper body, simply put down your paddle and relax your arms. Stretch out your limbs or massage your arms and shoulders. One good way to avoid becoming too sore or stiff—if you've got plenty of room to maneuver and someone to be your eyes and ears—is to paddle backward for a while, which works a slightly different set of muscles. This is called reverse paddling.

To rest your lower body, lie back as far as you can and hold that position for a moment or two before returning to an upright position. Then lean forward as far as you can and hold that position for a moment. These exercises help de-stress your back, and the second exercise is particularly helpful for stretching your hamstrings.

Safety Practices

Always tell someone where you are going and when you expect to return—and what to do if you are not back by the designated time.

The "buddy system" applies to paddling as much as it does to swimming (which of course is always a possible, though unintended, outcome of paddling). Always paddle with a friend.

If you fall out of your watercraft in moving water, particularly white water, always point your feet downstream to absorb the impact should you collide with an obstacle. If you are in fast-moving water, don't try to stand up in the stream; should your foot become caught on an obstacle below, the force of the current could bend you over like a bow despite your struggles, possibly drowning you in only chest-deep waters.

Keep a safe distance from dams and waterfalls, whether above or below them. Treacherous hydraulics can wreak havoc on even experienced paddlers. If you are launching near a dam or waterfall, check the strength of the current before putting in. If the current is strong and a dam or waterfall is downstream, choose a different location from which to launch.

If caught in a fast-approaching thunderstorm, head promptly to shore. Then, if there is no shelter, sit on your PFD (personal flotation device) to help keep yourself insulated from a possible lightning strike.

Be on the lookout for deer ticks and be aware of the possibility of contracting Lyme disease, a threat that has grown more severe with each passing year. Always make it a point to visually inspect your body after every paddle to make sure no ticks are attached, especially if you have been near brush or pushed your way through areas of overhanging trees and weeds.

Avoid marshlands during duck-hunting season. Leave the area immediately if you hear gunfire.

What to Pack, What to Wear

Always—repeat, ALWAYS—wear a brightly colored personal flotation device (PFD) with reflective tape when you are on the water. Most paddlers wear a Coast Guard–approved Type 3 vest. Insist that anyone with you do the same. This applies even if you are an expert swimmer.

• Take along a whistle or signaling device in case you need assistance or need to alert an oncoming, inattentive motorboat. To maximize your readiness, attach the whistle to your personal flotation device, preferably on the zipper pull.

• Take a flashlight with you, just in case. If your trip lasts longer than you expected and dusk is falling, you'll be glad to have a spare light in your emergency pack—particularly if you need to signal large boats of your presence. Better yet, pack a waterproof headlamp, which will leave your hands free to paddle.

• Pack a waterproof dry bag with all the small items that may be needed during the trip. These include, but are not limited to: sunblock, SPF-rated lip balm, bug repellent, compass, sunglasses, gloves (in case blisters develop on your hands), car keys, money, first-aid kit, cell phone, waterproof matches, extra clothing layers to keep warm, a Swiss army knife or "Leatherman," and duct tape. While you're at it, also pack toilet paper, a trowel, and a plastic bag (just in case …). It is also advisable to stash a tow rope, and a bilge pump is a basic necessity (along with a sponge). A waterproof waist pouch is particularly handy for storing items you may want to access quickly, such as a camera or binoculars.

• Be sure to have an extra change of clothing in your car. You may return from the paddle soaking wet even if you don't fall in—it's a wet sport.

• For long paddles, wear paddling gloves to minimize blisters.

• Always take along three to four liters of water per person to ward off dehydration and hyperthermia. If the weather is hot, increase it to five to six liters per person. Also pack some food and snacks to maintain proper energy levels. Keep them stored in a waterproof container when you're not munching.

• Take along an extra paddle in case the one you're using becomes lost or broken. A paddle leash will help prevent you from losing the paddle in your hands.

• Wear a spray skirt, even if not attached to the kayak, in case the river suddenly gets rough and you need to keep water from entering the kayak. This is also good for sun protection for the legs.

• Be sure to apply liberal portions of suntan lotion, and wear sunglasses if you are paddling under a hot, glaring sun. Wear a wide-brimmed hat as well. Remember that water reflects light and heat, intensifying both.

• Always take along personal identification, including emergency contacts and relevant medical information should you become unconscious and require emergency treatment.

• Do not wear bulky clothing unless you are paddling in cold weather. Should you capsize, soaked-through bulky clothing could interfere with swimming.

• For more information concerning safety and safety equipment, visit the Web sites uscgboating.org or nysparks.com/boats.

Kayaks come in all sizes, shapes, and colors. Photograph 2010.

Your Responsibilities as a Paddler

1. Life is hard enough for birds and other wildlife without additional pressures being caused by thoughtless humans. Keep at a respectable distance, particularly during nesting season.

2. Maintain a considerate distance when paddling past private residences and properties. Never trespass on private property unless there is an emergency.

3. Be considerate of others on the water, whether anglers, boaters, swimmers, or fellow paddlers. Steer clear of duck blinds and familiarize yourself with hunting seasons.

4. Cart out whatever you take along with you on your trip. If you see a stray piece of litter lying about or in the water, pick it up and haul it out. Nature has been good to you; it doesn't hurt to reciprocate.

5. Be sure to properly clean your watercraft and gear each time after entering a different body of water to avoid inadvertently transporting invasive aquatic species. Invasive plants such as Eurasian water milfoil, curlyleaf pondweed, and water chestnuts, invasive organisms such as zebra mussels, and invasive fish such as alewife, have already infiltrated some bodies of water in the region and threaten to spread to others. All boaters, including paddlers, need to be diligent about cleaning off their vessels every time they leave one aquatic area and move on to the next. Some of the larval stages of these species are microscopic; wash the vessel even if you can't see anything.

Invasive species are nonindigenous. Because they are not part of the original ecosystem, they will continue to proliferate and drive out native plants and organisms until a sufficient number of predators and natural defenses evolve to counterbalance their expansion.

6. Know the "rules of the road." As "captain" of your kayak or canoe, you are under the same obligations as commercial tugboat and ship captains. Generally, paddlers do not have the right of way in shipping channels.

Categories of River Difficulty

Class I: Easy—*Most of the paddles in this book fall into this category.* Flat or moving water, generally with few or no obstructions. Although risk to paddlers is slight, that doesn't mean that strong currents won't be encountered at times, particularly during the early spring or following intense rain.

Class II: Novice—Moving water; occasional obstructions and medium-sized waves; obvious channels. Some maneuvering may be necessary at times. Minimal risk to paddlers.

Class III: Intermediate—Current much stronger; channels more intricately strung together; potential for encountering medium-sized holes and short drops—obstacles that should be avoided. Irregular waves, sometimes difficult to avoid, are capable of swamping a canoe or kayak if you are not careful. More maneuvering in general is needed. Paddlers are unlikely to be injured.

Class IV: Advanced—Significant hydraulics; heavy, unavoidable waves; large rocks; moderate drops; constricted passages; paddlers must be able to react quickly and decisively under pressure; may require "must moves" above dangerous hazards. Risk of injury to paddlers is moderate to high.

Class V: Expert—Difficult and hazardous conditions, e.g., large drops that may contain large unavoidable holes, waves, or steep, congested chutes; major crosscurrents; huge, obstructed, turbulent waves; aerated holes, pronounced rocks and boulders; precise maneuvering required. Risk of injury or death to paddlers is significant.

Class VI: Almost Impossible—Potentially lethal; experts only (and then only after much deliberation and soul-searching); huge waves, rocks, boulders, and hazardous drops; rescue may be impossible. The likelihood of death and/or serious injury is high.

It's off to adventure! Photograph 2010.

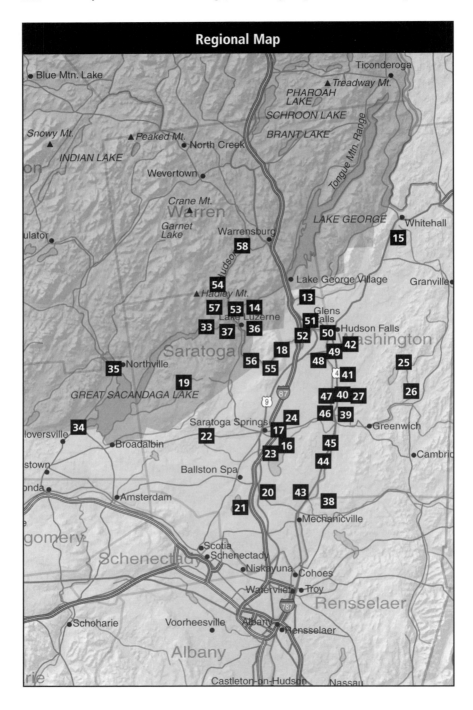

Regional Map

REGIONAL MAP KEY

13. Glen Lake

14. Fourth Lake Campgrounds

15. Halfway Creek

16. Saratoga Lake

17. Lake Lonely

18. Moreau Lake

19. Lake Desolation

20. Round Lake

21. Ballston Lake

22. Kayaderosseras Creek: Upper Section

23. Kayaderosseras Creek: Lower Section

24. Fish Creek: Saratoga Lake to Grangerville Dam

25. Cossayuna Lake

26. Carter's Pond State Wildlife Management Area

27. Champlain Canal Pond

33. Stewart Pond

34. Mayfield Lake

35. Northville Lake

36. Lake Luzerne

37. Sacandaga River: From Stewart Bridge Dam to Hudson River

38. Champlain Canal Lock C-4

39. Clarks Mills Lower Dam, Access #1

40. Champlain Canal above Lock C-6

41. Moses Kill

42. Fort Edward Public Dock

43. Stillwater Bridge

44. River Road Access

45. Fishing Access Site #1

46. Schuylerville Boat Launch

47. Champlain Canal Lock C-5, Upriver

48. Former West Shore Marina

49. Rogers Island

50. Feeder Canal from Richardson Street Access

51. Murray Street Access

52. Hudson River Park

53. Upper Hudson River Boat Launch

54. Hudson River Recreation Area

55. Sherman Island Boat Launch

56. Spier Falls Boat Launch

57. Hadley Canoe Take-out

58. Warren County Canoe Access

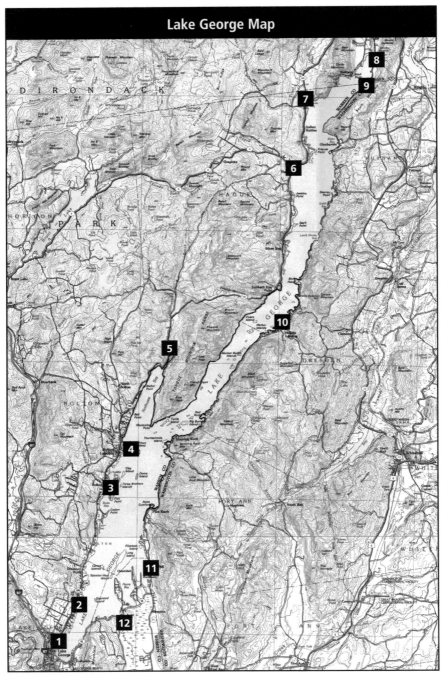

Lake George Map

LAKE GEORGE MAP KEY

1. Lake Avenue Park

2. Hearthstone Point Campgrounds

3. Huddle Beach

4. Green Island

5. Northwest Bay

6. Hague Town Beach

7. Rogers Rock Campground

8. Mossy Point

9. Black Point Public Beach

10. Washington County Beach

11. Warner Bay

12. Dunham Bay

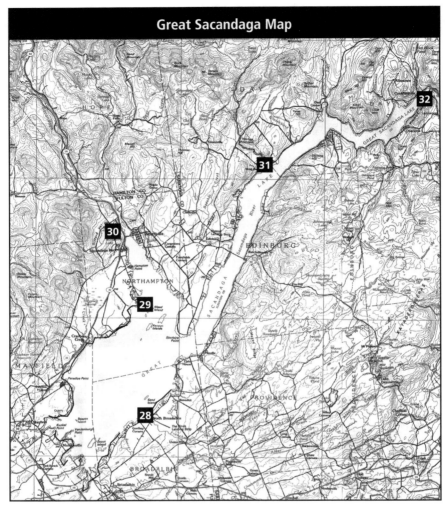

TOPO! © 2010 National Geographic.

GREAT SACANDAGA MAP KEY

28. DEC North Broadalbin State Boat Launch

29. DEC Northampton Beach Campground

30. DEC Northville State Boat Launch

31. DEC Saratoga County State Boat Launch

32. Conklingville Dam

Lake George Region

Advisory

Do not venture away from the shoreline and out into open water on Lake George unless you are at least an intermediate level paddler, capable of handling a variety of water and weather conditions and able to self-rescue.

Extra care must be taken when paddling on Lake George. This is a very large lake and one that quickly fills with powerboats during the summer months, especially on weekends and holidays. Large sailboats also come out in force and are potentially even more of a hazard to small craft because of a sailboat's inability to maneuver out of the way as quickly as a powerboat.

Operators of small watercraft like kayaks and canoes must be ever-vigilant. Don't assume boats can see you. Wear bright colors. Know where the boat channels are and avoid those waters. If you must cross open water, cross in a group and keep the group together. If you see a boat in the distance, let it pass before you set out. Some large boats move surprisingly fast, and distance can be hard to judge. Take into account current and wind when planning your trajectory across open water. Be prepared for an increase in boat traffic as you pass by marinas.

Unlike any of the other lakes described in this book, Lake George also has commercial traffic in addition to the many smaller private boats zooming about. A number of large tour boats regularly leave the south end of the lake and proceed north for excursions of varying lengths. Because these boats often follow close to the shoreline to give customers a view of historic or ostentatious homes, even paddlers close to the shore must remain vigilant when one of these large vessels is approaching.

Because Lake George is such a large lake, waves, wakes, and wind are ever-present forces to reckon with. Strong winds create large, capsizing waves. Paddlers must always stay alert for sudden changes in weather and surface conditions. Learning to expect the unexpected is a must if you want to paddle Lake George.

Stay close to the shoreline unless island-hopping is on your itinerary. When planning to cross open water, choose a calm day and watch the weather. Current and wind can be severe. The wind tends to be quietest in the early morning and early evening. Always check the forecast and weather before setting out. Do not leave shore if storms and/or high winds are predicted or if the weather forecast is at all questionable. Be aware that the weather can change abruptly, often with little warning and in spite of the forecast. Wind and current increase as you move away from the shoreline.

Wind, waves, and wakes are factors on the smaller lakes in this section as well, such as Glen Lake and Fourth Lake, and extra care must always be exercised if paddling away from shore on open water.

Memorize the shoreline as you leave so that you can return to the same starting point.

Introduction: Lake George, Queen of American Lakes

Lake George is 32 miles long on a northeasterly to southwesterly axis, up to 3 miles across (with an average width of 1.3 miles), and nearly 200 feet at its deepest. It is the largest body of water contained entirely within the Adirondack Park. The lake is constantly recharged by multiple springs (it is estimated that nearly 20 percent of Lake George's water may come from this source) and tributaries as its waters slowly drain north through the LaChute River into Lake Champlain—which is 226 feet lower than Lake George—and eventually flow into the St. Lawrence Seaway. Lake George's watershed (the area it drains), however, is only 233 square miles which, as watersheds go, is of meager size and one of the reasons why the lake's waters are so pure. The streams coming in are simply not of sufficient length and in great enough numbers to introduce much sediment to muddy up the waters. In fact, only eight streams of any significant size enter the lake.

The other major reason for the lake's unusual clarity is a plant called nitella (basswood), whose growth on the bottom of the lake helps keep the waters clear.[1]

Lake George is part of a natural corridor of rivers and lakes including the Hudson River, Lake Champlain, and the Richelieu River, that extends north and south between New York and Canada. It was the primary transportation route between New York City and Canada during colonial times and was much faster, even with the portages, than traveling overland. It served as backdrop to numerous skirmishes between early Native American tribes and as a maritime battleground between the French and British during the French and Indian War, and the British and Americans during the Revolutionary War.

Native American tribes consisted of the Huron and Algonquin to the north and the Mohawk to the south. Split Rock Mountain along the west side of Lake Champlain was the boundary that separated the two groups territorially. Opposing war parties would occasionally meet and fight on or near the waters of Lake Champlain and Lake George.

Both England and France had designs on this New World and approached Lake George from different directions—the English from the south and the French from the north via what is now Canada. The inevitable result was that the region became a heated battlefield between these two rival powers. Warfare on Lake Champlain and Lake George intensified during the eighteenth century after the French built Fort St. Frederic at Crown Point and Fort Carillon (Fort Ticonderoga) at Ticonderoga. Initially the conflict between France and England centered on Lake Champlain, but the war spilled over to Lake George in 1755 when three separate battles were fought in one long, bloody day. The mêlée soon became known collectively as the Battle of Lake George.

Later in the year Fort William Henry was erected by Major-General William Johnson, who had earlier been wounded in the leg at the Battle of Lake George.

Fort William Henry became a prized trophy for both sides and was attacked in 1757 by General Montcalm of France, who overwhelmed it with artillery fire. British Colonel George Munro, the commander of the fort during the siege, was forced to surrender. Although Munro was promised safe passage by Montcalm, the French-allied Indians had their own grievances against the English and massacred many of them—men, women, children—once the soldiers and their families had left the protection of the fort.

Montcalm then burned down the fort, immolating the dead and covering the remains with sand. However, Fort William Henry and the epic battle fought there were not forgotten and were later immortalized in James Fenimore Cooper's *The Last of the Mohicans*. A replica of Fort William Henry was constructed during the twentieth century and remains a favorite tourist attraction at the south end of Lake George.

Following the French and Indian War a short period of peace reigned, only to be shattered again in 1777. This time it was the early years of the Revolutionary War and America's fight to gain independence from England. As war efforts mounted, Lake George was seen by the British as a strategic link in their plan to divide and conquer the colonies. In October of 1777, however, General John Burgoyne and his army of Redcoats were defeated at the Battle of Saratoga south of Lake George while advancing on Albany. This victory became a turning point in the American Revolution and one that served to convince France that it should offer its help to the fledgling patriots against a common enemy. Even with France's help, however, many subsequent battles had to be fought before the final peace treaty was signed in Paris between England and America in 1783.

The Narrows, dominated by Black Mountain, the highest point along the perimeter of Lake George. Postcard ca. 1940.

Burgess Island. Postcard ca. 1910.

During all of this, Lake George was never far from the action.

Fast-forward to the beginning of the nineteenth century. New York State had begun encouraging the migration of populations northward in the state. It was hoped in particular that the lands around Lake George could be developed. Although settlers responded by moving into the area, the terrain proved too rugged for farming.

The construction in 1882 of the Lake George branch of the Delaware & Hudson Railroad, however, changed the picture forever. Within virtually no time at all Lake George turned into a mecca for tourism, with numerous hotels sprouting up along different parts of the lake. The picture changed even further with the introduction of the automobile. Seizing upon the newfound freedom and independence created by the "horseless carriage," the masses began leaving the cities to vacation or to acquire secondary homes in the country. The result was that thousands of homes and camps were built around the lake during the twentieth century.

Despite all of the changes wrought upon it over the last four centuries, however, Lake George has managed to retain much of its original beauty. Many travelers, in fact, have likened the lake's beauty to that of Lake Tahoe in Nevada and Lake Como in Italy.

Native Americans called Lake George *An-di-a-ta-roc-te*—translated variously as the "lake that shuts itself in"[2] or "where the mountains touch the water." This was not a name that was fancied by Europeans, however. In 1646 Father Isaac Jogues, the first European to visit the lake, named it Lac du St. Sacrement, which translates from the French as "Lake of the Blessed Sacrament." In 1755 Sir William Johnson, the Mohawk Valley's most distinguished historical figure, named it Lake George in honor of King George II, then-ruler of England. James Fenimore Cooper called the lake "Horicon" (an early Native American word) in *The Last of the Mohicans* and pushed for its adoption as the lake's official name. Cooper's rationale was that Lac du St. Sacrement was too complicated, *An-di-a-ta-roc-te* too unpronounceable, and Lake George too dull and ordinary. Cooper's suggested name, however, never stuck.

The lake is blessed with a number of notable geographic features. At the southwest end is 2,030-foot-high Prospect Mountain, one of two mountains in the Adirondacks with a commercial highway leading to its summit. Rogers Rock, near the northwest end of the lake, displays a steeply inclined slide and holds fascinating legend and lore from the military days of the eighteenth century. Tongue Mountain overlooks an area of islands called the Narrows and offers one of the grandest views of the lake. And 2,646-foot-high Black Mountain, on the east side, is the highest point on the mountainous bowl that encircles the lake.

For paddlers, probably the most striking feature about Lake George is its islands, particularly at The Narrows, where the lake is not only compressed but broken up into a constellation of islands. It was through The Narrows that Cooper's fictitious characters Hawkeye, Chingachgook, Uncas, Alice, Cora, and Duncan Heyward paddled as they tried to elude a pursuing war party of Hurons and Mingos.[3]

The Narrows has changed dramatically over the last 10,000 years. Prior to the last ice age it consisted of a slender upthrust of land that divided the valley into two sections. On one side of the ridge, a river flowed north into Lake Champlain; on the other side a stream raced south through Dunham's Bay, eventually flowing into the Hudson River. During the last glaciation, however, this ridge was ground down to stubble by the abrasive weight of glaciers over a mile high that, upon retreating north, left behind an enormous deposit of glacial debris at the south end of the valley. This debris dammed up the valley, leaving the rising waters to form Lake George. What remained of the ridge became the islands that we see today in The Narrows. Once filled, the overflow from Lake George poured into an outlet at the north end of the lake and rushed through Ticonderoga into Lake Champlain.

There are hundreds of islands on the lake, a number that varies greatly depending upon one's definition of an island. Estimates go as high as 395 islands, a figure that clearly includes bodies of the tiniest size. The Village of Lake George's Web site offers a figure of 245 islands.[4] Others are happier with a figure of around 175 islands.[5] What's important to remember is that the islands are in constant flux, continually eroded by wind, snow, ice, and, of course, water. In millennia to come they will eventually all disappear. Many of the islands are now state owned and have signs prominently displayed indicating the islands' names.

The islands have been clustered into three main groups by New York State: the Long Island Group, at the south end of the lake; the Glen Island Group (The Narrows), in the central part of the lake; and the Narrow Island Group (the

Mother Bunch Group), toward the northern part of the lake, extending from the base of Black Mountain to Mallory Island (east of the Silver Bay shoreline).

The Long Island Group includes Long Island, which is the longest island on Lake George. This group contains 90 campsites.

Regarding the Glen Island Group, The Narrows takes its name from a narrowing in the lake where a vast swarm of islands have clustered between Phelps Island (north of Pilot Knob) and Black Mountain. This group contains 170 campsites and 42 cruiser (pleasure vessel) sites.

The Narrow Island Group's alternate name, the Mother Bunch Group, comes from a particular rock formation or arrangement of the islands that suggested to some the shape of an old woman's head.[6] Although the nomenclature may be a bit confusing, the Narrow Island Group has nothing to do with The Narrows. This group contains 85 campsites.

DEC headquarters are located on Long Island in the Long Island Group, Glen Island in the Glen Island Group, and Narrow Island in the Narrow Island Group, which explains how the modern nomenclature for the groups arose.

There is also a collection of islands near Hague called the Waltonian Group, named after the Waltonians Sportsmen Club of Glens Falls. The sportsmen's club, in turn, derived its name from the English author Izaak Walton (known as the "Father of Angling"). Except for Prison Island—a singleton—this is the northernmost grouping of islands.

Altogether there are 387 shoreline campsites on 44 state-owned islands, and 116 day-use sites on 8 state-owned islands and 2 state-owned mainland areas. Most of these sites were built during the 1930s by the Civilian Conservation Corps (CCC) and contain a dock for at least one boat, a fireplace, a picnic table, and toilet facilities. Permits to use an island for overnight camping or day use must be obtained from the appropriate island group headquarters in advance. Permit fees are charged during the peak season from mid-May through Columbus Day. At all other times there is no charge.

Paddlers should bear in mind that privately owned islands are not to be landed upon and that a respectful distance should be maintained from all private land. Landing upon state-owned islands occupied by campers should also be avoided.

To reserve an island campsite, contact:

Long Island Group—(518) 656-9426. Headquarters are located on east side of Long Island.

Glen Island Group/The Narrows—(518) 644-9696. Headquarters are located on Glen Island.

Narrow Island Group/Mother Bunch Group—(518) 499-1288. Headquarters are located on Narrow Island.

Waltonian Group—(518) 585-6746. Headquarters are located at Rogers Rock Campground.

Regional Office—(518) 623-1200, dec.ny.gov/outdoors/24474, lakegeorge-vacations.com/lake_george_island_camping.htm.

Reservations can also be made at the Norowal Marina in Bolton Landing, (518) 644-9125, Thurs.–Mon., 9:30 AM–6 PM.

Lake George is replete with history not only around the lake and on its islands, but also on its watery bottom, where a number of eighteenth-century ships as well as newer vessels lie in repose. For more information on underwater sites contact:

Lake George Submerged Heritage Preserve
Department of Environmental Conservation—Region 5
Route 86, Box 296
Ray Brook, NY 12977
(518) 897-1200
dec.ny.gov/lands/315.html

What is Lake George like today? Ignoring the fact that the west section of the lake's shoreline south of Bolton and the east section of the lake's shoreline south of Pilot Knob are filled with summer camps, four-season homes, marinas, and motels, much of Lake George still resembles what Father Jogues saw four hundred years ago. The lake continues to be surrounded by a lowland boreal forest mix near the water, and upland northern hardwood forests along its mountain ridges. Land development has taken its toll on the lake, but efforts continue to be mounted to rein in what could become tantamount to loving the lake to death.

In 1885 the Lake George Association was formed. It remains one of, if not the, oldest continuously operating lake association in the United States.[7] It was initially established by fishermen who were interested in protecting the quality of the water. The role has since expanded to include the protection, conservation, and improvement of the entire Lake George basin. In 1961 Lake George Park, encompassing an area of 300 square miles, was established[8] by the New York State legislature to ensure that the lake remain the "Queen of American Lakes"—a title popularized by Seneca Ray Stoddard, the famous Adirondack photographer, writer, and illustrator. In 1987 the Lake George Park Commission was given additional authority by the legislature to consolidate power over the land and water uses in the Lake George basin. Previously a myriad of towns, villages, and counties, all with competing interests, had jurisdiction over the lake and its use.

The Lake George Land Conservancy (LGLC), founded in 1988, has been highly instrumental in preserving the lake's water quality and protecting the natural beauty of its lands. As of 2009 the LGLC had protected more than 12,530 acres of Lake George wilderness and 48,500 feet of shoreline.

The islands, villages, bays, and points of interest on Lake George have names that go back hundreds of years. How some of these places were named remains open to much speculation. Folklore seems to be the norm. For this reason readers should keep in mind that the line separating fact and fiction can be a wavy, permeable one.

Lake George is a haven for powerboats, and has been for over a century. As early as 1912 over 700 motorboats were operating on the lake—a number that has increased exponentially over the ensuing years. In 2009 the Lake George Park Commission's official registered boat count had the number at 10,214. For this reason you may wish to tailor your outings to between Monday and Friday, when there is considerably less boat traffic as opposed to the weekends when the lake is churning with powerboat activity. Likewise, you may want to head out during the off season, before July or after August, when fewer powerboats are likely to be encountered.

Paddlers should always give motorized boats the right-of-way for safety's sake. Accidents with powerboats happen and can prove deadly. In June 2010 near Long Island, a kayaker was hit by a powerboat and killed. His wife, nearby, barely escaped the same fate.

Things can get terribly out of control in an instant, no matter how proficient or experienced a paddler might be. Unless you are island-hopping, stay as close to the shoreline as possible. Motorboats are not as prevalent near shore nor moving as quickly. Most of the paddles in this section have been written with that caution in mind.

Paddlers should also be aware that strong winds and storms can come up fast over the mountains. Prevailing north winds can whip up quite a bit of power and produce sizeable waves. For this reason paddlers should always consult the forecast and keep a watchful eye on the sky.

It is always helpful to carry broad maps of the lake when venturing out on its waters. The following two are well worth the investment: *Lake George Boaters Map* (waterproofed 7th edition) published by JIMAPCO; *Chart of Lake George, 1948 Hydrographic Survey by Lake George Power Squadron Inc.*, 2008 edition (a collection of navigational charts).

1 Lake Avenue Park (Lake George Village)
Shoreline Views of Lake George Village

■ **Launch Site:** Lake Avenue Park Launch at end of Lake Avenue, Lake George Village (Warren County); parking meters; 200-foot carry to sandy beach
■ **Delorme NYS Atlas & Gazetteer:** p. 80, A4; **GPS:** 43°25.81'N; 73°42.56'W
■ **Destinations & Mileages:** *Northeast:* to Tea Island—0.7 mile; to Harman Point—0.8 mile; to Westover Cove—1.2 miles. *Southeast:* to Shepard Park—0.4 mile; to Lake George Shoreline Cruises—0.5 mile; to Steel Pier/Lake George Steamboat Company/Fort William Henry—0.7 mile; to Million Dollar Beach—1.0 mile; to Ushers Park—1.2 miles; to Plum Point—3.4 miles.
■ **Comments:** Read "Caution" beginning on page xxi and Lake George Region Advisory on page 2.
    Kayak rentals are available at Kayak Lake George (part of Shore Meadows Motel) at 22 Lake Avenue. The shop is open daily from 7 AM–7 PM, April through September. (518) 302-6005; kayaklakegeorge.com.

Directions: From the center of Lake George Village (junction of Canada Street/Rte. 9 & Beach Street/Rte. 51), proceed north on Canada Street (Rte. 9) for 0.6 mile. Turn right onto Lake Avenue just before the junction of Rtes. 9 & 9N and drive southeast for over 0.1 mile to the end of the road. Park to the right.

From the Adirondack Northway (I-87), get off at Exit 22 for Diamond Point and Lake George Village, and head east on Rte. 9. When you come to a fork in the road after 0.3–0.4 mile, bear right, following signs for Lake George Village. In 0.05 mile you will come to a traffic light. Immediately after the traffic light turn left onto Lake Avenue and proceed to the parking area at the end of the road. Park to the right.

Take note that you must pay to park, using parking meters, or else drop off your watercraft and park at some distance away. By feeding enough coins into the parking meter, you can park legally for up to five hours.

The Paddle:
Lake Avenue Park is unique on the lake. It is a collaborative demonstration project to show the benefits of establishing a vegetative buffer along the shoreline to reduce the impact that humans are having on the lake. It was set up through the combined efforts of the Village of Lake George, Lake George Association, BOCES Landscape Architect Program, Cornell Cooperative Extension, CT Male Engineering, and Warren County Soil & Water Conservation District.

Because of its strategic location at the south end of the lake, Lake George Village has always been a major stepping-stone in eastern New York State's waterways. Originally known as Caldwell in honor of its founder, James Caldwell, the name changed to Lake George Village in the early twentieth century.[1]

▶ **Lake Avenue Park (Lake George Village)**

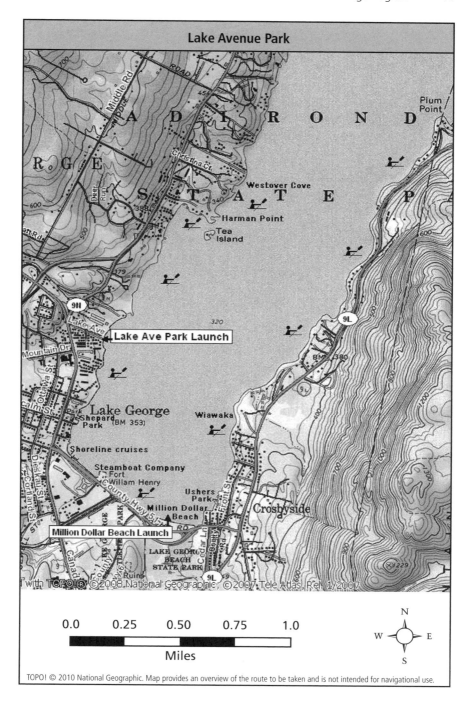

Lake Avenue Park

Lake Ave Park Launch

Million Dollar Beach Launch

0.0   0.25   0.50   0.75   1.0

Miles

N
W ⟷ E
S

TOPO! © 2010 National Geographic. Map provides an overview of the route to be taken and is not intended for navigational use.

The launch site is located on a section of the lake from Tea Island to east of the steel pier on Beach Street where private powerboats are prohibited.

Northeast—Following the west shoreline you will come to privately owned Tea Island, southeast of Harman Point, in 0.7 mile. The island is a tiny point of land almost connected to the mainland, just east of Boulder Bay. Its name comes from a teahouse that once operated on the island as far back as 1828.[2] Guests from Fort William Henry Hotel would row out to the island—an ideal half-day destination. One of the guests who did so was Teddy Roosevelt, in 1871. Legend has it that British General James Abercromby buried gold and valuables on the island. No treasure has ever been found, however, although many have dug in hopes of being handsomely rewarded for their efforts.[3]

Prior to the eighteenth century the island was called Two Mile Island. At that time it was believed that Tea Island was two miles from Fort William Henry.[4] Today we know that it is a mere 1.2 miles distant. In 1895 Tea Island was sold by New York State to Egbert J. Gale. Over the years the island has passed down through multiple owners, and to this day remains privately owned.[5] The rustic cottage that occupies the island was built in the late 1920s by Eugene Small and renovated by Helene Tuttle in 1936.

The 1758 battleship *Land Tortoise* (the oldest intact warship in North America) lies under 107 feet of water roughly 0.2 mile east of Tea Island at 43°26.40'N, 73°41.55'W. The ship was built by colonial and British troops at the south end of Lake George just east of today's Million Dollar Beach. It was deliberately sunk for safeguarding during the winter, but the ship—literally a raft with cannons on it—descended into deeper waters than expected and could not be retrieved the following spring.

Continuing northeast from Tea Island you will pass by Harman Point in another 0.1 mile and Westover Cove in 0.3 mile beyond that (or 1.2 miles from the launch site). A small stream that originates from a pond near Flat Rock Road enters Westover Cove.

Were you to continue farther north, you would reach the Hearthstone Point Campground at 1.9 miles.

Southeast—This paddle, which passes three public beaches, docking cruise ships, and a steel pier, is fun if you enjoy a lot of commotion, but probably not a good choice for the paddler who wants to get away from it all.

Following the shoreline south you will pass by the 350-foot-long beachfront of Shepard Park at 0.4 mile. The park, consisting of a small grassy area and public beach, was donated to the town by Edward Morse Shepard, a wealthy corporate lawyer who purchased the property in 1904.[6] The beach provides access for swimmers, but boat launches from the park are not allowed.

Rounding the southwest corner of the lake, the docking area for two cruise ships—the *Adirondac* and the *Horicon*—belonging to Lake George Shoreline Cruises is passed at 0.5 mile. Their office is located at 2 Kurosaka Lane and they can be reached at (518) 668-4644 or lakegeorgeshoreline.com.

▶ Lake Avenue Park (Lake George Village)

Aerial view of the south end of Lake George. Postcard ca. 1940.

In 0.7 mile you will paddle by a steel pier used by the Lake George Steamboat Company for docking its large boats. The steamboat company offers visitors an opportunity to tour sections of the lake in one of its three large vessels—the *Minne-ha-ha* (an authentic paddle wheeler), the *Mohican*, and *Lac Du Sacrement* (the lake's largest cruise ship). Their office is located at 57 Beach Road and they can be reached at (518) 668-5777 ext. 4, or lakegeorgestreamboat.com.

Fort William Henry is located directly behind the pier on the opposite side of the road on a promontory above the Steamboat Company. The fort was short-lived, lasting only from 1775–1777.[7] During the nineteenth century the fort was immortalized in James Fenimore Cooper's novel *The Last of the Mohicans*. In 1953 the fort finished reconstruction and again became a physical reality, opening to the public as a museum.[8]

Just east of Fort William Henry, along West Brook Road, is the site of the former Gaslight Village amusement complex, which was developed in 1959 by Charles Wood and endured until 1989. The land is now owned by the Village of Lake George and three environmental groups—The Lake George Association, the Fund for Lake George, and the Lake George Land Conservancy. An environmental park and wetland restoration project have begun to replace what remains of the amusement park.[9]

In 1.0 mile you will reach Million Dollar Beach, created in 1949 when New York State turned a wetland at the south end of Lake George into an expansive public beach. The name arose from the enormous cost involved in bringing in tons of sand to create the beach. Before Million Dollar Beach was created, a branch of the Delaware & Hudson (D&H) railroad ran tracks through the shallow wetland[10] to bring passengers up to Lake George from Glens Falls. A historic marker 0.1 mile west of Million Dollar Beach mentions that a 205-foot spur from the track survives underwater. Boats would be launched right into the water from boxcars on the tracks. The line operated from 1910–1950.[11] By good fortune some of the lands close to the beach have survived into the twenty-first century as wetlands.[12] Look for them to the south of Beach Street.

The south end of Lake George is framed by 1,500-foot-high French Mountain to the east and 2,030-foot-high Prospect Mountain to the west. Prospect Mountain is one of two Adirondack Mountains that offers a toll road up to its summit. At one time 1,224-foot-high Rattlesnake Cobble (Prospect Hill) afforded a view of the lake. Tourists staying at the Fort William Henry Hotel would follow a 0.7-mile-long path west from the hotel across to the base of the hill and then scramble up to the top of the cobble for a view.[13] Rattlesnake Cobble is accessed today along the pathway leading up to the summit of Prospect Mountain.

Looking north from the south end of the lake you will gaze across 12 miles of uninterrupted water, save for an occasional island.

Continuing on your way and staying close to the east shoreline, you will immediately pass by a former wetland area (now confined to the south side of Beach Street), and then Ushers Park in 0.2 mile (1.2 miles from the launch). Although Ushers Park is open to the public, launching kayaks and canoes from the park is prohibited.

At 1.5 miles you will pass near or over the underwater site of seven sunken eighteenth-century boats called bateaux, part of the Wiawaka Bateaux Cluster. The seven bateaux were purposely sunk in 1758. The site was named for its proximity to Wiawaka resort, established by feminist activists during the industrial revolution as a vacation spot for women who worked in the Troy shirt factories. *Wiawaka* is a Native American word that translates as "Great Spirit of Woman."

At 3.4 miles you will reach Plum Point. Near the middle of the lake, opposite Plum Point, is one of the deepest sections of Lake George. The fairly low-level French Mountain Range ("Top of the World") rises above the east shoreline along this part of the paddle.

Were you to continue paddling along the east shoreline beyond Plum Point, you would pass by Woods Point at 2.8 miles and Crooked Tree Point at 3.4 miles. Dunham Bay lies just beyond Crooked Tree Point.

▶ **Lake Avenue Park (Lake George Village)**

Alternate Launch Site

Million Dollar Beach (Lake George Village)

■ **Launch Site:** DEC boat launch at Million Dollar Beach State Park off of Beach
Street, Lake George Village (Warren County); watercraft launches are not permitted when the beach is in use for swimming (Memorial Day weekend through
Labor Day weekend); short carry from parking lot to launch site; hard-surface
ramp; parking for 200 cars & trailers (no fee for parking except during beach
season); restrooms closed after beach season; open daily, 10 AM–6:30 PM starting first week after Labor Day to first week before Memorial Day. For more information: 139 Beach Road, Lake George, NY 12845, (518) 668-3352, lakegeorge.
com.

■ **Delorme NYS Atlas & Gazetteer:** p. 80, A4; **Estimated GPS:** 43°25.03'N;
73°42.22'W

■ **Destinations & Mileages:** *Northwest:* to Steel Pier/Lake George Steamboat
Company/Fort William Henry—0.3 mile; to Tea Island, following shoreline—
1.7 miles; to Harman Point—1.8 miles; to Westover Cove—2.2 miles. *Northeast:*
to Ushers Park—0.2 mile; to Plum Point—2.4 miles.

■ **Comments:** Read "Caution" beginning on page xxi and Lake George Region
Advisory on page 2.

　　**Watercraft launches are not permitted during the summer between
Memorial Day and Labor Day when the beach is in use.**

Directions: From the Adirondack Northway (I-87), take exit 21 for Lake George
& Lake Luzerne and proceed northeast on Rte. 9N for around 0.1 mile. Turn left
onto Rte. 9 and head north for over 1.2 miles. At the center of Lake George Vil-
lage (junction of Canada Street/Rte. 9 & Beach Street), bear right onto Beach
Street and proceed southeast for 0.6 mile until you reach the parking area for
Million Dollar Beach on your left.

　　From the parking lot, carry your watercraft through a culvert under Beach
Road that leads immediately to the beach. It is a carry of only several hundred
feet to a concrete ramp.

2

Hearthstone Point Campgrounds (Lake George Village)
Paddling along the Southwest Shoreline

■ **Launch Site:** Hearthstone Point Campgrounds off of Rte. 9N (Warren County); slip-in at side of beach; day-use fee; restrooms; open mid-May through mid-September. For more information: 3298 Lake Shore Drive, Lake George, NY 12845, (518) 668-5193, lakegeorge.com.

■ **Delorme NYS Atlas & Gazetteer:** p. 80, A4; **Estimated GPS:** 43°27.24'N; 73°41.55'W

■ **Destinations & Mileages:** *North*: to Cramer Point, following the shoreline— 0.6 mile; around perimeter of Green Harbor—0.5 mile; from Cramer Point to Cooper Point—0.1 mile (0.7 mile from launch); from Cooper Point, following the shoreline of Still Bay, to Cannon Point—1.0 mile (1.7 miles from launch); from Cannon Point to mouth of Orcutt Bay and Reids Rock—0.1 mile (1.8 miles from launch); around Orcutt Bay—0.3 mile. *Northeast*: to Diamond Island—0.8 mile; around Diamond Island—0.4 mile; from Diamond Island to Dicks Islands—0.05 mile (1.0 mile from launch).

■ **Comments:** Read "Caution" beginning on page xxi and Lake George Region Advisory on page 2. Do not leave the shoreline to cross open water to Diamond Island and Dicks Islands unless the weather is calm and you are a skilled and experienced paddler.

Directions: From the center of Lake George Village (junction of Canada Street/ Rte. 9 & Beach Street), proceed north on Canada Street/Rte. 9 for 0.6 mile. At the junction of Rtes. 9 & 9N, turn right onto Rte. 9N and head north for 1.9 miles. The campground is on your right.

From the Adirondack Northway (I-87), get off at Exit 22 for Diamond Point and Lake George Village, and head east on Rte. 9. When you come to a fork in the road after 0.3–0.4 mile, bear left, following signs for Diamond Point. When you come to Rte. 9N after another 0.5 mile, turn left and proceed north for over 1.5 miles. Look for the campground on your right.

From either approach to the campground entrance, turn immediately right after the contact station and follow the road downhill for 0.3 mile to the lake for beach parking. Carry your kayak or canoe to the right of the beach to put in.

Although nearby Diamond Point has a public beach, the launching of watercraft from there is prohibited.

The Paddle:
The Hearthstone Point Campground[1] was created thanks to George Foster Peabody, a well-known banker and philanthropist who generously gifted the property to New York State.[2]

A tiny, pretty cove leading up to Cramer Point is noticeable to the left of the launch site. Cramer Point is named after George Cramer, who established a large

▶ **Hearthstone Point Campgrounds (Lake George Village)**

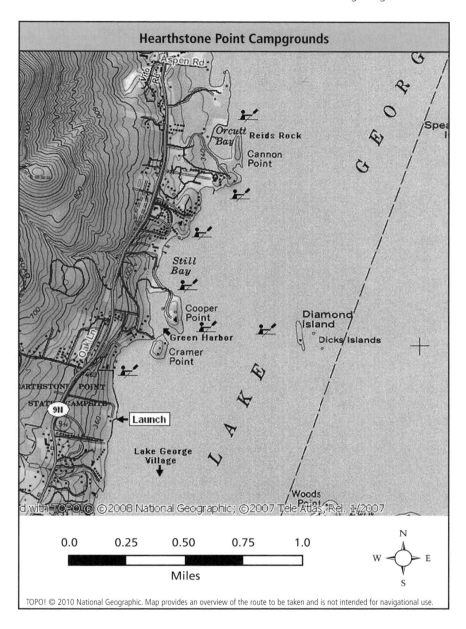

Hearthstone Point Campgrounds

0.0   0.25   0.50   0.75   1.0

Miles

TOPO! © 2010 National Geographic. Map provides an overview of the route to be taken and is not intended for navigational use.

villa called Trinity Rock here during the mid-nineteenth century.[3]

Don't be surprised to see parasailers off in the distance as you paddle along.

North—Head north along the west shoreline for 0.6 mile to reach Green Harbor, which is defined by Cramer Point to the south and Cooper Point to the

A spectacular man-made waterfall cascades into Lake George at Cooper Point. Photograph 2011.

north. Both of these high points have artificial waterfalls cascading into the lake. The waterfall at Cooper Point is particularly attractive, dropping fifteen feet over a rock face. The harbor's shoreline can be explored for nearly 0.5 mile and contains an extensive number of docks along its west, north, and east sides. Because boats are not allowed to speed in the cove, it is a fairly safe place to paddle.

The name Cooper Point would seem to be an obvious nod to James Fenimore Cooper, author of *The Last of the Mohicans*,[4] whose imprimatur is all around the lake. In fact, however, the point is named after John Cooper, who bought the property from Sarah P. Tuttle in 1860.

From Cooper Point, 0.1 mile north of Cramer Point, continue paddling north, now along the shoreline of Still Bay. The bay could well have been named for its calm waters, but one source contends that the bay was named for its stilbite—a lustrous mineral composed of hydrated calcium aluminum silicate—and that over the course of many decades the bay's name was shortened from Stilbite to Still. Considering that the wetlands at the bay were once called the Stilbite Swamps lends credence to this supposition.[5]

The north tip of Cannon Point is reached in 1.0 mile after leaving Cooper Point. Cannon Point may have been named after Revolutionary War artifacts that were allegedly recovered from its nearby waters, including an eighteenth-century cannon.[6] Another theory is that the point served as a staging area for

▶ **Hearthstone Point Campgrounds (Lake George Village)**

British cannon. Coincidentally, Cannon Point resembles the vague shape of a mounted cannon when viewed on a topo map or from the air. Rounding Cannon Point, proceed south into Orcutt Bay, which can be circumnavigated in 0.3 mile. The bay was named after Joseph Orcutt, an early settler who purchased land there in 1847.[7]

The rock formation near the mouth of Orcutt Bay is called Reids Rock, named after Rud Reid, who was found frozen to death on the rock.[8]

Northeast—By heading northeast across open waters, 0.1-mile-long state-owned Diamond Island is reached in 0.8 mile. Only venture out to Diamond Island if the weather is calm and you are a skilled and experienced paddler. Diamond Island was named for its abundance of six-sided quartz crystals.[9] Members of a family living on the island began selling the crystals as early as 1829.[10] Although interest in mining the island's quartz crystals has since waned, Diamond Island remains an attraction to scuba divers who plumb the lake's depths nearby, exploring the many shipwrecks that lie scattered about on the bottom. A ten-foot-high stone monument called the Peace Stone[11] is located at the north end of the island and is named for one of its inscriptions, which reads, "Peace/Here the Conqueror/of many Wars. 1666–1777." The monument was erected by Katrina Trask,[12] wife of Spencer Trask who founded Yaddo, an artists' retreat in Saratoga Springs. Paddlers may want to land on the island to see the Peace Stone close up. Although there are two docks on the island's east side, the waters are generally choppy. Far better is a tiny inlet on the southwest side of Diamond Island that permits an easier landing.

State-owned Dicks Island, also called Dix Island—a relatively flat scrap of treeless rock occupied by gulls—is just east of Diamond Island, a scant 0.05 mile away. Dicks Island is well known to local residents who occasionally wake up in the morning to find a motorboat stranded atop the island, having run aground during the night after straying off course from the main channel.

The Peace Stone can be seen at the north end of Diamond Island. Photograph 2010.

3 Huddle Beach (Bolton Landing)
Island-Hopping near Bolton Landing

- ■ **Launch Site:** Huddle Beach off of Rte. 9N between Bolton & Bolton Landing (Warren County); portable toilet; sandy beach & dock
- ■ **Delorme NYS Atlas & Gazetteer:** p. 89, D4; **GPS:** 43°32.53'N; 73°39.91'W
- ■ **Destinations & Mileages:** *Northeast:* to Sweetbriar Island—0.3 mile; to Bixby Beach—0.9 mile; to Green Island bridge—1.4 miles; around Green Island—1.8 miles; from Green Island to Crown Island—0.2 mile (2.4 miles from launch); around Crown Island—0.7 mile; from Green Island bridge to Finkle Brook—0.4 mile (1.8 miles from launch); from Crown Island to Oahu Island (start of the Narrows; refer to "Green Island" map)—0.9 mile (3.3 miles from launch). *South and East:* to Hiawatha Island—0.3 mile; from Hiawatha Island to Huddle Brook—0.3 mile (0.5 mile from launch); from Hiawatha Island to Clay Island—0.3 mile (0.6 mile from launch); around Clay Island—0.9 mile; from Clay Island to Leantine Island—0.3 mile; from Clay Island to Recluse Island—0.1 mile (1.1 miles from launch); from Clay Island to Dome Island—0.5 mile (1.5 miles from launch); around Dome Island—0.8 mile; from Dome Island to Three Brothers Islands—0.6 mile (2.2 miles from launch); around Three Brothers Islands—0.5 mile.
- ■ **Comments:** Read "Caution" beginning on page xxi and Lake George Region Advisory on page 2.

   Crossing open waters to The Narrows is a trek best undertaken with a group of paddlers and only when the weather is calm. We would further recommend that you consult with the Lake George Kayak Company before undertaking that paddle.

   Exercise extra caution near Green Island bridge. This is a fairly busy part of the lake because of the number of marinas located near the west end of the bridge.

Directions: From the Adirondack Northway (I-87) get off at Exit 24 for Bolton Landing and follow Rte. 11 (Bolton Landing/Riverbank Road) east for 4.7 miles. During the last mile on Rte. 11, you will have magnificent views of the lake and mountains as you come down a steep hill into the Lake George basin. When you reach Rte. 9N, turn right and drive south for 3.0 miles, then turn left onto Huddle Beach Road.

   If you are driving north on Rte. 9N from Bolton (junction of Rte. 9N & Trout Lake Road), continue north for 0.4 mile until you come to Huddle Beach Road on your right.

   From either direction, proceed east on Huddle Beach Road to its end at 0.1 mile. Park to the side of the road after dropping off your watercraft.

   This section of Rte. 9N was once called Millionaire's Row because of the number of palatial homes that were built here by nineteenth-century aristocrats. The millionaires who lived in these homes coyly referred to their Tudor, Georgian, and Italianate mansions as "cottages." Following the adverse economic

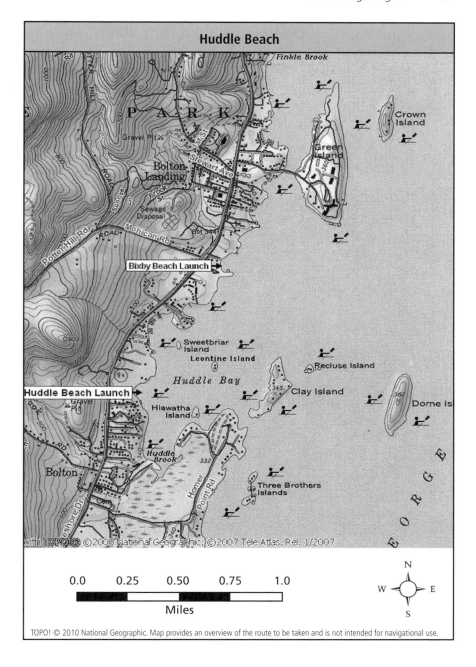

Huddle Beach

Finkle Brook

Crown Island

Green Island

P   A   R   K

Gravel Pit

Bolton Landing

Sewage Disposal

BM 344

Bixby Beach Launch →

Sweetbriar Island

Leontine Island

Recluse Island

Huddle Bay

Clay Island

Dome Is

← Huddle Beach Launch

Gravel Pit

Hiawatha Island

Huddle Brook   332

Bolton

Three Brothers Islands

G   E   O   R   G   E

with TOPO! © 2008 National Geographic; © 2007 Tele Atlas, Rel. 1/2007

| 0.0 | 0.25 | 0.50 | 0.75 | 1.0 |

Miles

N
W — E
S

consequences of the Great Depression and World War II, most of these mammoth homes were unsustainable because of expensive upkeep and high taxes and were demolished. A burgeoning middle and upper-middle class became the dominant population around the lake.

The Paddle:

The name Huddle Beach is a carryover from the days when Bolton Landing was known as Huddle.[1]

Look directly east and you will see Clay Island, 0.6 mile from the launch site. The island is separated from the land mass that delineates the northeast side of Huddle Bay.

Northeast—Follow along the west shoreline and you will reach state-owned Sweetbriar Island in 0.3 mile. The island was named for the sweetbriar bushes that once grew there. It has also been called Huckleberry Island.[2] In the later part of the nineteenth century, a narrow three-story house built by William A. Wait stood on the island.

Bixby Beach is reached at 0.9 mile. The beach is named after William Keeney Bixby, former president of the American Car and Foundry Company, who purchased the Mohican House on Mohican Point. After determining that the hotel was unsalvageable, Bixby had it razed and then erected a summer home in its place in 1902. This home is still standing today.[3] You can see it with its enormous white pillars on the east side of the Bixby Beach Cove overlooking the bay. Farther along the southeast shore of the peninsula are impressive boathouses, also belonging to the Bixby estate.

Directly east across the lake is Shelving Rock Bay, approximately 2.4 miles away. Several prominent mountains can be seen along the east shore—1,130-foot-high Shelving Rock Mountain slightly to the north, 1,605-foot-high Little Buck Mountain slightly to the south, and towering 2,334-foot-high Buck Mountain (earlier known as Deer Pasture Mountain) still farther south.

In another 0.5 mile from Bixby Beach, at the north end of Bolton Bay, you will come to the Green Island bridge (Sagamore Road), which connects the mainland with Green Island. Along the way there are great views of the Sagamore Hotel located at the southeast end of Green Island. This is a fairly busy part of the lake because of the number of marinas located near the west end of the bridge. For this reason use extra caution near the bridge. Green Island can be paddled around in 1.8 miles. Crown Island is only 0.2 mile east of Green Island and can be circumnavigated in 0.7 mile. Oahu Island (refer to "Green Island" map), at the beginning of The Narrows, can be reached in 0.9 mile from the northeast end of Crown Island. Once you reach The Narrows and its plethora of islands, there is much to explore. That is a trek best undertaken with a group of paddlers and only when the weather is calm, and we would further recommend that you consult with the Lake George Kayak Company before undertaking this paddle.

▶ **Huddle Beach (Bolton Landing)**

Views of the Sagamore Hotel from Huddle Bay. Photograph 2011.

Following the west shoreline north from the Green Island bridge, you will reach Finkle Brook at 0.4 mile. Were you to continue farther north, you would pass by Braley Point at 0.7 mile, Jacobie Point at 1.1 miles, and Bell Point at 1.7 miles. Once you reach Bell Point you are within the large expanse of Northwest Bay, a bay the size of a lake.

South and East—From Huddle Beach, paddle east and slightly south to reach privately owned Hiawatha Island in 0.3 mile. The name Hiawatha is sure to conjure up images of the Native American chief featured in Henry Wadsworth Longfellow's epic poem "The Song of Hiawatha." At one time Drs. Abraham and Mary Jacobi lived on the island, accessing it by boat.

From Hiawatha Island you can go 0.3 mile southwest into Huddle Bay to reach Huddle Brook. The stream is also known as Trout Lake Brook because it drains Trout Lake.

From Hiawatha Island you can also head northeast, skimming the north tip of the mainland peninsula, to reach privately owned Clay Island in 0.3 mile. The island, originally called Belvoir Island, can be circumnavigated in 0.9 mile, allowing you to pass through an area of shallow waters called The Gut that separates Clay Island from the mainland. It remains a tight squeeze only for motorboaters who, unlike paddlers, must be concerned about the depth and location of underlying rocks. Although the name of the island likely came about from the abundance of clay underlying its gravel and sand,[4] another theory contends that during the Revolutionary War a Scottish two-edged sword, called a claymore, was found on the island and that the name was eventually shortened from Claymore to Clay.[5]

Privately owned Leantine Island, also called Whortleberry Island and occasionally spelled Leontine, is 0.3 mile northwest of Clay Island.

From Clay Island head northeast for 0.1 mile to privately owned Recluse Island. Recluse Island's name came about after Pere St. Bernard, a Jesuit missionary, sought sanctuary on the island after escaping from his Native American captors. The island has also been called Picnic Island[6] and Hermitage Island.[7] It is believed that Rufus Wattles may have established the lake's first private residence on the island. He named the cottage "Hermitage."

Adjacent to Recluse Island is state-owned Little Recluse Island, also known as Sloop Island.[8] At one time a small bridge connected the two islands. The famous Hudson River School painter John Frederick Kensett spent two consecutive summers on Little Recluse Island painting the magnificent scenery before him. The painting now hangs in the Metropolitan Museum of Art.

From Recluse Island head 0.4 mile east to Dome Island, which rises 76 feet above the water level, giving it the highest elevation of any island on Lake George. Geologists consider it to be a glacial moraine that was left behind at the end of the last ice age.[9] The name of the island is self-explanatory; it has been described as "a singularly rounded form, covered with trees, with utmost regularity."[10]

Dome Island was purchased in the 1920s by John S. ("Appy") Apperson, a General Electric engineer and prominent advocate for the preservation of Lake George's natural beauty. Apperson saw to it that access to the island was limited in order to ensure that its shoreline remained stable. The island was acquired by the Northeastern Chapter of the Nature Conservancy in 1956. Today it can only be landed on by special request.[11] Like many of Lake George's islands, the windward side is more subject to blowdown and, because Dome Island towers above all the others, it is more often struck by lightning. The island can be circled around in 0.8 mile.

From Dome Island head southwest back toward the mainland to privately owned Three Brothers Islands, which is reached in 0.6 mile. Actually three islands, the Brothers can be paddled around in 0.5 mile. In the nineteenth century the islands were acquired by the Trask family, which proceeded to join all three together by two colonnaded bridges. Three Brothers Islands has also been known as Three Sisters Island and Triuna Island. It was Katrina Trask who came up with the name Triuna, which means "three-in-one."[12]

▶ **Huddle Beach (Bolton Landing)**

Alternate Launch Site

Bixby Beach (Bolton Landing)

■ **Launch Site:** Bixby Beach at end of Bixby Road in Bolton Landing (Warren County); slip-in at beach; limited parking
■ **Delorme NYS Atlas & Gazetteer:** p. 89, D4; **GPS:** 43°33.11'N; 73°39.38'W
■ **Destinations & Mileages:** *North:* to Green Island bridge—0.6 mile; around Green Island—1.8 miles; from Green Island to Crown Island—0.2 mile (1.6 miles from launch); around Crown Island—0.7 mile; from Green Island bridge to Finkle Brook—0.4 mile (1.0 mile from launch). *South:* to Sweetbriar Island—0.6 mile; from Sweetbriar Island to Huddle Beach—0.3 mile (0.9 mile from launch); from Sweetbriar Island to Hiawatha Island—0.3 mile (0.9 mile from launch); from Hiawatha Island to Huddle Brook—0.3 mile (1.2 miles from launch); from Sweetbriar Island to Clay Island—0.4 mile (1.0 mile from launch); around Clay Island—0.9 mile; from Clay Island to Recluse Island—0.1 mile (1.5 miles from launch); from Clay Island to Dome Island—0.5 mile (1.9 miles from launch); around Dome Island—0.8 mile; from Dome Island to Three Brothers Islands—0.6 mile (2.7 miles from launch); around Three Brothers Islands—0.5 mile. *Northeast:* from northeast end of Crown Island to Oahu Island (start of The Narrows)—0.9 mile (2.5 miles from launch).
■ **Comments:** Read "Caution" beginning on page xxi and Lake George Region Advisory on page 2.
   The paddle to Oahu Island and the Narrows is best undertaken with a group of paddlers and only when the weather is calm, and we would further recommend that you consult with the Lake George Kayak Company before undertaking that paddle.

Directions: From the Adirondack Northway (I-87), get off at Exit 24 for Bolton Landing and follow Rte. 11 (Bolton Landing/Riverbank Road) east for 4.7 miles. During the last mile on Rte. 11, you will have magnificent views of the lake and mountains as you come down a steep hill into the Lake George basin. When you reach Rte. 9N, turn right and drive south for 2.1 miles, then turn left onto Bixby Road just before Mohican Road (on your right). Bixby Road ends within 0.05 mile at a beach roughly 50 feet in width. Park along the side of the road.

   If you are driving along Rte. 9N and approaching Bolton Landing from the south, turn right onto Bixby Road as soon as you pass by Mohican Road (on your left), and follow the instructions above.

   If you are driving along Rte. 9N and approaching Bolton Landing from the north, continue south past Sagamore Road (which leads to Green Island and the Sagamore Hotel) for 0.5 mile and turn left onto Bixby Road. From that point, follow the instructions above.

4 Green Island (Bolton Landing)
Launching Midway on the Lake

■ **Launch Site:** Lake George Kayak Company's boathouse on Green Island (Warren County). No fee required. For more information: Lake George Kayak Co., 4973 Main St., Bolton Landing, NY 12814, (518) 644-9366, lakegeorgekayak.com.
■ **Delorme NYS Atlas & Gazetteer:** p. 89, D4-5
■ **Destinations & Mileages:** *Around Green Island*—1.8 miles. *East:* from Green Island to Crown Island—0.2 mile (0.8 mile from launch); around Crown Island—0.7 mile. *North*: to Finkle Brook—0.3 mile; to Braley Point—0.6 mile; to Bell Point—1.6 miles. *Northeast:* to Oahu Island—1.8 miles; from Oahu Island to nearby islands in The Narrows—variable mileages.
■ **Comments:** Read "Caution" beginning on page xxi and Lake George Region Advisory on page 2.

Kayaks and canoes can be launched without charge from a site on Green Island owned by the Lake George Kayak Company. Stop by their shop to let them know that you will be using their facilities. First-time users will also need to get directions to the boathouse. The Lake George Kayak Company offers a wide range of equipment and supplies for paddlers, and they are always well versed in up-to-date information on the lake's current conditions and advisories.

Although Bolton Landing contains two public beaches—Rogers Memorial Park Beach (off of Rte. 9N just south of Sagamore Road) and Veterans Memorial Park Beach (off of Rte. 9N just north of Sagamore Road)—neither can be used for launching watercraft.

The paddle from Green Island to Oahu Island and The Narrows takes you across a very broad expanse of open water. You should only attempt this excursion if the weather is calm, you are an experienced paddler, and you are with a group of similarly proficient paddlers.

Directions to Lake George Kayak Company: From the Adirondack Northway (I-87), get off at Exit 24 for Bolton Landing and follow Rte. 11 (Bolton Landing/Riverbank Road) east for 4.7 miles. When you reach Rte. 9N, turn right and drive south for 1.6 miles. Stop in at the Lake George Kayak Company, just past the traffic light on the west side of Rte. 9N, for directions to their boathouse.

The Paddle:
Green Island encompasses 66 acres of land. It is the largest privately owned island on the lake and the second-largest overall.[1] The island's undulating surface rises as high as 70 feet in places. Green Island can be circumnavigated in 1.8 miles. Most of the large structures, such as the Sagamore Hotel, are located near the south end of the island. The north tip is fairly undeveloped.

The island's long history dates back to Native Americans, who were the first to establish an encampment there. During the Revolutionary War the island was

▶ **Green Island (Bolton Landing)**

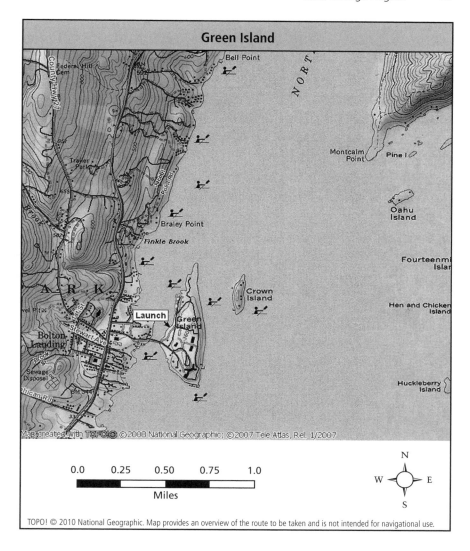

fortified. In 1794 the land was acquired by Wheeler Douglas and subsequently passed through a number of private owners. The first house on the island was built by Ferdinand Theriot in 1870.

In 1881, Myron O. Brown, manager of the Mohican House in Bolton Landing, along with several other businessmen, formed the Green Island Improvement Company. They built the first of three bridges in 1882 that connected the island to the mainland, and began work on the Sagamore Hotel, which opened in 1883. The hotel was severely damaged by fire in 1893 and again in 1914.[2] In 1930 the hotel was fully reconstructed, but gradually fell into disrepair and

The Sagamore Hotel, Bolton Landing. Postcard ca. 1950.

finally closed in 1981. In 1983 the hotel was purchased by Norman Wolgin of Philadelphia and restored to its former grandeur.

The launch site on Green Island is located on the east side of Sawmill Bay, which is north of the Green Island bridge.

East—Once you reach the east side of Green Island, you can easily paddle east over to privately owned Crown Island, which is only 0.2 mile away. Crown Island is quickly circumnavigated in 0.7 mile. At one time Crown Island had a large population of rattlesnakes. Hogs were brought in to eliminate them, and for a time the island was known as Hog Island. [3] It has also been called, not surprisingly, Snake Island.[4] Back in the 1930s the island was owned by Dr. Irving Languir, an eminent General Electric research scientist.[5]

North—Heading north you will pass by Finkle Brook at 0.3 mile and reach Braley Point at 0.6 mile. Braley Point was named after Fred Braley, an early resident.[6] Continuing farther north, Bell Point is reached at 1.6 miles. One account states that Bell Point was named for a large church bell that was rung three times a day from the porch of a summer resident named M. B. White.[7]

Northeast—The closest main island in The Narrows is Oahu Island, which can be reached in 1.8 miles. Using Oahu Island as a home base (but not landing on it, since the island is privately owned) you can visit the other islands in The Narrows by hopping from one to the next. Because you will be crossing 1.0 mile of open water northeast of Crown Island, however, you should only attempt this excursion if the weather is calm and you are an experienced paddler. Ideally, you should be with a group of similarly proficient paddlers, and we further recommend that you consult with the Lake George Kayak Company regarding the weather and lake conditions before setting out.

All of the islands in The Narrow are state owned except for Oahu Island (also called Floa Island, Flea Island, Flora Island, & Bellinger Island) and Fourteen Mile Island. The state-owned islands include Ship Island, Bouquet Island, Mingoe Island, Chingachgook (Little Pine) Island, Oahu Island, As You Were Island, Pine Island, Turtle Island, Mohican (Pleasure, Phelps) Island, Juanita (Centipede) Island, Phantom Island, Gravelly Island, Gem Island, Little Gem Island, Hermit Island, Watch Island, Gourd Island, Little Harbor Island, Fork (Kettle) Island, Hazel Island, Bass (Perch) Island, Commission Island, Hen & Chicken Islands, Ranger Island, and Big Burnt Island.

▶ Green Island (Bolton Landing)

Northwest Bay (North Bolton)
A Riverlike Section of Lake George

5

- **Launch Site:** Northwest Bay Launch Site off of Rte. 9N (Warren County); parking for 15 cars
- **Delorme NYS Atlas & Gazetteer:** p. 89, D4–5; **GPS:** 43°37.55'N; 73°36.45'W
- **Destinations & Mileages:** *Northwest Bay Brook to Northwest Bay*: 1.3 miles + side excursions. *From Northwest Bay Brook southwest along east shore of Northwest Bay*: to Bear Point—0.3 mile (1.6 miles from launch); to Fan Point—1.7 miles (3.0 miles from launch); to Montcalm Point—2.8 miles (4.1 miles from launch). *From Northwest Bay Brook southwest along west shore of Northwest Bay:* to Walker Point—1.3 miles (2.6 miles from launch); to Indian Brook—2.3 miles (3.6 miles from launch); to Bell Point—2.8 miles (4.1 miles from launch); to Braley Point—3.8 miles (5.1 miles from launch).
- **Comments:** Read "Caution" beginning on page xxi and Lake George Region Advisory on page 2. Under most conditions, wind and current are not significant factors in paddling on Northwest Bay Brook.
   Map #2 is a continuation south of Map #1.

Directions: From Bolton Landing (junction of Rte. 9N & Sagamore Road), head north on Rte. 9N for 6.1 miles. The launch site is on your right just before Rte. 9N crosses Northwest Bay Brook. From Hague (junction of Rtes. 8 & 9N), proceed south on Rte. 9N for 12.9 miles. Turn left onto a dirt road just after crossing Northwest Bay Brook.

Drive down to a cul-de-sac at the end of the road in 0.05 mile to drop off your kayak, and then park in the designated parking area.

The Paddle:
The east shore of Northwest Bay is bounded by the Tongue Mountain Range, named for its tapering, tongue-like shape. The range was acquired by New York State in 1923[1] and includes a number of substantial peaks that overlook Northwest Bay. Going southeast to northeast are First Peak (1,586'), French Point Mountain (1,756'), Fifth Peak (1,813'), and Five Mile Mountain (2,256').

Part of the land along the west side of the brook belongs to the Loines Preserve, a 37-acre parcel of land donated to the Nature Conservancy in 1964 by Hilda & Elma Loines and Sylvia Loines Dalton. In 2004 the lands were transferred from the Nature Conservancy to the Lake George Land Conservancy.

Northwest Bay Brook to Northwest Bay—Northwest Bay Brook flows through a vast wetland until it enters Northwest Bay (also called Ganouskie Bay).[2] It is a wild and seemingly remote area that invites exploration. In earlier times Northwest Bay Brook was called Beaver Brook.

While it is possible to go upstream from the launch site, you can only advance for 0.05 mile (or about several hundred feet downstream from the Rte. 9N bridge)

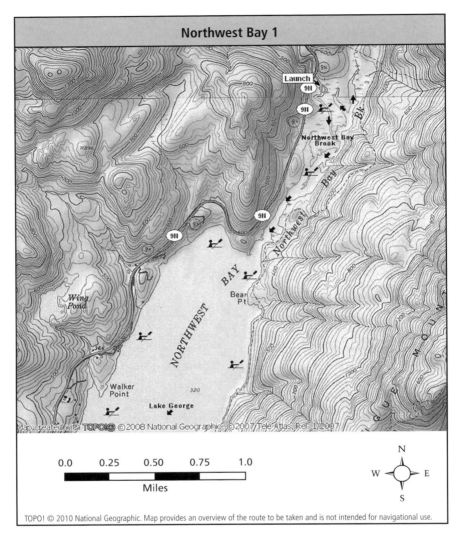

Northwest Bay 1

Map created with TOPO!® ©2008 National Geographic ©2007 Tele Atlas, Rel. 1/2007

0.0   0.25   0.50   0.75   1.0

Miles

N
W ← → E
S

TOPO! © 2010 National Geographic. Map provides an overview of the route to be taken and is not intended for navigational use.

before rapids force you back. The best course is to head straight downstream from the launch site, following a brook that is sinuous for the first 0.4 mile. You will then reach a junction. Turning left takes you away from Northwest Bay Brook, but allows you to go farther into the interior of the marshlands by following the stream's east branch into a wide open area. In 0.2 mile you will reach a fork. The left fork ends after 0.2 mile, but not before veering right and momentarily entering a forest-like area. The wider right fork goes northeast for over 0.2 mile, but you will probably not be able to paddle it that far during the summer because of the density of underwater plants.

▶ **Northwest Bay (North Bolton)**

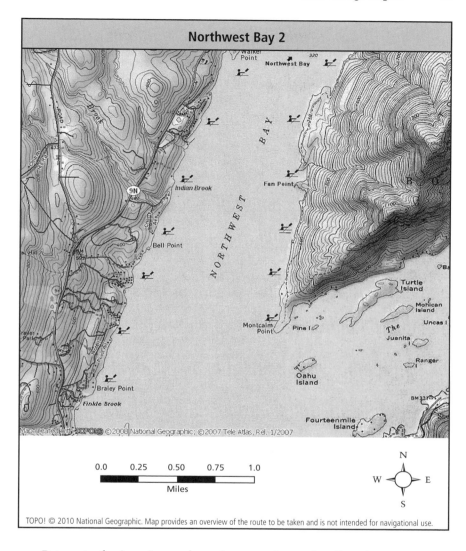

Northwest Bay 2

TOPO! © 2010 National Geographic. Map provides an overview of the route to be taken and is not intended for navigational use.

Return to the junction and continue southwest, heading downstream on Northwest Bay Brook for 0.8 mile (or 1.3 miles from the launch site) until you reach Northwest Bay. During this part of the paddle you will observe red and green buoys on the water, signifying that you may have to share this section with an occasional motorboat.

Look for a pine-covered corner of land on your left just before you enter the bay. You may get out there and stretch your legs or have a bite to eat if you wish. A 200-foot-long path leads uphill from the point to a main hiking trail that parallels the bay. Keep in mind that your feet are less protected than those of hikers

Looking across Montcalm Point toward Crown Island, Green Island, and village of Bolton Landing. Postcard ca. 1940.

wearing boots, so be on the lookout for rattlesnakes, which do inhabit the area but generally do their best to avoid contact with humans.

Northwest Bay—Venturing out onto Northwest Bay, you will discover that it is a lake within a lake, and one without islands. At this point you have two choices—either paddle along the bay's east shore, or paddle along its west shore, the two shores being separated by a distance of roughly 0.5 mile.

From Northwest Bay Brook southwest along east shore of Northwest Bay—You will pass by Bear Point at 0.3 mile, Fan Point at 1.7 miles, and Montcalm Point at 2.8 miles. Be prepared for the possibility of significantly more wind and waves if you round Montcalm Point. Fan Point got its name from being constantly fanned by breezes.[3] Montcalm Point is a nod to General Louis-Joseph de Montcalm who, while close to this point of land during the French and Indian War, saw a prearranged signal that reassured him that his troops from Ticonderoga had successfully crossed the nearby mountains.[4] A hiking trail parallels the shoreline to your left, but remains fairly well concealed in the woods. From Montcalm Point you can look northeast across the lake at the many islands contained in The Narrows.

From Northwest Bay Brook southwest along the west shore of Northwest Bay—Head southwest along the west shoreline for 1.3 miles to pass by Walker Point, a fairly pronounced projection of land. Indian Brook is reached at 2.3 miles, Bell Point at 2.8 miles, and Braley Point at 3.8 miles. Walker Point was named for an early resident who preferred walking over any other form of locomotion.[5] Indian Brook, like Northwest Bay, Finkle, Huddle, and Edmunds brooks—the four other major brooks in the Town of Bolton—was the site of numerous sawmills and grain mills. Farther upstream from the lake is Indian Falls, but it is on private property.

During most of this paddle, Rte. 9N will be close at hand but separated from the water by a distance of 0.2 mile, including 100–200 feet of elevation. You will occasionally hear the sound of a car or motorcycle passing by, but not too frequently.

▶ **Northwest Bay (North Bolton)**

Hague Town Beach (Hague)
Accessing the Waltonian Islands

6

- **Launch Site:** Hague Town Beach at Robert E. Henry Memorial Park off of Rte. 9N in Hague (Warren County); hard-surface ramp with parking for ten cars & trailers; public restrooms in Visitor Center; open Memorial Day through Columbus Day. Motorboats are charged a fee, but there are currently no fees to launch a canoe or kayak. For more information: Hague Town Beach, Lake Shore Drive, Hague, NY, (518) 543-6273, townofhague.org/townofhague/Calendar/Park.htm.
- **Delorme NYS Atlas & Gazetteer:** p.89, BC5–6; **GPS:** 43°44.67'N; 73°29.93'W
- **Destinations & Mileages:** *Northeast:* to Temple Knoll Island (shown on map as Temple Island)—0.8 mile; from Temple Knoll Island to Waltonian Island—0.05 mile (1.0 mile from launch); from Waltonian Island to Asas Island—0.05 mile (1.05 miles from launch); from Asas Island to Lenni-Lenape Island—0.05 mile (1.15 miles from launch); from Lenni-Lenape Island to Lover's Rock Island (an island so small it is not on the map)—0.05 mile (1.3 miles from launch); from Lover's Rock Island to North Huckleberry Island—0.05 mile (1.4 miles from launch); from North Huckleberry Island to Flirtation Island—0.1 mile (1.5 miles from launch); from Flirtation Island to Friends Point—0.1 mile (1.7 miles from launch). *South:* to Jenkins Point—1.1 miles; to Jabe Pond Brook—1.4 miles; to Pardo Point—1.8 miles.
- **Comments:** Read "Caution" beginning on page xxi and Lake George Region Advisory on page 2.

  Map #2 is a continuation south of Map #1.

  Visitors must park in spaces facing the road; town residents park in spaces facing the beach.

Directions: From the Adirondack Northway (I-87), get off at Exit 25 for Chestertown and drive east on Rte. 8 for roughly 18 miles until you reach the village of Hague (junction of Rtes. 8 & 9N). Turn right onto Rte. 9N and then, within a hundred feet, turn left into the parking area for Hague Town Beach, which is located next to the Visitor Center. The launch site is directly south of the beach.

Coming from Bolton Landing along Rte. 9N, the drive is roughly 19 miles to reach Hague Town Beach, on your right just before the junction of Rtes. 9N & 8. The parking area for Hague Town Beach is located next to the Visitor Center, and the launch site is directly south of the beach.

Approaching from southwest of Ticonderoga (junction of Rtes. 9N & 77), proceed south on Rte. 9N for 8.2 miles to reach The Hague Town Beach on your left, just past where Rte. 8 enters on your right.

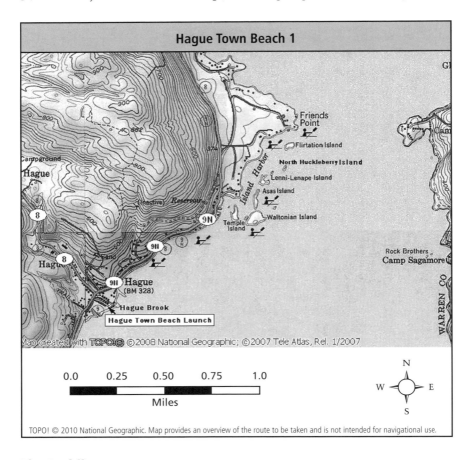

The Paddle:

The Memorial Town Park, including the town beach, was created in July 1955 through the generosity of Mrs. Robert E. Henry, whose gift in memory of her late husband helped purchase 1.5 acres of land including more than 300 feet of shoreline.[1]

Hague Brook, which parallels Rte. 8 as it descends through Hague, flows into Lake George near the public beach. It is too shallow to paddle upstream for any distance and, in fact, a shallow delta extends offshore for about 450 feet. Directly across the lake, at a distance of 1.8 miles, can be seen the eastern shoreline dominated by low-lying, 600-foot-high ridges.

Until 1808 Hague was known as Rochester.[2] The name Hague came from The Hague (Den Haag) in the Netherlands.[3] More recently the village has been dubbed "Basstown USA" for its annual bass fishing tournament held each June.

Northeast—By following along the west shoreline, the mouth of Hague Brook is immediately passed as you leave the beach behind. At 0.8 mile you will come

▶ **Hague Town Beach (Hague)**

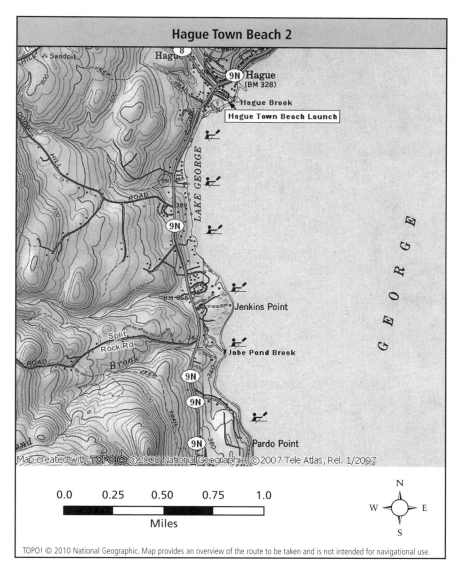

Hague Town Beach 2

Miles

TOPO! © 2010 National Geographic. Map provides an overview of the route to be taken and is not intended for navigational use.

to state-owned Temple Knoll Island, also known as Waltrous Island[4] and Temple Noe Island—the first of a series of nine, small, state-owned islands that have formed off the west mainland, all contained within a span of 0.5 mile and separated from each other by only 0.05–0.1 mile. The islands are located in an area where boaters are restricted from speeding, providing paddlers with a modicum of security from onrushing boats. It is a fascinating area where you can weave your way around and in-between the islands as you go from one to the next.

Temple Knoll Island. Photograph 2011.

Starting from Temple Knoll Island, you will reach Waltonian Island, named after the Waltonian Sportsmen Club of Glens Falls, in 0.05 mile. In the late 1890s Col. William D'Alton Mann erected a house on the island that lasted for only a short length of time. Asas Island, named after an old fisherman named Asa Leach who lived in a shack on the island, is reached in another 0.05 mile.[5] Next, in another 0.05 mile, is Lenni-Lenape Island, also called Lewanee Island, which pays homage to the Delaware tribe and their belief that they were the first inhabitants of the world (hence *Lenni-Lenape*, which means "true men").[6] Two tiny islands, Lover's Rock Island and North Huckleberry Island, follow in another 0.1 mile. And in another 0.1 mile, you'll find Flirtation Island (only 0.1 mile from the mainland), named either for Native Americans who came to the island to court their lovers[7] or from an eighteenth-century British word for "darting," which was suggested by the island's trees swaying wildly about on windy days.[8]

Friends Point, 0.1 mile from Flirtation Island, is the turnaround point for this trek. Its name likely comes from William Friend and his family, who settled there in 1790,[9] but another version contends that the name arose following an incident when two eighteenth-century scouting parties, meeting in the dark, were ready to skirmish until they discovered at the last possible moment that they were on the same side and therefore "friends."

▶ **Hague Town Beach (Hague)**

Friends Point is located at one of the narrowest sections of the lake, a mere 0.5 mile from Browns Point on the opposite side of the lake, where Camp Adirondack is located. From Friends Point, you can obtain excellent views of distant Rogers Slide to the north and Anthony's Nose, much closer, to the northeast.

It was near Friend's Point in July of 1856 that the 150-ton steamboat *John Jay* (named after Supreme Court Chief Justice John Jay) caught fire and had to be abandoned. A number of lives were lost in the process.[10] The wreck lies under 10 feet of water just south of Temple Knoll Island.

South—Heading south along the west shoreline you will come to Jenkins Point, which was named after an early settler, at 1.1 miles.[11] Look for Jabe Pond Brook, at 1.4 miles, between Jenkins Point and Pardo Point, which is reached at 1.8 miles. Pardo Point was possibly named after the nineteenth- and twentieth-century Spanish author and environmentalist Emilia Pardo Bazan, whose writings significantly contributed to the halting of lumbering and mining in northern New York.[12] In the eighteenth century Pardo Point was a favorite spot for British scouts wishing to keep track of French movements around the lake.[13]

Were you to continue farther south from Pardo Point, you would round the crescent-shaped shoreline of Arcady Bay and then reach Stark Point at 2.6 miles. From Stark Point it would be but a scant 0.1 mile to privately owned Scotch Bonnet Island, named because the island, with its solitary tree, resembled a Scottish cap or bonnet.[14]

7 Rogers Rock Campground (Hague)
Paddling by Rogers Slide and Indian Kettles

■ **Launch Site:** Rogers Rock State Campground off of Rte. 9N (Warren County); concrete ramp; parking for twenty-four cars and trailers; restrooms; modest day-use fee; open early May–Columbus Day. For more information: Rogers Rock State Campground, 9894 Lake Shore Drive, Hague, NY 12836, (518) 585-6746, Regional Office: (518) 623-1200, dec.ny.gov/outdoor/24493.html.

■ **Delorme NYS Atlas & Gazetteer:** p. 89, B6; **GPS:** 43°47.58'N, 73°28.85'W

■ **Destinations & Mileages:** *Northeast:* to Juniper Island—0.8 mile; to Rogers Slide—1.0 mile; to Echo Bay (North)—1.5 miles; to Windmill Point—1.8 miles. *South:* to Indian Kettles—1.3 miles.

■ **Comments:** Read "Caution" beginning on page xxi and Lake George Region Advisory on page 2.

Directions: From the Adirondack Northway (I-87), get off at Exit 25 for Chestertown and head northeast on Rte. 8 for roughly 18 miles until you reach the village of Hague. Turn left onto Rte. 9N and drive north for 3.8 miles. Turn right into the entrance for the Rogers Rock State Campgrounds.

From Ticonderoga (junction of Rtes. 9N & 74), head south for 5.6 miles (or 4.3 miles south of Rte. 77) and turn left into the entrance to Rogers Rock Campground.

From either direction proceed 0.6 mile from the entrance to Rogers Rock State Campground to reach the boat launch adjacent to the public beach.

The Paddle:
New York State purchased the lands at Rogers Rock State Campground in 1936. The Civilian Conservation Corps (CCC) worked for a number of years making the area habitable, and the campground was opened to the public in 1947.[1]

Both the mountain and the campground are named after Major Robert Rogers, a feared colonial fighter whose exploits during the French and Indian War were legendary. Rogers purportedly eluded a pursuing war party by engaging in a death-defying slide down the sloping rock face on Rogers Rock. Earlier Rogers Rock was called Mt. Pelee.[2]

The beach and boat launch at Rogers Rock Campground are located at Cooks Bay, named after Joseph Cook, a prominent historian and religious leader.[3] Presumably Cooks Mountain, just slightly to the northeast, is named for him as well.

Northeast—Heading northeast for 0.8 mile you will come to Juniper Island at the southern tip of the Rogers Slide massif (a block of the Earth's crust that has shifted as a unit). The island is named for its red cedar trees (*Juniperis virginiana*)[4] Rogers Slide is reached at roughly 1.0 mile and continues along the edge of the lake for an appreciable distance. The mountain rises up nearly 1,000 feet

Rogers Rock Campground

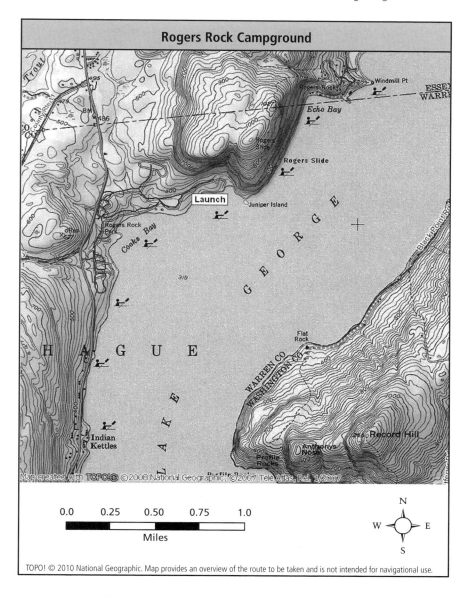

0.0   0.25   0.50   0.75   1.0

Miles

N
W — E
S

above the lake and is notable for being particularly rich in granite and graphite. Peregrine falcons can often be observed near the massive rock face.

Farther beyond is the site of Roger's Rock Hotel, a grand three-story edifice built by the Treadway Brothers in 1874. In 1903 the hotel became the Rogers Rock Club, a private establishment that lasted until 1948 when it was razed. During the time that the hotel operated, guests could follow a path that led up to the summit of the mountain. The private club remains today as a collection of new and revamped cottages.

Echo Bay is reached at 1.5 miles. Listen closely for an echo if you give a yell.

By continuing northeast you will come to Windmill Point at 1.8 miles. This point has also been known as Hawkeye Point, after the main protagonist in James Fenimore Cooper's novel *The Last of the Mohicans*.

South—Proceeding south for less than 0.2 mile you will pass by Haymeadow Brook, which runs through the south end of the campground. The Indian Kettles are reached at 1.3 miles along the rocky shoreline by The View Restaurant, which as of 2011 remained closed after operating continuously since 1947. The Indian Kettles consist of a grouping of naturally formed potholes that historians believe were used by Native Americans for cooking, pounding corn, and storing produce. The holes range in size from that of a pail to larger than a barrel.[5]

Across the lake from Indian Kettles is Anthony's Nose, which extends west along the north side of Blairs Bay. Were you to continue south for another 0.5 mile, you would reach Forest Bay.

Rogers Rock and slide. Postcard ca. 1920.

▶ Rogers Rock Campground (Hague)

Mossy Point (Ticonderoga)
Exploring the Northern Terminus of Lake George

8

- ■ **Launch Site:** Mossy Point Boat Launch off of Black Point Road (Essex County); hard-surface double ramp; parking for 100 cars & trailers; restrooms
- ■ **Delorme NYS Atlas & Gazetteer:** p. 89, B6; **GPS:** 43°49.34'N; 73°25.63'W
- ■ **Destinations & Mileages:** *North:* to Rte. 77 bridge—1.2 miles; to dam—1.3 miles. *Southwest*: to Prison Island—0.8 mile; to Black Point—1.2 miles.
- ■ **Comments:** Read "Caution" beginning on page xxi and Lake George Region Advisory on page 2.

Directions: From the junction of Rtes. 9N & 77 at the north end of Lake George near Ticonderoga, turn onto Rte. 77 (Alexandria Avenue) and proceed east for 1.3 miles, crossing over the tail end of Lake George in the process. Turn right onto Water Street and head south for 0.3 mile. You will reach a "V" intersection where The Portage (a road) comes in on your left. From there continue south on Black Point Road (Rte. 3) for another 0.7 mile. Turn right into the entrance for the Mossy Point Boat Launch, approximately 0.1 mile before you reach Mossy Point Road. Drive west for 0.05 mile and park in the large parking area provided.

The Paddle:
You are near Ticonderoga, an Iroquois word for "the land between the waters" or "the junction between two waterways"—the waters being Lake George and Lake Champlain. For thousands of years Native Americans portaged their canoes back and forth between these two lakes. Today you can paddle as far as the bridge before the dam at the northernmost end of Lake George, but no farther.

Look across the lake to see 1,285-foot-high Bear Mountain to the west and 1,223-foot-high Cooks Mountain to the southwest. Directly before you is a "choke point"—a place on the lake so narrow that a person with a good throwing arm could toss a rock across to the opposite side. Slightly north of the launch site the lake narrows again, contracting to a width of no more than 0.03 mile.

In 1759 a blockhouse stood at the site of the boat launch, taking advantage of the marked narrowing in the lake that provided an ideal strategic military position.[1] Henry Knox came overland to this spot with his train of cannons captured from Fort Ticonderoga on his way to Boston to help besiege the British in 1776.[2]

On the mainland northwest of Prison Island is the spot where British General James Abercromby and his army landed in preparation for an assault on Fort Ticonderoga during the French and Indian War. It was near there that General William Howe—Abercromby's main field general—was killed in a chance encounter with the enemy. His demise seriously undercut the troops' morale, causing Abercromby to postpone the attack on Fort Ticonderoga for a day. This

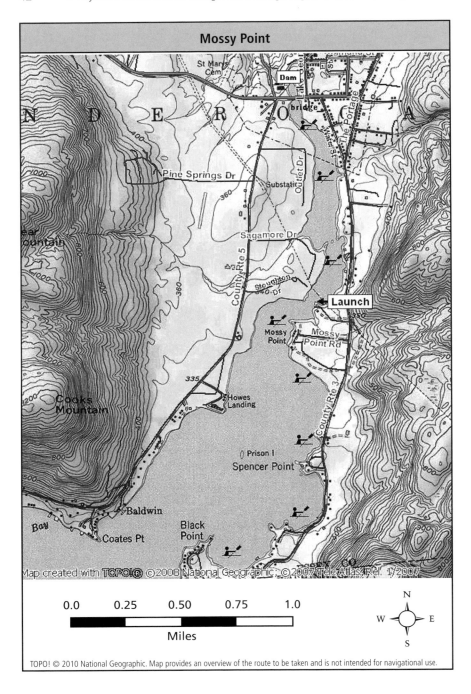

0.0   0.25   0.50   0.75   1.0

Miles

N
W ⬦ E
S

TOPO! © 2010 National Geographic. Map provides an overview of the route to be taken and is not intended for navigational use.

▶ **Mossy Point (Ticonderoga)**

small but significant delay allowed the French to shore up their defenses and may have contributed ultimately to Abercromby's defeat. Ever since then the site on the mainland has been known as Howes Landing.[3]

North—Heading north, you will paddle along a riverlike section of the lake. At 0.4 mile an area of shallow water and a series of tiny rocky outcroppings are encountered, the largest outcropping being near the middle of the narrow. This bedrock obstruction, known as the Natural Stone Dam, poses no difficulty for paddlers but does represent a serious hazard for motorboats. A tiny channel near the west shore was blasted out in the 1800s to allow boaters to (carefully) pass through.

Look for a plaque at the south end of the middle island, which is called Diane's Rock. The plaque commemorates Diane Struble, a 25-year-old divorced mother of three who, in August of 1958, became the first person to swim the entire length of Lake George. It took her 35 hours to go from the outlet at Ticonderoga to Lake George Village.

Directly southeast of the shallows is the Snug Harbor Marina. The cliffs visible to your right are along the west shoulder of Mt. Defiance. In 1.2 miles the Rte. 77 bridge that you drove over to get to the launch is reached. This is the turnaround point; a series of blue and white buoys warns against continuing any farther. Less than 0.1 mile beyond is a rusted iron bridge and, several hundred feet beyond that, an 80-foot-long dam built on top of a waterfall in 1903. The dam marks the north end of Lake George.

Diane's Rock. Photograph 2011.

Southwest—Proceeding south down the lake you will come to tiny state-owned Prison Island—variously known as Prisoner's Island[4] and Mutten Island—at 0.8 mile, less than 0.2 mile west of Spencer Point and 0.2 mile southeast of Howes Landing on the west mainland. Prison Island is heavily eroded and probably only half the size today as when it was described in the mid-1800s. In 1996 the DEC laid down riprap around the shoreline to fortify the island's perimeter. The island was allegedly used at different times by both the French and English to hold prisoners. The island apparently wasn't much of a prison. According to one account, 148 French soldiers being held by the English were able to escape by wading through shallow waters to the mainland.[5] This tale has a certain ring of plausibility to it, since the entire area northwest of Prison Island consists of rocky shoals. According to another source, however, the English took their prisoners to the south end of the lake after holding them for a few days on the island.[6] In the end, what makes the islands of Lake George so interesting are the many and varied stories that surround them. The French also used the island as a prison as a means of protecting their English captives from their sometimes overzealous Indian allies on the mainland.[7]

From Prison Island continue south for 0.4 mile to Black Point, where the lake narrows appreciably again to a width of 0.3 mile. If you wish, you can round Black Point and head past Turtle Rocks into Weeds Bay. The bay may have been named for Thurlow Weed who, as chief manager for Governor William Seward, discouraged rampant industrialization of Lake George.[8]

▶ **Mossy Point (Ticonderoga)**

Black Point Public Beach (Ticonderoga)
Paddling to Anthony's Nose

9

- ■ **Launch Site:** Town Beach at Black Point off of Black Point Road (Washington County); restrooms and changing rooms; open daily from 10 AM–6 PM.
  For more information: 11 Tiroga Beach Lane, Ticonderoga, NY, (518) 585-7139, townofticonderoga.com/index.php?page_id+160.
- ■ **Delorme NYS Atlas & Gazetteer:** p. 89, B6; **GPS:** 43°48.14'N; 73°26.16'W
- ■ **Destinations & Mileages:** *North*: to Turtle Rocks—0.1 mile; to Black Point—0.5 mile. *Southwest:* to Flat Rock—2.0 miles; to Profile Rocks/Anthony's Nose—2.9 miles.
- ■ **Comments:** Read "Caution" beginning on page xxi and Lake George Region Advisory on page 2.

Directions: From the junction of Rtes. 9N & 77 at the north end of Lake George near Ticonderoga, turn onto Rte. 77 and proceed east for 1.3 mile, crossing over the north end of Lake George in the process. Turn right onto Water Street and head south for 0.3 mile. When you reach the point where The Portage (a road) enters on your left, continue south for 2.3 miles and then turn right on Tiroga Beach Lane. In a couple of hundred feet you will reach the entrance to the beach, on your left. A 10-foot-wide lane has been created on the east side of the beach to enable paddlers to readily access the lake while bypassing bathers. This access was created thanks to the efforts of David Pahl, a summer resident at The Portage in Ticonderoga.

View of Cooks Mountain from Black Point Public Beach. Photograph 2010.

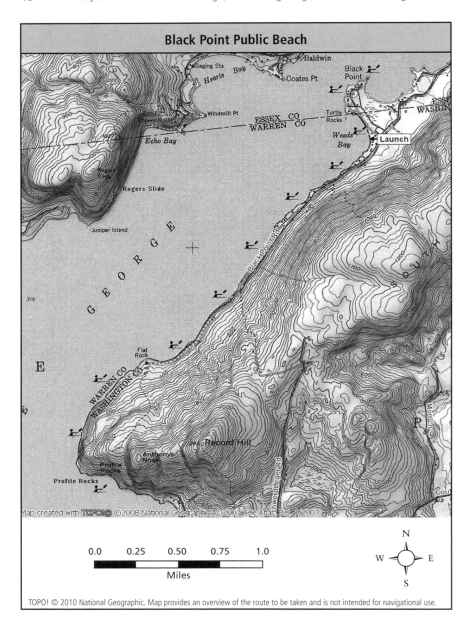

Black Point Public Beach

TOPO! © 2010 National Geographic. Map provides an overview of the route to be taken and is not intended for navigational use.

▶ **Black Point Public Beach (Ticonderoga)**

The Paddle:

Northwest across the lake is Cooks Mountain, which dominates the skyline. Rogers Rock, with its distinctive rock face descending to the water's edge, is farther southwest. You are looking at what some have dubbed the "million dollar view" of Lake George.

North—Head northwest initially, passing Turtle Rocks (whose upper surface has been painted white to help boaters avoid mishaps) in 0.1 mile and then rounding Black Point, which is at the end of a long peninsula, at 0.5 mile.

Southwest—Follow the east shore along the base of South Mountain to reach Flat Rock in 2.0 miles. Continue south for another 0.9 mile and you will come to the south end of Profile Rocks, a towering cliff face and rock formation on the west shoulder of Anthony's Nose. Look closely and you may catch a glimpse of Peregrine falcons on the upper cliff ledges.

One of the deepest basins in the lake, with a depth of 175 feet, is located next to Anthony's Nose.

10   Washington County Beach (Hulett's Landing)
Exploring a Seemingly Endless Number of Islands

■ **Launch Site:** Washington County Beach on Sunset Bay at Hulett's Landing near the terminus of Rte. 6 (Washington County); open daily 8 AM–8 PM; launch restricted to canoes and kayaks only

■ **Delorme NYS Atlas & Gazetteer:** p. 89, CD5–6; **GPS:** 43°38.58'N; 73°30.47'W

■ **Destinations & Mileages:** *South:* up Sunset Bay Creek—0.1 mile. *North:* to Fredericks Point—0.2 mile; to Rock Dunder Island—0.3 mile; to Loon Island—0.6 mile; to Meadow Point—0.7 mile; from Meadow Point to Little Gibraltar Island—0.5 mile (1.2 miles from launch); from Little Gibraltar Island to Agnes Island—0.2 mile (1.4 miles from launch); around Agnes Island—0.5 mile. *Southwest:* to Narrow Island—0.2 mile; from Narrow Island to Huletts Island—0.1 mile (0.3 mile from launch); from Huletts Island following shoreline to Gardner Point—0.7 mile (1.0 mile from launch); around Cook Bay—0.5 mile; from Gardner Point to Burgess Island—0.1 mile (1.1 miles from launch); from Burgess Island to Pederson Point—0.2 mile (1.3 miles from launch); alternately, from Gardner Point to Pederson Point—0.3 mile (1.3 miles from launch); from Pederson Point to Nobles Island—0.1 mile (1.4 miles from launch); around Kitchal Bay—0.4 mile; from Nobles Island to Vicars Island—0.5 mile (2.1 miles from launch); around Vicars Island—0.6 mile; alternately, from Nobles Island to Harbor Islands—0.4 mile (1.9 miles from launch); around Harbor Islands—1.3 miles; from Harbor Islands to St. Sacrament Island (Mother Bunch Islands)—0.6 mile (2.9 miles from launch).

Mother Bunch Islands: St. Sacrament Island is located at the north end of the Mother Bunch Group. From here ten islands can be paddled around within a span of 1.0 mile as you proceed southwest. From St. Sacrament Island to Coopers Island—0.05 mile (3.2 miles from launch); from St. Sacrament Island to Horicon Island—0.05 mile (3.3 miles from launch); from Horicon Island to Picnic Island—0.05 mile (3.5 miles from launch); from Picnic Island to Sagamore Island—0.05 mile (3.55 miles from launch); from Sagamore Island to Little Burgess Island—0.1 mile (3.8 miles from launch); from Little Burgess Island to Duran Island—0.05 mile (3.9 miles from launch); from Duran Island to Hatchet Island—0.2 mile (4.2 miles from launch); alternately, from Duran Island to Phenita Island—0.05 mile (4.0 miles from launch); alternately, from Duran Island to Floating Battery Island—0.2 mile (4.3 miles from launch); from Floating Battery Island to Three Sirens Islands—0.5 mile (5.2 miles from launch).

Should you continue even farther south you would reach the trailhead to Black Mountain to your left in another 0.7 miles (5.9 miles from launch).

■ **Comments:** Read "Caution" beginning on page xxi and Lake George Region Advisory on page 2.

Map 2 is a continuation south of Map 1.

▶ **Washington County Beach (Hulett's Landing)**

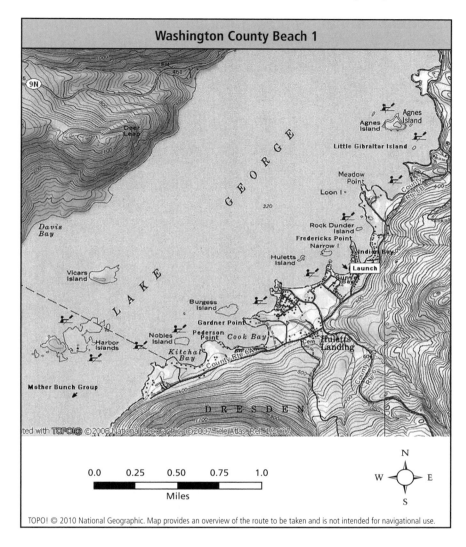

Washington County Beach 1

TOPO! © 2010 National Geographic. Map provides an overview of the route to be taken and is not intended for navigational use.

Directions: From Whitehall (junction of Rtes. 4 North & 22), head north on Rte. 22 for 7.3 miles. From Ticonderoga (junction of Rtes. 22 South & 74), proceed south on Rte. 22 for 18 miles.

From either direction, turn onto Hulett's Landing Road (Rte. 6) and drive west for 4.4 miles. As soon as you pass by a left-hand turn for Rte. 6A, bear right onto Rte. 6B. Go north for 0.2 mile and then turn left onto Sunset Bay Road, following signs to the Washington County Beach. After 100 feet turn left and drive for 0.1 mile to the parking area. The dock and car-top launch are located on the north (right) side of Washington County Beach in Sunset Bay.

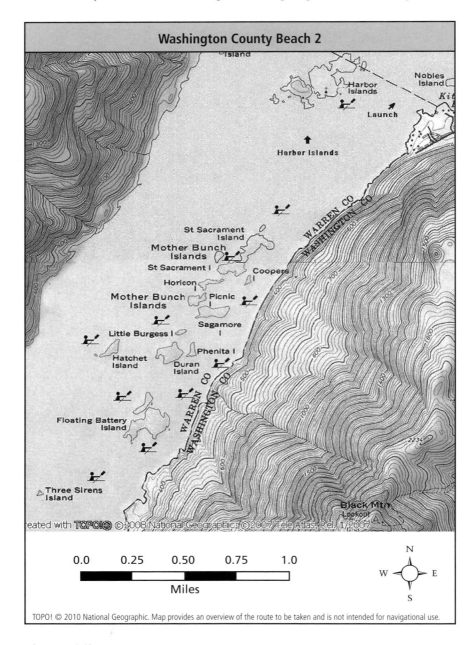

The Paddle:

Hulett's Landing is named after Philander Hulett, a nineteenth-century settler who established a farm near the landing.[1]

▶ **Washington County Beach (Hulett's Landing)**

South of Hulett's Landing is 1,954-foot-high Elephant Mountain rising up from the east shore of the lake. With a liberal dose of imagination the mountain's profile can be likened to that of an elephant's head and trunk.[2]

Across the lake is the distinctive vertical bluff of Deer Leap Mountain and, behind it, 1,605-foot-high Bloomer Mountain. Together the two are unofficially called the Twin Mountains.[3] Across the lake to the southwest lies historic Sabbath Day Point.

South—Paddle around the perimeter of the roped-in beach to reach the mouth of a tiny stream that rises from Hogback Mountain and flows into Sunset Bay along the west side of the beach. This creek, although shallow, can be paddled upstream for roughly 0.1 mile, passing between the town park to your left and private camps to your right.

North—Proceed north for 0.2 mile to reach Fredericks Point at the northwest end of a peninsula separating Sunset Bay from Indian Bay. From Fredericks Point it is but a scant 0.1 mile north to state-owned Rock Dunder Island and, from there, less than 0.3 mile northwest to Loon Island, whose name is a reminder that indigenous loon populations have been largely driven off the lake by development and other human use.[4] Returning to the mainland, Meadow Point is reached in another 0.1 mile.

From Meadow Point follow the shoreline east, then north until you come to state-owned Little Gibraltar Island in 0.5 mile (1.2 miles from launch). From Little Gibraltar Island it is less than 0.2 mile northwest to state-owned Agnes Island (1.4 miles from launch), named after the daughter of Delorm Knowlton, owner of a large estate opposite the island.[5] Agnes Island can be paddled around in 0.5 mile. Adjacent to Agnes Island is tiny Gillette Island, also called Alletete Island, and also state owned.

Southwest—Head northwest for 0.2 mile, passing by the Huletts Island View Marina (on your left) to reach state-owned Narrow Island, which is separated from the mainland by 0.05 mile. The island can be circumnavigated in 0.3 mile. The Narrow Island Group Headquarters is located on the southwest side of the island.

From Narrow Island head west for 0.1 mile (0.3 mile from launch) to state-owned Huletts Island, also known as Whale Island, which consists of three tiny islands almost joined together.

Leaving Huletts Island behind, paddle south for 0.2 mile (0.5 mile from launch) to the mainland and then follow the shoreline southwest for another 0.5 mile (1.0 mile from launch) to Gardner Point, located at the northwest tip of Cook Bay. Cook Bay can be paddled around in 0.5 mile.

From Gardner Point head northwest for 0.1 mile (1.1 miles from launch) to reach state-owned Burgess Island, a moderate-sized island named after John Burgess, a prominent local figure.[6] From Burgess Island it is a 0.2-mile paddle (1.3 miles from launch) southwest to the mainland at Pederson Point, which is located at the tip of a small peninsula separating Cook Bay from Kitchal Bay.

From Pederson Point head west for 0.1 mile (1.4 miles from launch) to state-owned Nobles Island, also called Cooks Island, formed at the mouth of Kitchal Bay, a tiny cove that can be paddled around in 0.4 mile. Nobles Island was named after Elijah Nobles, who maintained a log cabin on the mainland across from the island.[7]

From Nobles Island, paddle northwest for 0.5 mile (2.1 miles from launch) to 0.2-mile-long state-owned Vicars Island, which can be circumnavigated in 0.6 mile, or west for 0.4 mile (1.9 miles from launch) to the 0.3-mile-long Harbor Islands, which can be circumnavigated in 1.3 miles. Vicars Island, now state owned, was once occupied either by a vicar[8] or a man named Vicar.[9] The 8-acre island contains a small chapel visible from the water.

The five privately owned Harbor Islands, of which Hecker and Hewitt are the most prominent, are historically significant. The islands were the site of a terrible ambush during the French and Indian War in which 131 English troops out of a total force of 350 men were killed by French-allied Indians.[10] The islands provide excellent harborage today, which explains how their name came about.[11] The narrow passage between the two large islands, Hecker and Hewitt, is called the Needle's Eye. The chapel at the southeast end of Hecker Island was built in 1906 by the Paulist Fathers to honor Saint Isaac Jogues, the first European to set eyes on the lake.

Mother Bunch Islands—From Harbor Islands continue following the east shoreline southwest to reach a grouping of twelve principal islands called the Mother Bunch Islands. They lie between Black Mountain to the east and the Tongue Mountain Range to the west.

State-owned St. Sacrament Island, the northernmost island of the Mother Bunch Group, is reached at 0.6 mile from Harbor Islands (or 2.9 miles from the launch). Its name recalls the lake's original European appellation—Lac du St. Sacrement.[12]

From St. Sacrament Island, the Mother Bunch can be leisurely explored as you hop from one island to the next. Proceed 0.05 mile southeast from St. Sacrament Island to state-owned Coopers Island, also called Pine Island,[13] or 0.05 mile southwest to state-owned Horicon Island. James Fenimore Cooper fans may remember that Horicon was the name for Lake George in Cooper's novel *The Last of the Mohicans*. Although Cooper's name failed to take hold, two different steamboats on the lake have made use of it.

From Horicon Island it is a 0.05-mile jump south to its immediate neighbor, state-owned Picnic Island which, like several other islands on the lake, is designated for picnicking only. State-owned Sagamore Island, due south, is only 0.05 mile away. "Sagamore" was a title for a lesser Native American chieftain.

From Sagamore Island head 0.1 mile southwest to state-owned Little Burgess Island, then 0.05 mile south to state-owned Duran Island. Because of its size, Little Burgess Island only contains one state-operated campsite, an obvious enticement for those who wish to have their own island for the night. Duran

▶ **Washington County Beach (Hulett's Landing)**

Island was allegedly used by Native Americans to confine prisoners until ransom was paid. The name may have come from the French *durance vile*, meaning "imprisonment."[14]

From Duran Island head 0.2 mile west to state-owned Hatchet Island, also called Tomahawk Island,[15] 0.05 mile east to state-owned Phenita Island, or 0.2 mile south to Floating Battery Island. Hatchet Island vaguely resembles a tomahawk when seen from the air. The fact that three tomahawks were found hidden away in its rocks may also have given rise to its name.[16] A more lurid account claims that a British scout was killed on the island by Hurons in 1756.[17] Phenita Island's alternate name, Fanita Island, has an unusual origin. It may have arisen from fanions—small flags used by sailors to mark off position or territory—that were displayed on the Mother Bunch Islands whenever enemy scouts were sighted on Black Mountain, an obvious lookout post.[18] Floating Battery Island acquired its name from a gunboat that sank near the island.[19]

From Floating Battery Island proceed southwest for 0.5 mile to state-owned Three Sirens Island, which lies 0.4 mile west of the mainland. The name and the island's rocky shoreline and shoals hearken back to the classic mythological tale of sailors lured to their deaths on rocky shoals by the call of Sirens.[20]

If you wish to combine a hike with a paddle, continue south to Black Mountain Point, 4.7 miles from the launch site (or 5.9 miles if you are following along the islands), where obscure ruins of an old hotel can be seen near the trailhead. A three-mile-long trail leads up to the summit. Native Americans called Black Mountain *Tehaghweangaraneghton*, meaning "the masterful one."[21] Bring hiking boots and a pack to carry essentials if you decide to hike.

The Narrow Island Group's headquarters is located on Narrow Island. Photograph 2010.

11 Warner Bay (Kattskill Bay)
Coves and Islands Dominate This Paddle

■ **Launch Site:** Fischer's Marina off of Pilot Knob Road at Kattskill Bay (Washington County); seasonal hours; modest launch & parking fee; restrooms. For more information: Fischer's Marina Launch, 1215 Pilot Knob Road. Kattskill Bay, NY 12844-1701, (518) 656-9981.

■ **Delorme NYS Atlas & Gazetteer:** p. 81, A4–5; **GPS:** 43°28.47'N; 73°37.59'W

■ **Destinations & Mileages:** *North:* to Elizabeth Island—1.4 miles; to Travis Point—1.7 miles; to Triplet Islands—1.8 miles; to Echo Bay—1.9 miles; to Barber Bay—2.4 miles; to Point Comfort—3.6 miles; to Phelps Island—4.5 miles; to Calf Pen—4.9 miles. *Northwest & West:* to Sheldon Point—0.4 mile; to Ripley Point—0.9 mile; around Sandy Bay from Sheldon Point to Ripley Point—1.3 miles; from Ripley Point to Long Island—0.5 mile (1.4 miles from launch); around Long Island—2.8 miles; from Long Island to Speaker Heck Island—0.05 mile (2.3 miles from launch); around Speaker Heck Island—0.6 mile; from Long Island to Canoe Islands—0.5 mile (3.0 miles from launch); around Canoe Islands—0.9 mile. *Continuing South from Ripley Point:* from Ripley Point along perimeter of Harris Bay to Assembly Point—3.5 miles (4.4 miles from launch); around Happy Family Islands—0.5 mile. *South:* to end of Warner Bay—0.9 mile; under Rte. 9L and up inlet stream—0.3–0.4 mile (1.2–1.3 miles from launch).

■ **Comments:** Read "Caution" beginning on page xxi and Lake George Region Advisory on page 2.

This section of the lake, with the exception of Sandy Bay, can be very congested with boat traffic at times.

Crossing open waters from Long Island to the Canoe Islands should only be attempted if the weather is calm and you are an experienced and skilled paddler with a group of similarly capable paddlers.

The Town of Fort Ann Beach, near the end of Pilot Knob Road, is open for swimming only to residents of the Town of Fort Ann.

Directions: From the center of Lake George Village (junction of Canada Street/ Rte. 9 & Beach Street) drive southeast on Beach Street for 1.0 mile. Turn left onto Rte. 9L and head north for 6.3 miles, then turn left onto Pilot Knob Road and proceed north for 0.9 mile to Fischer's Marina, on your left.

The Paddle:
Fischer's Marina is located on Irish Bay in a larger area known as Kattskill Bay (there is no village, just a post office designation), whose name according to folklore arose from an incident in which a mountain lion was shot and killed.[1]

Warner Bay is named after an early settler.[2] On the opposite side of Warner Bay is a slender peninsula, called Rockhurst, lined with camps and homes—one of four similar communities that have developed at the south basin of Lake

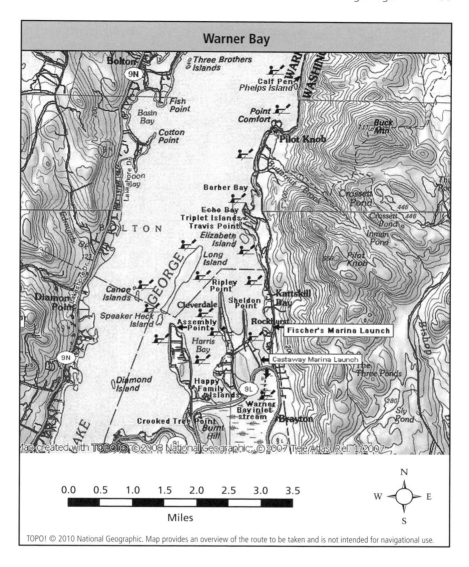

Warner Bay

Bolton

Three Brothers Islands

9N

Calf Pen
Phelps Island

Fish Point

Basin Bay

Point Comfort

Buck Mtn

Cotton Point

Pilot Knob

Lakeshore Dr

Loon Bay

Barber Bay

Crossett Pond

446

Echo Bay
Triplet Islands
Travis Point

Crossett Pond

446

Elizabeth Island

Inman Pond

Long Island

Pilot Knob

BOLTON

GEORGE

Ripley Point

Canoe Islands

Kattskill Bay

Diamond Point

Cleverdale

Sheldon Point

Speaker Heck Island

Assembly Points

Rockhurst

Fischer's Marina Launch

Harris Bay

Castaway Marina Launch

9N

Three Ponds

Diamond Island

Happy Family Islands

9L

Warner Bay inlet stream

Sly Pond

Crooked Tree Point
Burnt Hill

Brayton

LAKE

Map created with TOPO! © 2008 National Geographic; © 2007 Tele Atlas, Rel. 1/2007

0.0   0.5   1.0   1.5   2.0   2.5   3.0   3.5

Miles

N
W ⟡ E
S

TOPO! © 2010 National Geographic. Map provides an overview of the route to be taken and is not intended for navigational use.

George. The tip of Rockhurst Peninsula is called Sheldon Point, after Allen Sheldon, an early settler on the peninsula.[3] At one time the Sheldon House, a hotel, stood near the tip of the point.[4] The tip has also been known as Willard Point, named after the Hotel Willard owned by Deak and Mary Howland. That hotel burned down in the 1960s.

North—Heading north from Fischer's Marina along the east shoreline, at 0.2 mile you will see Sheldon Point close by, off to your left. To your right is a large, old, wooden pier with a broad expanse of lawn behind it—all that remains of the Trout Pavilion Hotel, which burned down in the mid-1970s. In 1.4 miles you will reach 0.2-mile-long Elizabeth Island, also called Little Green Island, likely named after Elizabeth de France, an eighteenth-century French monarch.[5] Early on, the island served as a summer camp for an elite group of New York University graduates who called themselves the Manhattan Club.[6] Elizabeth Island remains privately owned today.

From the south end of Elizabeth Island, continue north for another 0.4 mile to reach Triplet Islands (three tiny, privately owned islands in a row). Farther beyond, the paddle takes you past Echo Bay, which extends 0.3 mile into the mainland, and Barber Bay, a much smaller cove. Point Comfort at Pilot Knob, the site of the YMCA's Camp Chingachgook, is reached at 2.0 miles from Elizabeth Island.

Paddle around the north end of Pilot Knob and follow the east shoreline past Andrews Bay for another 0.9 mile until you come to 0.1-mile-long Phelps Island. Take note that this section of the east shoreline follows along the sloping shoulders of Buck Mountain and Little Buck Mountain. Most of the eastern shore from here past The Narrows and most of the islands are state owned. Continue north for another 0.4 mile to reach a tiny recess in the rock face called Calf Pen (or Calf's Pen). Boaters frequently stop here to watch daredevils jump off the notch's 43-foot-high cliff, a dangerous activity. As recently as July 2011 a 42-year-old Long Island woman was seriously injured when she slipped and fell. Although strangely named, there may be a certain logic to Calf Pen's appellation. The word "calf" is colloquial for a "foolish young man," and a "pen" is an enclosure. Draw your own conclusions. The deepest sounding on the lake was taken a quarter of a mile west of Calf Pen.

There are a number of similar rocky bluffs around the lake, including Jumping Rock (a 30-foot sheer granite slide owned by the Lake George Land Conservancy), 15-foot-high Diver's Rock, and 30-foot-high Double Diver's Rock.

Northwest & West—Take note that this section of the lake, with the exception of Sandy Bay, can be very congested with boat traffic. Exercise the utmost caution. Do not assume that powerboat operators can see you. Heading northwest across the bay from Fischer's Marina, you will reach Sheldon Point in 0.4 mile. Turn left to explore 0.4-mile-long Sandy Bay, which follows the shoreline all the way from Sheldon Point to Ripley Point and can be paddled in 1.3 miles. If you go straight from Sheldon Point to Ripley Point, it is a crossing of 0.5 mile. Ripley Point is associated in name with Reuben Ripley.

From Ripley Point continue west for another 0.5 mile until you reach 1.2-mile-long state-owned Long Island, which can be circumnavigated in 2.8 miles. If you have proceeded due west from Ripley Point, you will end up close to the harbor where the Long Island Group Headquarters is located. The two small islands here are called the Sanford Islands, after Dr. Drurie Sanford, who at one time owned both Long Island and Speaker Heck Island. Long Island was originally called North Island to differentiate it from adjacent South Island (now called Speaker Heck Island). Long Island covers over 97 acres with nearly 3 miles of shoreline[7] and 90

▶ **Warner Bay (Kattskill Bay)**

Long Island and Goose Island, Lake George, N. Y.

Paddling near Long Island. Postcard ca. 1940.

campsites. Some of the best views of the northern part of the lake and its soaring mountains are from near the north tip of Long Island, near Hogback Reef.

From the west side of Long Island, the Canoe Islands are clearly visible 0.5 mile away and can be reached by crossing open waters, but only if the weather is calm and you are an experienced and skilled paddler with a group of similarly capable paddlers. The Canoe Islands were named after twenty-three members of the American Canoe Association held their first meeting on the islands in August 1880.[8] They have also been known as Three Sisters Island[9] and originally as the Seven Mile Islands. The islands can be circled in 0.9 mile. The largest of the Canoe Islands is owned by the Canoe Island Lodge, located directly west across on the mainland. Its shape vaguely resembles that of an arrowhead. The smaller island, called Little (Baby) Canoe Island, is privately owned and there is a small summerhouse on it.[10] Major Robert Rogers and his men are said to have camped on the islands in 1758 following their defeat at Ticonderoga.[11]

Near the southwest end of Long Island is state-owned Speaker Heck Island, separated from Long Island by a narrow strait. Speaker Heck Island was earlier known as South Island (because it is south of Long Island), but the name was changed to Speaker Heck Island in 1968 in honor of Oswald Heck, former speaker of the New York State Assembly and longtime advocate for preserving the natural beauty of Lake George. A plaque honoring Heck's contributions was erected at the picnic shelter on the south end of the island.[12] The island can be circled in 0.6 mile.

Both Long Island and Speaker Heck Island are very close to Assembly Point— a long peninsula that forms the west perimeter of Harris Bay. Assembly Point was named for the Lake George Assembly, which gathered here for religious and recreational pursuits in 1888.[13] Should the weather suddenly deteriorate and you need an exit strategy, Assembly Point on the east mainland is only 0.1 mile away.

Continuing South from Ripley Point—Harris Bay can be explored by following the shoreline from Ripley Point to Assembly Point, a distance of 3.5 miles. The bay is named after Gilbert Harris,[14] an early settler, and is one of the principal wetlands on the lake. It was at this bay that General Montcalm moored his vessels before launching an attack on Fort William Henry in 1757. At the southeast end of Harris Bay are the state-owned Happy Family Islands. These islands, like many on the lake, are in constant danger of being eroded away. In the fall of 2000, volunteers piled 25 tons of stone around the islands' shorelines to slow down the erosive process.[15]

There is a charming, but possibly fanciful, story behind how the Happy Family Islands came to be named. A child was sketching a drawing of the islands for the Harris family and incorrectly labeled them the Harri Family Islands. In addition, insufficient pressure on the pen was applied to the front legs of the r's, leaving the caption to read Happi Family Islands.[16] They have been the Happy Family Islands ever since, if this story is to be believed.

South—From Fischer's Marina, head left into Warner Bay and proceed south for 0.9 mile to the Rte. 9L bridge. By paddling through a culvert under Rte. 9L, you can continue your voyage south through the wetlands for about 0.4 mile, following the inlet stream.

Alternate Launch Site

Castaway Marina (Warner Bay)

- ■ **Launch Site:** Castaway Marina's launch (Washington County); boat ramp; restrooms; fee charged for launching & parking. For more information: Castaway Marina, 1212 Bay Rd. Rte. 9L, Lake George, NY 12845, (518) 656-3636.
- ■ **Delorme NYS Atlas & Gazetteer:** p. 81, A4–5; **Estimated GPS:** 43°27.77'N; 73°37.78'W
- ■ **Destinations & Mileages:** *North:* to Elizabeth Island—2.1 miles; to Travis Point—2.4 miles; to Triplet Islands—2.5 miles; to Echo Bay—2.6 miles; to Barber Bay—3.1 miles; to Point Comfort—4.3 miles; to Phelps Island—5.2 miles; to Calf Pen—5.6 miles. *North & West:* to Sheldon Point—1.0 mile; to Ripley Point—1.5 miles; to Long Island—2.0 miles; around Long Island—2.8 miles; from Long Island to Speaker Heck Island—0.05 mile (2.9 miles from launch); around Speaker Heck Island—0.6 mile; from Long Island to Canoe Islands—0.5 mile (3.6 miles from launch). *Continuing South from Ripley Point:* from Ripley Point along perimeter of Harris Bay to Assembly Point—3.5 miles (5.0 miles from launch); around Happy Family Islands—0.5 mile. *South:* to culvert and inlet stream—0.1 mile; under Rte. 9L and along inlet stream—0.3–0.4 mile.
- ■ **Comments:** Read "Caution" beginning on page xxi and Lake George Region Advisory on page 2.

Directions: From the center of Lake George Village (junction of Canada Street/ Rte. 9 & Beach Street), drive southeast on Beach Street for 1.0 mile. Turn left onto Rte. 9L and head northeast for roughly 6.0 miles (or 0.5 miles past Cleverdale Road). The Castaway Marina is on your left.

▶ **Warner Bay (Kattskill Bay)**

Dunham Bay (Lake George Village)
Paddling a Narrow Section of the Lake

12

■ **Launch Site:** Dunham's Bay Launch off of Bay Road (Warren County); privately owned ramp site; seasonal hours; restrooms; modest launch fee. For more information: Dunham's Bay Launch, Route 9L & Bay Rd., Lake George, NY 12845, (518) 668-2729, (518) 744-2627.

■ **Delorme NYS Atlas & Gazetteer:** p. 81, A4–5; **GPS:** 43°26.49'N; 73°39.25'W

■ **Destinations & Mileages:** *South:* along Dunham Bay inlet stream—2.0 miles. *North & West:* to Crooked Tree Point—0.8 mile; to Dark Bay—1.3 miles; to Woods Point—1.5 miles; to Plum Point—1.8 miles.

■ **Comments:** Read "Caution" beginning on page xxi and Lake George Region Advisory on page 2.

  Under most conditions wind and current are not a significant factor on the Dunham Bay inlet stream.

Directions: From the center of Lake George Village (junction of Canada Street/ Rte. 9 & Beach Street) drive southeast on Beach Street for 1.0 mile. When you come to Rte. 9L (East Shore Drive), turn left and head northeast for 3.8 miles, then turn right onto Bay Road and immediately left into the parking area for the Dunham Bay Launch, located on the inlet stream.

  From there you can either paddle upstream along the inlet stream through marshlands, or head downstream through the culvert under Rte. 9L and directly into Dunham Bay.

The Paddle:
Dunham Bay (also spelled "Dunham's" and "Dunhams") is formed between 564-foot-high Burnt Hill to the east and 525-foot-high Joshua Rock to the west. The bay was named after Elijah Dunham, an early merchant, lumberman, and sloop operator.[1] The 1,400-acre bay wetland complex was purchased by the Nature Conservancy in 1977 and became part of the Adirondack Forest Preserve in that same year.[2] The marshlands serve as a spawning ground for bass, perch, pike, crappies, and other species of fish. They also provide shelter nests and lairs for many mammals, reptiles, amphibians, and birds[3] including otters, minks, beavers, raccoons, muskrat, and waterfowl. Powerboats are restricted to no more than 5 MPH within the bay and for a short distance outside of it.

  South—From the boat launch turn right and follow the inlet creek upstream (south) through a marshy area for 2.0 miles. This area is enclosed by Ridge Road to the east, East Shore Drive (Rte. 9L) to the north, Pickle Hill Road to the south, and Bay Road (Rte. 7) to the west. The stream is consistently over 60–70 feet wide and very serpentine, with many false leads that are still fun to explore anyway. Although you will paddle a respectable distance, it is not far as a crow

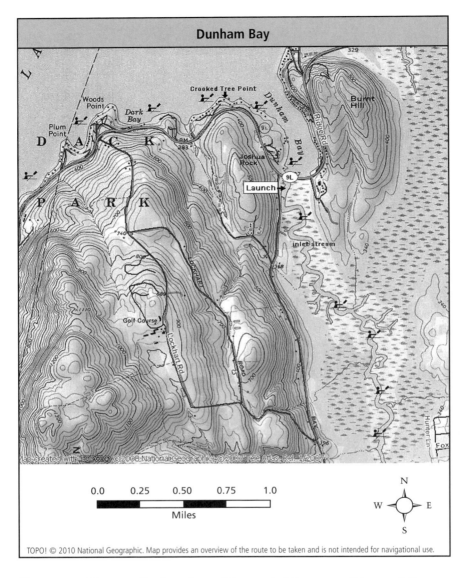

flies. At roughly 1.6 miles into the paddle, a subsidiary arm of the creek forms a nearly circular oxbow that at high water closes in on itself.

Overall you will find this to be a relatively peaceful paddle since motorboats are not permitted any farther south inland than 0.2 mile from the Rte. 9L bridge.

During certain times of the year, you can expect to hear the sound of rifle fire emanating from the Dunham Bay Fish & Game Club, which is located along the north end of Ridge Road.

▶ Dunham Bay (Lake George Village)

North & West—Paddle into Dunham Bay, passing under the Rte. 9L bridge (roughly 59 inches above the average waterline), and proceed north for 0.8 mile, rounding Crooked Tree Point at the northwest mouth of the bay.

Heading west now, you will reach Dark Bay in another 0.5 mile and then Woods Point 0.2 mile after that. Dark Bay's name arose from the tall pine trees that once grew around it and markedly reduced the amount of sunlight falling on the water.[4]

From Woods Point continue southwest for another 0.4 miles to reach Plum Point, supposedly named for its once-abundant plum trees.[5] You have now gone 1.9 miles from the launch site. If you were to continue south following the shoreline, you would reach Million Dollar Beach at 2.4 miles.

Views of Lake George from "Top of the World." Postcard ca. 1930.

Lake George Marinas

Lake George Village Area

Boardwalk Marina
Lower Amherst Street
(518) 668-4828

Castaway Marina
1212 Bay Road
(518) 743-8433

Gilchrist Marina
3686 Lake Shore Drive
(518) 668-2028

Diamond Point

Beckley's Boats
3950 Lake Shore Drive
(518) 668-5225

Lake George Marina & Boat Rentals
3910 Lake Shore Drive
(518) 668-5696

Yankee Boating Center
3910 Lake Shore Drive
(518) 668-5696

Bolton Landing

Bay View Marina
4762 Lake Shore Drive
(518) 644-9633

Bolton Landing Marina
PO Box 1058
(518) 644-3474

Chic's Marina
4782 Lake Shore Drive
(518) 644-2170

F. R. Smith & Sons
36 Sagamore Road
(518) 644-2988

Norowal Marina
Sagamore Road
(518) 644-3741

Waters Edge Marina
Sagamore Road
(518) 644-2511

Hague

Dockside Landing Marina
9130 Lakeshore Drive
(518) 543-8888

Hulett's Landing

Huletts Island View Marina
6069 Lakeside Way, Whitehall, NY
(518) 499-0801

Ticonderoga

Snug Harbor Marina
92 Black Point Road
(518) 585-2628

Kattskill Bay

Dunham's Bay Docks and Launch
Corner of Rte. 9L & Bay Road
Lake George, NY
(518) 744-2627

Dunham's Bay Sea Ray
10 Dunham's Bay Road
Lake George, NY
(518) 656-9244

Fisher's Marina
1215 Pilot Knob Road,
Kattskill Bay, NY
(518) 656-9981

Cleverdale

Boats by George (Cleverdale Location)
291 Cleverdale Road
(518) 656-9353

Harris Bay Yacht Club
2712 Rte. 9L
(528) 656-9028

Mooring Post Marina
291 Cleverdale Road
(518) 656-9206

13 Glen Lake (Queensbury)
A Lake with Hundreds of Years of History

■ **Launch Site:** Queensbury Park & Recreation Glen Lake Boat Launch Site, public boat launch for car-top watercraft only, 290 Glen Lake Road (Warren County); slip-in next to parking area; dock; parking for ten cars; porta-sans; park open from 6 AM–9 PM. For more information: Glen Lake Protective Association, ny-glen-lake.org.
■ **Delorme NYS Atlas & Gazetteer:** p. 81, B4–5; **GPS:** 43°21.93'N; 73°40.81'W
■ **Destinations & Mileages:** *Northeast:* to Osprey Point—0.6 mile; to outlet stream—1.2 miles; up outlet stream—0.2 mile. *East:* to islands—0.4 mile; around islands—0.3 mile. *Southwest:* to inlet stream—0.6 mile; up inlet stream—0.6 mile; *around perimeter of lake*—3.8 miles.
■ **Comments:** Read "Caution" beginning on page xxi and Lake George Region Advisory on page 2. Stay a safe distance back from the small dam at the north end of the lake.

Directions: From the Adirondack Northway (I-87) get off at Exit 20. When you come to Rte. 9, turn right and head south for 0.2 mile (mileage might vary slightly depending on whether you are exiting the Northway southbound or northbound), then turn left onto Glen Lake Road and proceed east for 1.3 miles. Pull into the parking area on your right for the Queensbury Park & Recreation Glen Lake Boat Launch Site, directly next to the Docksider Restaurant. The 0.5-acre park was established in 1985.[1]

The Paddle:
Glen Lake is 1.6 miles long and 0.5 mile across at its widest. The lake rises from a swampy area to its west and flows into Halfway Creek south of Queensbury. It is fed by Meadow Run, Rocky Brook, and Brown's Pond.[2]

You will quickly notice that Glen Lake, with few exceptions, is ringed by private homes and cottages, and that most of the houses have powerboats moored out in front of them.

Glen Lake has been known by a variety of names, including French Pond, Moon's Pond (after Robert Moon, who established a mill at the outlet), Valentine's Pond, Big Pond, Long Pond, and Great Lake. The name Glen Lake was affixed sometime between the Civil War and the turn of the century.

Prior to European occupation Glen Lake was inhabited by the Iroquois, who established a village at the lake's outlet, Glen Lake Brook. The north and west rim of the lake were part of a route between the Mohawk Valley and Canada that Native Americans used during their hunting forays and seasonal traverses.[3]

Benedict Brown was the first European settler to live near the lake. His son, Valentine, built a sawmill on the lake's outlet stream. By 1808 six mills were operating along Glen Lake Brook between the lake and Halfway Creek.[4]

▶ **Glen Lake (Queensbury)**

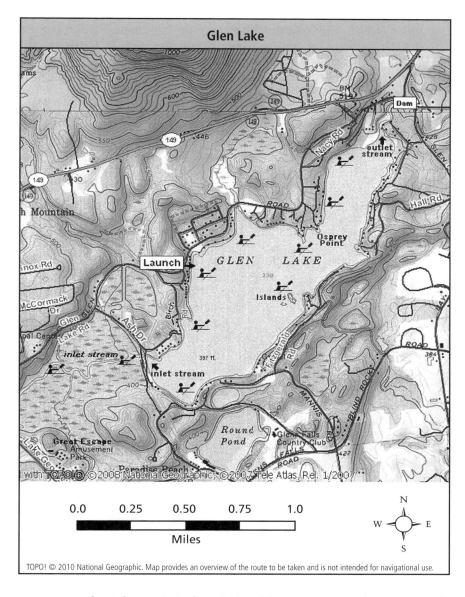

In 1882 the Delaware & Hudson Railroad (D&H) ran a line from Glens Falls to Lake George that passed by the west end of Glen Lake, but no railroad station was ever built near the lake. That didn't prevent Glen Lake from undergoing gradual development, however, and by the turn of the twentieth century a number of camps, small resorts, and boardinghouses had been constructed. Development was further accelerated when a trolley line to the lake from Glens Falls was established in 1901. The trolley line endured until 1929 when the Great Depression and the emerging age of the automobile caused its demise. Today it is part of the bike path between Glens Falls and Lake George.

The 1930s to 1940s at the lake were marked by a feeling of community, with the multitude of camps united by a public path that circled the lake. Following World War II and newfound prosperity, however, the character of the lake changed dramatically as more affluent residents came to settle in the area. Land became more privatized, and the public path around the lake gradually became a thing of the past.[5]

Today the lake's overseer is the Glen Lake Protective Association, which is committed to maintaining the quality of Glen Lake for future residents and lake-users to enjoy.

Northeast—Follow along the west shoreline for 0.5 mile to reach the southwest point of a tiny cove. Along the way you will pass by an inlet at 0.2 mile where a tiny stream rises from a swampy area just north of Glen Lake Road. At 0.5 mile look for a tiny faux lighthouse as you pass by the tip of the cove. After another 0.1 you will reach the southeast tip of the cove. Look for a weathered sign on a tree that reads "Osprey Point." This projection of land, probably once an island, is now connected to the mainland via a tiny footbridge built over a bed of rocks.

From Osprey Point continue following the mainland north. Look to your right to see a series of buoys in long rows near the center of the lake. They mark

Reflections of camps on Glen Lake. Photograph 2010.

▶ Glen Lake (Queensbury)

a slalom waterskiing course. Stay near the shore to avoid the water skiers who use this feature extensively.

In 1.2 miles you will come to the outlet stream, Glen Lake Brook, at the north end of the lake. The opening is delineated by a tiny marshland to the left and pine trees to the right. The outlet creek can be followed downstream for 0.2 mile before a small cement dam is reached. Stay a safe distance back from the dam.

East—Looking east (and slightly south) across the lake from the launch site, an island can be seen close to the opposite shoreline. Head east across the lake for 0.4 mile to reach the larger of two islands. This private, 250-foot-long, oval-shaped spot of land has a cottage on its west end (with a tiny lighthouse in front) and a teepee at its east end. To maintain a stable shoreline and prevent the inevitability of erosion, the entire perimeter of the island has been lined with stones. A smaller island, less than 0.1 mile due south, is no more than 50 feet across and unoccupied. Taken as a pair, the islands can be circumnavigated in 0.3 mile.

The hills clearly visible along the northeast side of the lake are part of the French Mountain range.

Southwest—Follow the west shoreline for 0.6 mile until you come to the lake's inlet stream, located near its southwest corner. The mouth of the creek can be difficult to see until you are almost upon it. Follow the creek west for 0.2 mile to a small private bridge (an offshoot of Ash Drive), which is easily paddled under. Within another 75 feet you will pass under a second bridge, which is used by a bike path. Be sure to duck, for this footbridge has an appreciably lower clearance.

The creek now opens up into a marshland that is 0.7 mile long and 0.4 mile wide. Continue following the main channel west as it slowly narrows and becomes shallower. Under most conditions you will have to turn back after you have gone another 0.4 mile. The trip can be extended, however, by following a number of leads into secondary channels.

In case you are wondering where the carnival-like sounds and the riot of voices are coming from, this part of the paddle puts you within earshot of the Great Escape—a large amusement park that nearly abuts the southeast end of the swamplands.

From the put-in, the lake can be circumnavigated in 3.8 miles.

14

Fourth Lake Campgrounds (Lake Luzerne)
Paddling One of a Series of Interlocking Adirondack Lakes

■ **Launch Site:** DEC Campgrounds at Fourth Lake (Warren County); open from early July through Labor Day; day-use fee; parking for three cars; rowboat and canoe rentals available; restrooms. For more information: Fourth Lake Campgrounds, 892 Lake Avenue, Rte. 9N, Lake Luzerne, NY 12846, (518) 696-2031, dec.ny.gov/outdoor/24480.html.

■ **Delorme NYS Atlas & Gazetteer:** p. A80, B3; **Estimated GPS:** 43°21.63'N; 73°49.50'W

■ **Destinations & Mileages:** *Following the lake perimeter clockwise:* to inlet stream—0.2 mile; up inlet stream—0.1 mile or more, depending upon conditions; to campground beach—0.4 mile; past Fourth Lake Community Association to cove entrance—0.7 mile; down outlet stream—0.15 mile; to day-use beach— 1.0 mile; back to launch—1.2 miles.

■ **Comments:** Read "Caution" beginning on page xxi and Lake George Region Advisory on page 2.

Stay a respectful distance back from the private beach run by the Fourth Lake Community Association.

Directions: From the Adirondack Northway (I-87) get off at Exit 21 and take Rte. 9N south for 7.0 miles. The entrance to Fourth Lake Campgrounds is to your left, opposite Potash Mountain Road.

From Lake Luzerne (junction of Rte. 9N & Mill Street by Wayside Beach) head north on Rte. 9N for 2.9 miles. The campground entrance is to your right, opposite Potash Mountain Road.

From either direction, as soon as you pull into the campground entrance and pass by the contact station, turn left and proceed north for 0.1 mile, then turn right onto a secondary road at a sign stating "No motorized boats." Drive downhill for 0.1 mile to the slip-in at the end of the road. Park in the little area to the left, just before the end of the road.

The Paddle:
The Fourth Lake Campgrounds opened in 1967. Because no motorboats are allowed, the 51-acre lake with a maximum depth of 41 feet maintains a serene, peaceful atmosphere.[1]

Following the lake perimeter clockwise—Within several hundred feet you will see a tiny cove to your left that can be entered for a hundred feet or so, but which tapers off quickly.

At 0.2 mile you will reach the inlet stream near the northeast corner of the lake. The stream's water is very shallow, particularly during late summer. The creek can be followed upstream for a distance that varies depending upon water depth, blowdown, beaver activity, and one's own willingness to persevere

▶ **Fourth Lake Campgrounds (Lake Luzerne)**

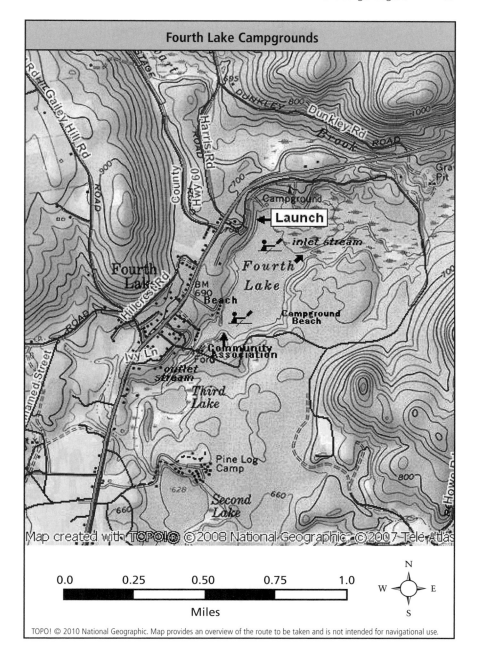

Fourth Lake Campgrounds

Launch

inlet stream

Fourth Lake

Campground

BM 690

Beach

Campground Beach

Community Association

Ford

outlet stream

Third Lake

Ivy Ln

Pine Log Camp

628

660

Second Lake

660

Fourth Lake

Harris Rd

Hillcrest Rd

Galley Hill Rd

County Hwy 60 Rd

ROAD

DUNKLEY

Dunkley Rd

Brook

ROAD

Gra Pit

unnamed Street

Howe Rd

800

1000

695

700

800

Map created with TOPO!® ©2008 National Geographic. ©2007 Tele Atlas

0.0   0.25   0.50   0.75   1.0

Miles

N
W ◇ E
S

TOPO! © 2010 National Geographic. Map provides an overview of the route to be taken and is not intended for navigational use.

despite hardships. A sizeable beaver dam, 50 feet across, is encountered at 0.1 mile and may be as far as most paddlers will choose to go. Portages after this are required. (The upper part of the creek can be checked out by driving north from the contact station along the campground road for 1.0 mile. You will pass by the "Field of Dreams" ball field and come to where the road crosses the inlet stream. From there a secondary road leads immediately right to a parking area.)

From the northeast end of the lake, continue making your away around the perimeter clockwise. In another 0.2 mile you will pass by a small beach area that serves as lake access for campers on the east side of Fourth Lake, far away from the sounds of traffic on Rte. 9N. Take a moment to look northwest across the lake to see the striking visage of Potash Mountain (1,751'), whose form rises high above the lake. Potash Mountain has also been called Potash Kettle Mountain because of its resemblance to an overturned kettle. Native Americans called it *Se-non-go-wah*.[2] It is an impressive sight with its bare rocky peak.

At 0.7 mile you will pass by an expansive beach along the south end of the lake belonging to the Fourth Lake Community Association, Inc. Only members of the association are allowed to use the beach and facilities.

Immediately after the private beach you will come to a cove that can be readily entered. Several private homes can be seen along the west bank. In less than 0.2 mile the lake narrows abruptly, turning into the outlet stream. Just before you reach a green-colored bridge (the continuation of Ivy Lane Extension), rapids and shallows are encountered that make continuation untenable.

Paddling out of the cove, continue around the perimeter of the lake. In 1.0 mile you will pass by the main campground beach area & boat rentals (which can be used as an alternate access site in the event that the parking space at the boat launch site is full). You will return to your launch site at 1.2 miles.

Potash Mountain as seen from Fourth Lake. Photograph 2010.

▶ Fourth Lake Campgrounds (Lake Luzerne)

Halfway Creek (Fort Ann)
Paddle Upstream to a Large Waterfall

15

■ **Launch Site:** Town dock on Champlain Canal next to Ann Street bridge (Washington County)
■ **Delorme NYS Atlas & Gazetteer:** p. 81, A5–6; **GPS:** 43°24.85'N; 73°29.12'W
■ **Destinations & Mileages:** *North:* to Halfway Creek—0.2 mile. *Continuing West:* to Route 4 bridge—0.3 mile; to tributary to Halfway Creek—0.4 mile; up tributary to Halfway Creek—0.3 mile; to small rapids/stronger current—1.0 mile; to high-tension power line—1.1 miles; to Kane Falls—1.4 miles.
■ **Comments:** Read "Caution" beginning on page xxi and Lake George Region Advisory on page 2.

Directions: At Fort Ann (junction of Rtes. 4 & 149) turn onto Ann Street (opposite Rte. 149 West) and drive east for 0.1 mile. Immediately after crossing railroad tracks and just before the Champlain Canal, turn left onto a dirt road and drive downhill for 70 feet to a small parking area at the town dock.

The Paddle:
The dock is 50 feet upstream from the new Ann Street bridge, built in 2007, which replaced a plate girder bridge erected in 1911.[1]

The village of Fort Ann is named after a small fort built during Queen Anne's War (1702–1713). It was one of four similar forts constructed in Fort Ann during the French and Indian wars.[2] Later, Fort Ann played a pivotal role during the Revolutionary War. As British troops were advancing south toward Albany in 1777, the retreating colonial army kept felling trees across the road in order to slow down the Redcoats' progress. This delayed the British just long enough to allow colonial defenses to be further shored up at Saratoga. During the brief skirmish at Fort Ann, the British were able to capture the American flag with its thirteen red and white stripes and constellation. Some have speculated that this may have been the first time the American flag flew in battle.

North—Head to your left, following the Champlain Canal for 0.2 mile. Turn left onto Halfway Creek, a medium-sized stream that rises from the Wilkie Reservoir northwest of Glens Falls. The creek was named because of its position halfway between Lake George and Fort Edward.[3] You will immediately pass under an old railroad bridge. As soon as you clear the bridge, look to your left to see one of the original three locks of the old Champlain Canal in Fort Ann several hundred feet away at the end of a short channel. Although the water in the channel is shallow, thanks to deposits of sediment, it is possible to paddle up to the lock and examine its limestone blocks more closely. When the original canal opened, Fort Ann was an inland port with considerable river-based activity. Prior to the Civil War it also served as part of the

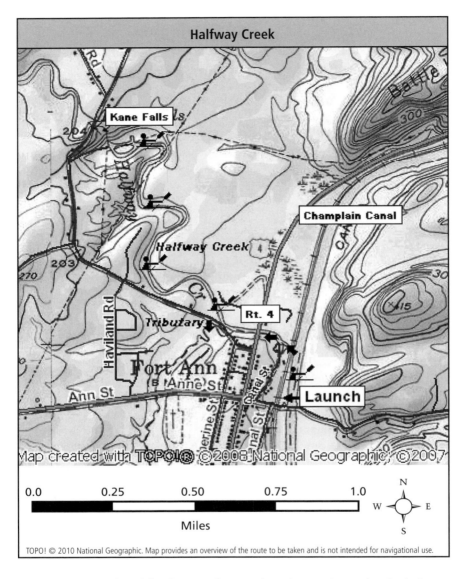

Underground Railroad for fugitive slaves.[4] There is a NYS Permitted Discharge Site on the southwest corner of the inlet.

Continuing upstream on Halfway Creek from its confluence with the Champlain Canal, you will come to the Route 4 bridge in 0.1 mile. The highway crossing the bridge follows an old path used by Native Americans and contending European armies to travel between the Hudson River and Lake Champlain. Fort Ann lies midway between those two points.

▶ **Halfway Creek (Fort Ann)**

A tributary to Halfway Creek leads upstream through a culvert. Photograph 2010.

In another 0.1 mile look for a large drainpipe to your left where a tributary to Halfway Creek passes under Route 16. There is plenty of clearance to allow paddlers to maneuver through the pipe, but watch out for riprap that lies just below the water's surface. Proceed carefully. Once through the pipe you can easily paddle upstream, heading southwest, for at least 0.3 mile depending upon blowdown and water level. This sizeable tributary rises from southeast of Vaughns Corners.

Back on Halfway Creek, continue paddling north. At 1.0 mile from launch you will have to pick up the pace slightly as an area of increased current is encountered, with the possibility of small rapids if the water level is low. A string of large boulders is visible to your left. At 1.1 miles from launch you will cross under high-tension power lines, which parallel the creek for another 0.2 mile before vanishing into the woods.

At 1.4 miles from launch you will come to the base of Kane Falls, named after Charles Kane, who constructed several mills and a forge at the site. Be prepared to be impressed, for Kane Falls is a large cascade, roughly 50 feet high. During early spring or late fall you can see the waterfall through the trees. A huge pool at the base of the fall provides for fairly calm waters even when Kane Falls is raging. Take note that the land around Kane Falls is private and posted.

The fall was the site of a blockhouse and sawmill during the Revolutionary War. At that time it was called Cheshire Falls, after John Cheshire, who erected the first sawmill. Lumber from the sawmill was used by Major General Benedict Arnold to build his fleet of ships at Whitehall—a village that has since become known as the "Birthplace of the American Navy."

Additional Site of Interest:
One of the original canal locks is visible from roadside at Fort Ann. Just before crossing the railroad tracks on Ann Street and reaching the launch site, turn right onto South Canal Street and you will immediately come to a very well-preserved lock on your right.

II

Saratoga Region

Advisory

The Saratoga region is characterized by a series of interconnected lakes of varying sizes, and streams that contain substantial volumes of water year-round. All of the lakes explored in this section encourage boat traffic, so paddlers need to stay alert at all times. Saratoga Lake, because of its size and proximity to the Capital District region, features the greatest number of powerboats in this section. Fewer powerboats are encountered on Ballston Lake (a more elongated, river-like body of water), and only a handful on Round Lake, Lake Lonely, and Lake Desolation. All of these bodies of water, however, as well as Moreau Lake, are large enough for wind, waves, and wakes to be a potential safety factor for small craft.

Operators of small watercraft, like kayaks and canoes, must be ever-vigilant. Don't assume boats can see you. Wear bright colors. It is best to stay close to the shoreline, but if you must cross open water, cross in a group and keep the group together. If you see a boat in the distance, let it pass before you set out. Some large boats move surprisingly fast, and distance can be hard to judge. Take into account current and wind when planning your trajectory across open water. Be prepared for an increase in boat traffic as you pass by marinas.

When leaving the shoreline to cross open water, choose a calm day and watch the weather. Current and wind can be severe. The wind tends to be quietest in the early morning and early evening. Always check the forecast and weather before setting out. Do not leave shore if storms and/or high winds are predicted or if the weather forecast is at all questionable. Be aware that the weather can change abruptly, often with little warning and in spite of the forecast. Wind and current increase as you move away from the shoreline.

Both Kayaderosseras Creek (the inlet stream to Saratoga Lake) and Fish Creek (the outlet stream to Saratoga Lake) are impressive rivers. Strong current can be a factor on Kayaderosseras Creek after heavy rainfall or following spring's snowmelt. Current is much less of a factor on the dammed segment of Fish Creek explored in this book, but paddlers should always be vigilant for small powerboats. The wakes from powerboats can be especially rough on Fish Creek because the boats will be passing fairly close to paddlers on this relatively narrow stream.

Memorize the shoreline as you leave so that you can return to the same starting point.

Saratoga Lake (Saratoga Springs)
A Lake Historically Associated with Saratoga Springs

16

▓ **Launch Site:** NYS Boat Launch at northeast end of Saratoga Lake (Saratoga County); cement ramp; seasonal fee; parking for 40 cars & trailers. For more information: Saratoga Lake Association, P.O. Box 2152, Ballston Spa, NY 12020, (518) 580-0656, saratogalake.org.

▓ **Delorme NYS Atlas & Gazetteer:** p. 80, D4; **GPS:** 43°03.21'N; 73°43.23'W

▓ **Destinations & Mileages:** *Clockwise around lake from Rte. 9P bridge:* to Cedar Bluff—1.3 miles; to Maple Shade/Mill Creek—2.9 miles; to Snake Hill—4.0 miles; to Riley Cove—8.2 miles; to Mannings Cove—8.8 miles; to Kayaderosseras Creek—11.0 miles; back to Rte. 9P bridge—12.0 miles.

▓ **Comments:** Read "Caution" beginning on page xxi and Saratoga Region Advisory on page 76.

It is best to stay close to the shoreline, venturing out into open water only if the weather is calm and you are a skilled and experienced paddler.

See chapters "Kayaderosseras Creek: Lower Section" and "Fish Creek: Saratoga Lake to Grangerville Dam" for additional launch sites.

Directions: From the Adirondack Northway (I-87) take Exit 14. Proceed east on Union Street (Rte. 9P) for 2.2 miles. As soon as you cross over the bridge spanning Fish Creek/Saratoga Lake, drive south for another 0.05 mile and then turn left onto a road that leads to the entrance to the state boat launch in 0.1 mile. This entrance is opposite the Point Breeze Marina.

The wide launch ramp used by powerboats is located next to a 610-foot bridge that in May 2011 replaced an earlier bridge that had deteriorated; 100 feet north is a sandy, beach-like area where you can easily slip in a kayak or canoe without having to go shoulder to shoulder with powerboats.

Two other waterways and a second lake can be reached from Saratoga Lake. See chapters "Fish Creek: Saratoga Lake to Grangerville Dam," "Kayaderosseras Creek: Lower Section," and "Lake Lonely."

The Paddle:

Saratoga Lake is a sizable body of water, 5 miles long and nearly 2 miles across at its widest point opposite Snake Hill. It encompasses an area of 6.3 square miles with a depth approaching 95 feet in places. Most of the lake is fairly shallow, however, with much aquatic vegetation. Bald eagles are regularly seen, and it is a staging ground for waterfowl during spring and fall migration, at which time you are likely to see Canada & snow geese, American black duck, bufflehead, and hooded mergansers.[1]

Although the lake is named "Saratoga," a corruption of the Native American word *Saraghtoga*, for "place of swift water,"[2] it was never called that by Native Americans.[3] They called the lake *Caniad-eri-os-se-ra*, meaning the "lake of crooked

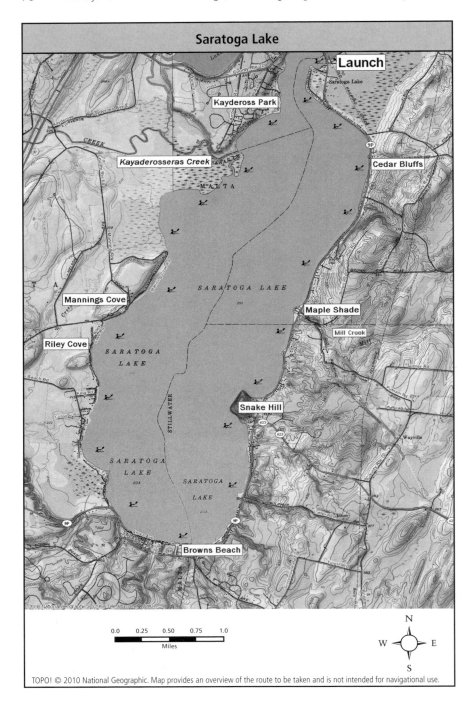

▶ Saratoga Lake (Saratoga Springs)

stream." Over time this was altered to *Cai-ad-er-ros-se-ra*, and then to *Kayad-ros-se-ra*, which is now used to identify the inlet stream, Kayaderosseras Creek, and not the lake itself. The lake was officially named Saratoga Lake in 1772.[4]

The lake's popularity increased dramatically when the Saratoga Railroad line was established in 1880 to take tourists directly to the lake.[5]

A number of significant hotels along the lakeshore were erected in the mid- to late 1800s. Moon's Lake House, owned and operated by Carey Moon, was located on a 50-foot-high bluff along the lake's western shore, near the outlet.[6] It was at Moon's Lake House where the "Saratoga Chip" was invented, which later was renamed the potato chip.[7] Carey's son Henry set up Capt. Abel's Lakeside Hotel near Moon's Lake House, and actually competed with his father for business. Brigg's Hotel, operated by John P. Conkling, was located north of Moon's Lake House, just before the bridge that spanned the outlet. Briggs had the novel idea of setting up an ice track for trotting horses on the lake during the winter. Over 800 people attended the first event.[8] Myer's Hotel was located south of Moon's Lake House and was also directly on the lake.

On the opposite side of Saratoga Lake was the White Sulphur Springs Hotel, approximately one mile south of Snake Hill. It was erected in the early 1870s and torn down in 1957.[9]

There were a number of other hotels, including: The Arrowhead (mentioned in the chapter "Kayaderosseras Creek: Lower Section"), which burned down in 1969; Newmans, which opened prior to the 1900s and was razed in 1972; and Riley's, which was started up in the mid-1800s by James and Hanna Riley and was destroyed by fire in the 1930s.[10] For a period of time Saratoga Lake was truly a lake of hotels, as well-to-do Victorians left the sweltering, odorous cities during the summer for the fresh air and balm of the countryside.

A famous legend is associated with the lake. Native Americans believed that silence was sacred to the Great Spirit, so much so that if any human uttered a sound while traveling across the lake, the offender's canoe would tip over and the occupants would be drowned. A white woman, while being taken across the lake by a party of Native Americans, decided to put this legend to the test. She waited until about halfway across, and then began making loud noises. Unable to stop her, the crew glumly continued paddling, expecting the worst, until they reached the other side of the lake. The woman leaped out and announced triumphantly, "See—I told you this was just a foolish superstition." Whereupon one Indian, unfazed, replied, "The Great Spirit took pity this time, for he knew that no white woman can hold her tongue."[11] One can only imagine what the Great Spirit must think of the lake today with all its noise and commotion.

The lake has long been a mecca for boaters. The first regatta on the lake, sponsored by John Morrissey, took place in 1871.[12] In the late 1800s many collegiate rowing competitions were hosted at the lake, and some prominent eastern colleges had boathouses on the shores.

Snake Hill (seen in the distance) is an instantly recognizable feature of Saratoga Lake. Postcard ca. 1930.

Today, the land surrounding Saratoga Lake doesn't look at all like it did in the nineteenth century. In Park Clinton's novel *Glanmore: Romance of the Revolution,* the lake is exquisitely described: "Its banks at this time [1853] are lined with cultivated farms, neat farm-houses, and stately old orchards, with occasionally a tract of woodland skirting its borders."[13] A hundred and fifty years later, the pastoral setting has turned into suburbia.

Clockwise around the lake from the Rte. 9P bridge—From the launch proceed along the east shore of Saratoga Lake in a clockwise direction. After you clear the Rte. 9P bridge you will immediately pass by the Point Breeze Marina and then the community of Cedar Bluffs at 1.3 miles, Maple Shade (another tiny community) and Mill Creek at 2.9 miles, and reach Snake Hill, the lake's most distinguishing geological feature, at 4.0 miles. Snake Hill is a rocky profile above the southeast shoreline that was named by a group of early settlers who encountered a den of rattlesnakes halfway up the hill.[14] You will easily recognize the hill by its dome-shaped appearance. Take note that during most of this paddle Rte. 9P follows closely along the shoreline.

From Snake Hill continue around the south end of the lake. You will pass by the 7-acre former site of Browns Beach, which opened in the early 1900s. It contained a bathhouse, dance hall, refreshment stand, and a number of rides.[15] You will also pass by the South Shore Marina at the southwest end of the lake, located opposite where Rte. 108 comes into Rte. 9P.

▶ **Saratoga Lake (Saratoga Springs)**

Heading north, following the west shore, you will pass by Riley Cove at 8.2 miles and Mannings Cove at 8.8 miles. Riley Cove is named after Jim Riley, who won the U.S. Amateurs rowing championship in 1876. In 1878, Riley founded the Riley Lakehouse, which lasted more than 60 years until it burned down in 1939.[16] The Saratoga Sailing Club is located at the start of Manning's Cove. A large parcel of marshy land just beyond the sailing club has been acquired by the Saratoga PLAN (the county's open-space organization). A small public dock for paddlers might be built there at some future point.

For the next 2.0 miles you will be paddling along an area of marshland. This is one of the few sections of the lake where no development has taken place. There are several tiny inlets that can be explored for short distances, including one channel that goes north for nearly 0.2 mile.

At 11.0 miles the wide mouth of Kayaderosseras Creek is reached. Just beyond, near the northeast end of the lake, you will pass by the site of the former Kaydeross Amusement Park, which operated on the lake from 1910 to 1987. It was first owned by the Saratoga Traction Company and then, in 1905, by the Hudson Valley Railroad.[17] The park offered a variety of rides, including a Ferris wheel, tilt-a-whirl, water slide, and carousel. All of the rides were disposed of when the park closed. A grassroots public effort to save the carousel was organized, and instead of the carousel being dismantled and sold as twenty-eight separate pieces, it was restored to its original condition and relocated to Congress Park in Saratoga Springs in 2002, where it can now be seen (and still ridden).[18] The park area has since been converted into the private Water's Edge/Woodlands residential development, and the dance hall (called "The Rafters" in its later years) has been boarded up. It's hard to imagine, looking at the area today, but centuries ago it was the site of a seasonal Native American encampment.

At roughly 11.5 miles you will pass by a 4-acre parcel of lakefront land that was acquired by the City of Saratoga Springs, with plans to develop it as a public park. The possibility thus exists that this parcel may in the future offer paddlers another access point to the lake.

In a little over 12.0 miles you will be back at the launch site and the Rte. 9P bridge.

17

Lake Lonely (Saratoga Springs)
A Pretty Lake, but You Won't Feel Lonely

■ **Launch Site:** Lake Lonely Boat Livery at southwest end of Lake Lonely off of Crescent Avenue (Saratoga County); portable toilet; slip-in; modest launch fee; open daily, 6 AM–6 PM; open seasonally from early May. For more information: Lake Lonely Boat Livery, 378 Crescent Avenue, Saratoga Springs, NY 12866, (518) 587-1721.

■ **Delorme NYS Atlas & Gazetteer:** p. 80, D4; **GPS:** 43°03.21'N; 73°45.23'W

■ **Destinations & Mileages:** *Up outlet stream to Lake Lonely and around perimeter of lake:* Up outlet stream to Lake Lonely—0.3 mile; around perimeter of lake—2.3 miles. *South down outlet stream and continuing east on Kayaderosseras Creek:* down outlet stream to Kayaderosseras Creek—0.9 mile; from confluence of the two streams down Kayaderosseras Creek to Saratoga Lake—1.0 mile (1.9 miles from launch).

■ **Comments:** Read "Caution" beginning on page xxi and Saratoga Region Advisory on page 76.

Only paddle down Lake Lonely's outlet stream if the current seems manageable to you for a return trip back to your starting point. Under most conditions it will be.

Fast currents can make entering the Kayaderosseras dangerous following heavy rainfall or during early spring.

The livery generally locks its gate at closing time, so be sure to plan your trip accordingly and return before 6 PM.

Directions: From Exit 13 of the Adirondack Northway (I-87), drive north on Rte. 9 for approximately 2.7 miles. Turn right onto Crescent Avenue (Rte. 22) and drive east for 1.8 miles. The Lake Lonely Boat Livery is directly to your right, just before you cross over Lake Lonely's outlet stream.

From the north end of Saratoga Lake at the Fish Creek bridge, drive northwest on Rte. 9P for over 0.3 mile and turn left onto Crescent Avenue (Rte. 22) at traffic light. Proceed west on Crescent Avenue for over 1.6 miles, and then turn left into the Lake Lonely Boat Livery as soon as you cross over the outlet stream from Lake Lonely.

The put-in is next to the Lake Lonely Boat Livery.

The Paddle:
Lake Lonely is 0.9 mile long, 0.2 mile wide, covers 153 acres, and is separated from Saratoga Lake by a scant 0.4 mile. It is fed by Bog Meadow Creek, coming in from Barnes Corner, and Spring Run, flowing in from northeast of Saratoga Springs.

Lake Lonely was known as Little Lake until 1858, at which time it was given its present name by Judge James B. McKean.[1]

▶ **Lake Lonely (Saratoga Springs)**

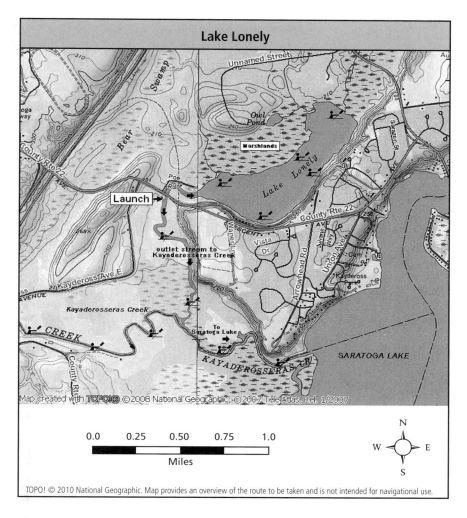

Not everybody has been suitably impressed by the lake. In the mid-1800s, one author had this to say: "It is rather pretty and has a good echo on the eastern shore, but beyond this it has no special interest."[2] All of this has changed in the twenty-first century, for the lake has become an oasis of natural beauty in the Capital Region, with its east side dotted with private homes.

The Lake Lonely Boat Livery is over 100 years old. Bill Parry is the current owner.

In 2001 the City of Saratoga Springs purchased Ramsdill Park, named after Lester Ramsdill III. The 30 acres of land can be found at the outlet to Lake Lonely and along Kayadeross Avenue East. The park provides public access to Lake Lonely and Kayaderosseras Creek at the Lake Lonely Boat Livery.[3]

Up outlet stream to Lake Lonely and around perimeter of lake—From the boat livery, paddle upstream, immediately passing under the Crescent Ave. bridge. Within 0.3 mile you will reach Lake Lonely proper, where you can follow along the lake's perimeter—a paddle of 2.3 miles round-trip. The northeast end of the lake consists of wetlands, as does the west side of the lake, which ends before reaching Owl Pond. This is an area with good fishing opportunities. Several tiny tributaries come into the north end of the lake, one being from Owl Pond. The Saratoga National Golf Club, an 18-hole public course, is also visible at the north end of the lake. The south end of the lake is more bowl shaped, with the shoreline rising up steeply for 50 feet or more.

South down outlet stream and continuing east on Kayaderosseras Creek—Follow the lake's outlet creek downstream for 0.9 mile to Kayaderosseras Creek. From the confluence of the two streams, you can go downstream on Kayaderosseras Creek for 1.0 mile to Saratoga Lake, or upstream until the current and shallows force you back. Heading downstream you will see huge piles of logs lining the bank, debris that was removed from the stream to facilitate navigation. Turtles like to sun themselves on these logs. (See chapter "Kayaderosseras Creek: Lower Section".)

Kayaderosseras Creek can be accessed by following Lake Lonely's outlet downstream. Photograph 2008.

▶ **Lake Lonely (Saratoga Springs)**

Moreau Lake (Gansevoort)
Two Bodies of Water Form One Lake

18

■ **Launch Site:** Moreau Lake State Park off of Old Saratoga Road (Saratoga County); hard-surface ramp; parking for ten cars & trailers; restrooms; day-use hours 8 AM–sunset; campground contains 148 campsites and is open from May–October; modest fee; no motorboats are allowed on the lake. For more information: Moreau Lake State Park, 605 Old Saratoga Road, Gansevoort, NY 12831, (518) 793-0511, nysparks.state.ny.us/parks/150/details.aspx.

■ **Delorme NYS Atlas & Gazetteer:** p. 80, BC4; **GPS:** 43°13.63'N; 73°42.80'W

■ **Destinations & Mileages:** *Around perimeter of Moreau Lake, clockwise:* to public beach—0.3 mile; to causeway footbridge—0.6 mile; through causeway and around smaller section of Moreau Lake—0.8 mile; from causeway footbridge to east-side cove—0.9 mile; into cove—0.2 mile; from cove following perimeter back to launch—0.4 mile (1.3 miles from launch); around perimeter of entire lake, including the smaller section—2.1 miles.

■ **Comments:** Read "Caution" beginning on page xxi and Saratoga Region Advisory on page 76.

Directions: From the Adirondack Northway (I-87) take Exit 17 South. Proceed west on Rte. 9 for 0.1 mile and then turn right onto Old Saratoga Road, heading southwest. After 0.7 mile turn right at the large sign for Moreau Lake State Park. You will immediately come to the contact station. The boat launch is 0.3 mile beyond to your right, near the southwest end of the lake. The launch site is identified by a sign, and there is parking available on both sides of the road.

The Paddle:
Moreau Lake is 0.6 mile long and 0.3 mile wide, with 0.8 mile of wetland extending north from its northern end. It was created when retreating glaciers left behind a huge block of ice whose weight caused a deep depression to form as the ice melted.[1] The deepest part of the bowl-shaped lake is 50 feet. The upper bay is 3–5 feet deep.[2]

The state park containing Moreau Lake consists of 4,100 acres of land, an additional 3,216 acres having been acquired by New York State along both sides of the Hudson River in 1998. It is New York's ninth-largest state park.[3] Its name honors a French general, Jean Victor Moreau.[4]

Around the perimeter of Moreau Lake, clockwise—From the launch site, paddle clockwise, proceeding north along the west side of the lake. In 0.3 mile you will pass by the public beach. In another 0.3 mile you will come to a causeway, where you can paddle under a footbridge and enter a smaller, less visited section of Moreau Lake. This section can be circumnavigated in 0.8 mile. Look for a beaver lodge, farther out on the lake to your right, after you go under the footbridge.

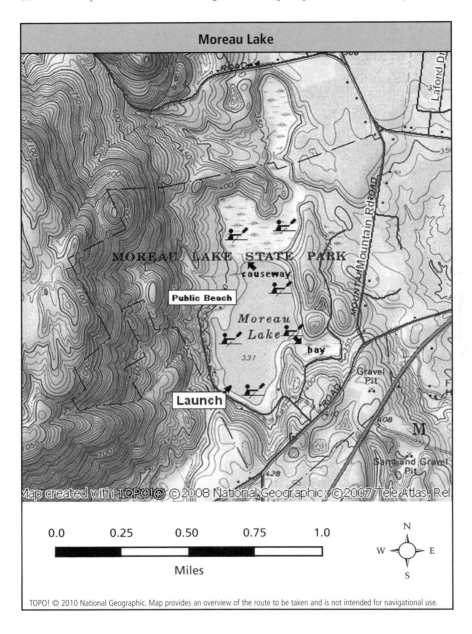

Moreau Lake

MOREAU LAKE STATE PARK

causeway

Public Beach

Moreau Lake
331

bay

Gravel Pit

Launch

Sand and Gravel Pit

Mount Mountain Road

Lafond Dr

Map created with TOPO!® © 2008 National Geographic; © 2007 Tele Atlas, Rel.

0.0   0.25   0.50   0.75   1.0

Miles

N
W ⟷ E
S

TOPO! © 2010 National Geographic. Map provides an overview of the route to be taken and is not intended for navigational use.

▶ **Moreau Lake (Gansevoort)**

Return to the main section of Moreau Lake and continue paddling clockwise. In another 0.3 mile you will reach a cove on your left that can be explored for nearly 0.2 mile of its length. The cove is located just south of a log cabin visible along the southeast shoreline.

When you are back out on the main section of the lake, continue paddling clockwise and you will end up back at the launch site in another 0.4 mile. If you paddle the perimeter of the entire lake, including the bay, you will have gone over 2.1 miles.

The Hike: A quick, 0.8-mile-long hike with a 300-foot ascent will take you up to the top of 650-foot-high Grant Mountain for overviews of the area. Trailheads begin just west of the launch site at the south end of the lake near the causeway. Trail maps may be picked up on the way into the park. Be sure to bring along hiking boots and a pack for essentials

Beavers are clearly in charge of this section of Moreau Lake. Photograph 2010.

19   Lake Desolation (Lake Desolation)
A Pretty Lake High in the Mountain

- ■ **Launch Site:** Across from Tinney's Tavern at Lake Desolation (Saratoga County); slip-in at water's edge; modest launch fee. For more information: Tinney's Tavern, 498 Lake Desolation Road, Middlegrove, NY 12850, (518) 584-8040, tinneystavern.com.
- ■ **Delorme NYS Atlas & Gazetteer:** p. 80, CD2; **Estimated GPS:** 43°07.84'N; 73°58.22'W
- ■ **Destinations & Mileages:** to tiny island—0.4 mile; around island—0.2 mile; around perimeter of lake—1.8 miles.
- ■ **Comments:** Read "Caution" beginning on page xxi and Saratoga Region Advisory on page 76.

  Please note that Lake Desolation is a private lake. Lake access is presently provided across from Tinney's Tavern on lakefront property owned by the tavern. Go to the east end of the fence to reach the lake and place the posted admission fee ($5.00 in 2011) into the locked box. Although it is not a requirement, it would be a nice gesture of goodwill to stop in at Tinney's for refreshments before or after paddling. (Be sure to check out their pulled-pork sandwiches.)

Directions: From Saratoga Springs (junction of Rtes. 9N North & 9) drive northwest on Rte. 9N North for roughly 3.0 miles. Turn left onto Middle Grove Road (Rte. 21) and proceed west for 4.5 miles, then turn right onto Lake Desolation Road and drive north for 5.0 miles until you reach Lake Desolation.

From the Great Sacandaga Lake at the east end of the Batchellerville Bridge, go north on South Shore Road (Rte. 7) for 0.1 mile, then turn right onto Fox Hill Road and head southeast for 9.8 miles to the south end of the lake.

From either direction, pull into the parking area at Tinney's Tavern, or if the parking lot at Tinney's looks like it's filling up with customers, drive east for 100 feet, turn left onto Main Street, and park along the side of the road, then carry your watercraft back to the launch across from the tavern.

The Paddle:

Lake Desolation is a pretty, 0.7-mile-long mountain lake that is 40 feet deep and fed both by springs and tiny tributaries. It rests at an elevation of 1,558 feet. Because of the lake's heavy iron content, the waters appear black, even on the brightest day.[1] Lake Desolation's main tributary is Balsam Creek, which enters from the southeast. The lake was a swamp at one time until the stream was impounded.

In the early 1900s a lakeside inn was established and operated through the 1950s until it burned down. It is believed that the foundation now lies buried under the parking lot at Tinney's Tavern.

Years ago Harwood's Dance Hall was located on the side of the lake near the outlet stream. What made the dance hall particularly enchanting was that it was

▶ **Lake Desolation (Lake Desolation)**

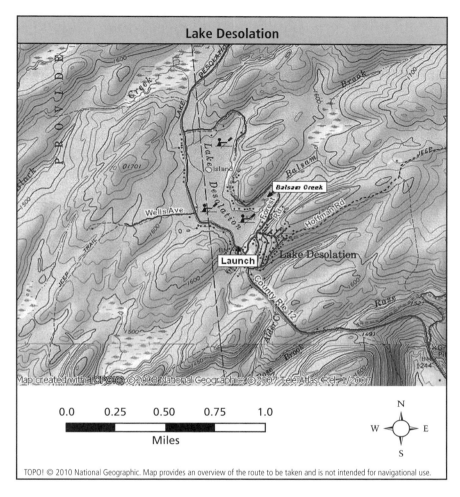

Lake Desolation

Map created with TOPO!® ©2008 National Geographic; ©2007 Tele Atlas (Rel. 1/2007)

| 0.0 | 0.25 | 0.50 | 0.75 | 1.0 |

Miles

TOPO! © 2010 National Geographic. Map provides an overview of the route to be taken and is not intended for navigational use.

supported by piers and extended out onto the lake.[2]

At nearby Mount Pleasant (a vanished community roughly one mile north of Lake Desolation where several hundred people once lived) faint ruins of a glass factory remain. The factory made bottles for Saratoga Springs water. The area close to Lake Desolation at one time was also involved in graphite mining.[3]

Around the perimeter of the lake—From the put-in you can travel around the perimeter of the lake in 1.8 miles. There are some wild sections along the lake, but most of the shoreline views consist of camps and year-round residences. Balsam Creek, which enters near the southeast end of the lake, is shallow and weed infested by early summer.

North from Tinney's Tavern is a tiny island 0.4 mile away. It can be circled around in 0.2 mile.

20 | **Round Lake (Round Lake)**
An Intriguing Body of Water with Numerous Opportunities for Exploration

- ▓ **Launch Sites:** Round Lake at Round Lake Village (Saratoga County); Ballston Creek access—slip-in at water's edge; parking for 6–8 cars
- ▓ **Delorme NYS Atlas & Gazetteer:** p. 66, A3; **GPS:** 42°56.45'N; 73°47.25'W
- ▓ **Destinations & Mileages:** *North:* up Ballston Creek—0.2 mile. *South:* to Round Lake—0.1 mile. *East:* from launch to Little Round Lake—0.6 mile; around perimeter of Little Round Lake—0.8 mile. *Southeast:* from launch to Anthony Kill—1.2 miles; down Anthony Kill—1.0 mile. *Around perimeter of Round Lake*—2.5 miles.
- ▓ **Comments:** Read "Caution" beginning on page xxi and Saratoga Region Advisory on page 76.
  Anthony Kill—Minimal current up to the beaver dam.
  Ballston Creek—Minimal current on the short, upstream trek.

Directions: From the Adirondack Northway (I-87) take Exit 11 for Burnt Hills/Round Lake. Go east on Round Lake Road for 0.7 miles (passing by the outskirts of Round Lake Village at 0.3 mile). Round Lake Road turns into George Road along the way. At the intersection with Rte. 9, turn left onto Rte. 9 and drive north for 0.2 mile. When you come to Goldfoot Road, turn right and head east for 0.1 mile, then turn right onto Maltaville Road (Rte. 80), which crosses over Ballston Creek and comes to a cul-de-sac at 0.1 mile. Park here and slip in at southwest end of the bridge.

Paddlers have previously been able to access the lake from Rte. 9, but "no parking" signs are now posted along the road. The town is concerned that incautious paddlers could be struck by speeding vehicles while trying to take their canoes or kayaks off the tops of their cars. Meanwhile the Malta Town Board and DEC are looking into the possibility of creating another lake access, most likely at the lake's southeast end.

The Paddle:

Part of the attraction of this paddle is the charm of Round Lake Village, located just uphill heading west from the lake. The village has religious roots, going back to 1868 when it was a Methodist Episcopal Church summer retreat.[1] Each summer the faithful would gather in tents, forming a vast transitory community. Gradually the tents gave way to permanent structures—quaint, Victorian, wooden houses—nestled together just as the tents had been. The community has survived twentieth-century modernization and retains a look and style that is unique in the Capital Region.

North up Ballston Creek—Ballston Creek rises from Ballston Lake and flows into Round Lake just east of Round Lake Village. There the creek immediately loses its identity, emerging from the lake as the Anthony Kill and flowing south-

▶ **Round Lake (Round Lake)**

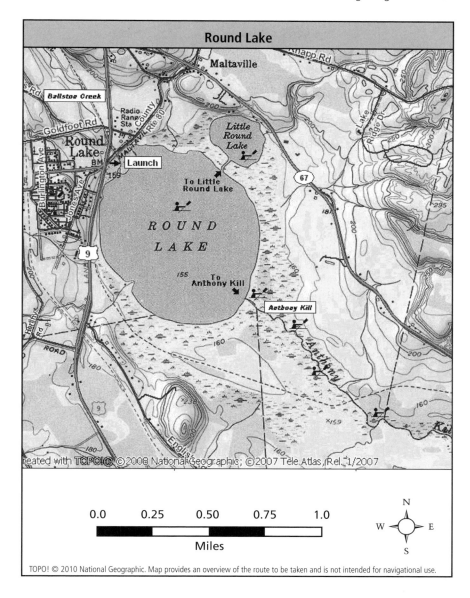

Round Lake

east to the Hudson River at Mechanicville.

What's interesting about Round Lake, Ballston Creek, and the Anthony Kill is that they are part of an old channel abandoned by the Mohawk River thousands of years ago when its waters were redirected to a different course at Rexford.

Native Americans used the waterway as a natural water trail, following the Anthony Kill up from the Hudson to East Line, and from there to the salt springs at Ballston Spa or on to Saratoga Lake. Archaeological evidence shows that the Algonquians frequently camped around the shore.[2]

The general area around the Ballston Creek put-in at the convergence of Goldfoot Road, Maltaville Road, and Route 9 was once a tiny amusement park. Howard Goldfoot and his brother purchased a merry-go-round, two electric pianos, a hurdy-gurdy, and a band organ, and housed them in a large wooden building close to the lake. The business ultimately was abandoned and the merry-go-round was subsequently sold to Kaydeross Amusement Park in Saratoga in 1940.[3]

If the lake level is low enough (which it generally is later in the summer), follow Ballston Creek upstream, immediately passing under the Maltaville Road bridge. Be sure to duck low, for clearance is limited. Once you have cleared the first bridge, you will immediately come to a second one where the double-barreled drain pipes loom ahead under the Route 9 bridge. A large, 50-foot-long tunnel invites entry, and this time no ducking is required.

From the other side of the bridge, continue paddling upstream. As soon as the creek veers sharply left by Goldfoot Road, little navigable water remains ahead. The end comes quickly, just downstream from where Ballston Creek runs under Goldfoot Road, roughly 0.2 mile from the put-in. Return the way you came.

South to Round Lake—To reach Round Lake head downstream from the launch site. In less than 0.1 mile you will come out onto Round Lake. You will likely have to push your way through mats of plants at the mouth of Ballston Creek as the season progresses.

Blue heron rookery. Photograph 2009.

▶ Round Lake (Round Lake)

Water lilies are everywhere. Photograph 2009.

Round Lake is formed at an elevation of 155 feet above sea level and has a diameter of 0.8 mile.[4] Its depth is no greater than 30 feet, which means that you could scuba dive for any length of time without having to deal with decompression tables.[5] The lake's name is derived from its nearly round shape. Little Round Lake (also round in shape) is considerably smaller, with a diameter of only 0.2 mile. It is located northeast of Round Lake and connected to Round Lake by a tiny channel. Both lakes are surprisingly pristine, with little development around their perimeters.

Round Lake has gone by other names. Native Americans called it *Topoondehowa, Dionoondehowa, Tanendahowa,* or *Shanandohawa,* all meaning "place of encampment" or "great plains."[6] Native Americans had no written language. As a result, these names were written down by Europeans who tried to approximate what they were hearing spoken in a language not familiar to them—hence, the variations in spelling.

Five tiny rivulets bring water into the main lake, but none invites exploration for any length except Ballston Creek.[7]

Round Lake contains a surprising amount of history for a body of water of such modest size. In 1878 an unusual attraction called Palestine Park was constructed by Rev. W. W. Wythe along the west shore of the lake. Palestine Park was meant to be a miniature replica of the Holy Land. It was 500 feet long and

250 feet wide, and built on a scale of 2.5 feet = 1.0 mile. The park's landscape contained mountains, valleys, rivers, and a scale model of Jerusalem.[8] Round Lake itself served to represent the Mediterranean Sea.

The park was very popular for a number of years, but folded in 1885. By the early 1920s, boaters reported that little of it remained other than unidentifiable mounds.[9]

The lake had its own steamboat. In 1875 the 45-foot-long *Ordelia*—named after the wife of prominent resident Joseph Hillman—was launched and could carry up to forty passengers.[10] In the early 1900s a casino and boathouse were erected along the tiny strip of land between Round Lake and Route 9, offering a 500-foot-long sandy beach. It operated during the 1920s and 1930s. In the 1940s the property was purchased by Lewis F. Lavery, who ran an airplane service as well as maintaining the bathing beach and boat livery for ten years.

When World War II erupted, the military designated Lavery's as a storage basin for planes. Anyone in the area who owned a plane had to stow it there. Many of the planes were fitted with pontoons to facilitate ease of takeoff and landing on the lake. And, although it sounds incredible today, traffic on Route 9 would be temporarily halted by state police for planes to take off or land along a one-mile stretch of straight highway. In the winter such measures weren't needed. Planes would simply use the frozen lake as an airfield.[11]

East on Round Lake—Once out on the lake, veer left and follow the shoreline east, clockwise. In 0.6 mile you will come to a tiny channel between Round Lake and Little Round Lake, which are otherwise separated only by marshland. Once reached, Little Round Lake's perimeter can be explored for 0.8 mile. The only signs of civilization are at the lake's north end, where the backs of several houses along Rte. 67 can be seen along with boats docked behind them.

Southeast—From the channel connecting Little Round Lake with Round Lake, continue clockwise around Round Lake for another 0.6 mile to a spacious wetland area between two sections of forest. Here the Anthony Kill, Round Lake's outlet stream, begins.

Down the Anthony Kill—The Anthony Kill is also called Tenandaho Creek, which explains why an event held on the stream each spring since the 1970s has been called the Tenandaho White Water Race. The race starts near Willow Glen next to Rte. 67 and ends up in Mechanicville at the confluence of the Anthony Kill and the Hudson River. It is more of a fun race than a competitive one.

The Anthony Kill can be explored for up to 1.0 mile of its length as it meanders east through an open marsh that contains a proliferation of purple pickerel weed and white water lilies. The marshland extends 0.2–0.3 mile on both sides. A line of ghostly, dead trees, and behind them a dense green forest, creates a sense of perimeter. There is virtually no current during most of the paddle.

▶ Round Lake (Round Lake)

At 0.8 mile you will pass by a beaver lodge to your left. If you are visiting during early to mid-July, be sure to look to your right toward the line of tall dead trees in the near-distance. Blue herons build large nests at the top of these trees and can be seen feeding their young. The entire scene has a prehistoric look to it. Paddlers should take note, however, that the nesting colony has been on the decline over recent years and may soon abandon the Anthony Kill for a new rookery. Blue herons move on to colonize elsewhere once the trees of their nesting grounds become uninhabitable.

At 0.9 mile the Dwaas Kill, rising west of Clifton Park Center, enters on your right. It can be explored upstream, but only for a short distance. Several miles farther upstream is the Dwaas Kill Nature Preserve, a 250-acre passive recreational area between Pierce and Kinns roads.

A large beaver dam is encountered at 1.0 mile, and this marks the navigable end of the Anthony Kill for most paddlers. The water level drops 1–2 feet here.

Continuing around Round Lake—Back at Round Lake, continue clockwise for 1.2 miles until you again reach Ballston Creek. Take note of the broken-down cement wall along the west shore, just opposite East Covel Avenue—a relic from days gone by.

21

Ballston Lake (Burnt Hills)
An Unusually Elongated Lake

- **Launch Site:** Ballston Lake off of Outlet Road (Saratoga County); public access developed by the Town of Ballston; seasonal portable toilet at parking lot; put-in near outlet stream, or a 400-foot carry from parking lot to fishing pier/dock
- **Delorme NYS Atlas & Gazetteer:** 66, A2–3; **GPS:** 42°57.43'N; 73°51.15'W
- **Destinations & Mileages:** *South*: to Good Times Restaurant—0.4 mile; to former White Beach—1.6 miles; to south end of lake and former Forest Park—3.4 miles.
- **Comments:** Read "Caution" beginning on page xxi and Saratoga Region Advisory on page 76.

Directions: From the Adirondack Northway (I-87) take Exit 12 for Ballston Spa/Malta and drive west on Rte. 67 for approximately 1.5 miles. Turn left onto East Line Road (Rte. 82) and proceed south for 0.5 mile. When you come to Lake Road, turn right and drive southwest for 1.1 miles, then turn right onto Outlet Road. In 0.1 mile you will cross over Ballston Creek at the point where the stream exits Ballston Lake. Several hundred feet beyond is a long pull-off to your left. Drop off your watercraft here—a site favored by locals—then continue driving west for another 0.1 mile and turn right into a parking area. Return on foot to the pull-off.

If you are approaching from Rte. 50, either 2.3 miles north of Burnt Hills (junction of Rtes. 146A & 50) or 2.4 miles south of Ballston Spa (junction of Rtes. 50 & 67 East), turn onto Outlet Road at a stoplight and drive east for 0.6 mile to a parking area on your left. 0.1 mile beyond the parking lot is a long pull-off to your right. Drop off your watercraft here, return to the parking area (now on your right) to park your car, and return on foot to the pull-off.

From the pull-off, slip your watercraft into the water and then follow a tiny channel that parallels Outlet Road for a couple of hundred feet. As soon as you reach the outlet stream, which is near a low bridge to your left, bear right and proceed onto the main body of the lake.

Kayaks and canoes can also be launched from the fishermen's dock, which is right across Outlet Road from the paved path leading down from the parking area. This launch involves a 200-foot carry from the road along a railed boardwalk that crosses a swampy area near the north shore of the lake. Some paddlers, however, may find it difficult to enter the cockpit of their watercraft from a dock. As a general rule, if a dock is more than 6–9 inches above water, it is difficult—if not dangerous—to try to enter a kayak from the dock.

Paddlers should take note that watercraft can be launched from the Good Times Lake View Restaurant during boating season from 11 AM–9 PM daily except for Tuesday. A modest launch fee is charged, but will be waived if more than $50 is spent in the restaurant.

▶ **Ballston Lake (Burnt Hills)**

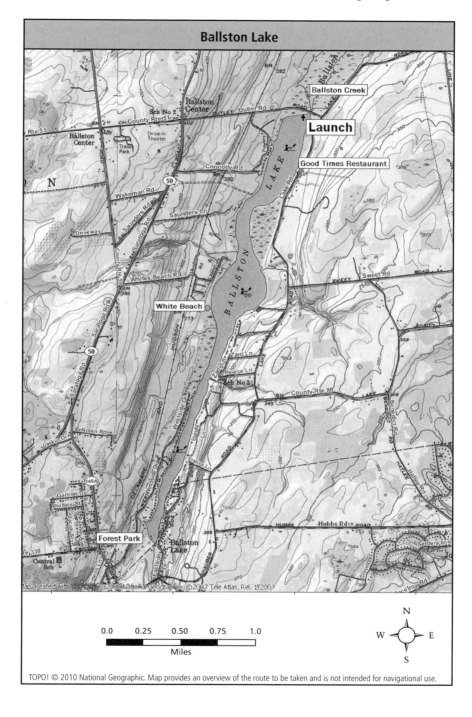

Ballston Lake

Launch

Ballston Creek

Good Times Restaurant

White Beach

Forest Park

Ballston Lake

0.0   0.25   0.50   0.75   1.0
Miles

TOPO! © 2010 National Geographic. Map provides an overview of the route to be taken and is not intended for navigational use.

The Paddle:

Ballston Lake is over three miles long and less than one-half mile across at its widest, making it an exceedingly narrow body of water.[1] Many millenniums ago it was a river. Formed in the Saratoga-McGregor fault zone, which extends from east of Ballston Spa to the Mohawk River at Alplaus, the lake possesses a number of freshwater springs that are rich in iron and other minerals.[2] It is quite deep, going down to a depth of 120 feet at its south end, possibly even deeper.[3] The lake is one of the few meromictic bodies of water in the United States, meaning that there is little exchange of water between the top and bottom of the lake.

Ballston Lake's elevation of 251 feet above sea level puts it higher than Round Lake (155 feet).[4] By the time water from Ballston Lake reaches Round Lake, it has dropped nearly 100 feet. A number of tiny streams enter the lake on both sides, but none are named on topographic maps and are easy to miss as you paddle along.

Because of its prime location in the Capital District region, Ballston Lake's shoreline has become heavily populated with primary residences as well as second homes and camps. Much of the scenery now consists of waterfront homes and wetlands, particularly as you approach the south end of the lake.

Ballston Lake is historically significant. Archaeologists have found Native American artifacts on the banks that date back to the Lamoka tribe of 3,500 BC.[5] Native Americans called the lake *Shenantaha*, meaning "deer water." It has also been known as Long Lake, which is not surprising given its slender shape.

The north part of the lake was first settled in 1763 by Michael & Nicholas McDonald.[6] Around 1771, Rev. Eliphalet Ball, a Congregational clergyman from Bedford, built a log cabin above the northwest end of the lake,[7] and that became the nucleus for a settlement of twenty families that formed by 1772.[8] It was only a matter of time until the area became known as Ball's Town, later to be shortened to Ballston.[9] An interesting historical footnote is that Reverend Ball's father and George Washington's mother were first cousins.

South—The paddle begins from the outlet stream, called Ballston Creek, at the north end of the lake. Proceeding clockwise, head southwest along the east shoreline. At 0.4 mile you will pass by a dock in front of the Good Times Lake View Restaurant, a well-known and popular restaurant that has been in operation since 1890 (and which offers its own public boat launch). At 0.8 mile the lake narrows appreciably, to 0.05 mile, and stays especially narrow for the next 0.4 mile. At 1.2 miles, however, Ballston Lake once again becomes more lakelike and reaches its widest point, at 0.3 mile across.

At 1.7 miles, the lake narrows again, this time for the remainder of the paddle south. Here the lake is generally no wider than 0.05 mile, which makes it easy to view the shoreline and the numerous camps and houses along both sides. Be sure to look for the Lighthouse (a private home) along the west bank. Also be sure to note the high banks on both sides of the lake, relics from the days when the lake was a river.

▶ **Ballston Lake (Burnt Hills)**

Ballston Lake, Ballston, N. Y.

Paddlers have enjoyed the lake for centuries. Postcard ca. 1910.

At 3.4 miles you will reach the south end of the lake, which is dominated by marshland. An amusement park called Forest Park once operated here, just west of the marshlands by the southwest corner. Forest Park was created in 1904 with the support of the Schenectady Railroad Company, which would bring customers up from the Capital District Region to enjoy the more rural setting of an amusement park. The 50-acre park featured a steam-driven boat called the *Comanche*,[10] dancing, clambakes, canoe rentals, a 100-foot dock, a baseball diamond, a casino, and a merry-go-round. Eighteen steel rowboats provided additional access to the water.

The merry-go-round has had an interesting history of its own. It started at Luna Park in Rexford, where it operated from 1910–1912. It was moved to Forest Park, where it operated from 1912–1930. Next it was at Round Lake from 1930–1940, and then it was part of Kaydeross Amusement Park on Saratoga Lake from 1940–1978.[11] It is now located at Congress Park in Saratoga Springs. Forest Park, also known at times as Demerest Park,[12] lasted until the beginning of the 1930s.[13] Since then the park's lands have been parceled out, and individual camps now occupy the site.

Head back north, following the west shoreline now. In 1.7 miles from the south end, you will reach the point where the lake widens. In less than another 0.1 mile you will pass by the former site of White Beach, an amusement park established in 1932 after the demise of Forest Park and located not far from where the McDonald brothers settled in 1763.[14] White Beach has also vanished. At one time you could paddle into a small pond off of the lake here, but this area is no longer accessible.

At 2.1 miles from the south end, the lake narrows again and remains constricted for another 0.4 mile. Then, for the last 0.9 mile of the paddle the lake becomes wider again. At 3.4 miles from the south end, you will find yourself back at the outlet stream entrance to the lake, a round-trip of 6.8 miles.

22

Kayaderosseras Creek: Upper Section (Rock City Falls)
A Paddle Made Possible by Dams

■ **Launch Site:** Fishing Access Site at Kayaderosseras Creek (Saratoga County); challenging 15-foot carry down rocky embankment
■ **Delorme NYS Atlas & Gazetteer:** p. 80, D2; **GPS:** 43°04.02'N; 73°56.10'W
■ **Destinations & Mileages:** *North:* upstream to shallows—0.3 mile. *East:* downstream to old factory dam—0.7 mile.
■ **Comments:** Read "Caution" beginning on page xxi and Saratoga Region Advisory on page 76.

Kayaderosseras Creek passes through a considerable portion of Saratoga County. There are a number of access points along the creek in addition to the ones described in this chapter and the next. These include the access points below the lower Rock City Falls dam at Milton Center, Factory Village, Kelly Park, Gray's Crossing, and Driscoll Road. All of these points access sections of the creek with faster-moving and much shallower waters. This increases the likelihood of blowdown and strainers being encountered, which means that advanced paddling skills are needed to respond to rapidly changing conditions. Readers interested in tackling these middle sections of Kayaderosseras Creek can consult the Adirondack Mountain Club's *Canoe and Kayak Guide: East-Central New York State* by Kathie Armstrong and Chet Harvey, or contact the Friends of Kayaderosseras at kayadeross@hotmail.com. The Friends is a nonprofit organization formed in 2004 to promote the river and ensure its preservation (kayaderosseras.org).

Directions: From Saratoga Springs (junction of Rtes. 50/9 & 29 West) drive west on Rte. 29 for roughly 7.0 miles. At Rock City Falls (junction of Rock City Road/ Rte. 49 and Rte. 29), continue west on Rte. 29 for another 1.0 mile. Just before you cross over the Hatch Bridge, which spans Kayaderosseras Creek, turn right onto Creek Road.

From North Galway (junction of Rtes. 29 & 147) drive east on Rte. 29 for 6.5 miles and turn left onto Creek Road immediately after crossing over Kayaderosseras Creek.

From either direction, the fishing access site is immediately to your left, next to the bridge where a DEC sign reads "Kayaderosseras Creek Public Fishing Stream." From the parking area for the access site, carry your watercraft 15 feet down a rocky embankment to the water's edge.

The Paddle:
Kayaderosseras Creek is a medium-sized stream that rises from the southern slopes of the Kayaderosseras Range in Greenfield and flows into Saratoga Lake along its northwest shore. It is the only creek in Saratoga County whose entire route is contained within the county borders.[1] Today the stream is commonly called Kaydeross Creek by paddlers.

▶ **Kayaderosseras Creek: Upper Section (Rock City Falls)**

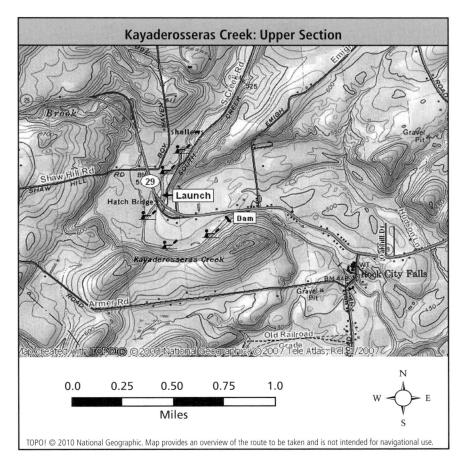

Kayaderosseras Creek: Upper Section

TOPO! © 2010 National Geographic. Map provides an overview of the route to be taken and is not intended for navigational use.

Kayaderosseras is Mohawk for "the land of the beautiful lake of the winding river."[2] During the French and Indian War in the mid-1700s, the stream was occasionally used by Native American war parties.[3]

During the nineteenth century the Kayaderosseras and its tributaries played host to numerous mills and factories, including paper mills, foundries, cotton mills, tanneries, wheel shops, sawmills, gristmills, and lumber and cabinetry mills. Prior to the 1800s, Rock City Falls was known as Hatch's Mill, which explains the name of the bridge next to the fishing access site. In 1840, Chauncey Kilmer and H. R. Rowland built a paper mill in Rock City Falls. It was later purchased by George West, the inventor of the paper bag.

North—Head upstream from Hatch Bridge, paddling over a rocky streambed that poses little difficulty as long as the creek's water level is sufficiently deep. It's a very pretty trek as your watercraft glides over a rock garden of boulders for the first 0.1 mile. After 0.3 mile you will reach a point where rapids prevent further advancement without a portage.

If you find yourself hitting bottom along the creek, which could happen late in the season, turn around and take the downstream paddle.

East—Paddle downstream, immediately passing under Hatch Bridge. From that point on the stream opens up and becomes wider and more languid as you proceed southwest. In 0.3 mile you will reach a point where the Kayaderosseras veers left. Here it is possible to turn right (west) momentarily into a tiny cove that can be explored briefly.

Continuing east on the Kayaderosseras, follow the creek downstream for another 0.4 mile, paralleling a high embankment to your right. You will come to a dam by an old factory building; this provides a good turnaround point. If you wish to make this a one-way paddle, there are several places to take out along the left (north) bank before the dam is reached.

Note: The take-out sites also provide an alternate put-in. The sites are located 0.4 mile east of Hatch Bridge, or 0.6 miles west of the junction of Rtes. 29 & 49, directly across from the Mansion Inn, a Victorian-style bed & breakfast that was originally built in 1866 and served as a summer home for industrialist George West.

The tiny hamlet of Rock City Falls is named after its waterfall. Photograph 2004.

▶ **Kayaderosseras Creek: Upper Section (Rock City Falls)**

Kayaderosseras Creek: Lower Section (Saratoga Springs)
A Stream That's Had a Little Help from Its Friends

23

- ■ **Launch Site:** Lake Lonely Boat Livery (Saratoga County); modest launch fee; open daily, 6 AM–6 PM; portable toilet; open seasonally from early May. For more information: Lake Lonely Boat Livery, 378 Crescent Avenue, Saratoga Springs, NY 12866, (518) 587-1721.
- ■ **Delorme NYS Atlas & Gazetteer:** p. 80, D3–4; **GPS:** 43°03.21'N; 73°45.23'W
- ■ **Destinations & Mileages:** *South*: down Lake Lonely outlet stream to confluence with Kayaderosseras Creek—0.9 mile. *East (downstream) on Kayaderosseras Creek*: to trail leading up to the Arrowhead Casino Archaeological Preserve—0.9 mile (1.8 miles from launch); downstream on Kayaderosseras Creek to Saratoga Lake—1.0 mile (1.9 miles from launch); downstream on Kayaderosseras Creek and across north end of Saratoga Lake to NYS Boat Launch—2.3 miles (3.2 miles from launch). *West (upstream) on Kayaderosseras Creek*: to the Adirondack Northway (I-87)—1.7 miles (2.6 miles from launch); upstream on Kayaderosseras Creek to Rte. 9 bridge—2.8 miles (3.7 miles from launch).
- ■ **Comments:** Read "Caution" beginning on page xxi and Saratoga Region Advisory on page 76.

  See previous chapter, "Kayaderosseras Creek: Upper Section," for general information and history on Kayaderosseras Creek and environs.

  The livery generally locks its gate at closing time, so be sure to plan your trip accordingly and return prior to 6 PM.

  Paddlers should be vigilant for new accumulations of deadfall, which are particularly likely to occur when the stream is engorged, eroding the banks and toppling trees that have a tenuous purchase.

Directions: From Exit 13 of the Adirondack Northway (I-87), proceed north on Rte. 9 for 2.6 miles. Turn right onto Crescent Avenue (Rte. 22) and drive east for 1.8 miles. You will see the Lake Lonely Boat Livery directly to your right, just before you cross over Lake Lonely's outlet stream. Park at the livery and launch just south of the building.

From the north end of Saratoga Lake at Fish Creek bridge on Rte. 9P, proceed northwest on Rte. 9P for over 0.3 mile. At a traffic light turn left onto Rte. 22 and head west for over 1.6 miles. As soon as you cross over the outlet stream from Lake Lonely, turn left into the Lake Lonely Boat Livery. Park at the livery and launch just south of the building.

The Paddle:
South—Follow the outlet stream from Lake Lonely downstream for 0.9 mile to Kayaderosseras Creek.

East (downstream) on Kayaderosseras Creek —At the confluence of the outlet stream and Kayaderosseras Creek, turn left onto Kayaderosseras Creek and

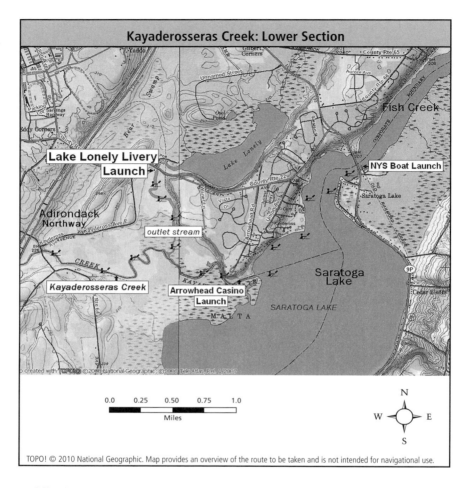

Kayaderosseras Creek: Lower Section

TOPO! © 2010 National Geographic. Map provides an overview of the route to be taken and is not intended for navigational use.

paddle downriver. Along the way you will see huge piles of logs lining the riverbank—debris that until recently had clogged up the river and created several unwanted dams. The logs and debris were removed through the concerted efforts of the Friends of Kayaderosseras Creek and contractors.

To the left at 0.9 mile (1.8 miles from the launch, and 0.1 mile before reaching Saratoga Lake), is a trail leading up to the Arrowhead Casino Archaeological Preserve, a 26-acre nature and historic preserve. If you get out of your watercraft and follow the trail uphill for 0.1 mile, you will come to stone walls near a parking lot. This is all that remains of the Arrowhead Inn Restaurant & Casino, which burned down in 1969. A kiosk next to the parking area recounts the history of the area going back in time to the prehistoric people who camped here in 6,500 BC, and possibly even as far back as 11,000 years ago.[1]

▶ **Kayaderosseras Creek: Lower Section (Saratoga Springs)**

Back on the creek, it is only another 0.1 mile downstream until you reach the northwest sweep of Saratoga Lake. You can paddle around the shoreline for any distance you please, returning to the Lake Lonely Boat Livery launch when you are done. If you wish to make this paddle a one-way trip, the NYS Boat Launch site at the mouth of Fish Creek, 1.3 miles northeast across the lake from the mouth of the creek, makes for a nice exit point.

West (upstream) on Kayaderosseras Creek—It is also possible to paddle upstream on Kayaderosseras Creek for a considerable distance. From the confluence of Lake Lonely's outlet stream with Kayaderosseras Creek, turn right. You will go under the Adirondack Northway (I-87) at 1.7 miles (2.6 miles from launch) and reach the Route 9 bridge at 2.8 miles (3.7 miles from launch).

Alternate Launch Site #1

Arrowhead Casino Archaeological Preserve (Saratoga Springs)

◼ **Launch Site:** Arrowhead Casino Archaeological Preserve (Saratoga County); 0.1-mile carry to slip-in at edge of Kayaderosseras Creek. The deeply worn path is on private property. A posted sign informs visitors that the owner is not liable for any mishaps that may occur while on his property.
◼ **Delorme NYS Atlas & Gazetteer:** p. 80, D3–4; **GPS:** 43°02.47'N; 73°44.40'W
◼ **Destinations & Mileages:** *East*: to Saratoga Lake—0.1 mile; to NYS Boat Launch—1.4 miles. *West*: to confluence of Kayaderosseras Creek with Lake Lonely's outlet stream—0.9 mile; up Lake Lonely's outlet stream to Lake Lonely—0.9 mile (1.8 mile from launch); to Adirondack Northway—2.6 miles; to Rte. 9—3.7 miles.
◼ **Comments:** Read "Caution" beginning on page xxi and Saratoga Region Advisory on page 76.

Directions: From Exit 13 of the Adirondack Northway (I-87), proceed north on Rte. 9 for 2.6 miles. Turn right onto Crescent Avenue (Rte. 22) and drive east for 2.7 miles.

From the north end of Saratoga Lake at Fish Creek bridge on Rte. 9P, proceed northwest on Rte. 9P for over 0.3 mile. At a traffic light, turn left onto Rte. 22 and head west for over 0.7 mile.

From either direction, turn on to Arrowhead Road and drive south for 0.7 mile to its end at a small parking lot at the Arrowhead Casino Archaeological Preserve.

From the parking area carry your watercraft along a wide, well-worn path that leads downhill in 0.1 mile to Kayaderosseras Creek. Upon reaching the creek the path turns left and follows the shoreline. Instead of putting in your watercraft when you first come to the stream, where it tends to be muddy, you may want to follow the trail left for several hundred feet and launch where the footing is drier.

Alternate Launch Site #2

NYS Boat Launch (Saratoga Springs)

- ◼ **Launch Site:** New York State Boat Launch (Saratoga County); modest fee during summer and on weekends during the spring and fall
- ◼ **Delorme NYS Atlas & Gazetteer:** p. 80, D4; **GPS:** 43°03.21'N; 73°43.23'W
- ◼ **Destinations & Mileages:** *West*: across north end of Saratoga Lake to mouth of Kayaderosseras Creek—1.3 miles; to trail to Arrowhead Casino Archaeological Preserve—1.4 miles; to confluence of Kayaderosseras Creek and Lake Lonely's outlet stream—2.3 miles; up Lake Lonely's outlet stream to Lake Lonely—0.9 miles (3.2 miles from launch); upstream along Kayaderosseras Creek to Adirondack Northway (I-87)—4.0 miles; upstream along Kayaderosseras Creek to Rte. 9—5.1 miles.
- ◼ **Comments:** Read "Caution" beginning on page xxi and Saratoga Region Advisory on page 76.

Directions: From the Adirondack Northway (I-87) take Exit 14. Proceed southeast on Union Street (Rte. 9P) for 2.2 miles. As soon as you cross over Fish Creek/Saratoga Lake, drive 0.05 mile farther and then turn left onto a road that leads to the entrance to the NYS Boat Launch site in 0.1 mile. The put-in is just downstream from the bridge.

From the north end of Saratoga Lake at Fish Creek bridge on Rte. 9P, drive to the south end of the bridge and turn northeast onto a small road that leads to the NYS Boat Launch within 0.1 mile. The put-in is just downstream from the bridge.

The NYS Boat Launch at Fish Creek. Photograph 2010.

▶ **Kayaderosseras Creek: Lower Section (Saratoga Springs)**

Fish Creek: Saratoga Lake to Grangerville Dam (Saratoga Springs)
The Outlet Stream from Saratoga Lake

24

- ■ **Launch Site:** NYS Boat Launch (Saratoga County); cement ramp; modest daily charge during summer and on weekends during the spring and fall
- ■ **Delorme NYS Atlas & Gazetteer:** pp. 80–81, D4; **GPS:** 43°03.21'N; 73°43.23'W
- ■ **Destinations & Mileages:** *Northeast*: to Fish Creek Marina—2.0 miles; to pilings from old railroad bridge—3.3 miles; to Sucker Brook—3.7 miles; to Bryants Bridge—4.5 miles; to Gold Brook—5.5 miles; to Grangerville Dam— 6.8 miles. *Southwest*: to Saratoga Lake—0.6 mile; around perimeter of Saratoga Lake—12.0 miles.
- ■ **Comments:** Read "Caution" beginning on page xxi and Saratoga Region Advisory on page 76.

Directions: From the Adirondack Northway (I-87) take Exit 14. Proceed southeast on Union Street (Rte. 9P) for 2.2 miles. At the end of the bridge spanning Fish Creek/Saratoga Lake, drive 0.05 mile farther and then turn left onto a road that leads northeast to the entrance to the NYS Boat Launch in 0.1 mile.

The Paddle:
The put-in is close to the new bridge that opened in May 2011 and replaced the 609-foot-long steel truss bridge that had stood next to the launch site since 1923.

Fish Creek for much of its length is a friendly, easily navigable stream. Many consider it to be the continuation of Kayaderosseras Creek, which flows into Saratoga Lake and emerges from the lake as Fish Creek (just as Ballston Creek emerges from Round Lake as the Anthony Kill). Meandering northeast, Fish Creek flows into the Hudson River at the south end of Schuylerville, where it passes by the historic Philip Schuyler mansion. Paddlers will find the stream to be as wide as a river as far downstream as the Grangerville Dam. It would be a natural assumption to anticipate that the size and depth of Fish Creek would keep diminishing as you paddle downstream from Saratoga Lake, but in actuality the stream grows in size because of being dammed at Grangerville. For this reason, you will note that many camps and homes along the stream have powerboats moored by their backyards.

Fish Creek has witnessed at least one dramatic scene. In 1689 a flotilla of 250 canoes carrying over 1,300 Iroquois warriors made their way down the creek past Victory Mills and then on to the Hudson River, where they headed north and took part in the Ville de Lachine massacre in present-day Montreal, Quebec.[1]

Northeast—From the launch, head downstream on Fish Creek. For the first 1.3 miles the land to your right is fairly level and marshy, while the shore to your left is more elevated. In 2.0 miles you will arrive at the Fish Creek Marina.

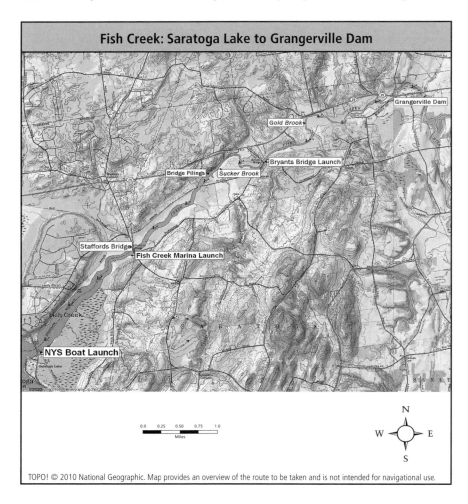

Fish Creek: Saratoga Lake to Grangerville Dam

Grangerville Dam

Gold Brook

Bryants Bridge Launch

Bridge Pilings   Sucker Brook

Staffords Bridge

Fish Creek Marina Launch

NYS Boat Launch

N
W ←⊕→ E
S

0.0   0.25   0.50   0.75   1.0
Miles

TOPO! © 2010 National Geographic. Map provides an overview of the route to be taken and is not intended for navigational use.

Continuing downstream you will pass by pilings from an old railroad bridge at 3.3 miles and then, at 3.7 miles, Sucker Brook, coming in along the south bank. Sucker Brook can be paddled upstream for a very short distance.

Bryants Bridge (another access site) is reached at 4.5 miles. You will pass by Gold Brook, coming in on your left, at 5.5 miles. Rte. 29 becomes noticeable to your left at 5.6 miles and stays close to the stream for another 0.2 mile.

At 6.8 miles you will reach the impassable Grangerville Dam (also known as Winnie's Reef Dam), whose two sections connect to a midstream island.[2] Blue and white buoys span the river to warn against going any farther. Turn around at this point and return to the starting point.

For details on paddling sections of Fish Creek below the Grangerville Dam, which involves stronger current and the potential for obstacles and

▶ **Fish Creek: Saratoga Lake to Grangerville Dam (Saratoga Springs)**

rifts, interested readers should consult the Adirondack Mountain Club's *Canoe and Kayak Guide: East-Central New York State* by Kathie Armstrong and Chet Harvey.

The hamlet of Grangerville and the dam were named after Harvey Granger, who operated a gristmill on Fish Creek prior to 1800.[3] In the early days the stream was heavily populated by migratory eels, many of which were caught when a weir (a low dam) was constructed across the river at Grangerville.

Southwest—Saratoga Lake is reached in 0.6 mile paddling southwest from the boat launch. Once you are out onto Saratoga Lake proper, you can follow its perimeter clockwise or counterclockwise. A complete paddle around the lake's perimeter would entail a trek of 12.0 miles (see chapter "Saratoga Lake").

Alternate Launch Site #1

Fish Creek Marina (Hickeys Corners)

■ **Launch Site:** Fish Creek Marina, Saratoga Springs Outdoor Center (Saratoga County); ramp; portable toilet; modest launch fee; open seasonally May 15 through Oct. 15. For additional information: 252 Staffords Bridge Road, Saratoga Springs, NY 12866, (518) 584-1901, fishcreekmarina.com. The Fish Creek Marina features the Kayak Shak (518) 587-9788, specializing in kayak, canoe & rowboat rentals.

■ **Delorme NYS Atlas & Gazetteer:** p. 80, D4; **Estimated GPS:** 43°04.42'N; 73°41.70'W

■ **Destinations & Mileages:** *Southwest*: to NYS Boat Launch—2.0 miles. *Northeast*: to old railroad bridge pilings—1.3 miles; to Sucker Brook—1.7 miles; to Bryants Bridge—2.5 miles; to Gold Brook—3.5 miles; to Grangerville Dam—4.8 miles.

■ **Comments:** Read "Caution" beginning on page xxi and Saratoga Region Advisory on page 76.

Directions: From the Adirondack Northway (I-87) take Exit 14 and proceed southeast on Union Avenue (Rte. 9P). At 0.8 mile turn left onto Dyer Switch Road (Rte. 66) and head southeast for 0.8 mile. When you come to Meadowbrook Road (Rte. 65), turn right and proceed northeast for 1.2 miles to Staffords Bridge Road.

From Saratoga Springs (junction of Rtes. 29 East & 50/9), drive east on Rte. 29 for 4.3 miles until you reach Staffords Bridge Road.

From either direction, upon reaching Stafford Bridge Road (Rte. 67) turn right and go south for 0.3 mile. As soon as you cross over Staffords Bridge spanning Fish Creek, turn right into the Fish Creek Marina. The Kayak Shak is the colorful building closest to the bridge.

Alternate Launch Site #2

Bryants Bridge (Burgoyne)

- ■ **Launch Site:** Bryants Bridge (Saratoga County); moderately difficult (sloping bank and rocky footing) 20-foot carry down embankment; limited parking
- ■ **Delorme NYS Atlas & Gazetteer:** p. 81, D4; **Estimated GPS:** 43°05.54'N; 73°39.59'W
- ■ **Destinations & Mileages:** *Southwest*: to Sucker Brook—0.8 mile; to old railroad bridge pilings—1.1 miles; to Fish Creek Marina—2.5 miles; to NYS Boat Launch—4.5 miles. *Northeast*: to Gold Brook—1.0 mile; to Grangerville Dam—2.3 miles.
- ■ **Comments:** Read "Caution" beginning on page xxi and Saratoga Region Advisory on page 76.

Directions: From the Adirondack Northway (I-87) take Exit 14. Go southeast on Rte. 9P for 0.7 mile. Turn left onto Gilbert Road and drive northeast for 1.2 miles, then turn right onto Rte. 29 and drive east for 4.2 miles until you reach Bryants Bridge Road.

From Saratoga Springs (junction of Rtes. 29 East & 50/9), drive east on Rte. 29 for 6.3 miles until you come to Bryants Bridge Road.

From either starting point, at Bryants Bridge Road turn right and drive southeast for 0.3 mile. As soon as you cross over the bridge spanning Fish Creek, park immediately to your left. There is *very* limited parking here—perhaps enough for 4–5 cars if people park carefully. A carry of 20 feet down a moderately steep bank will take you to the river.

The Grangerville Dam marks the end of this portion of the paddle.
Photograph 2010.

▶ **Fish Creek: Saratoga Lake to Grangerville Dam (Saratoga Springs)**

Cossayuna Lake (Cossayuna)
A Lake with an Unusual Island

25

■ **Launch Site:** DEC Boat Launch off of East Lake Road at northeast end of Cossayuna Lake (Washington County); hard-surface ramp; seasonal portable toilet; parking for 30 cars & trailers. For more information: Cossayuna Lake Improvement Association, P.O. Box 97, Cossayuna, NY 12823, (518) 692-9270.
■ **Delorme NYS Atlas & Gazetteer:** p. 81, C6; **Estimated GPS:** 43°13.10'N; 73°24.71'W
■ **Destinations & Mileages:** *West*: to Big Island—0.2 mile; around Big Island—0.6 mile; to Oak Point, going counterclockwise around lake—2.3 miles; *around perimeter of lake*—7.0 miles.
■ **Comments:** Read "Caution" beginning on page xxi and Saratoga Region Advisory on page 76.

Directions: From Schuylerville (junction of Rtes. 4/32 & 29 East) proceed east on Rte. 29 for 3.8 miles. When you come to a traffic rotary, head north on Rte. 40 for 5.9 miles. At South Argyle turn right onto Rte. 49 and proceed east for 3.8 miles until you reach the tiny hamlet of Cossayuna. (Along the way, at 3.2 miles, you will pass by Rte. 48, which parallels the west side of the lake). At 3.9 miles, in Cossayuna, turn left onto Bunker Hill Road and then immediately left again onto East Lake Road. Proceed north for 2.5 miles, then turn left onto a dirt road at a sign for the DEC Boat Launch and drive west for less than 0.1 mile to the launch site.

The Paddle:
Cossayuna Lake is a sizeable body of water, roughly 3 miles long and 1 mile across at its widest, covering 649 acres. It is fed by a watershed of 11 square miles. The lake is not deep, possessing a maximum depth of 25 feet and an average depth of 11 feet.[1] There are sections near Big Island where you can walk out from the island for hundreds of feet and still only be up to your thighs in water.

The village of Cossayuna was settled in 1780.[2] It was originally known as Hog Hollow, and then simply as Lake. Three dams were built along the lake's outlet, and several mills were established, including a blanket factory and a cheese factory.[3]

Cossayuna is a corruption of the Native American word *Quabbauna*, meaning "lake of the three pines." It is said that at one time three large pines grew on Oak Point.[4]

West—From the put-in, head west for over 0.2 mile to Big Island, which can be circumnavigated in 0.6 mile. The island is roughly 0.25 mile long and 0.05 mile wide. What is so unusual for an island so narrow is its high ridge line, which towers above the lake.

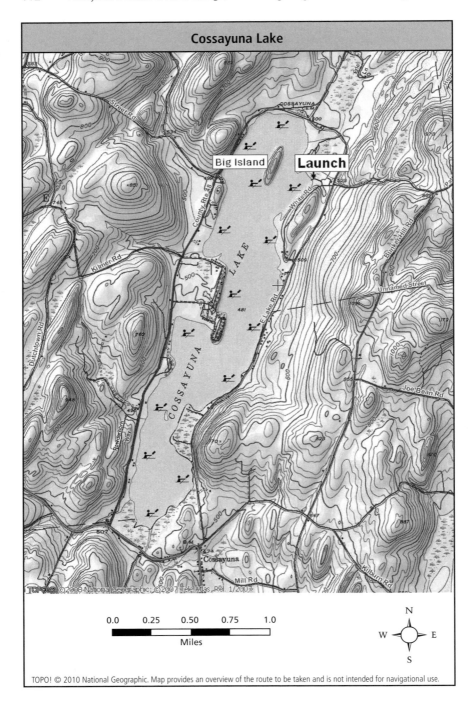

Cossayuna Lake

TOPO! © 2010 National Geographic. Map provides an overview of the route to be taken and is not intended for navigational use.

▶ **Cossayuna Lake (Cossayuna)**

The paddle around Cossayuna Lake, following the shoreline closely, is 7.0 miles in length. At 2.3 miles you will pass by Oak Point, midway along the west shore. With the exception of the south end, the lake is ringed by seasonal camps and year-round residences, but it remains a very pretty setting. Stewart Hill and Browns Mountain dominate the view at the south end of the lake.

The Island, Lake Cossayuna, N. Y.

Big Island rises high above the waters of Cossayuna Lake. Postcard ca. 1910.

26   Carter's Pond State Wildlife Management Area (Cossayuna)
A Sanctuary for Birds and Beavers

■ **Launch Site:** Carter's Pond/Phil A. Dustin Wildlife Management Area (Washington County); parking for 10 cars; 75-foot carry down gravel incline to slip-in at pond's edge. For more information: dec.ny.gov/outdoor/24402.html.

■ **Delorme NYS Atlas & Gazetteer:** p. 81, C6; **Estimated GPS:** 43°09.85'N; 73°25.40'W

■ **Destinations & Mileages:** *North*: to inlet stream—0.1 mile; up inlet stream—0.6 mile. *South*: to outlet channel—0.2 mile; down outlet channel—0.3 mile. *Around perimeter of pond*—0.9 mile.

■ **Comments:** Read "Caution" beginning on page xxi and Saratoga Region Advisory on page 76.

    Be careful not to disturb the wildlife.

Directions: From Schuylerville (junction of Rtes. 4/32 & 29 East) proceed east on Rte. 29 for 3.8 miles. At the traffic circle, head north on Rte. 40 for 5.9 miles. When you come to South Argyle, turn right onto Rte. 49 and proceed east for 5.2 miles, passing through the tiny hamlet of Cossayuna along the way, and turn left into the first (northernmost) pull-off, on your left.

The Paddle:
Carter's Pond/Phil A. Dustin Wildlife Management Area (WMA) is an extensive, 43.5-acre marsh and upland complex that includes the pond, a wooded swamp, emergent marsh, shrub wetlands, old fields, grasslands, shrub lands, and forests. It is part of the Batten Kill River watershed in Washington County. The WMA's main feature is its diversity of bird species, encouraged and supported by the Bird Conservation Area signed into law by Governor George E. Pataki in 1997. The bill was modeled after National Audubon Society's Improvement Bird Area Program.

    A stone monument at the northernmost pull-off states: "Erected by Waterfowl Improvement Association Inc. Dedicated to improving habitat at Carters Pond and similar areas. In memory of its founder Phil. A. Dustin, devoted conservationist and sportsman. 4/13/1917–10/13/1975."

    A kiosk at the parking area gives additional information about the pond and its wildlife. The WMA's habitat supports a diversity of species including 51 mammals, 174 birds, 6 reptiles, 8 amphibians, and 11 fish.[1]

    Carter's Pond is surrounded by a huge wetland area. The open-water section comprises an area roughly 0.4 mile long and 0.2 mile wide, and can be paddled around in 0.9 mile.

    North—At the north end of Carter's Pond, the lake's inlet creek, which descends from nearby Cossayuna Lake, can be followed upstream through a maze-like marshland for well over 0.6 mile before portages over small obstructions make continuation increasingly frustrating.

▶ **Carter's Pond State Wildlife Management Area (Cossayuna)**

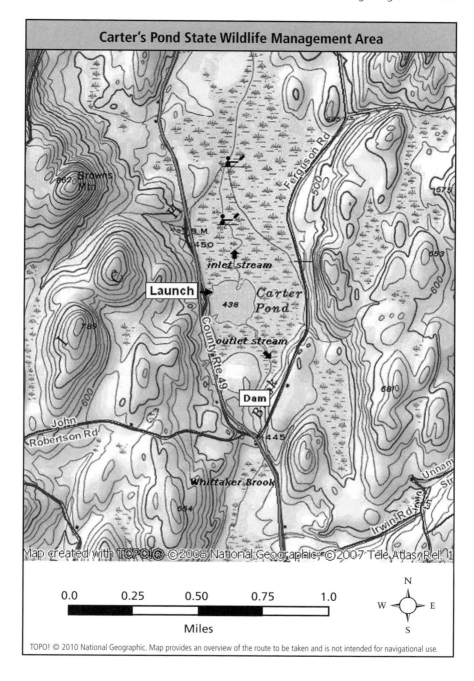

Carter's Pond State Wildlife Management Area

South—At the southeast end of the lake, a labyrinthine channel can be followed for roughly 0.3 mile before you reach a small dam. Whittaker Brook, the outlet stream, continues south beyond the dam and eventually flows into the Batten Kill at the village of Battenkill.

Hike: A short trail can be followed along part of the WMA. The trail was created in 1980 by the Youth Conservation Corp (YCC). A trailhead sign provides the names of the supervisor and the youths who worked on the project. Take note of the observation deck that overlooks the pond several hundred feet from the second (southernmost) pull-off for the WMA along Rte. 49.

Carter's Pond in the early morning mist. Photograph 2009.

▶ **Carter's Pond State Wildlife Management Area (Cossayuna)**

Champlain Canal Pond (Fort Miller)
A Quiet Paddle along Part of the Old Champlain Canal

27

■ **Launch Site:** West side of shallow pond off of Rte. 4 (Washington County); slip-in next to parking area
■ **Delorme NYS Atlas & Gazetteer:** p. 81, C5; **GPS:** 43°10.20'N; 73°34.71'W
■ **Destination & Mileage:** *Around perimeter of pond*—0.9 mile.
■ **Comments:** Read "Caution" beginning on page xxi and Saratoga Region Advisory on page 76.

Directions: From Schuylerville (junction of Rtes. 29 West & 4/32), go north on Rte. 4 for 5.0 miles. You will come to large pull-offs on both sides of the road. Turn right into the large, east-side parking area.

From Fort Edward (where Rte. 4 crosses over the Champlain Canal), head south for 6.7 miles. You will come to large pull-offs on both sides of the road. Turn left into the large, east-side parking area.

Your watercraft can be slipped into the pond directly to the rear and slightly to the right of the parking area.

The Paddle:
This unnamed pond is over 0.5 mile long, 0.2 mile wide, and is part of the old Champlain Canal, which can be seen occasionally paralleling the east side of Rte. 4 between Northumberland and Fort Edward. The pond can be circum-navigated in 0.9 mile. Although short, this paddle is great fun when combined with a trek along the Champlain Canal. (See chapter "Champlain Canal above Lock C-6.")

This pond was formerly part of the old Champlain Canal. Photograph 2010.

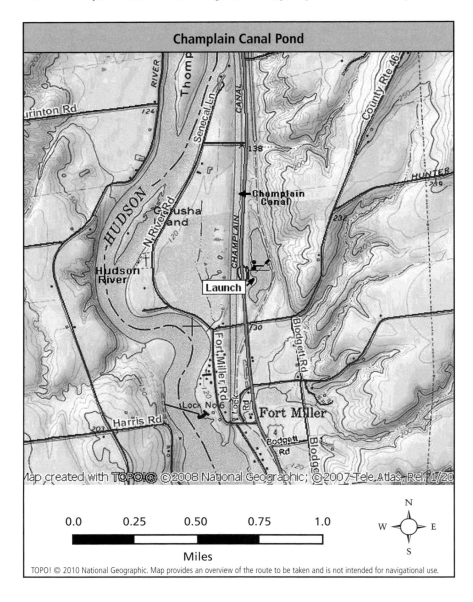

Champlain Canal Pond

▶ **Champlain Canal Pond (Fort Miller)**

III

Great Sacandaga Lake & Environs

Advisory

Do not venture away from the shoreline and out into open water on Great Sacandaga Lake unless you are at least an intermediate-level paddler, capable of handling a variety of water and weather conditions and able to self-rescue.

Great Sacandaga Lake is first cousin size-wise to Lake George and warrants the same degree of caution and respect. The lake is heavily populated by big powerboats, and many move at fast speeds. Personal watercraft such as Jet Skis are also abundant.

Operators of small watercraft, like kayaks and canoes, must be ever-vigilant. Don't assume boats can see you. Wear bright colors. If you must cross open water, cross in a group and keep the group together. If you see a boat in the distance, let it pass before you set out. Some large boats move surprisingly fast, and distance can be hard to judge. Take into account current and wind when planning your trajectory across open water. Be prepared for an increase in boat traffic as you pass by marinas.

Stay close to the shoreline unless you are planning to go island-hopping. Even then, do not venture away from the shore unless the weather is calm. Always check the forecast and weather before setting out. Do not leave shore if storms and/or high winds are predicted or if the weather forecast is at all questionable. Be aware that the weather can change abruptly, often with little warning and in spite of the forecast. Turn about at the first sign of inclement weather and return to shore.

Pay attention to wind, waves, and wakes, which can capsize an inattentive paddler. It is not unusual for the lake to produce intense winds and three-foot waves. Wind and current increase as you move away from the shoreline. The wind tends to be quietest in the early morning and early evening.

Memorize the shoreline as you leave so that you can return to the same starting point, and pack a compass and waterproof map.

Great Sacandaga Lake is a reservoir, which means that its water level varies with seasonal regularity (more water in the spring, less in the midsummer through fall). The lake will be rougher when it is near maximum capacity and gentler when it contains a smaller volume of water. When the water level drops sufficiently, later in the season, large boats generally are pulled out of the lake because of hidden shoals that can claim props. It is at this time that the lake becomes a heaven for paddlers.

Several of Great Sacandaga Lake's secondary bodies of water have dams on their outlet streams. Stay a safe distance back from all dams, and make sure that the current is not strong if you launch close to a dam.

Introduction

The Great Sacandaga may look natural and as long-lived as the mountains surrounding it, but the lake is anything but naturally formed. Until 1930 there was no lake—only a medium-sized river meandering through the Sacandaga Valley. When the Conklingville Dam impounded the Sacandaga River, however, a once-bustling river valley was transformed into a mighty reservoir within a matter of weeks.

The dam was built to help prevent the Hudson River from flooding annually. The year 1913 had been a particularly bad flood year, with extensive damage inflicted on downstream Hudson River-based communities and towns. Engineers correctly determined that if waters from the Sacandaga River were diverted into a reservoir each spring, then the Hudson—bereft of one of its main tributaries—would no longer imperil the river towns from Glens Falls to Albany as it had in the past. It took another decade and a half before the project became a reality.

There were secondary benefits from creating the reservoir as well. With the erection of dams at Conklingville and Stewart Bridge, hydroelectric plants were also installed so that the prodigious energy contained in the Sacandaga River's falling waters would not be wasted. In addition, the lake served as a holding tank, ready for its waters to be released in one mighty surge to help push back the Atlantic Ocean during the summer should an invading salt line move too far up the tidal Hudson River and begin contaminating local sources of water.

The result of this impoundment of the waters of the Sacandaga River is a man-made lake that is far bigger than most people realize; Great Sacandaga Lake is nearly the size of Lake George. It is 29 miles long, over 5 miles across at its widest, and contains 125 miles of shoreline. It holds 285 billion gallons of water and occupies what geologists call a graben—a valley created when a large tract of the Earth's crust drops between two fault lines.[1]

Because the Great Sacandaga Lake is a reservoir, its water level can change dramatically, but generally with seasonal predictability—rising in the spring and receding in the fall. Shoals that were hidden one week can emerge the next as the lake contracts in size; the contour of the shoreline can change significantly with alterations in the water level.

Great Sacandaga Lake's most notable features are its islands, which are principally found on the main body of the lake. Until 1930 these islands were rolling hills in the valley. When you step onto an island today, keep in mind that you are walking on the former Sacandaga Valley.

All of the islands are public land. They remain undeveloped and free of homes, camps, or structures. Since the lake falls within the "blue line" of the Forest Preserve, the islands are governed under the New York State constitution and can't be sold or leased. Some, like Mead Island and the Kenyon Island Group, are fairly inhospitable places and are rarely explored on foot.

The lake's principal island destination is Sand Island, where boaters gather by the hundreds during the summer, filling the beaches with throngs of sun worshippers. Sometimes boats are so numerous that they form concentric rings around the island.

During the summer all of the islands grow larger as the lake level gradually drops and exposes more land. Sand Island increases in size several times over, and if the lake gets low enough, an island 0.5 mile to the west of Sand Island occasionally emerges. The Trapp Islands link together, increasing in size tenfold, and a small island 0.2 mile to the north of Trapp Island often makes an appearance.

Scout Island stays fairly constant in size because of the depth of water around it, while neighboring islands to its southeast grow larger, sometimes becoming part of the mainland. Beacon Island often triples in size; Deer Island can quadruple in size if the lake's waters diminish enough.

Between Diamond Point and Silver Bay, two well-known areas along the southeast side of Great Sacandaga Lake, Rock Island emerges and grows rapidly in size, accompanied by several smaller raised shoals at times of low water volume. Stump Island, across from Silver Bay, rarely appears unless the lake is exceptionally low, but when it does, it is larger than several football fields.

Mead Island and the Kenyon Island Group, located at the shallowest part of the lake, quickly become joined as a huge section of lake bottom is exposed.

All of this is worth noting if you are paddling on the Great Sacandaga Lake in the late fall and the waters have been drawn down unusually low. It is then that you will find the main section of the Great Sacandaga Lake to be a lake of islands.

Although many small towns and villages were buried when the valley was flooded, there is little to see if you try to peer into the lake's watery depths from your watercraft. From 1927 to 1929, workers methodically razed everything in the valley to a height of no more than 12 inches. Eighty years of underwater erosion coupled with the constant pressure of treasure-hunters seeking artifacts have further obliterated whatever traces once remained from the pre-reservoir days.

Because the Great Sacandaga Lake is an enormous body of water, it can become turbulent at times, often without much warning, with wind gusts typically coming in from the southwest. Two- to three-foot waves are not uncommon, nor are whitecaps when the waters start to get churned up. Weather must always be taken into consideration when setting out onto the lake. Stay as close to the shoreline as possible, only venturing out to distant islands when the weather is favorable.

The lake also attracts a great number of high-speed motorboats, large pontoon boats, and Jet Skis; consequently, it is vital to stay alert when on the lake. It should never be assumed that boaters will slow down when they approach or pass near a canoe or kayak. Like Lake George, the powerboaters hold dominion over Great Sacandaga Lake. Most boats, however (but not Jet Skis!), tend to gravitate to the center of the lake, which means that the likelihood of encountering a fast-moving boat rapidly decreases the closer you are to the shoreline.

To navigate the Great Sacandaga Lake it is important to first be able to navigate its main highways so that you can get to the sections of the lake that you want to explore. On a map or gazetteer, Great Sacandaga Lake is shaped like a heart with two arteries branching from its upper body. One artery goes northwest past Northville; the other, and by far the longer, artery goes northeast toward Hadley. Paralleling the lake are a number of main highways: Rte. 30 follows along the lake's west side; Rte. 4 (called North Shore Road) parallels the west side of the northeast artery; Rte. 110 follows along the east shore of the main body; and Rte. 7 (called South Shore Road) stays close to the east side of the northeast artery.

Four NYS Department of Environmental Conservation (DEC) boat launches provide direct access to the lake. They are located at North Broadalbin, West Day, Northville, and Northampton. There are other less formal launch sites as well. Unfortunately, the launch sites are not evenly spaced around Great Sacandaga Lake, which means that the lake's southernmost end is inadequately served. Fortunately a number of private marinas have cropped up at the south end of the lake and provide kayakers with an opportunity to reach vital sections of the lake that would otherwise entail a lengthy paddle. There is a listing of private marinas at the end of this section.

The infrastructure of the lake has changed over the years. Seventy-five miles of road were buried when the reservoir was created, and fifty miles of new roads and ten new bridges had to be created. Since then the earlier little camps and oftentimes ramshackle structures that circled the lake have given way to a second generation of modern homes and permanent residences. The lake has acquired a more affluent look.

For more information: Great Sacandaga Lake Association, P.O. Box 900, Northville, NY 12134, (518) 863-6848, gsla.org; sloffice@gsla.org.

Mike Canavan seizes the moment as he paddles an old fiberglass kayak through the choppy waters of Great Sacandaga Lake. Photograph 2000.

28 | DEC North Broadalbin State Boat Launch (North Broadalbin)
Access to the Lake's Southernmost Islands

■ **Launch Site:** North Broadalbin State Boat Launch off of Lakeview Road in North Broadalbin (Fulton County); hard-surface ramp. For more information: Town of Broadalbin, 671 Lakeview Road, Broadalbin, NY 12025, (518) 883-4657.

■ **Delorme NYS Atlas & Gazetteer:** p. 79, CD7; **GPS:** 43°06.30'N; 74°10.44'W

■ **Destinations & Mileages:** *Northeast*: to Frenchman's Creek Bay—0.6 mile; to Benedict Bay—1.9 miles; up Benedict Bay & Hans Creek—0.3 mile; to Silver Bay—2.0 miles; to Diamond Point—2.9 miles; to Fish House—3.8 miles. *North*: to Sand Island—1.0 mile. *South & West*: to Beaver Creek—1.1 miles; around Beaver Creek Cove—0.3 mile; to Trapp Islands—2.1 miles; around Trapp Islands—1.5 miles; from Trapp Islands to Scout Island—0.3 mile (2.5 miles from launch); around Scout Island—1.4 miles; from Scout Island northwest to Beacon Island—1.0 mile (4.0 miles from launch); from Scout Island west to Vandenburgh Point—0.9 mile (3.9 miles from launch); from Scout Island west to Kunkel Point—1.4 miles (4.7 miles from launch); from Kunkel Point to end of Mayfield Bay—0.8 mile (5.5 miles from launch); from Scout Island south to Woods Hollow Bay—0.9 mile (3.6 miles from launch); from Scout Island south to Muscle Harbor—1.2 miles (3.9 miles from launch); from Scout Island south to mouth of Kenneyetto Creek—1.7 miles (4.5 miles from launch); up Kenneyetto Creek—mileage dependent on water depth.

■ **Comments:** Read "Caution" beginning on page xxi and Advisory on page 120.
Look carefully both ways while paddling to or between islands to avoid oncoming boats. Be prepared for increased wind and waves as you move away from the shoreline.

Directions: From Broadalbin (at the southeast end of Great Sacandaga Lake) head north following the main road (North Main Street) out of town. North Main Street quickly turns into Rte. 110. Continue northeast on Rte. 110 for a total of 3.4 miles from the center triangle of Broadalbin, then turn left onto Lakeview Road (you will see a DEC sign).

Approaching from Fish House (junction of Rte. 110 & Fish House Road/Rte. 109), drive southwest for 4.4 miles and turn right onto Lakeview Road (you will see a DEC sign).

From either direction, proceed northwest on Lakeview Road for 0.4 mile. The entrance to the launch site is on your right. Enter and bear to your right to the beach area, where car-top launches are encouraged.

The Paddle:
Northeast—Follow along the south shore to reach Frenchman's Creek Bay at 0.6 mile. Paddle into the bay to as far as the mouth of Frenchman's Creek, which begins just downstream from the Rte. 110 bridge in North Broadalbin.

▶ **DEC North Broadalbin State Boat Launch (North Broadalbin)**

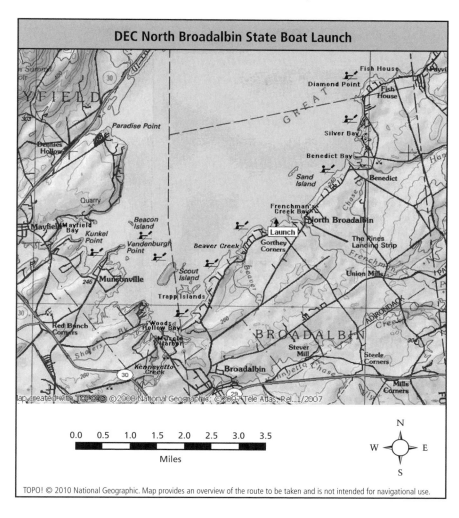

DEC North Broadalbin State Boat Launch

TOPO! © 2010 National Geographic. Map provides an overview of the route to be taken and is not intended for navigational use.

Frenchman's Creek is named after a French pioneer named Joseph de Golyer who settled nearby. In 1810 Duncan McMartin established a gristmill, sawmill, and woolen mill on the creek.[1]

Benedict Bay is reached in 1.9 miles. Turn right into the bay and head south, reaching a tiny island behind which Hans Creek emerges. The creek is named after John Conyne, who accidentally fell in the creek while fishing with Sir William Johnson in the 1700s. Originally Hons Creek ("Hons" is Dutch for "John"), the "o" was corrupted to an "a" over time.[2]

The creek can be paddled upstream for 0.05 mile as it leads into a fairly deep ravine. As soon as you reach a fork where the stream divides, however, both channels become impassable. Although it is not visible, the Rte. 110 bridge spanning Hans Creek is less than 0.1 mile away. A fishermen's path by the bridge leads from the shore to the road.

Paddle back down the creek and return to the lake by rounding the north end of Benedict Bay. An enormous mansion overlooks the lake to your right—an example of the lake's increasingly affluent look.

In another 0.1 mile you will come to Silver Bay, where a small, marshy island lies close to the mainland. Less than 0.2 mile north of Silver Bay is yet another bay that contains some interesting leads. It can be explored for nearly 0.3 mile of its length. Keep in mind, however, that this bay has a tendency to turn into a mudflat at the end of the season if the water level drops precipitously. The beach for Sacandaga Foothills—a recreational vehicle & mobile home park—is at the northwest point.

In another 0.3 mile you will pass by a beach belonging to Birch Haven— a large mobile home and recreational vehicle park on the east side of Rte. 110.

At 2.9 miles you will reach Diamond Point, where a wetland area in front of a series of distant camps offers a moderately protected retreat for geese and ducks.

Continue following the shoreline for another 0.9 mile to reach the hamlet of Fish House, named after Sir William Johnson's eighteenth-century hunting lodge & fishing outpost. Most of the village, including the famous Fish House Bridge that spanned the Sacandaga River, was buried under the lake, but a number of historic homes were hauled up from the valley to higher ground before the great inundation and can be found close to the intersection of Rtes. 110 & 109 (Fish House Road).

If you're far enough back from the shore, it is possible to see 1,600-foot-high Bald Bluff northeast of Fish House.

North—Most savvy paddlers will probably head north from the launch site to reach Sand Island, 1.0 mile away. If you undertake this paddle, however, be sure that the weather is calm and that you are a skilled and experienced paddler. Sand Island is hands down the lake's most popular boating destination, for it is blessed with sandy beaches extending in virtually every direction around the island. During the summer weekends and holidays, the island is literally surrounded by moored boats.

South & West—The collection of islands in the southwest part of Great Sacandaga Lake is located in what at one time was called the Vly (also spelled Vlaie and sometimes referred to as "the Fly")[3]—a marshland nourished by a network of incoming streams including Hans Creek, Frenchman's Creek, Beaver Creek, Kenneyetto Creek, Vly Creek, and Cranberry Creek. The Vly was frequented by Native Americans in pursuit of game, and later by European settlers for the same purpose. Until the creation of Great Sacandaga Lake, the Vly was considered to be a sportsman's paradise.

Follow the shoreline south to reach Beaver Creek in 1.1 miles. Turn left into the bay and head southeast, following the north shoreline as the bay gradually turns into a cove. You will see a line of boats moored at the Sacandaga Boat Club.

▶ DEC North Broadalbin State Boat Launch (North Broadalbin)

In 0.3 mile you will reach the end of the cove, demarcated by a 15-foot-high cliff of shale to your left and a tiny culvert that runs under the Lakeview Road bridge at the end of canoeable waters. An informal access that comes down to the water's edge at the northwest end of the bridge is also visible. On the way out take note of a tiny island, more shoal-like when the lake level is high, located near the south end of the bay.

From the bay at Beaver Creek, continue south following along the east shoreline. In 0.4 mile you will pass by an enormous boulder on your left whose visibility depends upon the season and the height of the reservoir. Once you have gone by this enormous rock, turn around and look back. Painted on the flat side of the boulder is an American Flag.

In 1.0 mile from the bay at Beaver Creek, you will reach the start of a series of small islands consisting of two medium-sized islands and three tiny ones. Known collectively as the Trapp Islands, they can be paddled around in 1.5 miles.

From the largest of the Trapp Islands, paddle west for 0.3 mile to reach the east side of Scout Island. This large island, once privately owned, can be circum-navigated in 1.4 miles.

Using Scout Island as a starting point, the following paddles can be under-taken, but only if the weather is calm and you are a skilled and experienced pad-dler, ideally accompanied by a group of similarly experienced paddlers.

Trip #1—From the west side of Scout Island, head northwest across open

Paddlers head toward a distant island. Photograph 2010.

water for 1.0 mile to reach 0.1-mile-long Beacon Island. This is an extremely narrow island, heavily eroded on both sides. A spiny ridge lined by a row of trees runs along its center, giving it the appearance of having a "Mohawk" haircut.

Trip #2—From the west side of Scout Island, head west and slightly north across open water to reach Vandenburgh Point in 0.9 mile. Vandenburgh Point is roughly 0.4 mile southwest of Beacon Island and is named after Frank Vandenburgh, whose home was farthest inland from the nearby village of Munsonville (another inundated community) when the lake was created.

From Vandenburgh Point continue west and slightly north for 0.4 mile to reach Kunkel Point, which forms the southern extremity of Mayfield Bay. Kunkel Point is named after Robert S. Kunkel, a prominent Gloversville physician who was one of the first to buy property in this area.

Proceed west into Mayfield Bay for less than another 0.3 mile and then turn left, following the bay southwest as it narrows significantly and finally dead-ends by the School Street bridge in another 0.5 mile. Beyond the bridge and dam is Mayfield Lake, at an elevation higher than Great Sacandaga Lake (see chapter "Mayfield Lake").

Trip #3—From the south end of Scout Island, proceed south to reach Woods Hollow Bay in 0.9 mile. Continue south through Woods Hollow Bay, passing by the Woods Hollow Marina in 0.3 mile, to enter Muscle Harbor. From there you can penetrate even farther south for another 0.5 mile. At that point you have arrived at the mouth of Kenneyetto Creek, which can be followed upstream (west) for a short distance, depending upon water levels.

▶ **DEC North Broadalbin State Boat Launch (North Broadalbin)**

DEC Northampton Beach Campground (Northampton)
Paddling near Historic Sacandaga Park

29

- ◼ **Launch Site:** Northampton Beach Campground at terminus of Houseman Street (Fulton County); hard-surface ramp and dock; restrooms; day-use charge for launch. For more information: Northampton Beach Campground, 328 Houseman Street, Mayfield, NY 12134, (518) 863-6000, dec.ny.gov/outdoor/24486.html.
- ◼ **Delorme NYS Atlas & Gazetteer:** p. 79, C7; **GPS:** 43°11.19'N; 74°10.38'W
- ◼ **Destinations & Mileages:** *West:* up campground cove—0.4 mile. *North:* to views of Christmans Bay—1.3 miles; to Hampton Point—1.5 miles; to views of Hunters Creek Dam—2.4 miles; to Northville Bridge—2.9 miles. *Southeast:* to Mead Island—0.6 mile; around Mead Island—1.7 miles; into cove northwest of Mead Island—0.3 mile; from Mead Island to Kenyon Island Group—0.4 mile (1.4 miles from launch); around Kenyon Island Group—2.7 miles. *Southwest:* to Deer Island—2.3 miles; to Cranberry Creek—3.7 miles; to Paradise Point/Sunset Bay—5.3 miles; along Sunset Bay—1.0 mile.
- ◼ **Comments:** Read "Caution" beginning on page xxi and Advisory on page 120.

  Look carefully both ways while paddling to or between islands to avoid oncoming boats. Be prepared for increased wind and current as you move away from the shoreline.

  Remember that you are on an expansive section of the lake, which means that it is easy to become disoriented as you paddle between peninsulas, bays, and islands. Look behind you periodically so that the route back looks familiar when it is time to return. Pack a compass and waterproof map.

  Be extra vigilant when paddling to Deer Island, which can be easily missed because of its small size.

Directions: From west of Northville (junction of Rte. 30 & Bridge Street), drive south on Rte. 30 for 0.8 mile. Turn left onto Rte. 152 and proceed east for 0.05 mile, then turn right, following Rte. 152 (Old Rte. 30) and head south. At 0.6 mile continue straight ahead on Houseman Road as Rte. 152 veers right (now becoming Hampton Point Road) and continues south for another 1.3 miles.

From southwest of Mayfield (junction of Rtes. 30 & 30A), drive northeast on Rte. 30 for 7.9 miles. When you come to Rte. 152 (Hampton Point Road), turn right and drive northeast for 1.3 miles until you come to Houseman Road on your right.

From either direction, take Houseman Road and look for the Northampton Marina at 0.9 mile and the Northampton Beach Campground's contact station at 1.1 miles. From the contact station continue straight ahead for over 0.1 mile until the road ends. Turn left and then immediately right into the parking area for the boat launch.

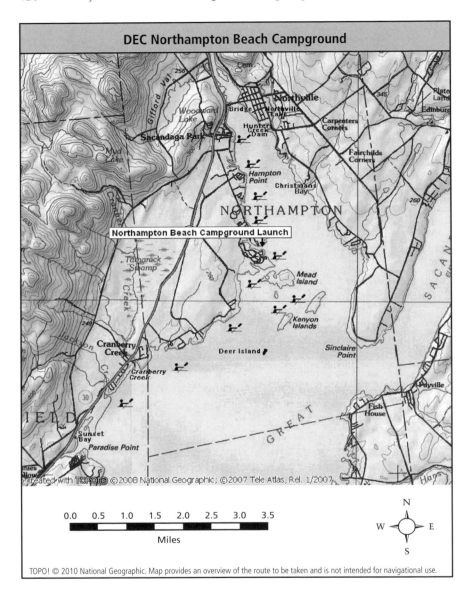

DEC Northampton Beach Campground

Northampton Beach Campground Launch

0.0   0.5   1.0   1.5   2.0   2.5   3.0   3.5

Miles

The Paddle:

The Northampton Beach Campground is one of the largest state-operated camp-grounds in the Adirondack Park. It opened to the public in 1954 after 232 acres of land were made available to New York State by the Hudson River Black River Regulating District (HRBRRD). Additional acres of land have been acquired since then.[1] Northampton is close to Mead Island and the Kenyon Island Group,

▶ **DEC Northampton Beach Campground (Northampton)**

making it an ideal starting point if you enjoy islands as a destination.

The launch site is in the shelter of a small cove. Directly across from the launch are numerous campsites along the opposite shore, all belonging to the Northampton Beach Campground.

West—Follow the cove inland from the launch site to explore the campground by water. You will find a number of fingerlike nooks and crannies to explore off the main channel. This trek will appeal to the gregarious paddler, as campsites line both banks for the entire route. The paddle takes you as far northwest as 0.4 mile from the launch.

North—Head east (left) for 0.2 mile to exit the cove, and then follow along the west shoreline, heading north toward Northville. At 1.3 miles you will be opposite Christmans Bay, 1.0 mile across the lake to your right but difficult to see because of the distance. (Do not paddle over to Christmans Bay unless the weather is favorable and you are an experienced paddler.)

At 1.5 miles you will reach Hampton Point. Until the Great Sacandaga Lake was created, this spot was only 0.2 mile away from the south end of the now-submerged Sports Island. In 0.2 mile beyond Hampton Point, two tiny coves are encountered to your left that can be entered for up to 0.1 mile each.

At 2.4 miles, Hunters Creek Dam is visible to your right (east), 0.6 mile across the lake at the south end of Northville. An impoundment called Northville Lake was created when Hunters Creek was dammed (see chapter "Northville Lake").

When you have paddled another 0.1 mile farther north, opposite the Sports Island Pub and beach to your left, you will be floating directly above the north end of former Sports Island, a nearly mile-long body of land once delineated by the Sacandaga River. Sports Island extended from east of present-day Park Marine Base to east of present-day Hampton Point. The island was named for the sporting events it hosted, including wrestling and boxing exhibitions and baseball. A little railroad ran between the island and the main part of Sacandaga Park. Sacandaga Park was created in 1875 by the Fonda, Johnstown & Gloversville (FJ&G) Railroad, and for many years basked in the title of "Gem of the Adirondacks." It was the upstate version of Coney Island Amusement Park. Sacandaga Park contained four large hotels—The Pines, Adirondack Inn, Old Orchard Inn, and High Rock Lodge—and offered attractions such as merry-go-round, roller-coaster, and shoot-the-chute rides, a rustic theater, a picnic grove, a regulation nine-hole golf course, Sports Island, and nearly a mile of beach shoreline. Such celebrities as Al Jolson, W. C. Fields, and Harry Houdini performed at the rustic theater. Sacandaga Park's glory days ended with the creation of the lake, which inundated most of the area.

Parts of Sacandaga Park still exist as lakeside terrain, but the community of Osborne Bridge was totally obliterated. It was located roughly 0.6 mile east from the Northampton Beach Campgrounds and was named for the covered bridge separating it from Denton's Corners (also buried under the lake). Osborne Bridge had a population of around 150 people.

The Northville Bridge is reached at 2.9 miles and is a good turnaround point.

Southeast—Head east for 0.2 mile to exit the cove, and then turn right, passing alongside a sizeable sandbar (which becomes very noticeable when the water level is down) on your right. You will come to Mead Island in 0.6 mile. Mead Island (also spelled Meade) is very irregularly shaped and can be paddled around in 1.7 miles, or even longer if you explore all the nooks and crannies that the island has to offer. The bay at the west side of Mead Island is called Mosquito Bay. Northwest of Mead Island is a pretty cove that can be entered for 0.3 mile. Just south of Mead Island's south shore are several small islands, one of which is particularly elongated.

A mere 0.4 mile beyond the east side of Mead Island is the Kenyon Island Group, which consists of two main islands 0.4 mile and 0.5 mile in length, respectively. Taken as one, the two islands can be circumnavigated in 2.7 miles. There are also a number of satellite islands in close proximity to these two. Two of these tiny, narrow islands with trees on them were visible due east as you initially made your way toward Mead Island.

It is not until you paddle to the south side of Mead Island or begin to circumnavigate the large Kenyon Islands that views of the main basin of the lake and its enormous reach emerge.

Mead Island and the Kenyon Island Group are located in one of the shallowest parts of the lake. The highest point on any of the islands is 13 feet above the regular lake level. When the water level drops sufficiently, the whole area can become a wide expanse of exposed land. It is said that the shallow area forms a shoal of five square miles.

Southwest—Deer Island can be reached in 2.3 miles from the Northampton Beach Campground. The island is located 0.9 mile southeast of the mainland and 1.4 miles east of the Hudson River Black River Regulating District's Sacandaga Field Office on Bunker Hill Road. Be alert if you decide to paddle out to Deer Island, for it is tiny spot of land and can be easily missed in the vastness of the lake. Only venture out to the island if weather conditions permit safe open-water paddling and you are an experienced paddler.

By continuing west along the shoreline, in 3.7 miles you will reach Cranberry Creek, a tributary to the Sacandaga River that rises in the hills west of Sacandaga Park. The village of Cranberry Creek, located midway between Mayfield and Northville along the former Fonda, Johnstown & Gloversville (FJ&G) Railroad line, was another settlement destroyed when the valley was flooded. The village was located just a short distance northeast of the mouth of Cranberry Creek and consisted of over 30 homes, with as many as 150 people who were mostly engaged in farming and trapping.[2] When the reservoir was created, only six homes were pulled out of the valley to higher ground. The rest were demol-

▶ **DEC Northampton Beach Campground (Northampton)**

ished and burned, along with trees and brush. What remains of their foundations now lie buried under the lake.

Distant mountains to the west are noticeable along this paddle route. From north to south they are Steele Mountain (1,963'), Peters Mountain (2,122'), Lawyer Mountain (2,044') and Bernhardt Mountain (2,285')—the highest mountains in the Sacandaga Valley.

At 5.3 miles you will come to Paradise Point and Sunset Bay. Sunset Bay can be explored along its cross-section for 1.0 mile.

Visitors come to Great Sacandaga Lake to worship sun, sand, and surf. Postcard ca. 1940.

30 DEC Northville State Boat Launch (Northville)
Exploring the Lake's Northwest Terminus

- **Launch Site:** Northville State Boat Launch off of Rte. 30 in Northville (Fulton County); hard-surface launching ramp. For more information: Northville State Boat Launch, 283 State Highway 30, Northville, NY 12134, (518) 863-4545.
- **Delorme NYS Atlas & Gazetteer:** p. 79, BC7; **GPS:** 43°13.78'N; 74°11.23'W
- **Destinations & Mileages:** *North*: to East Stony Creek Bay—2.1 miles; up East Stony Creek bay—0.6 mile (2.7 miles from launch); to Rte. 30 bridge—3.1 miles. *South*: to Northville Bridge—0.4 mile; to views of Hunters Creek Dam—0.9 mile; to Hampton Point—1.8 miles; to views of Christmans Bay—2.4 miles; to Mead Island—3.7 miles; from Mead Island to Kenyon Island Group—0.4 mile (4.5 miles from launch).
- **Comments:** Read "Caution" beginning on page xxi and Advisory on page 120.
  Look carefully both ways while paddling to or between islands to avoid oncoming boats. Be prepared for increased wind and current as you move away from the shoreline.
  Remember that you are on an expansive section of the lake, which means that it is easy to become disoriented as you paddle between peninsulas, bays, and islands. Look behind you periodically so that the route back looks familiar when it is time to return.

Directions: From west of Northville (junction of Rte. 30 & Bridge Street), drive north on Rte. 30 for 0.4 mile. Turn right into the entrance for the Northville State Boat Launch.

The Paddle:
Were it not for the Northville State Boat Launch, this section of the lake would undoubtedly be considerably quieter with much less boat traffic. Great Sacandaga Lake, however, is a haven for powerboats. For this reason you must stay keenly alert when out on the water in a kayak or canoe.

The village of Northville was founded in 1788 by Samuel Olmstead and Zadoc Sherwood, who established their home where the Main Street spillway is now located between Northville Lake and the Great Sacandaga Lake.[1]

Northwest—Following the west shoreline you will come to a noticeable narrowing of the lake in 0.7 mile. This stricture continues for the next 0.6 mile, becoming 0.05 mile wide at its narrowest. As you leave the narrow passageway behind, you will pass by a tiny island at 1.3 miles.

At 2.1 miles a divide is reached. By veering left you can follow the Sacandaga River north as far as the Rte. 30 Bridge, which is reached in 3.1 miles. Beyond this point the river becomes shallow and filled with rapids.

By veering right at the divide, you will enter into a bay formed by East Stony Creek. Head northeast for 0.6 mile, passing by several small islands to your left.

▶ **DEC Northville State Boat Launch (Northville)**

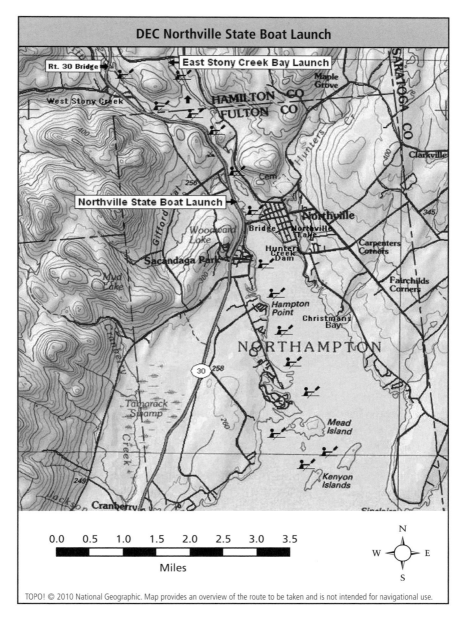

DEC Northville State Boat Launch

TOPO! © 2010 National Geographic. Map provides an overview of the route to be taken and is not intended for navigational use.

Along this section the west bank of the bay rises up nearly vertically 20–25 feet, creating a feeling of remoteness. The trek ends just upstream from a 15-foot-high bridge spanning East Stony Creek, where shallows and rapids prevent further progress. Prior to this point, little current will be felt.

Great Sacandaga Lake north of the Northville Bridge. Postcard ca. 1940.

South—Follow the west shoreline south for 0.3 mile to the Northville Public Beach, and then to the Northville Bridge at 0.4 mile. The Northville Bridge connecting Rte. 30 with the village of Northville was constructed in 1989, replacing the Blue Bridge (located just north of the present bridge), which was erected in 1930 at the time the reservoir was created. Prior to the reservoir's construction, two other bridges also spanned the Sacandaga River at roughly the same spot at different periods of time.[2] At the northeast end of the Northville Bridge is the Inn at the Bridge—a well-known establishment with its own docks next to the bridge.

At 0.9 mile look to your left to see the distant Hunters Creek Dam, 0.6 mile across the lake on the east side. The dam impounds Northville Lake (see chapter "Northville Lake"), a small body of water that offers quiet paddling opportunities.

Directly beneath your watercraft, 20–40 feet below the water's surface, lies the submerged Sports Island. Prior to 1930 this 1.0-mile-long body of land was a commercially developed island delineated by two channels of the Sacandaga River.

Hampton Point is reached at 1.8 miles, nearly across from the south end of now-buried Sports Island.

In another 0.6 miles you will be opposite Christmans Bay, which is roughly 1.0 mile across the lake on its east side. From this distance the bay is barely visible.

Continuing south you will reach a section of the lake containing large islands. Few motorboats venture into this area when the lake level has dropped substantially. The waters are simply too shallow. At 3.7 miles, Mead Island comes to port (left)—an island that is substantial in size, but otherwise offers little reason to land unless you have been invited by mosquitoes for lunch. The Kenyon Island Group lies just 0.4 mile from the east side of Mead Island (4.5 miles from the starting point). These islands also offer little to see if you debark from your craft.

▶ DEC Northville State Boat Launch (Northville)

Alternate Launch Site

East Stony Creek Bay (Northville)

■ **Launch Site:** East Stony Creek Bay off of Old Northville Road (Hamilton County); challenging carry down a steep 15-foot-high slope to informal put-in
■ **Delorme NYS Atlas & Gazetteer:** p. 79, BC7; **GPS:** 43°15.71'N; 74°12.43'W
■ **Destinations & Mileages:** *South:* from Old Northville Road bridge to south end of East Stony Creek Bay—0.6 mile. *Continuing west from south end of East Stony Creek Bay:* to West Stony Kill—1.3 miles (1.9 miles from launch); to Rte. 30 Bridge—1.6 miles (2.2 miles from launch). *Continuing southeast from south end of East Stony Creek Bay:* to Northville Bridge—2.2 miles (2.8 miles from launch); to views eastward of Hunters Creek Dam—2.7 miles (3.3 miles from launch); to Hampton Point—3.6 miles (4.2 miles from launch); to views eastward of Christmans Bay—4.2 miles (4.8 miles from launch); to Mead Island—5.5 miles (6.1 miles from launch); from Mead Island to Kenyon Island Group—0.4 mile (6.9 miles from launch).
■ **Comments:** Read "Caution" beginning on page xxi and Advisory on page 120.

Look carefully both ways while paddling to or between islands in order to avoid oncoming boats. Be prepared for increased wind and current as you move away from the shoreline.

Remember that you are on an expansive section of the lake, which means that it is easy to become disoriented as you paddle between peninsulas, bays, and islands. Look behind you periodically so that the route back looks familiar when it is time to return.

Directions: From the center of Northville (junction of Bridge Street & Main Street), drive north on Main Street for less than 0.2 mile. Before you start up a steep hill, turn left onto Reed Street. Continue following Reed Street as it leaves the village, becoming Old Northville Road (Rte. 15), and heads north along the east side of Great Sacandaga Lake. At 3.2 miles from the junction of Main Street and Reed Street, you will come to a bridge spanning East Stony Creek.

From the junction of Rte. 30 & Old Northville Road (north of where Rte. 30 crosses over the Sacandaga River), drive southeast on Old Northville Road for 1.2 miles until you come to a bridge that spans East Stony Creek.

You can access the river and lake from either the northwest or the southwest ends of the bridge, but be prepared for a difficult carry down a steep slope to the water's edge.

31 — DEC Saratoga County State Boat Launch (West Day)
Creeks, Bays, and a Bridge

- **Launch Site:** Saratoga County State Boat Launch off of Rte. 4 (Saratoga County); hard-surface launching ramp; parking for 44 cars and trailers
- **Delorme NYS Atlas & Gazetteer:** p. 80, B1; **GPS:** 43°16.26'N; 74°03.30'W
- **Destinations & Mileages:** *Northeast*: to Glasshouse Creek—1.2 miles; to Pauls Creek Bay—3.0 miles; north into bay—0.5 mile. *Southwest*: to Sand Creek—0.3 mile; to views of Gordons Point & Gordons Creek—3.0 miles; to Beecher Creek Cove—4.3 miles; to Batchellerville Bridge—4.9 miles.
- **Comments:** Read "Caution" beginning on page xxi and Advisory on page 120.
  Look carefully both ways while paddling to or between islands to avoid oncoming boats. Be prepared for increased wind and waves as you move away from the shoreline.
  Remember that you are on an expansive section of the lake, which means that it is easy to become disoriented as you paddle between peninsulas, bays, and islands. Look behind you periodically so that the route back looks familiar when it is time to return.

Directions: From the four corners in Edinburg (junction of Rtes. 4 & 5), proceed northeast on Rte. 4 for 5.2 miles and turn right at the site for the Saratoga County Boat Launch.

From Lake Luzerne (junction of Rte. 4 & Main Street) cross over the Bridge of Hope spanning the Hudson River and continue southwest for 16.3 miles (or 10.5 miles from the junction of Rtes. 4 & 8). Turn left into the boat launch site, which is less than 0.05 mile east of Snow Road.

From either direction drive downhill for 0.1 mile. A large parking area provides for ample parking.

The Paddle:

These paddles take place on a narrower section of Great Sacandaga Lake, following the original riverbed of the Sacandaga River before the valley was flooded. The large hill northwest of the put-in is 1,630-foot-high Youngs Mountain. To the east of the put-in, nearly straight across the lake, is 1,362-foot-high Deming Hill.

The Town of Day was named after Eliphaz Day, a prominent resident of the village who was heavily involved in the lumber industry and in farming. West Day was initially called Huntsville in honor of a tavern owner named Amos Hunt.

Northeast—Follow along the north shoreline to reach Glasshouse Creek on your left at 1.2 miles. The creek is named after a glass factory that once operated along its banks. In 3.0 miles you will come to Pauls Creek Bay, which can be explored north for 0.5 mile. The mountains northeast of the bay are 1,533-foot-

▶ **DEC Saratoga County State Boat Launch (West Day)**

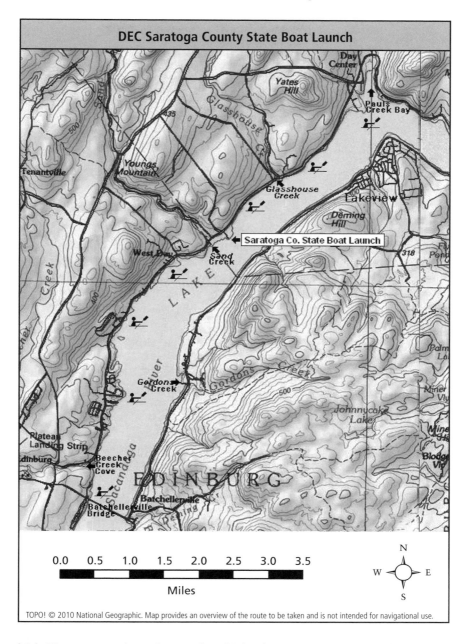

DEC Saratoga County State Boat Launch

Saratoga Co. State Boat Launch

0.0   0.5   1.0   1.5   2.0   2.5   3.0   3.5

Miles

N
W ⟵◇⟶ E
S

TOPO! © 2010 National Geographic. Map provides an overview of the route to be taken and is not intended for navigational use.

high Kings Mountain and 1,725-foot-high Clute Mountain. Across the lake on the east side looms 1,113-foot-high Gray Hill.

Southwest—Follow the north shoreline to reach Sand Creek, coming in to the lake to your right, at 0.3 miles. A small island near the north shore is passed at 2.3 miles. At 3.0 miles you will be in alignment with Gordons Point and Gordons Creek, which are 0.8 mile across the lake on its east side. An area called Penn Heights is passed at 3.7 miles.

Beecher Creek Cove, formed by the mouth of Beecher Creek, is reached on your right at 4.3 miles, roughly midway between the two ends of Great Sacandaga Lake. The cove and creek are named after Eli Beecher, an early settler. A small island is located just offshore from the mouth of the stream-produced cove.

The Edinburg Marina is Beecher Creek Cove's main attraction. If you pull ashore there, be sure to walk south up Rte. 4 for 0.3 mile to reach the historic Edinburg Covered Bridge, to your left. Beecher Creek runs directly under the bridge, forming an attractive 20-foot-high cascade just upstream from the bridge.

Continuing southwest along the lake, you will reach the Batchellerville Bridge at 4.9 miles. This is an excellent turnaround point. The Batchellerville Bridge connects the tiny village of Batchellerville with Edinburg. The first giant bridge to span Great Sacandaga Lake, it was finished in 1930 shortly after the valley was flooded and is 3,150 feet long, supported by 21 spans on concrete piers standing an average of 50–60 feet high. The bridge was refurbished in 1982. In 2010 work began on a new bridge at a cost of $46.6 million to replace the old one, which had progressively deteriorated. The new bridge is expected to be completed by the end of 2012. An earlier, much smaller bridge once spanned the Sacandaga River roughly 0.2 mile north of the present bridge and lasted until the reservoir was flooded.[1]

The village of Batchellerville was a much larger community with a population of 500 people by 1880, but most of the community relocated when the valley was inundated. The village and bridge are named after Sherman and Samuel Batcheller, two early settlers who moved into the area in the late 1830s to join their father, Ambrose, in the lumbering and woodenware business.

The Batchellerville Bridge bisects Great Sacandaga Lake, connecting Batchellerville with Edinburg. Postcard ca. 1940.

▶ **DEC Saratoga County State Boat Launch (West Day)**

Conklingville Dam (Conklingville)
Launching at the Northeast Terminus of the Lake

32

■ **Launch Site:** Small parking area off of Frank Kathan Road (Saratoga County); dirt ramp

■ **Delorme NYS Atlas & Gazetteer:** p. 80, B2; **GPS:** 43°18.93'N; 73°55.58'W

■ **Destinations & Mileages:** *North*: to north end of Conklingville Dam—0.3 mile. *Continuing southwest along north shore*: to Bell Brook Bay—0.8 mile; north up Bell Brook Bay—0.1 mile; to Kathan Bay—2.0 miles; north up Kathan Bay—0.3 mile; to Boulder Bay—4.0 miles. *Southwest along south shore*: to Overlook—1.8 miles; to Brooks Bay—2.7 miles; up Brooks Bay—0.2 mile; to South Shore Road Access—3.5 miles; to small bay—3.7 miles; to Ogden Cove—4.0 miles; up Ogden Cove—0.2 mile; to Lakeview—5.5 miles.

■ **Comments:** Read "Caution" beginning on page xxi and Advisory on page 120. Stay back from the Conklingville Dam spillway.

Directions: From Brooks Bay on Great Sacandaga Lake (junction of West Mountain Road [Rte. 10] and South Shore Road [Rte. 7]), proceed northeast on South Shore Road for 3.0 miles. Turn left onto Rte. 8 and head north for 1.1 mile. Just before you reach the Conklingville Dam, turn left onto Frank Kathan Road and go 0.05 mile, then turn sharply right onto a dirt road that leads to a dirt ramp in less than 150 feet.

From northeast of Conklingville (junction of Rtes. 4 & 8), turn onto Rte. 8 and drive south for 0.4 mile. As soon as you cross over the Conklingville Dam, turn right onto Frank Kathan Road, head west for 0.05 mile, and then sharply right onto a dirt road that leads to a dirt ramp in less than 150 feet.

The launch site is less than 0.1 mile from the south end of the Conklingville Dam.

The Paddle:

North—You can parallel the rocky base of this enormous earthen dam for 0.3 mile before reaching a line of buoys that warn of the dam's intake channel. The channel leads under Rte. 8 and down to the powerhouse near the north end of the dam. The Conklingville Dam is 1,100 feet long, with an interior made of hardened granite dust surrounded by earth and concrete. The village of Conklingville was named after Gurden Conklin, an early settler who established a tannery on the south bank of the Sacandaga River in 1848.[1] It was a bustling town in earlier days and during construction of the dam.

Continuing southwest along north shore—Cross over to the north shore and paddle southwest. To your left is the Woodcock Mountain Range looming high above the south shore. In another 0.5 mile you will come to a small bay produced by Bell Brook. The bay can be explored north for 0.1 mile, nearly up to Rte. 4.

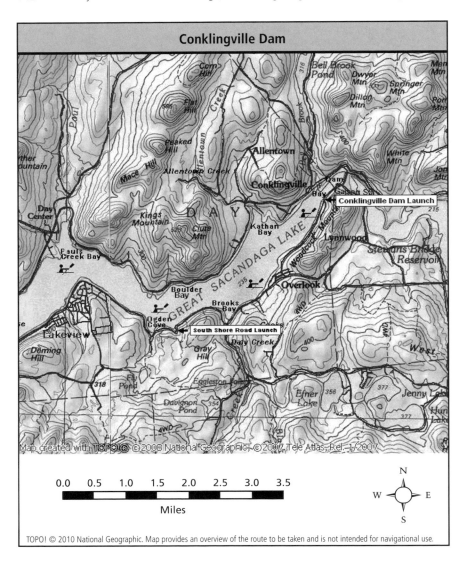

Continue paddling southwest, following along the north shoreline. At 2.0 miles you will come to Kathan Bay, a more substantial inlet that can be explored north for over 0.3 mile. It is produced by Allentown Creek, a shallow brook that is impassable upstream.

At 4.0 miles you will reach Boulder Bay, a good turnaround point. If you look across the lake, slightly to the southwest is Ogden Cove.

Southwest along south shore—Paddling southwest along the east shoreline you will pass by the tiny community of Overlook at 1.8 miles. Brooks Bay and its

▶ **Conklingville Dam (Conklingville)**

inlet stream, Daly Creek, are reached in another 0.9 mile. Brooks Bay is formed between 1,202-foot-high Cooks Hill to the east and 1,113-foot-high Gray Hill to the west. Daly Creek is too rocky to follow upstream for any distance. The bay is notable for being just downstream from camp Hi-'N'-Dry, home to the legendary woodsman, hunter, author, and nature lover Ira Gray ("Adirondack Ike"), who was to the Great Sacandaga Lake what Old Mountain Phelps was to the Adirondacks.

At 3.5 miles you will pass by the South Shore Road Access, followed by a tiny bay in another 0.2 mile whose inlet stream rises from marshlands south of Gray Hill. It is just far enough away from South Shore Road to provide a modicum of seclusion. At 4.0 miles you will come to a more substantial bay called Ogden Cove, which can be entered for 0.2 mile. It is formed by a small creek that flows out of Fly Pond (elevation 925'). Several scenes of Fly Pond, along with nearby Eggleston Falls, were included in the movie *Billy Bathgate*.[2]

This section of the paddle affords the opportunity to see first-hand the unbridled power of Great Sacandaga Lake as it continues to erode the shoreline, and the measures taken by homeowners to mitigate the damage being done to their property. High shoreline banks, some rising over twenty feet above the lake, are in various stages of collapse, with trees lying scattered about as if dashed by the hand of a petulant child. Where homes are close to the water, huge walls of riprap have been erected to fend off the lake.

Slightly northwest across the lake from Ogden Cove is the North Shore Marina.

By continuing along the shoreline northwest for another 1.5 miles, you will come to a major bend where the riverlike part of the lake alters direction from northwest to southwest. A tiny community called Lakeview is located there.

Alternate Launch Site

South Shore Road Access (Lakeview)

- ■ **Launch Site:** 150-foot carry to lake from South Shore Road (Saratoga County); informal launch from beach or area of flat bedrock
- ■ **Delorme NYS Atlas & Gazetteer:** p. 80, BC2; **GPS:** 43°16.96'N; 73°58.59'W
- ■ **Destinations & Mileages:** *Northeast*: to Brooks Bay & Daly Creek—1.0 mile; past the community of Overlook—1.8 miles; to Conklingville Dam—4.0 miles; to north end of Conklingville Dam—4.3 miles. *Continuing southwest on north shore*: to Bell Brook Bay—4.8 miles; north up Bell Brook Bay—0.1 mile; to Kathan Bay—6.0 miles; north up Kathan Bay—0.3 mile; to Boulder Bay—8.0 miles. *West*: to tiny bay—0.2 mile; to Ogden Cove—0.5 mile; to point at Lakeview—2.0 miles.
- ■ **Comments:** Read "Caution" beginning on page xxi and Advisory on page 120. Obey posted rules and regulations.
  Stay back from the Conklingville Dam spillway.

Directions: From junction of South Shore Road (Rte. 7) & West Mountain Road (Rte. 10) near the northeast end of the lake, drive west on South Shore Road for 0.9 mile. Park to your right at a pull-off.

From the tiny community of Fish House (junction of Fish House Road [Rte. 109] and South Shore Road [Rte. 7]), drive northeast on South Shore Road for 15.2 miles. Turn into a small pull-off on the left side of the road 0.05 mile after you complete a horseshoe turn around a small bay.

From the pull-off, a wide path leads down to the put-in within a couple of hundred feet. You can launch from either an area of flat bedrock or from a sandy beach.

The 1,100-foot-long Conklingville Dam holds back the massive Great Sacandaga Lake. Postcard ca. 1940.

▶ **Conklingville Dam (Conklingville)**

Marinas, Informal Lake Accesses, and Canoe Portage between Great Sacandaga Lake and Stewart Pond

In addition to the DEC Boat Launches, a significant number of marinas also operate around Great Sacandaga Lake to provide lake access. This can be particularly helpful in reaching those sections of the lake where no public access is available, turning what would otherwise be a very long paddle into a much shorter one. Most of the marinas charge a modest fee for launching watercraft, but such charges are well worth it if you are a half-day paddler wishing to see the lake in bits and pieces without having to paddle great distances to get to a new area.

Broadalbin

Dominick's Sand Bar
306 Woods Hollow Road
Mayfield, NY 12117
(518) 883-8080

McMurry's Boat Livery
245 Lakeview Road
Broadalbin, NY 12025
(518) 883-5068

Sandbar Restaurant & Marina
306 Woods Hollow Road
Broadalbin, NY 12025
(518) 883-8080

Mayfield

Cranberry Cove Marina
1840 St. Hwy. 30
Mayfield, NY 12117
(518) 661-5616

Driftwood Park
534 Vandenburg Point
Mayfield, NY 12117
(518) 661-9905

Gordon's Lakeside Marine
322 Lakeside Drive
Mayfield, NY 12117
(518) 661-5031

Holly's Service and Marina
P.O. Box 275
275 Lakeshore Drive
Mayfield, NY 12117
(518) 661-5512

Miller's Grandview Marine
342 Lakeside Drive
Mayfield, NY 12117
(518) 661-5824

Montoney's Marina
199 State Highway 30
Mayfield, NY 12117
(518) 661-6473

Northampton Marina
284 Houseman Street
Mayfield, NY 12117
(518) 863-8127

Sacandaga Marina
117 School Street
Mayfield, NY 12117
(518) 661-6021

Sunset Bay Vacation
   Resort RV Park & Marina
Paradise Point Road
Mayfield, NY 12117
(518) 661-6187

Hadley

Majestic Mountain Marina
2335 N. Shore Road
Hadley, NY 12835
(518) 696-3727

Edinburg & Northville

Edinburg Marina & Powersports
140 North Shore Road
Edinburg, NY 12134
(518) 863-8398

I-Go-Inn
241 South Shore Rd.
Edinburg, NY 12134
(518) 883-8900

Inn at the Bridge
641 Bridge St.
Northville, NY 12134
(518) 863-2240

Park Marine Base
199 County Highway 152
Sacandaga Park
Northville, NY 12134
(518) 863-8112

Informal Lake Accesses—A number of informal accesses can also be found around the lake. These are mostly used by fishermen and are typically located next to bridges spanning major streams that enter the lake—e.g., Rte. 30 crossing over Kenneyetto Creek northwest of Vail Mills; Lakeview Road crossing over Beaver Creek north of Broadalbin and south of Gorthey Corners; County Rte. 110 crossing over Frenchman's Creek in North Broadalbin; and Rte. 7 crossing over Fayville Creek in Fayville.

You will also find that a number of restaurants located on the lake have docks for their customers, and they may allow access to the lake if you are a patron and request permission to launch.

Canoe Portage between Great Sacandaga Lake and Stewart Pond—For those who wish to paddle Great Sacandaga Lake and then continue on to Stewart Pond (Stewart Bridge Reservoir), there is a portage between the northeast terminus of Great Sacandaga Lake at the Conklingville Dam and the west end of Stewart Pond. When you reach the northeast end of Great Sacandaga Lake, look for a takeout on your right less than 0.1 mile before arriving at the south end of the Conklingville Dam. From there, carry your watercraft up to Frank Kathan Road, turn left and walk up to Rte. 8, which is only a couple of hundred feet away. Once you are on Rte. 8, head southeast for a couple of hundred feet more. You will then see on the left side of Rte. 8 a dirt road with a sign reading "Hudson River

▶ **Marinas, Informal lake Accesses & Portage**

Canoe Route Portage." Follow this abandoned road that is slightly overgrown in places for 0.3 mile downhill until you reach an easy slip-in at Stewart Pond, roughly 0.4 mile downstream from the Conklingville Dam and powerhouse.

The portage can be undertaken in reverse—from Stewart Pond to the Great Sacandaga Lake—of course, but this is a slightly more difficult route, being steadily uphill for most of the carry.

See also the following chapter, "Stewart Pond."

33

Stewart Pond (Conklingville/Hadley)
A Quieter Section of the Sacandaga River

■ **Launch Sites:** Stewart Pond, also called the Stewart Bridge Reservoir (Saratoga County): public boat launch—put-in at tiny bay formed by Man Shanty Brook off of Rte. 4, or at end of road next to cemetery

■ **Delorme NYS Atlas & Gazetteer:** p. 80, B2; **GPS:** public boat launch #1—43°18.66'N; 73°54.29'W; public boat launch #2—43°18.45'N; 73°54.33'W; Stewart Pond Campsites—43°18.71'N; 73°53.65'W

■ **Destinations & Mileages:** *Southwest and then Northwest*: to Breen Brook Cove—0.9 mile; to Conklingville Dam—1.9 miles. *Southeast*: to Stewart Bridge Dam—1.5 miles. *Around perimeter of pond*—3.4 miles.

■ **Comments:** Read "Caution" beginning on page xxi and Advisory on page 120.
 Stay a safe distance back from the Conklingville Dam and the Stewart Bridge Dam.

Directions: *To Public Boat Launch*—From Lake Luzerne (junction of Rte. 4 & Main Street) head west, immediately crossing over the Bridge of Hope that spans the Hudson River. At 4.3 miles (or 1.4 miles west of the junction of Rtes. 4 & 7) turn left at a sign that reads, "Stewarts Bridge Development Federal Energy Regulating Comm. Project # 2047."

From Edinburg (junction of Rtes. 4 & 5) head northeast on Rte. 4 for 17.0 miles (or 1.4 miles east of the junction of Rtes. 4 & 8) and turn right at the sign for the Stewarts Bridge Development Project.

There are two boat launch sites. At 0.1 mile you will come to a launch site on your left with a large parking area to your right (public boat launch #1). The put-in here is at a tiny bay formed by Man Shanty Brook.

If you continue another 0.3 mile to the end of the road, you will reach a second, informal boat launch site, straight ahead, with an abundance of parking (public boat launch #2). The launch is directly to the left of a small cemetery.

To Stewart Pond Campsites—For those wishing to camp out and access the lake from the Stewart Pond Campsites, or for those who wish to launch from the south side of the lake for a fee, head west on Rte. 4 from Lake Luzerne (junction of Rte. 4 & Main Street) for 2.8 miles, bear left at a fork in the road and drive 0.1 mile. Turn left again onto Rte. 7 and go south for 0.7 mile, crossing over the Stewart Bridge Dam in the process. When you come to a junction, turn right and follow Rte. 7 northwest for another 1.1 miles. Turn right onto a dirt road at the sign that leads into the Stewart Pond Campsites. For more information: 4405 South Shore Road, Hadley, NY 12835, (518) 696-2779, adirondackcampgrounds.com, mail@stewartspond.com.

Coming in on Rte. 7 (South Shore Road) from the Great Sacandaga Lake, when you reach the junction of Rtes. 7 & 8, continue west for 1.0 mile farther on Rte. 7 and then turn left onto a road that leads north to the campsites.

▶ **Stewart Pond (Conklingville/Hadley)**

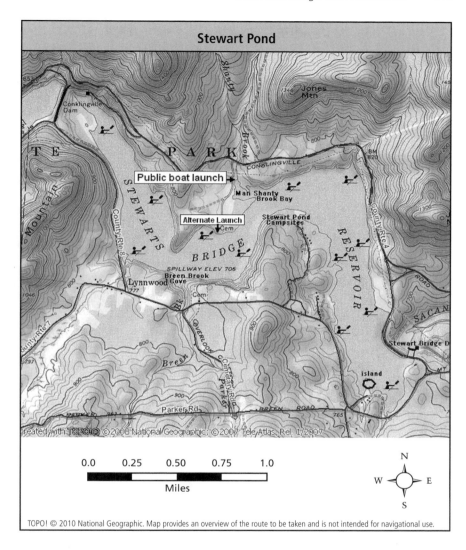

Stewart Pond

Public boat launch

Man Shanty Brook Bay

Alternate Launch

Stewart Pond Campsites

SPILLWAY ELEV 706
Breen Brook
Lynnwood Cove

Stewart Bridge D

island

```
0.0      0.25     0.50     0.75     1.0
                  Miles
```

N
W   E
S

TOPO! © 2010 National Geographic. Map provides an overview of the route to be taken and is not intended for navigational use.

The Paddle:

Stewart Pond is situated between the Conklingville Dam to the northwest and the Stewart Bridge Dam to the southeast. The Stewart Bridge Dam has impounded a portion of the Sacandaga River to create the reservoir. The following paddle describes the route as taken from the Man Shanty Brook Bay launch site (public boat launch #1). The routes and the distances from the Stewart Pond Campsite or informal public boat launch #2 will vary slightly from the routes below.

   Southwest and then Northwest—From Man Shanty Brook Bay, paddle 1.9 miles southwest and then northwest to reach the Conklingville Dam (staying a safe distance back from the dam). Along the way, at 0.9 mile, you will pass by a tiny cove on your left produced by Breen Brook that goes south for 0.05 mile.

Southeast—From Man Shanty Brook Bay, go 1.5 miles to the main part of Stewart Bridge Dam. Stay a safe distance from the top of the dam. You can continue south past the dam for another 0.2 mile before reaching the end of navigable waters. A tiny island-like projection of land is located near the south end of this section.

Around perimeter of pond—The shoreline of the entire pond can be paddled around in 3.4 miles.

Additional launch sites: It is also possible to access Stewart Pond from Great Sacandaga Lake via a canoe portage route (see "Marinas, Informal Lake Accesses, and Portage between Great Sacandaga Lake and Stewart Pond").

In addition there are blue-colored, diamond-shaped posted signs put up by Erie Blvd. Hydropower of Liverpool, New York, along the east side of Rte. 8 between the Conklingville Dam and Rte. 7 where foot access to Stewart Pond is allowed. There are several points along the road where you can pull in and park.

Stewart Bridge Dam prior to its completion in the 1950s. Postcard ca.1940.

▶ **Stewart Pond (Conklingville/Hadley)**

Mayfield Lake (Mayfield)
A Quiet Paddle on a Satellite of Great Sacandaga Lake

34

- ▓ **Launch Site:** Mayfield Lake in Mayfield off of North Main Street (Fulton County); 50-foot carry to informal slip-in; limited parking. For more information: Town of Mayfield, 28 North School Street. P.O. Box 00, Mayfield, NY 12117, (518) 661-5414, mayfieldny.org.
- ▓ **Delorme NYS Atlas & Gazetteer:** p. 79, D6–7; **GPS:** 43°05.87'N; 74°15.43'W
- ▓ **Destinations & Mileages:** *West*: to filtration plant—0.6 mile; to Mayfield Creek—0.7 mile; up Mayfield Creek—0.3 mile. *Southwest*: to Anthony Creek—0.8 mile. *Around perimeter of lake*—3.4 miles.
- ▓ **Comments:** Read "Caution" beginning on page xxi and Advisory on page 120.

  Stay a safe distance back from the six-slot spillway under the School Street bridge that drops the water level approximately 8 feet between Mayfield Lake and Great Sacandaga Lake. The height varies depending upon the water level of Great Sacandaga Lake.

  Always check the current before heading out when a dam is in close proximity to the launch site.

Directions: From Vail Mills (junction of Rtes. 30 & 29) head northwest on Rte. 30 for 3.6 miles. Turn right onto School Street and head north for over 1.3 miles. As soon as you cross over a small bridge, turn left into a tiny pull-off at the northwest end of the bridge next to a large sign reading "Welcome to Mayfield Village."

From north of Mayfield (junction of Rte. 30 & North School Street), turn south onto North School Street and go 1.0 mile. Pull into a small pull-off to your right next to a large sign reading "Welcome to Mayfield Village" just before crossing a bridge.

There is sufficient parking for only 2–3 cars. From the pull-off, carry your watercraft 50 feet to a slip-in next to the bridge.

The Paddle:
According to a historic marker on the bridge leading into Mayfield, the site was originally occupied by a mill erected in 1773 by Sir William Johnson, arguably the Mohawk Valley's most distinguished past resident. The mill burned down during the Revolutionary War. It was later rebuilt by Col. Abraham Romeyn, commander of the Montgomery County militia, and became known as Romeyn's Mill.

Mayfield Lake has been artificially enhanced by the damming of Mayfield Creek, which rises north of Gloversville, and Anthony Creek, which rises east of Gloversville.

Take note that the put-in is just 100 feet away from the spillway dam. Under most conditions there is little draw toward the dam, but it is best to give it a wide berth.

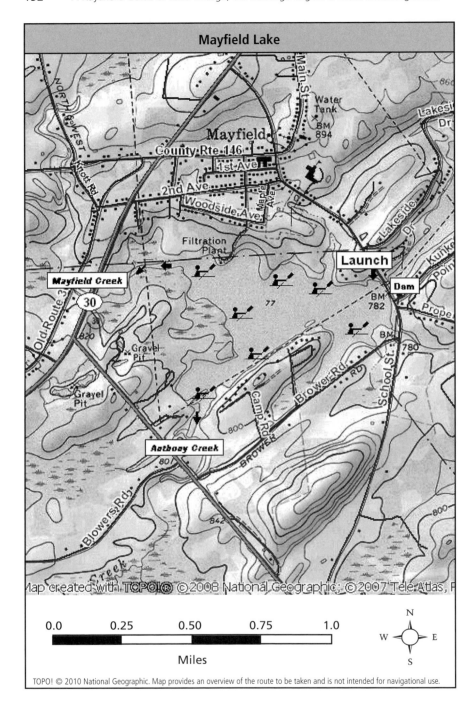

Mayfield Lake

TOPO! © 2010 National Geographic. Map provides an overview of the route to be taken and is not intended for navigational use.

▶ **Mayfield Lake (Mayfield)**

West—Follow along the north shore, heading west. At 0.6 mile you will pass by a filtration plant. After another 0.1 mile you will come to Mayfield Creek. You will have to paddle over a shallow-water sandbar to reach the creek, but once you start the trek you will find that Mayfield Creek stays reasonably deep and surprisingly wide on the section you will be exploring. After paddling 0.3 mile, you will come to a tiny island where rapids and jumbles of rocks in the stream-bed prevent further continuation.

Southwest—Head southwest along the south shore of the lake. After 0.6 mile you will reach a wide bay. In another 0.2 mile the bay narrows and becomes Anthony Creek, the canoeable end of the paddle.

Around perimeter of lake—The entire shoreline of the lake can be paddled around in 3.4 miles.

One small dam separates Mayfield Lake from Great Sacandaga Lake. Photograph 2009.

35 Northville Lake (Northville)
A Tiny Satellite of Great Sacandaga Lake

■ **Launch Sites:** Southwest shore of Northville Lake at village of Northville (Fulton County) next to Main Street as you leave the village going south; 20-foot carry to informal slip-ins. For more information: Northville Civic Association, northvilleny.com.

■ **Delorme NYS Atlas & Gazetteer:** p. 79, C7; **GPS:** southwest end of lake (first pull-off)—43°13.14'N; 74°10.11'W; south end of lake (second pull-off)—43°13.16'N; 74°10.10'W

■ **Destinations & Mileages:** *North*: to Water Street causeway—0.6 mile; to Hunters Creek—0.8 mile; up Hunters Creek—0.05 mile. *Around perimeter of lake*—2.0 miles.

■ **Comments:** Read "Caution" beginning on page xxi and Advisory on page 120.
Stay a safe distance back from the spillway dam at the southwest end of the lake. Always check the current before heading out when a dam is in close proximity to the launch site.

Directions: From the center of Northville (junction of Main Street & Bridge Street), drive south on Main Street for 0.5 mile. As soon as you reach the causeway separating Northville Lake from Great Sacandaga Lake, pull into the parking area on your left, where a 20-foot carry takes you down to the water's edge.

If you continue on Main Street for less than 0.2 mile farther, you will reach a second pull-off with lake access, also to your left.

Both accesses are informal entry points used by anglers.

The Paddle:

Northville Lake is a modest-sized body of water formed by the impoundment of Hunters Creek, a small stream that rises in the hills north of Maple Grove. Before the creation of Great Sacandaga Lake, Hunters Creek flowed past the south end of Northville and directly into the Sacandaga River. Northville Lake is separated from Great Sacandaga Lake by a small causeway whose spillway causes Northville Lake to remain slightly higher in elevation than Great Sacandaga Lake. As summer progresses and the level of Great Sacandaga Lake drops further because of water releases, this disparity increases even more.

In some respects, paddling on Northville Lake is more satisfying than paddling on Great Sacandaga Lake, for Northville Lake's diminutive size effectively discourages the proliferation of motorboats. Virtually all of the watercraft you will see along the shoreline are rowboats and canoes.

Northville Lake, combined with Great Sacandaga Lake, has turned the village of Northville into a large peninsula. Northville, located at the north end of Great Sacandaga Lake, rests on a "flat terrace of land which was once a glacial delta."[1] Northville was permanently settled in the 1780s and became incorpo-

▶ **Northville Lake (Northville)**

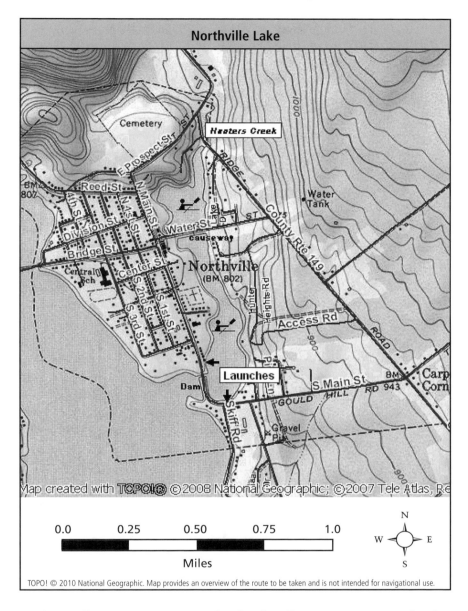

Northville Lake

rated as a village in 1873. During its heyday the village was a prosperous lumber town complete with mills, cooperages, tanneries, and woodenware industries.[2]

North—Head north from the launch site, paddling along the west bank of Northville Lake. You will notice that the west bank is much steeper than the east shoreline of the lake. At the top of the west bank is the village of Northville, which essentially extends along the full length of the west shoreline. Interestingly, most of Northville is hidden from sight, with homeowners and shopowners seemingly indifferent about exploiting the lakefront so close at hand. Just before you reach the Water Street causeway, at 0.6 mile, you will pass by Riverside Park to your left.

The paddle does not end at the Water Street causeway. A culvert under the causeway allows you to paddle into the smaller section of the lake. Proceeding north from the causeway for another 0.2 mile, you will reach the mouth of Hunters Creek, the lake's inlet stream. Under most conditions it is possible to paddle a short distance up the creek to a low bridge spanning Ridge Road. At times it is even possible to go under the bridge by ducking low, but blowdown will likely halt your progress after you have gone several hundred feet beyond the bridge.

Around perimeter of lake—The perimeter of Northville Lake can be paddled in 2.0 miles.

A paddler gets ready to go under the Water Street causeway. Photograph 2011.

▶ Northville Lake (Northville)

Lake Luzerne (Lake Luzerne)
A Lake at the Gateway to the Adirondacks

■ **Launch Site:** Wayside Beach (Saratoga County); parking area off of Rte. 9N; ramp between beach and parking area; beach open from late June–Labor Day; parking for 10 cars; no motorboats permitted; parking lot is closed from 9 PM to 7 AM except for the launching of watercraft. For more information: (518) 696-2711, townoflakeluzerne.com.

■ **Delorme NYS Atlas & Gazetteer:** p. 80, B3; **GPS:** 43°19.33'N; 73°50.30'W

■ **Destinations & Mileages:** *North:* to inlet stream—0.5 mile; from mouth of inlet stream upstream to Read Park Road bridge—0.3 mile (0.8 mile from launch); to Towner Road bridge—1.2 miles (1.7 miles from launch); to Second Lake—1.9 miles (2.4 miles from launch). *Around perimeter of lake*—2.3 miles.

■ **Comments:** Read "Caution" beginning on page xxi and Advisory on page 120. Keep a respectable distance away from Ivy Island, which is privately owned.

Directions: The village of Lake Luzerne can be reached by taking Rte. 9N either southwest from Lake George or north from Saratoga Springs. When you reach the village of Lake Luzerne, look for Wayside Beach (the entry point to the lake at Lake Luzerne) directly opposite Mill Street. The launch is from Wayside Beach, which involves a short carry and easy put-in next to the beach.

The Paddle:
Lake Luzerne encompasses 109 acres with several miles of shoreline. Just offshore from Wayside Beach is tiny Ivy Island. Lake Luzerne has been described as "a gem of pearl in a setting of emerald, and bearing on its tremulous bosom a solitary island, Ivy Isle, so small it seems to float."[1]

Lake Luzerne was named after Chevalier de la Luzerne, a French diplomat who was sent over to America by his government during the Revolutionary War to provide encouragement to General George Washington and feedback to France on the war's progress.[2]

In times past Lake Luzerne was called the "Gateway to the Adirondacks." The village started off as a mill town with a profusion of sawmills and gristmills. In the second half of the nineteenth century, it became a major producer of leather goods as well as a tourist town. The town's most famous visitor was President Ulysses S. Grant, who came to Lake Luzerne after the Civil War for relaxation.[3]

The paddle from the west side of Lake Luzerne begins at Wayside Beach, named after the former Wayside Inn, an imposing structure built in 1869 on a 20-acre plateau (now occupied by a school) overlooking the lake. The inn, a Victorian gothic structure, was built by Col. Benjamin C. Butler in 1869.[4] With modifications it lasted until it was destroyed by fire in 1938.[5]

Earlier this section of the west shore was a gathering place for Native Americans, principally the Iroquois, who maintained a fishing lodge.

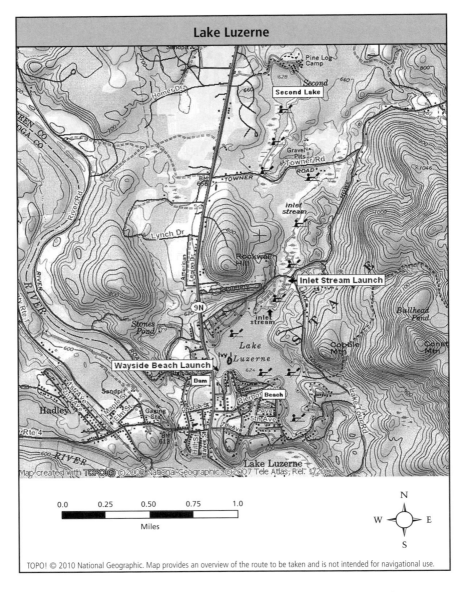

Map created with TOPO!® ©2008 National Geographic; ©2007 Tele Atlas; Rel. 1/2007

TOPO! © 2010 National Geographic. Map provides an overview of the route to be taken and is not intended for navigational use.

Listen carefully and you will often hear the sound of music wafting across the lake from the Luzerne Music Center, an international summer camp for young people ages 11 through 18 who wish to develop themselves further as vocalists, instrumentalists, composers, and conductors.

North—Leaving the public beach behind, paddle north to the left of Ivy Island (privately owned and posted) and continue following the shoreline north

▶ **Lake Luzerne (Lake Luzerne)**

to reach the mouth of Lake Luzerne's inlet stream in 0.5 mile. The inlet stream, which some call Berry Pond Brook, can be paddled upstream for 1.9 miles to Second Lake. Be prepared for a moderately challenging paddle, for you will encounter obstacles (blowdown and beaver dams) as well as having to make your way through a mazelike marshland. In several instances you may have to backtrack after coming to a dead end. The inlet stream drains a series of lakes to the north beginning, in ascending order, with Second Lake, then Third Lake, Fourth Lake, Lake Forest, and Lake Vanare.

Following the inlet stream from Lake Luzerne, you will pass under the Read Park Road bridge (where the alternate access site is located) at 0.3 mile. Soon after, you will enter a wide marshy area of shrubs and clumps of grasses. Rockwell Hill, 917 feet high and named after an eighteenth-century gristmill operator named Jeremy Rockwell, is off to your left. In another 0.05 mile a small beaver dam is encountered that you will have to portage around. Shortly after you pass by this barrier, follow a lead that goes left and then momentarily parallels the west shore of the marsh. Continue making your way through what can only be described as a labyrinth. Later you will find yourself along the east side of the marsh, following a stream that meanders. In 1.0 mile you will come to a circular pool of water where the creek comes in from the left. Private camps can be seen along the bank here, and the marshland turns into forest. You will immediately encounter small rapids that can sometimes be paddled through. Just upstream another set of rapids is encountered that is longer and shallower. You will have to carry around this natural barrier. At 1.2 miles you will come to the Towner Road Bridge. More rapids are encountered here. From this point it is another 0.7 mile up to Second Lake. Be prepared for further portages depending upon conditions.

Some kayakers have gone all the way from Lake Luzerne to Fourth Lake, or have made the trip in reverse, but this requires numerous carries to accomplish.

Around perimeter of lake—The paddle around Lake Luzerne is a leisurely 2.3 miles. Visible near the northwest end of the lake is 917-foot-high Rockwell Hill. Looming to the east is 953-foot-high Cobble Mountain.

At the southwest end of the lake near Wayside Beach, the outlet stream (Mill Creek) goes under Rte. 9N through an arched tunnel and immediately reaches a small dam. From there the stream cascades through a small gorge and flows west into the Hudson River approximately 0.2 mile upstream from the Bridge of Hope, which connects the village of Lake Luzerne with Hadley.

The lakefront is quite developed with private camps and full-time residences, particularly at its south end. A second public beach, called Luzerne Beach, is located off of Pierpoint Road, but there are no boat launches at that site.

Alternate Launch Site

Inlet Stream Access (Lake Luzerne)

■ **Launch Site:** Read Park Road bridge (Saratoga County); 20-foot carry to slip-in; no motorboats permitted. The launch site area is maintained by the Aquatic Conservation Taskforce.
■ **Delorme NYS Atlas & Gazetteer:** p. 80, B3; **GPS:** 43°19.80'N; 73°49.78'W
■ **Destinations & Mileages:** *South*: down inlet stream to Lake Luzerne—0.3 mile; to Wayside Beach—0.8 mile. *North*: up inlet stream to Towner Road bridge—0.9 mile; up inlet stream to Second Lake—1.6 miles. *Around perimeter of Lake Luzerne*—2.3 miles.
■ **Comments:** Read "Caution" beginning on page xxi and Advisory on page 120.

Directions: The village of Lake Luzerne can be reached by taking Rte. 9N either southwest from Lake George or north from Saratoga Springs. When you reach the village of Lake Luzerne, look for Wayside Beach (the entry point to the lake at Lake Luzerne), which is directly opposite Mill Street.

Starting from Wayside Beach/Mill Street, proceed north on Rte. 9N for over 0.2 mile. Turn right onto Read Park Road and head east for over 0.5 mile. As soon as you cross over the tiny bridge spanning the inlet stream to Lake Luzerne, turn right into a small pull-off. From there it is a 20-foot carry to a slip-in at the water's edge.

View of Lake Luzerne from its east shore. Postcard ca. 1940.

▶ **Lake Luzerne (Lake Luzerne)**

Sacandaga River: From Stewart Bridge Dam to Hudson River (Hadley)
One of the Northeast's Favorite Whitewater Treks for Intermediate Paddlers **37**

■ **Launch Site:** Below Stewart Bridge Dam (also spelled Stewarts and Stewart's), off of Bridge Street in Hadley (Saratoga County); 0.3-mile carry down graded pathway with 100 feet of elevation change.

The dam releases water daily from Memorial Day to Columbus Day, producing a fairly reliable flow of 4,000 cfs. To verify times, call Waterline after 7 PM the evening before your trip. Their automatic phone answering number is (800) 452-1737. Enter code 365122 for the Stewart Bridge Dam site. If you head out to paddle and your timing is wrong, you may reach the Sacandaga River only to find it a bed of rocks and boulders with minimal water flow. The controlled releases of water are provided through Brookfield Renewable Energy (operators of the hydroelectric plant). Brookfield Renewable Energy is part of a larger corporation that has been a power provider in northeastern North America and Brazil for almost a hundred years.

There is no charge to use the river unless you are rafting or paddling with a commercial company, using the shuttle service to avoid the necessity of placing cars at both ends of the paddle, or renting white-water equipment such as kayaks, inner tubes, or PFDs (personal flotation devices).

Guided rafting trips down the river began 33 years ago when the Hudson River Rafting Company and the former Adirondack Wildwaters company began operating commercially.

■ **Take-out Site:** Whitewater Recreation Area at Sacandaga Outdoor Center

■ **Delorme NYS Atlas & Gazetteer:** p. 80, B2–3; **GPS:** entrance gate—43°18.04'N; 73°53.23'W; parking area—43°18.19'N; 73°53.23'W; launch—43°17.98'N; 73°53.12'W; take-out at Sacandaga Outdoor Center—43°18.89'N; 73°50.62'W

■ **Destinations & Mileages:** *Northeast*: down Sacandaga River—3.5 miles (one-way only); *Continuing East & North*: from mouth of Sacandaga River to Rockwell Falls—0.4 mile (round-trip).

■ **Comments:** Read "Caution" beginning on page xxi and Advisory on page 120.

This is a paddle for intermediate white-water paddlers—not intermediate flat-water paddlers. It involves Class II & III rapids (see "Categories of River Difficulty") and is the only Class III white-water paddle contained in this book. You should expect to encounter not only swift current because of dam releases, but episodes of bouncy white water and occasional eddies. An intermediate flat-water paddler should first take a guided trip down the river with one of the rafting companies to get a feel for the river. It would also be wise to practice on the rapids at the beginning of the paddle before advancing farther downstream. If you find that negotiating those rapids may be beyond your abilities and comfort level, take out your craft at the earliest opportunity (there are many places along the north bank where this is possible).

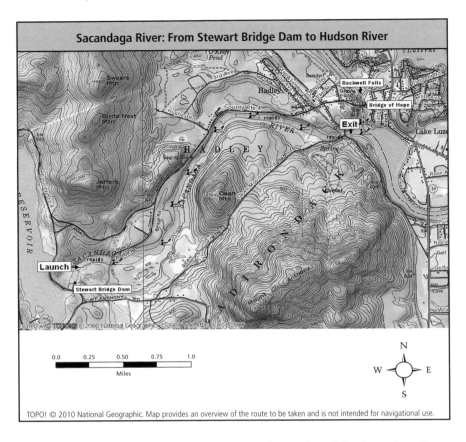

Sacandaga River: From Stewart Bridge Dam to Hudson River

0.0   0.25   0.50   0.75   1.0

Miles

N
W — E
S

TOPO! © 2010 National Geographic. Map provides an overview of the route to be taken and is not intended for navigational use.

Hundreds of paddlers and tubers go down this section of the Sacandaga River daily in rafts, kayaks, and inner tubes without mishaps. Heed all of the cautions in this book, follow all recommended safety practices, practice some basic white-water techniques, and familiarize yourself with the river first before becoming fully engaged in the trek to maximize your chances of enjoying this paddle without accident.

Should you become separated from your watercraft, keep your feet pointed downstream and make your way over to the shoreline. Do not attempt to stand up and walk along the river bottom. Although the water is frequently only waist deep, should your foot become stuck as you try to walk along the river bottom the force of the water could bow you over, pushing your face into the water and making it difficult to get air.

Stay a safe distance back from the Stewart Bridge Dam, just upstream from the put-in, and Rockwell Falls, 0.2 mile upstream on the Hudson River from its confluence with the Sacandaga River.

If you are undertaking the trip on your own and are not a client with a rafting

▶ **Sacandaga River: From Stewart Bridge Dam to Hudson River (Hadley)**

company, a canoe/kayak carrier would be helpful even though the carry to the launch site is essentially downhill.

Unless you are planning to use the shuttle, you will want to have two cars, one at the launch and one at the take-out.

Directions: From west of Saratoga Springs (junction of Rtes. 9N & West Ave.), drive north on Rte. 9N for 18 miles, passing through the village of Corinth in the process. Just before reaching the village of Lake Luzerne, you will come to a stoplight. Turn left onto Bay Road and drive northwest for 0.4 mile, then turn left onto Bridge Street (Rte. 4) and cross over the Hudson River via the "Bridge of Hope." Be sure to look to your right for views of Rockwell Falls as you drive over the bridge.

To take-out—From the "Bridge of Hope" drive west on Bridge Street (Rte. 4) for 0.4 mile until you come to an intersection. Turn left onto Old Corinth Road and drive south for 0.2 mile.

If you are approaching from the parking area by the put-in, follow Rte. 4 northeast for 2.5 miles. At an intersection turn right onto Old Corinth Road and drive south for 0.2 mile.

From either direction, just before going across the historic Bow Bridge that spans the Sacandaga River, turn left onto Whitewater Way and drive east for 0.05 mile to the end of the road and the parking area for the Whitewater Recreation Area. The Sacandaga Outdoor Center is located at the end of the parking lot. The hard-surface ramp take-out is virtually at the confluence of the Sacandaga River and the Hudson River. Leave a second car here.

To put-in—From the "Bridge of Hope" follow Rte. 4 southwest for 2.8 miles until you come to a fork in the road. Turn left onto Rte. 7 and drive west for 0.1 mile. Just as you reach a second intersection, take note of a large parking area on the right.

From the second intersection bear left and drive downhill, south, for less than 0.2 mile. You will see to your left a long pull-off with an abundance of "no parking" signs. Drop off your watercraft here and return to the parking area you noted 0.2 mile back. Note: in the future a parking area next to the entrance gate may be made available to white-water paddlers. At the writing of this book, however, the parking area remains locked.

From the pull-off where you dropped off your watercraft, carry your kayak down a 0.3-mile-long access trail to the Sacandaga River, just below the Stewart Bridge Dam. The last third of the trail is steep and the put-in is rocky, making the launch site moderately difficult to access.

The Paddle:

The Sacandaga River has undergone many changes, some caused by nature and some by human intervention. Geologists speculate that the Sacandaga River at one time was a tributary to the Mohawk River, running south from Northville and flowing into the Mohawk River west of Amsterdam. At the end of the last ice age, retreating glaciers created a moraine (an earthen barrier) that blocked the Sacandaga River's path south. The river was then diverted east around Sinclair Point (now a land mass that extends into the main basin of Great Sacandaga Lake) and northeast through Conklingville, finally ending up flowing into the Hudson River at Hadley/Lake Luzerne.[1]

Not only has the area been modified by nature, but humans have taken a hand as well. In 1930 a huge earthen dam and the E. J. West powerhouse were erected at Conklingville to impound the Sacandaga River, creating a reservoir whose surface area nearly rivals that of Lake George.

Then, in the 1950s, a second dam and power plant were built three miles downstream from the Conklingville Dam, creating the Stewart Bridge Reservoir. Controlled releases of water from the Stewart Bridge Reservoir cause the Sacandaga River to burst into life several times a day along a 3.5-mile stretch of river. Were it not for these controlled releases of water, there would be insufficient depth during the summer season to support a rafting business.

Northeast down the Sacandaga River—Put in downstream from the base of Stewart Bridge Dam. You will see the Stewart Bridge power plant across the river, slightly to your right. Also across the river, slightly downstream, is the launch site used by the shuttle raft service.

Right at the start there are many rapids and eddies, giving fledging paddlers a chance to practice and hone their skills.

Soon you will pass by the abutments of an abandoned bridge, where Stewart Bridge Road once continued across the Sacandaga River. After the bridge the waters become essentially calm for 1.0 mile. Following this stretch of quiet waters, the river starts to pick up again immediately after you pass under the old D&H Railroad Bridge. The bridge was earlier called the Adirondack Railroad Bridge. Prior to 1865 and the bridge's construction, the railway line from Saratoga stopped just before reaching the Sacandaga River. When the train trestle was erected over the river, however, the line was extended to the train depot in Hadley.[2]

The largest rapids are encountered by the Bow Bridge, where the river's natural turbulence has been augmented by the recent addition of more boulders to the river. A particularly lively area of white water (where most photos of paddlers coming downriver are taken) is called Sonny Hole, or sometimes Picture Hole.

The Bow Bridge spans the Sacandaga River just upstream from the Sacandaga's confluence with the Hudson River. One of only three lenticular truss bridges ever built in New York State, the Bow Bridge is the only one that is still standing. It is named for its bow-shaped arches, both above and below the deck, which give it a parabolic (or lenticular) shape. The Bow Bridge was built in 1885 to replace a wooden covered bridge that had been erected in 1813. In 1977 the Bow Bridge was put on the National Registry of Historic Sites.[3] It was closed in 1984 because of safety concerns, and for a time seemed destined for demolition. Vigorous community support developed, however, and a "Save the Bridge" campaign began, with the result that the bridge was rehabilitated and reopened

▶ **Sacandaga River: From Stewart Bridge Dam to Hudson River (Hadley)**

for one-lane traffic in 2006. A small gazebo at the northwest end of the bridge provides both excellent historical information and great views of the river and its paddlers.

The waters have always been turbulent below the Bow Bridge because of large boulders in the stream. In May 2006, however, 1,500 extra tons of native rocks were placed into the river under the bridge to make the waters even more spectacular and exciting for paddlers. John Duncan, owner of the Sacandaga Outdoor Center, is hopeful that the Whitewater Recreation Area will eventually become one of the top ten such sites in the country. The long-range plan is to create three distinct "park & play" sites along the river between the Stewart Bridge Dam and Hadley, thus turning the river into a white-water paddler's paradise.

Take out to your left at the Sacandaga Outdoor Center just before reaching where the Sacandaga River enters the Hudson River.

Continuing East & North—Continue downstream, east, past the take-out at the Sacandaga Outdoor Center to the confluence of the Sacandaga River with the Hudson River. Old foundation ruins are visible at the confluence along the west bank of the Hudson River.

Bear left onto the Hudson River, fighting against the current—which can be strong at times—and head north. You will paddle upstream through a rocky gorge and then under the "Bridge of Hope" spanning the Hudson River between Hadley & Lake Luzerne, where you will encounter a whirlpool that paddlers have named, in the vernacular of hyperbole, the "Room of Doom." Just beyond the bridge, a tiny cascade/rapid is encountered at a narrowing in the gorge. This may be as far as most paddlers will want to go. Should you continue farther, a second tiny cascade/rapid is reached in another 50 feet. Beyond that Rockwell Falls looms less than 100 feet away. Bear in mind that Rockwell Falls is rated Class V waters—significant risk of injury—with strong hydraulics and undercut ledges. Keep a safe distance away from the waterfall if you push on to reach it. Fortunately, the current is strong enough to propel you backwards the closer you get, as if to protect the unwitting.

Paddle back down the Hudson River and turn right onto the Sacandaga River. You will need to paddle hard to go back upstream for 0.05 mile to the take-out on your right.

It is also possible to white-water tube down the Sacandaga River and, in fact, many people do. Tubing provides a more intimate connection with the river without the enclosing walls of a kayak or canoe or the stiff rubber buffer of a raft. One such exhilarating trip was described in detail in this author's article "The Buoys of Summer" in *Adirondack Life* magazine.[4] Low-cost shuttle service is available at the Sacandaga Outdoor Center. To check on specific times when the shuttle is operating, which may vary depending upon water flow and customer demand, contact (518) 696-5710.

White-Water Rafting Companies: There are a number of white-water rafting companies that furnish equipment (rafts, tubes, kayaks, paddles, and life vests) for paddlers interested in checking out the river with a group and a guide before undertaking a solo trek:

ARO (Adirondack River Outfitters) Adventures
aroadventures.com   (800) 525-RAFT

Beaver Brook Outfitters
beaverbrook.net   (518) 696-5101

Hudson River Rafting Company
hudsonriverrafting.com   (800) 888-RAFT

Sacandaga Outdoor Center
4soc.com   (518) 696-RAFT

Wild Waters Outdoor Center
wildwaters.net/whitewater-rafting/Sacandaga-river-rafting   (800) 867-2335

Additional Point of Interest: Take note of the multiple pull-offs along Rte. 4 between Stewart Bridge Dam and Old Corinth Road, which provide sightings of the river.

Dean Mountain Whitewater Park, on the opposite side of the river from Rte. 4, provides outstanding views of a stretch of white water just upstream from the Bow Bridge. To get there from Rte. 4, turn onto Old Corinth Road and drive south for over 0.2 mile. As soon as you cross over the Bow Bridge, turn immediately right and follow the road west for 0.2 mile to Dean Mountain Whitewater Park, which is on your right. The park offers picnic tables from which you may enjoy great views of the river. Take note, however, that it is not intended as a river access.

Turbulent waters are encountered on the Sacandaga River near its confluence with the Hudson River. Postcard ca. 1910.

▶ **Sacandaga River: From Stewart Bridge Dam to Hudson River (Hadley)**

IV

Champlain Canal & Environs
From Stillwater to Fort Edward

Advisory

The Hudson River above the Federal Dam in Troy is very much like the Mohawk River—a series of interconnected, narrow lakes interposed by dams and canal locks. While powerboats abound, they tend to be cruisers, often "locking through" the canal system. The enormous barges and ocean vessels that characterize the lower Hudson River are not found here.

Even so, operators of small watercraft like kayaks and canoes must be ever-vigilant. Don't assume boats can see you. Wear bright colors. Know where the boat channels are and avoid those waters. If you must cross a boat channel, cross in a group and keep the group together. If you see a boat in the distance, let it pass before you set out. Some large boats move surprisingly fast, and distance can be hard to judge. Take into account current and wind when planning your trajectory across the river.

Wind, waves, and wakes can be factors. Even though this section of the Hudson River is generally fairly narrow (often 0.05 mile across or less), stay close to the shoreline where more protection is afforded from wind and waves.

When planning to leave the shoreline and cross open water, choose a calm day and watch the weather. Always check the forecast and weather before setting out. Do not leave shore if storms and/or high winds are predicted or if the weather forecast is at all questionable. Be aware that the weather can change abruptly, often with little warning and in spite of the forecast. Current and wind can be severe. The wind tends to be quietest in the early morning and early evening. Wind and current increase as you move away from the shoreline.

Stay a safe distance back from any dam to avoid being swept over its brink if you are approaching the top, or being caught up in its hydraulics if you are approaching from below. Make sure that the current is not strong if you launch near a dam.

At the writing of this book, environmental dredging continues to take place along designated sections of the Champlain Canal. Paddlers should refer to the General Electric dredging Web site for updates on the location and scope of dredging activities: hudsondredging.com.

Memorize the shoreline as you leave so that you can return to the same starting point.

Introduction: The Champlain Canal

The New York State Canal Corporation, the Erie Canalway National Heritage Corridor, and the Hudson River Valley Greenway are leading the way and part-nering with many local entities and the National Park Service's Rivers and Trails Program to work together to create a water trail that will extend all the way up the canal to Whitehall. In addition the Hudson River Valley Greenway is dili-gently laboring to extend the present water trail to Hadley in northeastern Sara-toga County.

The New York State Canal Corporation's stated goal is to establish "a coor-dinated 'trail' with boat launches and campsites along the shores of the 524-mile New York State Canal System, encouraging more types of motorized and nonmotorized boaters to explore this historic resource." When completed, the Canal Corporation's water trail "will allow small boaters to intimately explore the NYS Canal System's natural, cultural and historic wonders, for a day, a week or a lifetime."[1] This trail will connect with numerous other water trails including the Champlain Paddlers Trail to the north and the Hudson River Greenway Water Trail to the south. The Hudson River Greenway Water Trail, which includes the Champlain Canal, won several awards in 2011 as the best new trail in America.

The canal towpaths paralleling the waterways are also receiving a lot of attention these days. A Champlain Canalway Trail Action Plan for the 62 miles between Waterford and Whitehall was released in March 2011.

The reader should realize the limitless possibilities of combining water-trail paddles. For those wishing to "lock through" the parts of the canal covered in this book for a longer excursion, the following numbers will prove helpful:

Lock C-3, (518) 664-5171
Lock C-4, (518) 664-5261
Lock C-5, (518) 695-3919
Lock C-6, (518) 747-4614
Lock C-7, (518) 747-5520
Lock C-8, (518) 747-6021
Lock C-9, (518) 639-8964

The following chapters offer paddles from Stillwater to Fort Edwards* cov-ering sections of both the old and the new Champlain Canal. Although the Erie Canal, which connected Albany with Buffalo, comes most readily to mind when New York historic waterways are mentioned, most people are surprised to learn that the Champlain Canal, constructed in 1823, was almost as important and was built two years prior to the Erie Canal. Whereas the Erie Canal extended east to west, the Champlain Canal went south to north to link the Hudson River, Mohawk River, and Erie Canal at Albany with Lake Champlain at Whitehall.

A blue heron strikes a pose before taking flight. Photograph 2010.

Until that time, travel north and south by water had been exceedingly difficult, with no continuous water connection between the Hudson River and Lake George or Lake Champlain.

Militarily the Hudson River, Lake George, and Lake Champlain route proved crucial in the seventeenth and eighteenth centuries, culminating in fierce struggles to control the waterways during the French and Indian War (the Seven Years War) and the Revolutionary War. It was common knowledge that whichever country controlled these waterways controlled New York State. Route 4 is now popularly called the "Burgoyne Trail," roughly following the route that British General John Burgoyne took from Whitehall to just outside of Stillwater, where he was stopped by the Continental Army at Bemis Heights.

When military activities in New York State ceased for good after the War of 1812, the water routes along eastern New York State were finally free for commerce, and men with vision began to contemplate how the various components of these routes could be physically connected.

One result was the completion of the Champlain Canal in 1823, which connected the Hudson River at Albany with Lake Champlain at Whitehall. Lake George was bypassed (leaving it, as a result, relatively untouched and in its natural state). The long overland carries between Fort Edward and Whitehall that had plagued north-south travelers were eliminated. The canal extended for sixty-three miles. It paralleled the Hudson River north to Fort Edward, veered northeast from Fort Edward to Wood Creek, and then pushed on north again to Lake Champlain. To overcome changes in elevation along the way, a series of twenty-three locks were established to raise boats from near sea level at Cohoes to a height of 140 feet, and then to lower them down to a height of 96 feet above sea level as Lake Champlain was approached.

Even though the canal's significance was soon eclipsed by the advent of trains and, later, the internal combustion engine, significant parts of the old canal have survived into modern times. Several sections can be paddled today, and extensive parts of the old canal farther north remain in use, having been incorporated into New York State's modern canal system, which opened in 1918. Today there are eleven locks (numbered 1 through 12, with no #10) to be transited between the Hudson River and Lake Champlain, a trip of nearly sixty-four miles—forty miles from Troy to Fort Edward along the Hudson River, and another twenty-four miles following a dug channel from Fort Edward to Whitehall at the head of Lake Champlain.

*Paddles on the lower Champlain Canal, from Albany to Mechanicville, were explored in *A Kayaker's Guide to New York's Capital Region* (Black Dome Press, 2010).

East Shore:
Hudson River
& Champlain Canal

Champlain Canal Lock C-4 (Schaghticoke)
At the Confluence of the Hudson and Hoosic Rivers

38

■ **Launch Site:** Champlain Canal Lock C-4 Park, off of Stillwater Bridge Road in Schaghticoke (Rensselaer County); 0.3-mile carry along trail to put-in at confluence of the Hudson River and the Hoosic River; open daily from 7 AM–4 PM during regular boating season. For more information: Lock C-4, (518) 664-5261; Lock C-3, (518) 664-5171.

■ **Delorme NYS Atlas & Gazetteer:** p. 67, A4–5; **GPS:** Parking—42°55.86'N; 73°39.28'W; Launch—42°55.72'N; 73°39.51'W

■ **Destinations & Mileages:** *Northeast*: up Hoosic River and back—0.2 mile (round-trip). *South*: to south end of Green Island—0.7 mile; around Green Island—1.2 miles; from Green Island to Boston & Maine Railroad Bridge—0.3 mile (1.0 mile from launch); from Boston & Maine Railroad Bridge to Lock C-3— 0.4 mile (1.4 miles from launch). *North*: to Lock C-4—0.3 mile.

■ **Comments:** Read "Caution" beginning on page xxi and Champlain Canal & Environs Advisory on page 168.

Stay a safe distance back from Lock C-4 and Lock C-3 and dam (unless you are locking through) and from the Stillwater Dam on the west side of the Hudson River.

A carrier would be helpful to reach the put-in.

Keep an eye out for eagles below Lock C-4.

Directions: From Mechanicville (junction of Rtes. 67 East & 4/32) proceed north on Rte. 4/32. In 2.7 miles turn right at a blinking traffic light onto Rte. 125. Go east for 0.2 mile, crossing both the Hudson River and the Champlain Canal in the process. As soon as you reach the end of the bridge, turn right onto Stillwater Bridge Road (look for signs indicating Lock C-4), drive south for 0.5 mile to a parking area, and park your vehicle.

From where Stillwater Bridge Road turns abruptly right into the parking area, follow a path into the woods, heading south. It leads in less than 0.3 mile to a gentle descent to the edge of the water at the confluence of the Hudson and Hoosic rivers.

The Paddle:

The name Stillwater came from early settlers who found the waters by the village to be calm compared to the rapids farther downstream. The original name of the village, however, was Up-Town, which later shortened to Upton.[1] Except for Saratoga, which burned down in 1745, Stillwater is the earliest European settlement in New York north of the confluence of the Hudson and Mohawk rivers.[2] The area between Stillwater and Mechanicville was the site of many industries, some bound to the Champlain Canal and some to the Hudson River.

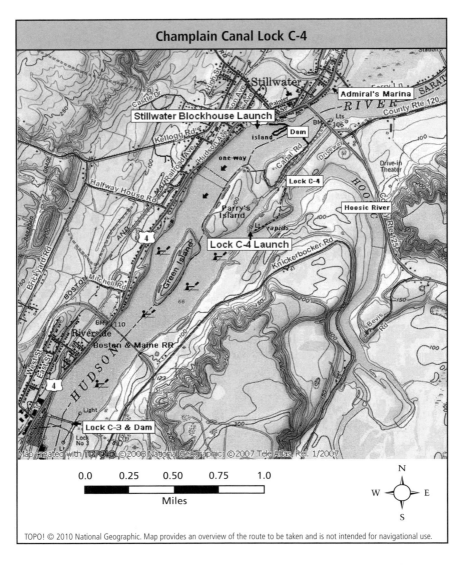

Champlain Canal Lock C-4

TOPO! © 2010 National Geographic. Map provides an overview of the route to be taken and is not intended for navigational use.

Northeast—The Hoosic River is a substantial stream that rises from the Cheshire Reservoir in Massachusetts and produces the Great Falls of the Hoosic River at Schaghticoke before it flows into the Hudson River after traveling a total of 70 miles. The river is fed by a 720-square-mile watershed that includes the Mt. Greylock Reservation (where Massachusetts's highest peak can be found). Hoosic (also spelled Hoosac and Hoosick) is a Native American word for "the stony place."[3] In addition the river has been called informally The Hoosey. The Hoosic has the distinction of being the only river to knit

▶ **Champlain Canal Lock C-4 (Schaghticoke)**

together Massachusetts, Vermont, and New York State.[4] At one time a main Algonquian Indian trail followed the Hoosic River Valley into New England from the Hudson River.[5]

The paddle up the Hoosic River starts off promising enough, but quickly degenerates into shallows and rapids by 0.05 mile, making further progress difficult and eventually impossible.

South—Excellent views of shale bluffs around the various islands are a dominant feature of this paddle. Many of these bluffs rise straight up to a height of 20–25 feet. Heading southwest you will reach the south end of Parry's Island in 0.2 mile. From there it is best to turn right (west) into the channel between Parry's Island and Green Island, and then circumnavigate 0.4-mile-long Green Island by going counterclockwise, a trek of 1.2 miles. Be prepared for a significant amount of current as you enter the channel between the two islands, as well as along the west side of Green Island.

As you round the south tip of Green Island, you will see the Boston & Maine Railroad Bridge 0.3 mile farther downstream, built in 1879 by the Boston, Hoosic Tunnel & Western Railway Company.[6] The bridge has an adjustable level, allowing it to be raised up and down to accommodate boats exceeding a height of 15.5 feet. A 10-foot-wide beach of crumbled shale at the south end of Green Island provides a convenient spot to pull in for a moment if you need a respite.

Farther downstream are Champlain Canal Lock C-3 and the Riverside Dam at a distance of 0.7 mile from the south end of Green Island, or 1.4 miles from the launch site. On the west bank next to the dam is the NYSEG Upper Mechanicville Hydroelectric Generating Facility.

As you paddle back north along the east side of Green Island, take note of how steeply cut the banks are on both sides of the river. Although Green Island is heavily forested, the woods curiously begin 75–100 feet back from the edge of this side of the escarpment.

North—Paddling north up the canal will take you to Lock C-4 in a distance of 0.3 mile. If you wish to enter Lock C-4 and be raised to the next elevation, further progress upstream is possible. Above Lock C-4 the dam created a much wider, lakelike portion of the Hudson, backing up the river for nearly 15 miles and significantly altering the topography of the Hoosic River's confluence with the Hudson. Before then three separate islands existed—Green Island, Parry's Island, and Vandenberg's Island. Vandenberg's Island is now the peninsula encompassing Lock C-4 and its nature trail. A tiny stream called the Dwaas Kill (Dutch for "connecting stream"), which separated Vandenberg's Island from the mainland, was filled in at the time of the lock's creation.[7]

Alternate Launch Site

Stillwater Blockhouse (Stillwater)

- ◼ **Launch Site:** Stillwater Blockhouse Park, off of Rte. 4/32 in Stillwater (Saratoga County); 25-foot carry down slope to water's edge; slip-in. For more information: (518) 664-1847 ext. 11; Lock C-4, (518) 664-5261; Lock C-3, (518) 664-5171.
- ◼ **Delorme NYS Atlas & Gazetteer:** p. 67, A4–5; **GPS:** 42°56.27'N; 73°39.41'W
- ◼ **Destinations & Mileages:** *North*: to upstream island—0.2 mile (round-trip). *South* (one-way): to south tip of Parry's Island—0.6 mile; to south tip of Green Island—1.2 miles; around Green Island—1.2 miles; to Riverside Dam & Lock C-3—2.0 miles; from south tip of Green Island to mouth of Hoosic River—0.6 mile; up Hoosic River—0.05 mile; from south tip of Green Island to Lock C-4— 1.0 mile.
- ◼ **Comments:** Read "Caution" beginning on page xxi and Champlain Canal & Environs Advisory on page 168.

  The paddle south should be considered a one-way paddle. The current along the west channel is consistently strong and its waters are shallow, making it a demanding and extremely difficult paddle the last 0.6 mile back to the block-house. Therefore, take out either at the Champlain Canal Lock C-4 launch (which involves a 0.3-mile portage) or "lock through" Lock C-4 and take out at the Admiral's Marina (see chapter "Stillwater Bridge"). Either exit will allow you to enjoy the fast ride downstream from the Stillwater Blockhouse launch without having to worry about fighting the current to get back upstream.

  Stay a safe distance back from the Stillwater dam, Lock C-3 and dam, and Lock C-4 (unless you are locking through).

Directions: From Mechanicville (junction of Rtes. 67 East & 4/32) proceed north on Rte. 4/32 for 2.5 miles. As soon as you cross over Schuyler Creek, turn right into the parking area for the Stillwater Blockhouse Park. The informal put-in is just upriver from where Schuyler Creek comes into the Hudson River.

The Paddle:

North—Head upstream for 0.1 mile to reach a slender, scraggly looking, 0.05-mile-long island. The rocky end of the island abuts the Stillwater Dam, making a circumnavigation of the island impossible. Stay a safe distance back from the dam to avoid hydraulics. The building next to the west side of the dam is the Stillwater Hydroelectric Project.

South—Head downstream, veering diagonally toward Parry's Island (the land mass to your east). The current will carry you along quickly. In over 0.6 mile you will pass by the south end of Parry's Island. From there the route duplicates the directions given on page 175.

▶ **Champlain Canal Lock C-4 (Schaghticoke)**

Additional Point of Interest: The Stillwater Blockhouse is a replica of an eighteenth-century fortification and once stood in the Saratoga National Historical Park. In the eighteenth century, blockhouses such as this provided shelter and protection to nearby settlers who were under attack. The replica was built in 1927 using timber borrowed from actual Revolutionary War structures, following the detailed drawings of Thomas Anburye in *Travels through the Interior Parts of America*. The replica originally served as the visitors center for the Saratoga National Historical Park, but eventually became too small and confining. It was then donated in 1975 to the town of Stillwater, which set it up on its present location in 1999.[8] The building is surrounded by two acres of land including a paved promenade, picnic tables, benches, and great views of the Hudson River. The interior of the blockhouse is open seasonally, Wednesday through Sunday from 12 PM–4 PM, from the first Saturday before Memorial Day to the Sunday before Columbus Day. For more information: (518) 664-1847.

PERIOD BLOCK HOUSE. BEMIS HEIGHTS. N. Y. SARATOGA BATTLEFIELD   9

The Stillwater Blockhouse was formerly located at Bemis Heights in the Saratoga National Historical Park. Postcard ca.1940.

39

Clarks Mills Lower Dam Access #1 (Clarks Mills)
Accessing the Batten Kill

- **Launch Site:** Batten Kill at Clarks Mills Lower Dam (Washington County); 200-foot carry on dirt road to put-in
- **Delorme NYS Atlas & Gazetteer:** p. 81, CD5; **GPS:** 43°06.93'N; 73°34.04'W
- **Destinations & Mileages:** *East*: to railroad bridge stone piers—0.3 mile; to Clarks Mills Upper Dam & island—0.8 mile.
- **Comments:** Read "Caution" beginning on page xxi and Champlain Canal & Environs Advisory on page 168.

  Stay a safe distance back from the Clarks Mills Lower Dam, immediately left of the launch site and set off by orange buoys. Don't put in if the current looks strong. If you have any doubts about your ability to handle the current, do not launch from this site.

  The Clarks Mills Lower Dam is located on the private property of the Hollingsworth & Vose Co., and access is allowed through their generosity and civic-mindedness.

Directions: From Schuylerville (junction of Rtes. 29 East & 4/32) go east on Rte. 29 for 0.7 mile, crossing over the Hudson River in the process. Turn left onto River Road (Rte. 113) and drive north for 1.3 miles, then turn right into a small pull-off just before crossing over a cement arch bridge spanning the Batten Kill.

Carry your watercraft along a dirt road for several hundred feet to the put-in (which can also be driven to, although you may then have to back out carefully).

The Paddle:

Maps and books have spelled the name of the hamlet in several different ways including Clark Mills and Clarks Mill. The hamlet was named after Hiram Clark, who in 1830 built a sawmill, a planing mill, and a plaster mill on the Batten Kill, all powered by a dam he had constructed.[1] These businesses prospered for fifty years.

In 1891, I. C. Blandy and three associates purchased land on both sides of the Batten Kill and opened a pulp mill in 1904. Later they established a paper mill, which is still operated today by the Hollingsworth & Vose Company.[2] Hollingsworth & Vose continue to be heavily involved in technical, filter, and specialty papers such as non-wovens and advanced composites.

The Clarks Mills Lower Dam has created a wide, bay-like area at the beginning of the paddle. If you keep veering to the right you will enter (or portage, when the water level is down) into a tiny cove where water is bled off by the Hollingsworth & Vose Co. for power generation.

▶ **Clarks Mills Lower Dam Access #1 (Clark's Mills)**

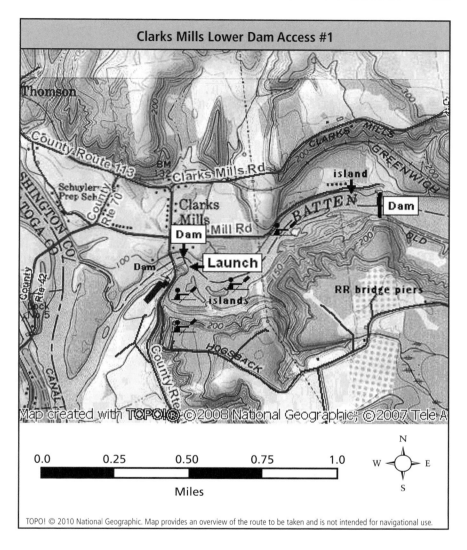

Clarks Mills Lower Dam Access #1

TOPO! © 2010 National Geographic. Map provides an overview of the route to be taken and is not intended for navigational use.

East—From the launch, paddle south momentarily and then east as you pass between a small marshy island to your left and the east bank of the river to your right. In 0.3 mile you will paddle between the stone piers of an abandoned railroad bridge that once crossed over the Batten Kill. Continue east for another 0.5 mile before encountering the upper dam. A tiny island, 0.1-mile downstream from the dam, is the turnaround point.

Historically, the Batten Kill is significant for being the latter part of the route Major General Arthur St. Clair chose in his 100-mile retreat in late June 1777 when Fort Ticonderoga was threatened by British cannon fire from Mt. Defiance. After reaching Manchester, Vermont, St. Clair took his men down to Fort Miller, following the Batten Kill.[3]

The Lower Dam at Clarks Mills has created a small impoundment. Photograph 2009.

▶ **Clarks Mills Lower Dam Access #1 (Clarks Mills)**

Champlain Canal above Lock C-6 (Fort Miller)
Bypassing an Impassable Section of the Hudson River

40

- **Launch Site:** Champlain Canal (Washington County); 20-foot carry to informal put-in at north end of parking area. For more information: Champlain Canal Lock C-6, (518) 747-4614.
- **Delorme NYS Atlas & Gazetteer:** p. 81, C5; **GPS:** 43°10.22'N; 73°34.77'W
- **Destinations & Mileages:** *North*: to North River Bridge—0.6 mile; to Crocker's Reef Guard Gate—1.4 miles; to Hudson River—2.0 miles. *South*: to Fort Miller Road bridge—0.2 mile; to Lock C-6—0.5 mile.
- **Comments:** Read "Caution" beginning on page xxi and Champlain Canal & Environs Advisory on page 168.

  Although Lock C-6 is close at hand, no direct access to the canal is provided from the grounds at the lock. Paddlers should stay back from Lock C-6 unless planning to "lock through."

  This paddle can be combined with a quick paddle on the small pond directly across the road (see chapter "Champlain Canal Pond").

Directions: From Schuylerville (junction of Rtes. 29 West & 4/32) go north on Rte. 4, crossing over the Hudson River at 1.8 miles. Along the way, at 2.5 miles, you will pass by a pull-off on your right for the Denton Wildlife Sanctuary. If you follow the sanctuary path east on foot for 100 feet you will see part of the old Champlain Canal to your right. At 5.0 miles you will come to large pull-offs on opposite sides of the road. Turn left into the pull-off on the west side of the road.

From Fort Edward where Rte. 4 crosses over the Champlain Canal, drive south for 6.7 miles. Turn right into the pull-off on the west side of the road.

The Paddle:

Fort Miller is named after Colonel Miller, who built a fort during the French and Indian War on the side of the river opposite today's Fort Miller.[1]

This paddle navigates a section of the Champlain Canal that bypasses the Hudson River. The river is mostly out of sight, some 0.4 mile to the west, during the bulk of this paddle. One section of the Hudson River west of Rte. 4 was called the Little Carrying Place because it was a good place to ford the river in the seventeenth and eighteenth centuries.[2]

North—Follow the canal upstream as it parallels Rte. 4 to your right. At 0.6 mile you will pass under the North River Road Bridge, then, at 1.4 miles, under the Crocker's Reef Guard Gate, whose metal gate looms overhead like the blade of a guillotine. The Hudson River is reached at 2.0 miles.

Although not visible during the paddle, Galusha Island and Thompson Island, both part of the Hudson River landscape, are nearby to the west but inaccessible because of rapids and dams 0.5 mile upstream on the Hudson River from its junction with the Lock C-6 channel.

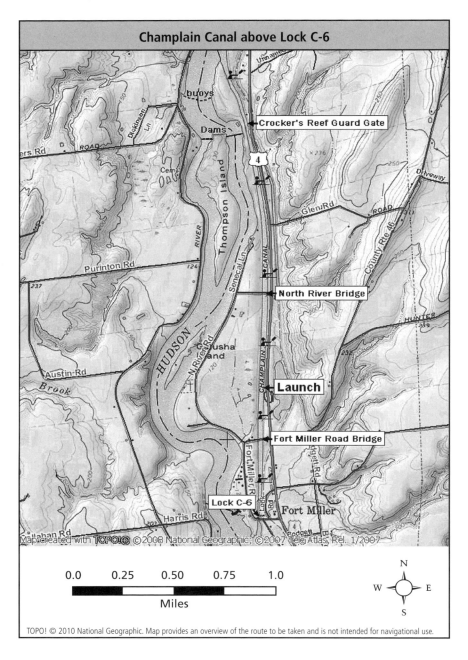

South—Heading downstream you will pass under the Fort Miller Road bridge in less than 0.2 mile. Lock C-6 is reached at 0.5 mile.

▶ **Champlain Canal above Lock C-6 (Fort Miller)**

Moses Kill (south of Fort Edward)
Backwaters of the Hudson River Have Created an Idyllic Paddle   **41**

- **Launch Site:** Moses Kill (Washington County); 0.05-mile carry to river's edge
- **Delorme NYS Atlas & Gazetteer:** p. 81, C5; **GPS:** 43°12.00'N; 73°34.88'W
- **Destinations & Mileages:** *Northeast*: to Moses Kill Aqueduct—0.3 mile; to old trolley bridge—0.4 mile; to Dead Creek—1.4 miles; to rusted bridge—1.6 miles; to Woodard Road bridge—2.3 miles. *North*: to south end of Griffin Island—0.3 mile; around Griffin Island—2.0 miles. *South*: to Lock C-6 canal channel—0.2 mile.
- **Comments:** Read "Caution" beginning on page xxi and Champlain Canal & Environs Advisory on page 168.

    Moses Kill—The current is generally mild, particularly the farther upstream you go, except following snowmelt or heavy rains.

    Hudson River—South from the Moses Kill, stay to the north of a string of buoys 0.3 mile upstream from dams located by Thompson Island.

Directions: From Schuylerville (junction of Rtes. 4/32 & 29 West) head north on Rte. 4 for 7 miles. After going less than 0.1 mile past the south end of the bridge over the Moses Kill, turn right into a small opening between the guardrails that leads immediately to an overgrown concrete road.

From Fort Edward (junction of Rtes. 4 & 197 East) drive south on Rte. 4 for 4.8 miles. Turn left into a small opening in the guardrails that leads immediately to an overgrown concrete road. If you reach the Moses Kill, you have gone too far.

From the opening in the guardrails, the concrete road heads back south toward the Moses Kill and pulls away from Rte. 4. It is possible to drive to the end of this abandoned 0.05-mile-long road, but invading bushes close in on the road and give the passageway a claustrophobic feel. You would be hemmed in at the end of the road should another paddler or angler pull in near the guardrails, blocking the exit. For this reason it makes sense to back into the opening between the guardrails and then pull forward so that you are not obstructing the road behind you but are clearly in sight. That way no one will pull in and inadvertently block your way out.

From the guardrails a 0.05-mile-long carry is required. When you come to the end of the concrete road—a continuation of Richardson Lane from the other side of the Moses Kill—proceed to your right and follow a short path that leads down to the stream, where you can put in approximately 100 feet upstream from the Rte. 4 bridge.

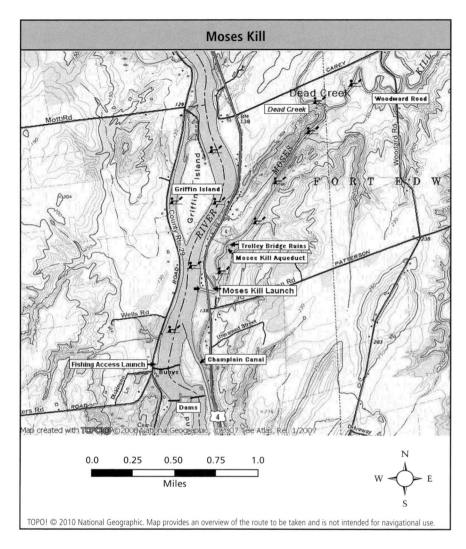

Moses Kill

0.0   0.25   0.50   0.75   1.0

Miles

N
W ⟡ E
S

TOPO! © 2010 National Geographic. Map provides an overview of the route to be taken and is not intended for navigational use.

The Paddle:

The Moses Kill is a substantial tributary to the Hudson River that rises north of North Argyle. Back in the mid-1800s a tiny hamlet called Moses Kill (also known as Mock) thrived nearby. For a brief period of time, the suffragette Susan B. Anthony taught school here.[1]

Northeast—Follow the Moses Kill upstream, quickly passing by an old bridge abutment on the south bank of the stream. This part of the stream is bay-like. At 0.3 mile you will pass by the ruins of the Moses Kill Aqueduct, which was built around 1862 as part of the enlarged Champlain Canal.[2] The large lime-

▶ **Moses Kill (south of Fort Edward)**

stone blocks are still well intact and form three enormous structures, the center one being near the middle of the stream. Take note of the center piling's tuning-fork shape, which supported the wooden canal trough.

Within another 0.1 mile you will paddle under the single-span, 200-foot arch of an old cement trolley bridge. From there the stream proceeds east in a fairly straight line for another 0.5 mile.

At 0.9 mile, turning right, you will begin making your way through a rocky gorge with walls of shale rising up as high as 20 feet. There are two shallow shale ledges with rapids extending across the full length of the stream that have to be negotiated. When you come to the first one, take out along the rocky shoreline to your left and put in above the rapids. This can easily be done. At the second shelf you may be able to push your way upstream through the shallows and rapids using your hands. If not, get out and portage.

At 1.4 miles you will reach Dead Creek, a small stream that enters on your left almost exactly where high-tension lines cross the Moses Kill. Dead Creek can be explored northwest for a short distance depending upon conditions.

From this point on the Moses Kill becomes narrower and more contorted, and the banks, ranging in height from 5–20 feet, are more earthen. It is likely that you will encounter blowdown, which you may be able to bypass (although this will vary from year to year). At around 1.6 miles you will pass under a rusted metal bridge. Look to your left to see a farm windmill in the adjacent field.

At 2.3 miles the Woodard Road bridge will come into view. Expect to portage around a tiny shelf with rapids just before reaching the bridge. This can easily be accomplished by getting out on the right-hand side of the creek.

If you need to exit the river, the Woodard Road bridge could be used in an emergency. The northeast end of the bridge is a fisherman's "catch & release" site, but it is not designed for river access.

Depending upon conditions, you can continue upstream from the Woodard Road bridge for another 0.2–0.4 mile.

North—Paddle downstream on the Moses Kill for less than 0.1 mile, going under the Rte. 4 bridge, and turn right onto the Hudson River. In 0.3 mile you will reach the south end of Griffin Island, to your left.

Griffin Island is 0.9 mile long and 0.3 mile across at its widest. Years ago a causeway extended out from the west shoreline, allowing farmers to access the island. During periods of high waters, however, the causeway would be temporarily submerged. A bridge near the northwest end of the island now connects it to the mainland and is high enough to allow paddlers to pass under. The island can be circumnavigated in 2.0 miles. Be sure to look for sea planes moored on the west side of the island.

The west side of the island provides one of only two backwater areas along a 40-mile length of the upper Hudson for largemouth bass to spawn and nurse.[3]

If you were to continue farther north, you would pass by Black House Creek, to your right, at 2.3 miles and then the mouth of the Snook Kill, coming in on your left, at 2.4 miles. The Snook Kill can be followed upstream, depending upon conditions (such as blowdown), for 1.0 mile. The south tip of Rogers Island is another 2.0 miles farther upstream.

South—Paddle downstream on the Moses Kill for less than 0.05 mile and then turn left onto the Hudson River. Within 0.2 mile you will reach the north end of a 2.7-mile-long canal that bypasses a hazardous, impassable section of the Hudson River. Were you to follow the canal south it would lead to Lock C-6 at Fort Miller in 2.7 miles.

Alternate Launch Site

Fishing Access Site (Jewell Corner)

- **Launch Site:** Catch & Release Fishing Access site off of West River Road (Saratoga County); slip-in
- **Delorme NYS Atlas & Gazetteer:** p. 81, C5; **GPS:** 43°11.67'N; 73°35.21'W
- **Destinations & Mileages:** *Northeast*: to Lock C-6 canal—0.2 mile; to Moses Kill—0.4 mile; up Moses Kill to aqueduct—0.7 mile; up Moses Kill to old trolley bridge—0.8 mile; up Moses Kill to Dead Creek—1.8 miles; up Moses Kill to rusted bridge—2.0 miles; up Moses Kill to Woodard Road bridge—2.7 miles. *North*: to south tip of Griffin Island—0.6 mile; around Griffin Island—2.0 miles.
- **Comments:** Read "Caution" beginning on page xxi and Champlain Canal & Environs Advisory on page 168.
  The put-in is at the mouth of a small stream next to a line of orange buoys that shepherd boaters to the east side of the river and into the Champlain Canal channel. For safety reasons stay on the north side of the buoys. Downstream, 0.3 mile farther, await the unnegotiable 4-foot-high Thompson Island dams.

Directions: From Schuylerville (junction of Rtes. 4/32 & 29 West) drive north on Rte. 32 for 1.8 miles until you come to a fork. Follow Rte. 32 northwest as Rte. 4 veers northeast and crosses over the Hudson River. Heading uphill you will reach the hamlet of Bacon Hill in 0.9 mile. Turn right onto West River Road (County Rte. 29) and proceed north for 4.9 miles. Along the way you will pass by Peters Road to your left, at 4.7 miles. Turn right onto a tiny, narrow dirt road that looks more like a driveway (it is very easy to miss). The dirt road is 0.2 mile after Peters Road, and 0.2 mile before Wells Lane, to your left.

From west of Fort Edward (junction of Rtes. 197 West & County Rte. 29) turn onto Rte. 29 (West River Road) and drive south for over 4.8 miles. Turn left onto a tiny narrow road that is more like a driveway, 0.2 mile after passing by Wells Lane to your right, and 0.2 mile before reaching Peters Road, also on your right.

The dirt road leads to the river's edge in less than 75 feet, but it is so narrow that only two or three cars can park one behind the other. For this reason it is

▶ **Moses Kill (south of Fort Edward)**

best to park on West River Road, off to the side. Otherwise it would be easy to get hemmed in by somebody thoughtlessly parked behind you.

Carry your watercraft 50 feet down this tiny earthen road. Just before you get to the water's edge, turn left and follow a faint path for 50 feet that leads to the inlet of the small unnamed tributary. Put in there, on the north side of the orange buoys whose protective line extends across the river several feet away to your right.

The old trolley bridge is abandoned but not forgotten. Photograph 2010.

42 | Fort Edward Public Dock (Fort Edward)
Accessing the Champlain Canal above Lock C-7

■ **Launch Site:** Fort Edward Public Dock & informal launch site (Washington County); short carry to put-in from public dock. For more information: The Fort Edward Historical Association, 22 Broadway, Fort Edward, NY, (518) 747-9600; Champlain Canal Lock C-7, (518) 747-5520; Champlain Canal Lock C-8, (518) 747-6021.

■ **Delorme NYS Atlas & Gazetteer:** p. 81, BC5; **GPS:** 43°15.64'N; 73°34.84'W

■ **Destinations & Mileages:** *Northeast*: to Rte. 197 bridge—0.4 mile; to East Street Bridge—1.1 miles; to Lock C-8—1.9 miles. *Southwest*: to Lock C-7—0.2 mile.

■ **Comments:** Read "Caution" beginning on page xxi and Champlain Canal & Environs Advisory on page 168.
  Stay back from Lock C-7 and Lock C-8 unless you are planning to "lock through."

Directions: From Fort Edward (junction of Rtes. 4 & 197 East) go south on Rte. 4 for 0.2 mile. Just before crossing over the Champlain Canal via the Rte. 4/Broadway Street Bridge, turn left into a large dirt parking area.

Carry your watercraft north for 50 feet to the public park adjacent to the parking area, and then across the lawn to the Fort Edward Public Dock, where access to the canal is provided from a long dock. This is a carry of no more than a couple of hundred feet from the car. Take note that the park is directly across the street from the Canal Maintenance Facility. The building adjacent to the public park is used by the John Burke Research Center and the Fort Edward Historical Association. The historical association was founded in 1925 and has played a vital role over the years in preserving the town's history.

The Paddle:

Fort Edward has the distinction of being both the site of the "Great Carrying Place," a colonial portage route that bypassed formidable waterfalls upstream, and a key location on the "Great War Path" between English and French colonies.

Northeast—Heading upstream you will come to the Rte. 197 Bridge that spans the Champlain Canal in 0.4 mile. The East Street Bridge is reached in 1.1 miles. At 1.9 miles you will arrive at Lock C-8, which is a good turnaround point unless you plan to lock through to go farther northeast. Should you continue through Lock C-8, you will be raised to an elevation of 140 feet above sea level.

Southwest—Unless you plan to go through Lock C-7 and out onto the Hudson River, this will be a short paddle.

In over 0.2 mile you will come to the lock where the Champlain Canal, for the first time since leaving the Waterford area, finally pulls away completely from the Hudson River and heads northeast toward Lake Champlain. Lock C-7

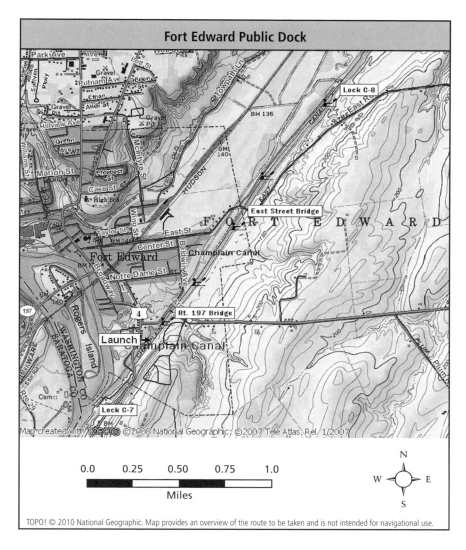

is a 10-foot-high lift-lock that brings the canal's waterway up to a height of 129 feet above sea level. (Between Locks C-8 and C-9 the waterway reaches a summit height of 140 feet. Starting between Locks C-9 and C-11 [there is no Lock C-10] the waterway drops back to 124 feet and continues to descend at each lock until it reaches Lake Champlain at Whitehall at an elevation of approximately 97 feet above sea level.[1])

Earlier versions of the Champlain Canal still exist. You can see vestiges of the old canal running from Fort Edward to Smiths Basin about 0.4 mile west of the current Champlain Canal. An even earlier version exists, however—at least on paper. Philip Schuyler, commander of the Northern Department of the Continental Army during the Revolutionary War, designed a canal that would link the Hudson River with Lake Champlain. After the Revolution he formed the Northern Inland Lock Navigation Company to carry out his plan. He figured that, if a canal was constructed between Bond Creek and Wood Creek, the two creeks could then be dredged and locks established, making them serviceable to boats. Schuyler already knew that, even without dredging and the construction of locks, Wood Creek was navigable to canoes and light bark boats during spring floods, so the plan seemed eminently feasible. Work commenced on the canal in June 1794, but quickly came to a halt when funds ran out.[2] Another thirty years had to go by before canal building began again at Fort Edward.

Today, Wood Creek can be seen entering the modern Champlain Canal just west of Smiths Basin, and Bond Creek enters the old Champlain Canal at Dunhams Basin near where Rte. 196 crosses the canals.

▶ **Fort Edward Public Dock (Fort Edward)**

West Shore: Hudson River & Champlain Canal

43

Stillwater Bridge (Stillwater)
Exploring the Hudson River North of the Stillwater Bridge

- **Launch Site:** Admiral's Marina off of Rte. 4/32 in Stillwater (Saratoga County); boat launch ramp; modest launch fee. The marina is closed Monday, opens 4 PM Tuesday through Friday, and noontime on Saturday & Sunday. For more information: Admiral's Marina, Rte. 4/32, Stillwater, NY 12170, (518) 664-9039; Lock C-4 (518) 664-5261.
- **Delorme NYS Atlas & Gazetteer:** p. 67, A4–5; **GPS:** 42°56.41'N; 73°38.94'W
- **Destinations & Mileages:** *Northeast*: to Mill Hollow Brook—0.8 mile; to Bemis Heights—3.0 miles. *Southwest*: to Stillwater Bridge—0.05 mile. *South*: to Lock C-4 canal—0.2 mile; down canal to Lock C-4—0.4 mile.
- **Comments:** Read "Caution" beginning on page xxi and Champlain Canal & Environs Advisory on page 168.
  Stay a safe distance back from the Stillwater dam. Do not approach Lock C-4 unless you are planning to "lock through."

Directions: From Stillwater (junction of Rtes. 4/32/Hudson Avenue & Rte. 125/Stillwater Bridge Road) drive north on Rte. 4 for 0.05 mile. Turn right into Admiral's Marina. If you reach Ferry Lane, you have gone too far.

The Paddle:
Stillwater played an important role in the eighteenth-century military conflicts in New York State. In 1709, Col. Peter Philip Schuyler built Fort Ingoldsby, a stockaded fort named after Lieutenant-Governor Major Richard Ingoldsby. It was located near present-day Stillwater and was used for storing provisions. In 1756 the fort was replaced by Fort Winslow, named after the general who had it built while engaged on a northern expedition. Later, during the American Revolution, the pivotal Battle of Saratoga raged nearby.[1]

Earlier, between 1730 and 1740, settlers began to take root in Stillwater, and the town became incorporated in 1816.[2] Today Stillwater is referred to as a "bedroom community"; many of its residents commute daily to jobs in the Capital District.

Northeast—From the put-in head upstream, going northeast. In 0.8 mile you will pass by Mill Hollow Brook to your right. This small brook, which rises north of Schaghticoke, can be explored upstream, but only for a short distance before it narrows and becomes too shallow to progress any farther.

Continuing upstream on the Hudson River, you will eventually reach Bemis Heights to your left at 3.0 miles where a small stream flows into the Hudson. Other than the stream, there is very little to distinguish this historic point from its surroundings, but Bemis Heights is the spot where the second and final engagement of the Battle of Saratoga, the Battle of Bemis Heights, took place on October 7, 1777.

▶ **Stillwater Bridge (Stillwater)**

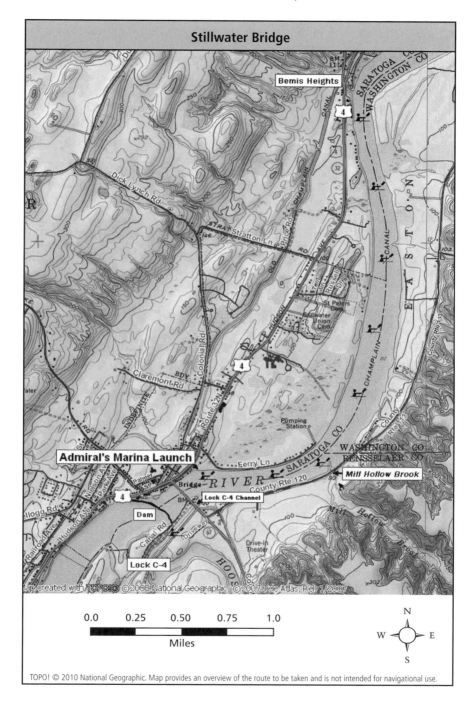

Stillwater Bridge

Bemis Heights

Admiral's Marina Launch

Mill Hollow Brook

WASHINGTON CO.
RENSSELAER CO.

Lock C-4 Channel

Dam

Lock C-4

map created with TOPO!® ©2008 National Geographic; ©2007 Tele Atlas, Rel. 1/2007

0.0   0.25   0.50   0.75   1.0

Miles

N
W   E
S

TOPO! © 2010 National Geographic. Map provides an overview of the route to be taken and is not intended for navigational use.

Southwest—In 0.05 mile you will pass under the Stillwater Bridge. Go no farther downstream. The unrunnable Stillwater dam is straight ahead, less than 0.2 mile away. Prior to the twentieth century the Stillwater dam powered a number of notable industries—the Newland & Denison knitting mill (1873), the Mosher & Allen paper mill (1847), the Ephraim Newland hosiery mill (1873), the D. & W. Pemble straw-board mill (1866), and the Gardner Howland & Sons paper mill (1863).[3]

To the right of the 0.3-mile-long dam is the Stillwater Hydroelectric Project, visible along the west bank. The plant, constructed in 1993, generates 3.4 megawatts of power.

South—Head downstream and across the river for nearly 0.2 mile until you reach the rock-cut channel leading to Lock C-4. You can paddle into the canal and head southwest for 0.4 mile before reaching Lock C-4. In doing so you will pass under the east end of the Stillwater Bridge.

Four birds share a quiet moment. Photograph 2009.

▶ **Stillwater Bridge (Stillwater)**

River Road Access (Bemis Heights)
A Section of the Hudson River Paralleled by the Old Champlain Canal

44

■ **Launch Site:** Fishing access site along rocky west bank of Hudson River (Saratoga County); rocky access

■ **Delorme NYS Atlas & Gazetteer:** p. 81, D5; **GPS:** 43°00.35'N; 73°36.12'W

■ **Destinations & Mileages:** *North*: to McAuley Brook—0.3 mile; to Schuyler Brook—0.9 mile; to Ensign Brook—1.7 miles; to Flately Brook—3.0 miles; to The Cove—3.3 miles; up The Cove—0.7 mile. *South*: to Kroma Kill—0.6 mile; to Kidney Creek—1.8 miles; to Mill Creek—2.6 miles; to Bemis Heights—3.1 miles.

■ **Comments:** Read "Caution" beginning on page xxi and Champlain Canal & Environs Advisory on page 168.

Getting into the river can be challenging because of the rocky shoreline.

Directions: From Bemis Heights (junction of Rtes. 4 & 32) drive north on Rte. 4 for 2.8 miles (at 2.3 miles you will pass by the entrance to the Saratoga National Historical Park on your left). Turn right onto River Road.

From Schuylerville (junction of Rtes. 32/4 & 29 East) drive south on Rte. 4 for 6.9 miles and turn left onto River Road (note: ignore the first left-hand turn for River Road, at 5.1 miles).

From either direction, go east on River Road for 0.1 mile and park at the fishing access site where the road bends sharply to the left and begins paralleling the Hudson River. Observe signs and park only where permitted.

The Paddle:
This entire paddle parallels the old Champlain Canal, which remains out of sight along the west side of Route 4. The trek leads you along a less-developed section of the Hudson River.

North—Heading upstream you will pass by a series of named streams, all to your right: McAuley Brook at 0.3 mile; Schuyler Brook at 0.9 mile; Ensign Brook at 1.7 miles; and Flately Brook at 3.0 miles. Several small unnamed streams will also be evident to your left as you make your way upriver.

When you reach 3.3 miles, bear left at a fork in the river and enter The Cove, which can be explored for 0.7 mile up to the Alcove (Coveville) Marina & Pub, and possibly even 0.2 mile farther with a portage.

South—Heading downstream you will pass by the Kroma Kill on your right at 0.6 mile as it flows out of the Saratoga National Historical Park. The creek can be followed upstream for several hundred feet to Rte. 4. Its name may be a corruption of an old Dutch word for "crooked."[1]

At 1.8 miles Kidney Creek comes in on your left. Back in the 1800s Kidney Creek was considered a "sluggish, clay laden brook" whose banks were constantly in a state of collapse. It wasn't until the twentieth century that highway department engineers were finally able to stabilize the creek.[2]

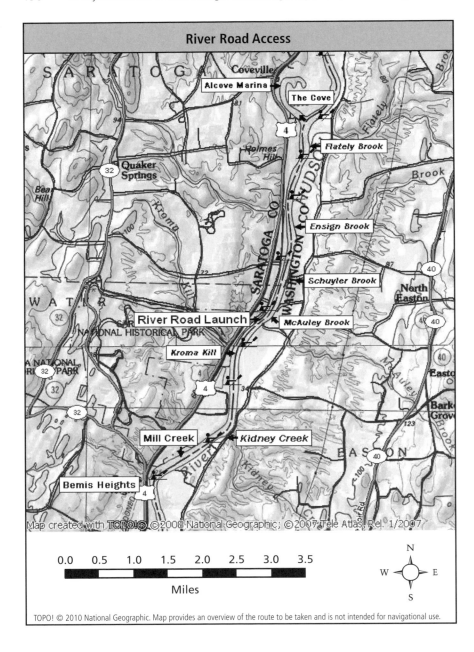

▶ **River Road Access (Bemis Heights)**

At 2.6 miles you will pass by Mill Creek, on your right, which rises from the Saratoga National Historical Park.

Bemis Heights, where a fairly nondescript stream enters on your right, is reached at 3.1 miles. Bemis Heights is named after Jotham Bemis, Jr., an early tavern owner.[3] The 102-foot elevation of the village, which is roughly 170 miles from the Atlantic Ocean, shows how little the Hudson River has to descend from this point to reach sea level.

Were you to continue south for another 2.9 miles, you would reach Lock C-4 & dam in Stillwater at 6.0 miles.

Additional Point of Interest: A 0.3-mile-long section of the old Champlain Canal can be seen by driving north on Rte. 4 for another 1.0 mile and turning left onto Wilbur Road (a Blue Star Memorial Highway). Within 100 feet you will come to a pull-off on your right. Park there, cross the road, and then walk south along a towpath following the old Champlain Canal for 0.3 mile. The towpath and canal both come to an end at the town line.

45 Fishing Access Site #1 (Coveville)
More Opportunities for Exploring the Hudson River

- ■ **Launch Site:** Fishing Access Site; slip in along west bank of Hudson River (Saratoga County)
- ■ **Delorme NYS Atlas & Gazetteer:** p. 81, D5; **GPS:** 43°02.17'N; 73°35.57'W
- ■ **Destinations & Mileages:** *North*: to Flately Brook—0.6 mile; to The Cove—1.0 mile; up The Cove to Alcove Marina & Pub—0.7 mile; to Fryer Brook—3.0 miles; to upriver island—3.2 miles; around island—1.0 mile. *South*: to Ensign Brook—0.8 mile; to Schuyler Brook—1.6 miles; to McAuley Brook—2.1 miles; to Kroma Kill—3.1 miles.
- ■ **Comments:** Read "Caution" beginning on page xxi and Champlain Canal & Environs Advisory on page 168.

Directions: From Bemis Heights (junction of Rtes. 4 & 32 North) continue north on Rte. 4 for 5.0 miles. Turn right onto a dirt road that leads immediately to the edge of the river.

From Schuylerville (junction of Rtes. 4/32 & 29 East) drive south on Rte. 4 for 4.7 miles (or 0.1 mile past Hanehan Road, on your right) and turn left onto a dirt road that leads immediately to the edge of the river.

The site is near 180-foot-high Holmes Hill, located on the opposite side of Rte. 4 and slightly to the northwest.

The Paddle:
Paddle either upstream or downstream, following the Hudson River as it meanders across lands that once served as a Revolutionary War battleground.

Coveville was originally called Do-ve-gat;[1] later it was known as Van Veghten's Cove after Colonel Cornelius Van Veghten. Van Veghten, along with his three sons, Herman, Cornelius, and Walter, were some of the first settlers in the area.[2] Because of its U-shape, The Cove has also been called the Horseshoe. It is one of two backwater areas within a 40-mile length of the upper Hudson River that provides a spawning and nursery area for largemouth bass.[3]

North—Heading upstream you will pass by Flately Brook to your right at 0.6 mile, then past a series of private camps to your left at 0.9 mile. A large cornfield can be seen to your right. The entrance to The Cove is reached at 1.0 mile. Turn left here, immediately paddling by a mock lighthouse on a dock advertising the Alcove Marina & Pub.

Proceeding up The Cove, in 0.2 mile you will pass by a narrowing in the channel whose rocky protrusions once served as abutments for a railroad bridge. The Alcove Marina & Pub is reached at 0.7 mile. Just north of the marina is a small marshland that can be explored west for 0.05 mile.

The Alcove Marina & Pub is historically significant. Its shed, which is over 100 years old, once served as an icehouse to store blocks of ice harvested from

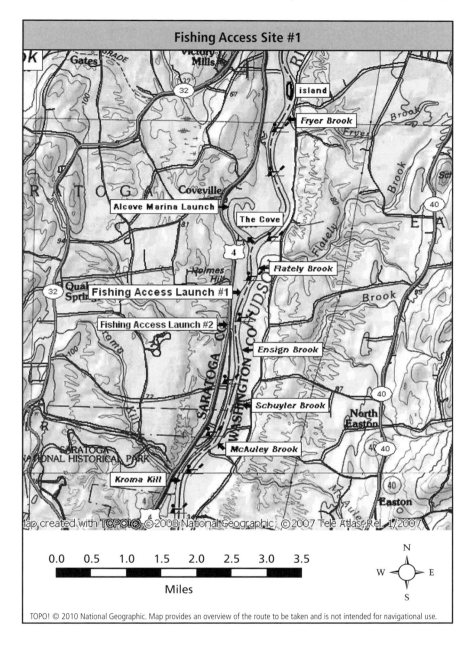

Fishing Access Site #1

island

Fryer Brook

Coveville

Alcove Marina Launch

The Cove

Flately Brook

Fishing Access Launch #1

Fishing Access Launch #2

Ensign Brook

Schuyler Brook

North Easton

McAuley Brook

Kroma Kill

Easton

Map created with TOPO!® © 2008 National Geographic; © 2007 Tele Atlas, Rel. 1/2007

0.0   0.5   1.0   1.5   2.0   2.5   3.0   3.5

Miles

The Cove, whose relatively still waters would freeze more readily than the fast-moving waters of the Hudson River.

Although the body of land across from the marina may look like an island (and probably was many centuries ago), its north end is connected to the mainland. Today, fields of corn are grown on its fertile soil.

If you paddle east, away from the marina, you will come to a large beaver dam in 0.05 mile. Paddlers who feel adventurous can carry their watercraft over the beaver dam and then continue onto a large marshy expanse of open water for another 0.2 mile. The best time to undertake this adventure, however, is at the beginning of the season; otherwise, the area by the beaver dam acquires the consistency of thick pea soup by late summer, and is too swampy and smelly to make for a pleasant trek.

Back on the Hudson River continuing upstream, you will pass by a small cove on your right at 1.1 miles and an inlet to your left at 1.2 miles. Farther upriver you will come to Fryer Brook on your right at 3.0 miles and then reach a slender, 0.3-mile-long island in 3.2 miles. The island can be circumnavigated in 1.0 mile.

South—Expect to see many camps and homes along both sides of the Hudson after you have gone 0.4 mile from the launch site. This will continue for the next two miles, particularly along the west bank of the river, which River Road closely parallels.

Proceeding downstream, you will pass by three named streams on your left—Ensign Brook at 0.8 mile, Schuyler Brook at 1.6 miles, and McAuley Brook at 2.1 miles—followed by the Kroma Kill on your right at 3.1 miles. The Kroma Kill can be paddled upstream, west, for several hundred feet to Rte. 4.

Were you to continue farther south for another 5.4 miles you would come to Lock C-4 & dam, 8.5 miles from the launch site.

Alternative Launch Site #1

Alcove Marina Launch (Coveville)

■ **Launch Site:** Alcove Marina & Pub off of Rte. 32/4 (Saratoga County); put-in from dock; modest launch fee
■ **Delorme NYS Atlas & Gazetteer:** p. 81, D5; **GPS:** 43°03.54'N; 73°35.64'W
■ **Destinations & Mileages:** *Southeast*: down The Cove to Hudson River—0.7 mile. *North*: from mouth of The Cove up Hudson River to Fryer Brook—2.2 miles (2.9 miles from launch); to island north of Coveville—2.4 miles (3.1 miles from launch); around island—1.0 mile. *South*: from mouth of The Cove down Hudson River to Flately Brook—0.4 mile (1.1 miles from launch); to Ensign Brook— 1.7 miles (2.4 miles from launch); to Schuyler Brook—2.5 miles (3.2 miles from launch); to McAuley Brook—3.0 miles (3.7 miles from launch).
■ **Comments:** Read "Caution" beginning on page xxi and Champlain Canal & Environs Advisory on page 168.

▶ **Fishing Access Site #1 (Coveville)**

Directions: From Bemis Heights (junction of Rtes. 4 & 32 North) drive north on Rte. 4 for 6.6 miles and turn right at the sign for the Alcove Marina & Pub.

From Schuylerville (junction of Rtes. 4/32 & 29 East) head south on Rte. 4 for 3.1 miles and turn left at the sign for the Alcove Marina & Pub.

Drive over 0.05 mile to the parking area for the marina.

Alternative Launch Site #2

Fishing Access Site #2 (Coveville)

- **Launch Site:** Fishing Access site (Saratoga County); gravel incline into water
- **Delorme NYS Atlas & Gazetteer:** p. 81, D5; **Estimated GPS:** 43°01.87′N, 73°35.59′W
- **Destinations & Mileages:** *North*: to Flately Brook—1.0 mile; to The Cove—1.4 mile; up The Cove—0.7 mile; to Fryer Brook—3.4 miles; to island upriver—3.6 miles; around island—1.0 mile. *South*: to Ensign Brook—0.4 mile; to Schuyler Brook—1.2 miles; to McAuley Brook—1.7 miles; to Kroma Kill—2.7 miles.
- **Comments:** Read "Caution" beginning on page xxi and Champlain Canal & Environs Advisory on page 168.

Directions: From the Coveville Fishing Access Site #1 drive south on Rte. 4 for 0.4 mile and turn left into a second Fishing Access Site, just before River Road. Carry your watercraft 50 feet down a gravel incline to a put-in at the water's edge.

At the mouth of The Cove. Photograph 2010.

46 Schuylerville Boat Launch (Schuylerville)
Accessing the Hudson River at Schuylerville

■ **Launch Site:** Schuylerville Boat Launch at Schuylerville (Saratoga County); cement ramp next to small floating dock. For more information: Lock C-6, (518) 747-4614.

■ **Delorme NYS Atlas & Gazetteer:** p. 81, CD5; **GPS:** 43°06.12'N, 73°34.54'W

■ **Destinations & Mileages:** *North*: to Lock C-5 channel—0.7 mile. *Northeast*: to Batten Kill—0.5 mile; up Batten Kill—0.7 mile (1.2 miles from launch). *South*: to Schuyler Island—0.05 mile; around Schuyler Island—0.8 mile; to Fish Creek—0.4 mile; up Fish Creek—0.1 mile.

■ **Comments:** Read "Caution" beginning on page xxi and Champlain Canal & Environs Advisory on page 168.

　　Hudson River—Look carefully both ways while paddling to or between islands to avoid oncoming boats. Stay back from Lock C-5 dam.

　　Batten Kill—The current can be strong following snowmelt or heavy rains.

Directions: From Schuylerville (junction of Rtes. 29 East & 4/32) drive east on Rte. 29 (Ferry Street) for 0.1 mile. Turn left onto Reds Street and proceed north for over 0.1 mile. At a barrier turn right onto a dirt road (a former towpath) that parallels the old Champlain Canal (on your left). Proceed north for 0.1 mile and then turn right onto a dirt road that leads east down to the parking area and launch site, next to the water treatment plant, within 0.1 mile.

The Paddle:

Schuylerville is strategically located at the four corners of a massive river valley system. Running north and south is the Hudson River; coming in from the west is Fish Creek, which drains Saratoga Lake, and from the east the Batten Kill, which rises in Vermont. This confluence of water routes gave the Iroquois, who occupied the land originally, ready access to Canada (to the north), the lower Hudson Valley (to the south), the Mohawk Valley (to the west), and the Connecticut River Valley (to the east).

Schuylerville was originally called Old Saratoga. It was renamed for General Philip Schuyler, a hero of the Revolution who lived in a mansion near the confluence of Fish Creek and the Hudson River. The original mansion was destroyed by the British in 1777 during the Battle of Saratoga, which marked the turning point in the Revolutionary War.[1] After the battle was won, Schuyler rebuilt the house in seventeen days. The mansion, with slight modifications, has survived into modern times and is now part of Saratoga National Historical Park (visit nps.gov/sara/index.htm). For more information: Schuyler House, Coveville Road, Schuylerville, NY 12871, (518) 695-3664.

The village grew up around Schuyler's house and the nearby site where British General Burgoyne and his troops were encamped at the time of their surrender

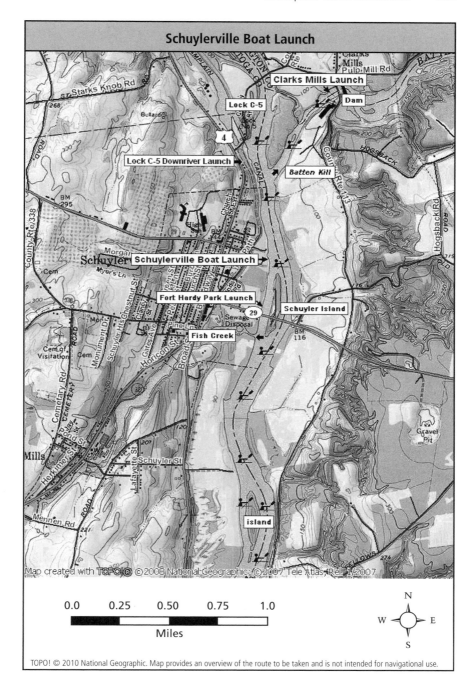

Schuylerville Boat Launch

to the Americans following the Battle of Saratoga.

Schuylerville's economic rise and fall was inextricably tied to the fortunes of the Champlain Canal. In its prime the village bustled with boatmen, teamsters, merchants, insurers, freight forwarders, and workers from many other walks of life. Between World War I and World War II, twelve factories turned out window sashes and blinds, and manufactured a variety of paper products using Adirondack pulp.[2] Today, little of this past industrial history remains.

North—Heading upriver you will pass by the mouth of the Batten Kill to your right at 0.5 mile. Lock C-5, which raises the river 19 feet higher, looms ahead. Continuing upstream you will reach the channel to Lock C-5 (on the west side of the river) at 0.7 mile. This is a good turnaround point. Stay back from Lock C-5 unless you are locking through.

Northeast—Head upriver for 0.5 mile until you reach the mouth of the Batten Kill, which comes in along the east bank of the Hudson River. The Batten Kill is a substantial river with a watershed of 441 square miles.[3] It rises north of Manchester, Vermont, and produces several waterfalls, including Dionondahowah Falls, along its length before flowing into the Hudson River after a 50-mile journey. The Batten Kill is the 301st tributary on the Hudson River as you go north from the Atlantic Ocean,[4] which should give you an appropriate sense of the grandeur of the Hudson River and the immensity of its watershed. Be prepared for some current as you make your way up the Batten Kill.

The Batten Kill can be explored upstream for 0.7 mile. You will immediately pass by a tiny 10-by-10-foot island just south of the confluence of the two rivers. Heading up the Batten Kill you will reach a small island in less than 0.4 mile. At 0.7 mile you will find yourself unable to paddle upstream any farther because of exposed bedrock and shallow waters, roughly 0.05 mile downstream from the Clarks Mills Lower Dam and the Rte. 113 bridge. The old arched cement bridge is known as the Clarks Mills Bridge and was erected 1915–1916. The Clarks Mills Lower Dam allows a significant portion of the Batten Kill's flow to be siphoned off by the Hollingsworth & Vose Company. The waters are returned to the stream 0.05 mile below the dam (see chapter "Clarks Mills Lower Dam Access #1" for additional information).

South—Going downstream you will immediately reach the north tip of Schuyler Island, on which the Route 29 bridge rests. The Rte. 29 bridge is not the first one to span this section of the Hudson River and Schuyler Island. In 1836 a private company established a toll bridge across Schuyler Island that lasted until 1906.[5]

Schuyler Island can be circumnavigated in 0.8 mile. Up until the early twentieth century, the island was known as Bridge Island. Prior to the Hudson River being dammed, it was possible to ford the river just north of the island when the water level was low. Later a man named De Ridder ran a ferry around the south end of the island. The ferry became known as the "Horse Boat" because it was propelled by horsepower.[6]

▶ **Schuylerville Boat Launch (Schuylerville)**

Continuing south you will pass by the Schuyler Yacht Basin (a private marina that has been in service since 1944) to your right. The Schuyler Yacht Basin is located at the confluence of the Hudson River and Fish Creek. It occupies the site where a blockhouse stood in the late 1600s or early 1700s. Later, Fort Hardy was constructed there in 1757.[7] Fort Hardy was named for Sir Charles Hardy, governor of New York, and served as an eighteenth-century supply fort during the French and Indian War. It is most renowned for being where the conditions of surrender were signed by British General Burgoyne following his defeat at the Battle of Saratoga and where his army stacked their weapons as they marched out with "Honors of War." The surrender of Burgoyne marked a major victory for the colonists, and served to convince France, Spain, and the Netherlands that America was worth backing in its fight against the British. The Fort Hardy site is now an athletic park along the west bank of the Hudson River.

The mouth of Fish Creek, also to your right (west), is reached at 0.4 mile. Fish Creek has formed a tiny bay that can be explored for a short distance upstream until further progress is blocked by several tiny cascades and rapids. These cascades are formed under a footbridge next to where an abandoned section of the Champlain Canal once crossed over the stream. The Fish Creek Aqueduct, which was completed in 1821, was rebuilt in 1844 to allow for the passage of two boats, and then was enlarged a second time between 1864 and 1873.[8] The canal is now truncated by Fish Creek. The part of the old canal that extends north is filled with water; the short section extending south is simply a wide, dry trench. It is possible, with considerable difficulty, to portage around the canal and put in on Fish Creek just above the footbridge crossing, but you can only go another 0.1–0.2 mile before further progress is permanently blocked by small cascades at the Rte. 4/32 bridge.

If you were to continue south on the Hudson River from Fish Creek for another 0.8 mile, you would reach the north tip of a 0.4-mile-long island that can be circumnavigated in 0.9 mile. An 1841 map shows no island on this section of the river. It is quite possible that the island is artificial and was created when the river was dredged.

The Batten Kill: The upper part of the Batten Kill is favored by flat-water paddlers, with numerous access sites to the river available in both New York State and Vermont. Many of these access sites are along or close to Route 313.

In addition, the following outfitters can be consulted to arrange for paddling trips down the Batten Kill:

Battenkill Canoe Ltd.
6328 Historic Route 7A, Arlington, VT 05250
(802) 362-2800, (800) 421-5268 battenkill.com

Battenkill Riversports Trips
937 State Route 313, Cambridge, NY 12816
(518) 677-8868, (800) 676-8767   battenkillriversports@netzero.net

Battenkill Valley Outdoors
1414 State Route 313, Cambridge, NY 12816
(518) 677-3311   battenkillvalleyoutdoors.com

Alternate Launch Site #1

Fort Hardy Park (Schuylerville)

■ **Launch Site:** Fort Hardy Park in Schuylerville (Saratoga County); 75-foot carry across lawn to slip-in. Restrooms, picnicking, ball fields, trails, and concerts are provided at the park. No motorboats allowed.
■ **Delorme NYS Atlas & Gazetteer:** p. 81, CD5; **GPS:** 43°05.94'N; 73°34.63'W
■ **Destinations & Mileages:** *North*: to Lock C-5 channel—0.9 mile. *Northeast*: to Batten Kill—0.7 mile; up Batten Kill—0.7 mile (1.4 miles from launch). *East*: to Schuyler Island—0.05 mile; around Schuyler Island—0.8 mile. *South*: to Fish Creek—0.1 mile; up Fish Creek—0.1 mile.
■ **Comments:** Read "Caution" beginning on page xxi and Champlain Canal & Environs Advisory on page 168.
   Watch out for boat traffic, and stay a safe distance back from the Lock C-5 dam.

Directions: From Schuylerville (junction of Rtes. 29 East & 4/32) drive east on Rte. 29 for 0.2 mile. Turn left at the easternmost section of Fort Hardy Park, just before crossing over the Hudson River. Park to your right as soon as you enter the park. The slip-in is directly across the lawn from the parking area.

The north tip of Schuyler Island, now residential. Photograph 2009.

▶ Schuylerville Boat Launch (Schuylerville)

Alternate Launch Site #2

Champlain Canal Lock C-5 (Schuylerville)

- **Launch Site:** Champlain Canal Lock C-5 Hudson Crossing Park (Saratoga County); several-hundred-foot carry to opening in guardrail, followed by a carry of a couple of hundred feet more to river's edge. For more information: Lock C-5, (518) 695-3919.
- **Delorme NYS Atlas & Gazetteer:** p. 81, CD5; **GPS:** parking lot—43°06.77'N; 73°34.66'W; river access—43°06.76'N, 73°34.71'W
- **Destinations & Mileages:** *Southeast*: to Batten Kill—0.2 mile; up Batten Kill— 0.7 mile (0.9 mile from launch). *South*: to Schuyler Island—0.8 mile; around Schuyler Island—0.8 mile; past Fort Hardy Park—0.9 mile; to Fish Creek— 1.0 mile; up Fish Creek—0.1 mile.
- **Comments:** Read "Caution" beginning on page xxi and Champlain Canal & Environs Advisory on page 168.

   Hudson River—Watch out for boat traffic and stay a safe distance back from the Lock C-5 dam.

   Batten Kill—Current can be strong following snowmelt or heavy rains.

   Fish Creek—Current is generally mild except in early spring following snowmelt or heavy rains.

   A kayak carrier would be helpful to reach the river access.

   Canal Tour Boats (champlaincanaltours.com) provides boat tours during the season and is located at the end of the northwest terminal wall.

Directions: From Schuylerville (junction of Rtes. 29 West & 4/32) drive north on Rte. 4/32 for 0.5 mile. Turn right at a sign for Lock C-5 and drive east for 0.1 mile, crossing over the canal. Sections of the old Champlain Canal are clearly visible to your right and left before you cross over the canal. On your left are the fairly intact remnants of a lock; on your right can be seen the old canal and towpath. Park in the small area next to the administrative building. You are now on what used to be an island roughly the size of Schuyler Island before it was modified by engineers and incorporated into the Champlain Canal system.

   Carry your watercraft back along the entrance road. About one hundred feet before reaching Rte. 4/32, turn left through a break in the guardrail marked by three yellow-and-orange-striped posts. Start down the gravel pathway and then veer left, heading across the lawn to the southwest end of the canal. Within several hundred feet you will reach a point where a tiny tributary enters the Hudson River. Put in here.

   You may be curious about the fairly loud sound produced by this tiny tributary and might think that it contains a waterfall. Walk upstream and you will see that the creek is issuing from a drainpipe whose waters are flowing out of the old Champlain Canal just a short distance uphill.

A grant has been approved to create a canoe/kayak access on the east side of the island, east of the lock and just south of the Dix Bridge. A path cut through the guardrail will lead down to the site, and additional parking will be available in close proximity to the path. This will be a designated Hudson River Greenway Water Trail site. For updates and more information: New York State Canal Corporation, (518) 436-2700.

Alternate Launch Site #3

Clarks Mills Lower Dam, Access #2 (Clarks Mills)

- **Launch Site:** Batten Kill below Lower Clarks Mills Dam (Washington County); 0.1 mile carry to put-in
- **Delorme NYS Atlas & Gazetteer:** p. 81, D–5; **GPS:** parking—43°06.97'N; 73°34.14'W; launch—43°06.93'N; 73°34.20'W
- **Destinations & Mileages:** *Southwest*: to Hudson River—0.7 mile; continuing north on Hudson River from mouth of Batten Kill to Lock C-5 channel— 0.1 mile (0.8 mile from launch); continuing south on Hudson River from mouth of Batten Kill to Schuyler Island—0.5 mile (1.2 miles from launch); around Schuyler Island—0.8 mile; to Fish Creek—0.9 miles (1.6 miles from launch); up Fish Creek—0.1 mile.
- **Comments:** Read "Caution" beginning on page xxi and Champlain Canal & Environs Advisory on page 168.
  Batten Kill—Current can be strong following snowmelt or heavy rains. Access is restricted to car-top watercraft and angler fishing, and is intended for recreational use only.
  Hudson River—Watch out for boat traffic and stay a safe distance back from the Lock C-5 dam.
  Fish Creek—Current is generally mild except after heavy rains or in early spring following snowmelt.
  A kayak/canoe carrier would be helpful.
  Access to the Batten Kill by Clarks Mills Lower Dam is made possible through the generosity and civic-mindedness of Hollingsworth & Vose Company.

Directions: From Schuylerville (junction of Rtes. 4/32 & 29 East) drive east on Rte. 29 for 0.7 mile. Turn left onto River Road (Rte. 113) and drive north for 1.4 miles. As soon as you cross over the old cement bridge spanning the Batten Kill, turn immediately left into a small off-road parking area. Follow a path for 0.1 mile that leads west across a tiny creek and then through an open field to the Batten Kill. Put in your watercraft along the exposed bedrock.

▶ **Schuylerville Boat Launch (Schuylerville)**

Champlain Canal Lock C-5, Upriver (Schuylerville)
Accessing the Canal and the Hudson River

47

■ **Launch Site:** Champlain Canal Lock C-5 Hudson Crossing Park; open seasonally; several-hundred-foot carry to public dock upstream from Lock C-5. For more information: Lock C-5, (518) 695-3919.
■ **Delorme NYS Atlas & Gazetteer:** p. 81, CD5; **GPS:** parking lot—43°06.77'N; 73°34.66'W; upriver access—43°06.83'N, 73°34.71'W
■ **Destinations & Mileages:** *North*: to Northumberland Bridge—1.1 miles; to Van Antwerp Creek—2.2 miles.
■ **Comments:** Read "Caution" beginning on page xxi and Champlain Canal & Environs Advisory on page 168.

Paddling north, watch out for the L-shaped Lock C-5 dam, 0.8 mile upriver to your right. The dam's west side closely parallels the canal for a short distance. Stay well to the left of the orange buoys and the large stone blocks.

A kayak carrier would be helpful to reach the launch site.

Canal Tour Boats (champlaincanaltours.com) provides boat tours during the season and is located at the end of the northwest terminal wall.

Directions: From Schuylerville (junction of Rtes. 29 West & 4/32) drive north on Rte. 4/32 for 0.5 mile. Turn right at a sign for Lock C-5 and drive east for 0.1 mile, crossing over the canal. Sections of the old Champlain Canal are clearly visible to your right and left before you cross over the canal. On your left are the fairly intact remnants of a lock that connected the old and new canal systems; on your right can be seen the old canal and towpath. Park in the small area next to the administrative building. You are now on what used to be an island roughly the size of Schuyler Island before it was modified by engineers and incorporated into the Champlain Canal system.

From the parking area carry your watercraft north for several hundred feet along a dirt road that closely parallels the canal. Turn left before reaching a pavilion, and follow a paved pathway that leads quickly down to a public dock set into the canal.

The Paddle:

North—Head upstream, following along the Champlain Canal channel for 0.7 mile before clearing the Lock C-5 dam, off to your right. According to some sources Lock C-5 served as a model for the Panama Canal locks.[1] Pay close attention along this section of the canal because you don't want to get too close to the edge of a dam that parallels the canal for 0.1 mile of its length. Stay well to the left of the orange buoys and the large stone blocks.

Before you get to the dam you will pass near historic Starks Knob, a Revolutionary War site and a hill that at one time was mistaken for being the cone of an extinct volcano. The triangular volcano-like shape, however, was caused by

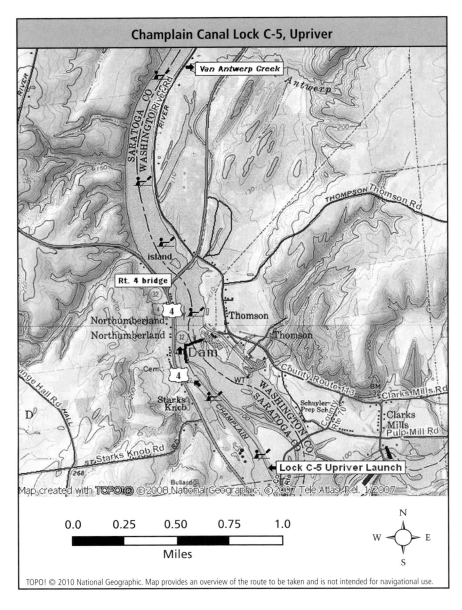

Champlain Canal Lock C-5, Upriver

TOPO! © 2010 National Geographic. Map provides an overview of the route to be taken and is not intended for navigational use.

early quarrying that removed the east side of the hill. Its geological significance is that it is formed of a submarine pillow lava called pillow basalt, and is one of very few such formations in the eastern United States. Starks Knob is 0.1 mile to the west of the river and is not visible from the water, but it is accessible by car off of Rte. 4/32.

▶ Champlain Canal Lock C-5, Upriver (Schuylerville)

At 1.1 miles you will reach the Rte. 4 Northumberland Bridge. In 1777 British General John Burgoyne and his army forded the Hudson near this spot.[2] A small island is passed just upstream from the bridge.

At 2.2 miles you will see the mouth of Van Antwerp Creek, to your right, which is the turnaround point.

If you continued farther north, you would come to Slocum Creek on your right at 3.0 miles and eventually reach Lock C-6 at 3.6 miles.

Champlain Canal Lock C-5. Postcard ca. 1920.

48 Former West Shore Marina (Moreau)
Putting in Just South of Rogers Island

- **Launch Site:** Cement ramp at end of inclined road-cut at former site of the West Shore Marina (Saratoga County)
- **Delorme NYS Atlas & Gazetteer:** p. 81, BC5; **GPS:** 43°15.27'N; 73°35.25'W
- **Destinations & Mileages:** *North*: to Rogers Island—0.2 mile; around Rogers Island—2.0 miles. *Northeast*: to Lock C-7—0.2 mile. *South*: to Snook Kill—1.8 miles; up Snook Kill—1.0 mile.
- **Comments:** Read "Caution" beginning on page xxi and Champlain Canal & Environs Advisory on page 168.

     Do not approach Lock C-7 unless you are planning to "lock through."

     As of the writing of this book, the launch site remains near the staging area for PCB-dredging. Stay clear of barges and heavy machinery. The dredging is expected to continue into the future for some time.

Directions: From Fort Edward (junction of Rtes. 4 & 197 West) go west on Rte. 197, crossing over the Hudson River and Rogers Island in the process. After 0.6 mile turn left at a traffic light onto West River Road (Rte. 29) and proceed southwest for nearly 0.4 mile. When you come to an unmarked dirt road, turn left. In less than 0.1 mile turn right and go 0.05 mile to a launch site by the river.

Dredging continues on the river to remove PCB contamination. Photograph 2009.

▶ **Former West Shore Marina (Moreau)**

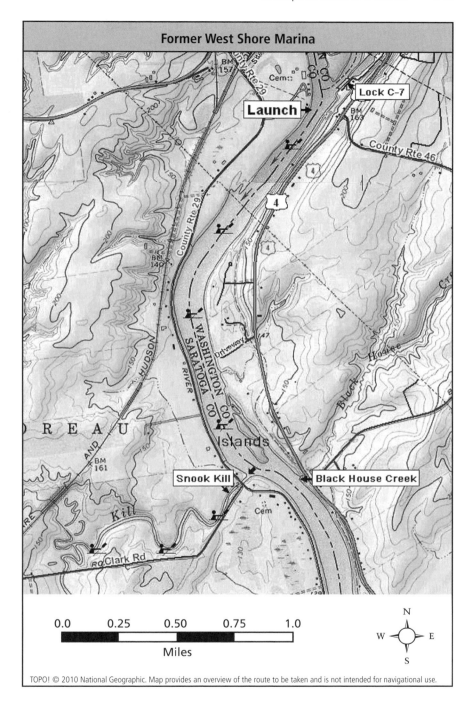

Former West Shore Marina

Lock C-7

Launch

Black House Creek

Snook Kill

Islands

0.0   0.25   0.50   0.75   1.0

Miles

N
W   E
S

TOPO! © 2010 National Geographic. Map provides an overview of the route to be taken and is not intended for navigational use.

The Paddle:

The launch is located at the site of the former West Shore Marina, sometimes called the West River Road Marina.[1] The site is now owned by the New York State Department of Environmental Conservation. It is situated on the Hudson River only a short distance downriver from Rogers Island and Lock C-7, both of which are clearly visible as you look upstream.

North & Northeast—Proceeding upriver you will come to the south end of Rogers Island in 0.2 mile or, if you divert slightly east, to Lock C-7, also in 0.2 mile. Rogers Island can be circumnavigated in 2.0 miles (see chapter "Rogers Island" and its map for further details).

South—Heading downriver takes you past a small island in 1.6 miles and up to the Snook Kill, which enters the Hudson River on your right, in 1.8 miles. The Snook Kill is a medium-sized stream that rises west of Kings Station and can be followed upstream for over 1.0 mile, depending upon blowdown and other variable conditions, possibly as far as (or even beyond) the Clark Road bridge, where a fishing access site is located. Note, however, that there is no way of either putting in or taking out a kayak or canoe at the fishing access site.

The name of the stream may have originated from the name of a large tropical game fish of coastal and brackish waters that resembles a pike.

▶ **Former West Shore Marina (Moreau)**

V

Hudson River
From Fort Edward to Thurman Station

Advisory

The complexion of the Hudson River changes dramatically from Glens Falls to Thurman Station. Near Glens Falls the shoreline is more urban, with the sights and sounds of the city in the near distance. There may be powerboats on the river, but they tend to be smaller ones, some of them carrying fishing enthusiasts to coveted "secret" spots where the big fish can be found.

Even so, operators of small watercraft like kayaks and canoes must be ever-vigilant. Don't assume boats can see you. Wear bright colors. If you must cross the river, cross in a group and keep the group together. If you see a boat in the distance, let it pass before you set out. Some large boats move surprisingly fast, and distance can be hard to judge.

The time of year can significantly affect conditions on the Hudson River. The earlier in the year, the faster the current and the greater your skills level will need to be to manage the variable conditions encountered, but generally the waters are paddler-friendly thanks to the presence of dams that help to control the pace of the river. By the time you reach the Spier Falls area, the river has become wide and wonderfully scenic, and powerboats are not all that prevalent.

However, because the dams have made the river much wider along this section than it is from Stillwater to Fort Edward, wind, waves, and wakes are greater potential hazards here. When heading out onto the river, choose a calm day and watch the weather. Always check the forecast before setting out. Do not leave shore if storms and/or high winds are predicted or if the weather forecast is at all questionable. Be aware that the weather can change abruptly, often with little warning and in spite of the forecast. Current and wind can be severe. The wind tends to be quietest in the early morning and early evening. Wind and current increase as you move away from the shoreline.

Always stay a safe distance back from the top of a dam, to avoid being swept over the brink, as well as from the bottom of a dam, to avoid being caught up in the hydraulics. Make sure the current is not strong if you launch near a dam.

Above Hadley/Lake Luzerne, the Hudson River becomes noticeably shallower and narrower. This is because there are no dams along this section of the river. Paddlers should keep in mind that some rapids will be encountered, as well as occasional underlying sandbars that may require pushing through or portaging around.

Memorize the shoreline as you leave so that you can return to the same starting point.

Rogers Island (Fort Edward)
An Island with Centuries of Accrued History

49

- ■ **Launch Site:** Terminus of Bradley Avenue in Bradley Park on Rogers Island (Washington County); slip-in at river's edge; open 7 AM–10 PM
- ■ **Delorme NYS Atlas & Gazetteer:** p. 81, BC5; **GPS:** 43°16.00'N; 73°35.45'W
- ■ **Destinations & Mileages:** *Around Rogers Island (clockwise):* to Rte. 197 bridge—0.3 mile; to D&H Railroad bridge—0.4 mile; to Lock C-7—1.1 miles; to south end of secondary island—1.5 miles; to D&H Railroad bridge west of island—1.7 miles; to Rte. 197 bridge west of island—1.8 miles; back to launch—2.0 miles. *North:* to upriver rapids—0.3 mile.
- ■ **Comments:** Read "Caution" beginning on page xxi and Hudson River Advisory on page 216.

  Be prepared for maneuvering around the bridge pilings as you paddle along the Hudson River by Rogers Island.

  Watch out for dredging rigs, which at the time of the writing of this book were still scooping up sediment containing PCBs.

  Stay clear of Champlain Canal Lock C-7 unless you plan to enter it to head upstream on the canal.

Directions: From the Adirondack Northway (I-87) take Exit 17 for South Glens Falls and drive northeast on Rte. 9 for 1.2 miles. When you come to Rte. 197, turn right and proceed east for 4.6 miles. You are now on Rogers Island. Turn left onto Riverside Drive before leaving the island, and proceed north for 0.1 mile, then bear right into Bradley Park and onto Bradley Avenue.

From Fort Edward (junction of Rtes. 4 & 197 West) head west on Rte. 197 for 0.1 mile, crossing onto Rogers Island. Turn right onto Riverside Drive and drive north for 0.1 mile, then turn right into Bradley Park and onto Bradley Avenue.

From either direction, Bradley Avenue leads within 0.05 mile to a large parking area by the launch site.

Bradley Park is named in honor of George and Margaret Bradley, former lumber industrialists and opera house owners. A stone monument commemorating their achievements can be seen at the junction of Bradley Avenue and Riverside Drive.

The Paddle:

Rogers Island by Fort Edward, like the identically named Rogers Island near the city of Hudson (see *A Kayaker's Guide to New York's Capital Region*, Black Dome Press, 2010), is rich with Native American history. During pre-colonial times it was the site of a Native American encampment. Many archaeological digs have been conducted there in recent times.

The island is named after Robert Rogers, who established an encampment with his rangers on the island from 1756 to 1759 during the French and Indian

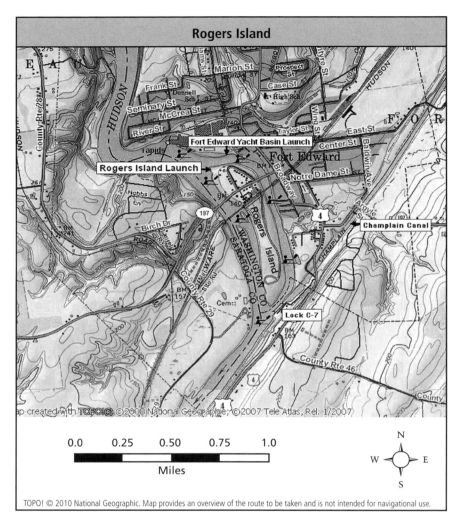

TOPO! © 2010 National Geographic. Map provides an overview of the route to be taken and is not intended for navigational use.

War. It was while here that Rogers developed his famous "Rules of Ranging," which still guide ground-fighting troops today. Roger's Rangers are considered by many to be the forefathers of today's U.S. Army Rangers.

Around Rogers Island (clockwise)—Rogers Island can be circumnavigated in 2.0 miles. Paddling clockwise around the island you will immediately pass by a tiny island at the northwest tip of Rogers Island. Clear the north tip of Rogers Island and head south along its east side. At 0.3 mile you will pass under the Rte. 197 bridge and then, at 0.4 mile, under the old D&H Railroad bridge, which was built in 1924 and then reconstructed in 1941. The bridge now serves a main rail line to Canada.[1]

▶ **Rogers Island (Fort Edward)**

At roughly 0.5 mile you will pass by the docking area for the Rogers Island Visitor Center. You will also pass by the historic site of old Fort Edward on the river's east bank, approximately 0.4 mile south of the Rte. 197 bridge and 0.3 mile north of Lock C-7. Fort Edward was known to Native Americans as *Wahcoloosencoocchaleva*, or the "Great Carrying Place," for it marked the start of a canoe carry from Bond Creek northeast to Lake Champlain.[2]

The first fortification here was a stockade erected in 1709 by Sir Francis Nicholson. In 1731 a Dutchman named John Henry Lydius built a trading post, which became known as Fort Lydius. A second fort was constructed during the French and Indian War by Phineas Lyman, and this became known as Fort Lyman. In 1755, Sir William Johnson changed the name from Fort Lyman to Fort Edward, in honor of Edward, Duke of York and Albany, grandson of King George II, and brother of King George III.[3] In 1766 the fort was evacuated, and nine years later it was razed.[4] The Old Fort House Museum was constructed by Patrick Smythe in 1772 with timbers taken from the ruins of Fort Edward. Smythe was arrested at the house in 1777 by Benedict Arnold for being a Loyalist. American General Stark erected a stockade around the house, and for a time the building was called Fort Stark.

You will reach Lock C-7, opposite the south end of Rogers Island, at 1.1 miles. Were you to continue downriver for another 2.0 miles, you would come to the mouth of the Snook Kill flowing in on your right down the west bank.

Rounding the south tip of Rogers Island, proceed north, heading upstream along the west side of the island. At 1.5 miles you will come to the south end of a 0.15-mile-long island. In another 0.2 mile you will pass by a tiny island next to Rogers Island, and then under the D&H Railroad Bridge, followed by the Rte. 197 bridge at 1.8 miles. From there it is but another 0.2 mile back to your starting point at Bradley Park.

North—While it is possible to paddle north up the Hudson for up to 0.3 mile, a line of rapids and shallows extending across the river makes it extremely difficult to make any further headway against the current. If you do head north, take note of the shallow sandbar in front of the launch site.

If it were possible to paddle 2.5 miles upriver, you would reach the base of Bakers Falls, an eighty-five-foot-high dammed waterfall. The cascade was named after Albert Baker, Sandy Hill's first settler, who owned the water rights by the falls.[5] It was at the General Electric plant along the east bank near the top of the falls, along with a GE plant in Fort Edward, that the problem of PCBs (polychlorinated biphenyl) in the Hudson River originated. Between 1946 and 1977 these two plants discharged into the river over 1.3 million pounds of PCBs, a toxic insulating fluid used in the production of heavy capacitors.[6]

Additional Point of Interest: Rogers Island Visitor Center, 11 Rogers Island Drive. P.O. Box 208, Fort Edward, NY 12828, (518) 747-3693, rogersisland.org. Open daily from June–August, Monday–Saturday 10 AM–4 PM, and Sunday 1 PM–4 PM; open from September–May, Wednesday–Sunday, 10 AM–4 PM.

The Visitor Center, located at the site of the 1756 base camp for Rogers Rangers, offers historical displays, archaeological artifacts, and early history of Fort Edward. Every September it hosts a French and Indian War encampment and reenactment, as well as serving as a six-week field placement for the Adirondack Community College Archaeological Field School.

The 0.1-mile-long road to the Rogers Island Visitor Center is 0.1 mile west of Riverside Drive, on the opposite side of Rte. 197.

It is possible to access the Hudson River from a short metal stairway leading down to a dock behind the stockade section of the visitor center (GPS: 43°15.93'N; 73°35.22'W), next to the railroad bridge. The dock is used primarily by boaters accessing the visitor center. Just downstream is a gravel and mud beach that is better suited for paddlers.

Alternate Launch Site

Fort Edward Yacht Basin (Fort Edward)

■ **Launch Site:** Fort Edward Yacht Basin at end of Terminal Street behind the Glens Falls National Bank in Fort Edward (Washington County); 0.05-mile carry from parking lot to informal put-in
■ **Delorme NYS Atlas & Gazetteer:** p. 81, BC5; **GPS:** 43°16.12'N; 73°35.25'W
■ **Destinations & Mileages:** *Around Rogers Island (clockwise)*: to Rte. 197 bridge—0.3 mile; to D&H Railroad bridge—0.4 mile; to Lock C-7—1.1 miles; to south end of secondary island—1.5 miles; to D&H Railroad bridge west of island—1.7 miles; to Rte. 197 bridge west of island—1.8 miles; back to launch—2.0 miles. *Northwest*: to upriver rapids—0.3 mile.
■ **Comments:** Read "Caution" beginning on page xxi and Hudson River Advisory on page 216.

Be prepared for maneuvering around the bridge pilings as you paddle along the Hudson River by Rogers Island.

Watch out for dredging rigs, which at the time of the writing of this book were still scooping up sediment containing PCBs.

Stay clear of Champlain Canal Lock C-7 unless you plan to enter it to head upstream on the canal.

▶ **Rogers Island (Fort Edward)**

Kayakers make their way around Rogers Island. Photograph 2010.

Directions: From Fort Edward (junction of Rtes. 4 and 197 West) drive north on Rte. 4 for over 0.1 mile. Turn left onto Terminal Lane and proceed west for 0.05 mile to the Yacht Basin parking lot.

From Hudson Falls (junction of Rtes. 4 & 254 at the roundabout) drive south on Rte. 4 for 2.5 miles and turn right onto Terminal Street where the sign directs you to the Yacht Basin.

From the parking lot carry your watercraft north for 0.05 mile to the north end of the wharf, where an informal access point can be found next to the wharf. The wharf itself is too high above the water to easily launch a canoe or kayak.

Glens Falls Feeder Canal

Introduction

The seven-mile-long Feeder Canal (including the Feeder Dam) was built in 1824 to carry a steady flow of water downhill from the Hudson River to the Champlain Canal. In doing so the massive falls at Glens Falls and Bakers Falls were bypassed. Water from the Feeder Canal entered the Champlain Canal at its highest point, located between Fort Edward and Smith Basin, and then ran north toward Whitehall and south toward Fort Edward. In this way an adequate water level throughout the entire length of the canal was assured.

This was not the first canal and feeder dam to be built for the Champlain Canal. In 1822 a dam downstream near Fort Edward was constructed to divert water 0.5 mile east into the Champlain Canal, but it was partially destroyed by floodwaters and never rebuilt. The new Feeder Canal and dam proved to be an immediate success, and with it came the recognition that the Feeder Canal might also serve as a waterway for commerce.

In 1832 the width and depth of the Feeder Canal were increased markedly to accommodate barge traffic, with blocks of limestone used to shore up the walls of the canal. At the same time, 13 masonry locks were constructed to allow boats to negotiate the 130-foot elevation change between Fort Edward and Glens Falls.[1] Each of the locks was 100 feet long by 15 feet wide except for one, which was 110 feet by 18 feet.[2] For nearly a hundred years the canal played a vital role in Glens Falls's industrial development, principally transporting lumber, limestone, and marble. The age of the locomotive and the dawning era of the automobile proved to be too much competition for the canal, however, and the last commercial boat to use the canal passed through it in 1928. From then on the canal simply served as a feeder for the Champlain Canal. In more recent times it has reopened for traffic again, but now just for canoes and kayaks.

The Champlain Canal continues to require an adequate volume of water for its daily operation. In order to replenish water lost while the Champlain Canal's locks operate, the Feeder Canal must keep up a constant flow of 100–200 cfs—a requirement that was established over 150 years ago and which is accomplished by maintaining a minimum flow on the Hudson River of 1,760 cfs from the Curtis Falls (Dam) impoundment at Corinth, where the variable water releases from the Sacandaga River are averaged out with the more steady flow from the Hudson River.[3] Generally the depth of the water in the Feeder Canal varies from 1 to 5 feet. From late November to late April, however, water is essentially removed from the Feeder Canal when the New York State Canal Corporation closes the Champlain Canal.

The paddle today takes you along a 5.5-mile-long section of the Feeder Canal that is no longer open to commercial traffic. The canal essentially parallels the Hudson River, which is to the southwest. The canal's towpath has been paved over and is now a 9-mile-long trail for walkers, joggers, and bicyclists. Together, the canal and towpath comprise the Feeder Canal Linear Park.

Were it not for the prodigious amount of work performed by the Feeder Canal Alliance—an organization formed in 1987 to preserve, promote, and protect the canal—there would be no canoeable waterway today, only a wide ditch grossly neglected and filled with trash. For more information on the Feeder Canal Alliance, go to feedercanal.com or call (518) 792-5363. Additional information can be obtained at nycanaltimes.com/pages/articledetail-sarch.asp?cat=57.

Paddling along the historic Feeder Canal. Photograph 2009.

50 Feeder Canal from Richardson Street Access (Glens Falls)

- **Launch Site:** Off of Richardson Street in Glens Falls (Warren County); several-hundred-foot carry to put-in at northeast end of footbridge that spans the canal; the dock is next to the limestone wall of the canal.
- **Delorme NYS Atlas & Gazetteer:** p. 81, B4–5; **GPS:** parking—43°17.56'N; 73°39.93'W; launch—43°17.49'N; 73°39.82'W
- **Destinations & Mileages:** *East*: to Bush Street access—0.5 mile; to Haviland Cove—0.8 mile; to Morgan Dry Dock Basin—1.4 miles; to Murray Street access—1.5 miles; to Cooper's Cave Bridge—1.9 miles; to Shermantown Road access—2.7 miles; to Rte. 254—3.7 miles; to Martindale Boat Basin access and eastern terminus of canal—5.5 miles.
- **Comments:** Read "Caution" beginning on page xxi and Hudson River Advisory on page 216.

    No map accompanies this paddle because the Feeder Canal is too narrow to show up clearly on the maps generated by the mapping software used for this book. A map of the feeder canal will be posted on the Feeder Canal Alliance Web site in the near future. Interested readers should consult feedercanal.org.

Directions: From the Adirondack Northway (I-87) take Exit 18 for Glens Falls and head east on Main Street for over 0.5 mile. At the traffic light turn right onto Richardson Street and proceed south for 0.6 mile. When you come to the junction of Richardson Street and Haviland Avenue, turn right into a paved parking area overlooking the river and dam.

Approaching from the north end of Cooper's Cave Bridge (junction of Rtes. 9 & 32), go west on Mohican Street for 0.4 mile. Turn right onto Murray Street and drive north for less than 0.1 mile. When you come to South Street, turn left and drive southwest for 0.4 mile, then turn right onto Knight Street and go west for 0.2 mile. Turn left onto Haviland Street and drive southwest for over 0.5 mile. The parking area is directly to your left, facing the river.

From the parking area carry your watercraft down a slight hill following a paved walkway for several hundred feet to the footbridge that spans the canal. Put in at the northeast end of the bridge from a fixed dock.

The Paddle:

Starting at the Moore Memorial (Foot) Bridge by the Feeder Dam, the paddle takes you on a quiet journey through Glens Falls's industrial history, past a turning basin/dry dock, factories, and lime kilns sites. Col. Zenas Van Dusen once operated a sawmill by the Feeder Dam,[1] and the Sherman Sawmill, operated by Augustus Sherman, was located directly across the river on the south shore.[2] Still visible today near the Feeder Dam are the remains of Lock #14.[3]

In 0.5 mile you will go under the Bush Street Bridge (an informal access

▶ **Feeder Canal from Richardson Street Access (Glens Falls)**

point). At 0.8 mile you will pass by Haviland Cove, located at the south end of Pruyn Island to your right. Parts of the cove can be glimpsed through the trees. Pruyn Island was created when the Feeder Canal was built and separated the island from the mainland.

The land next to this section of the canal was once stacked high with enormous piles of freshly cut, drying lumber awaiting shipment.[4] Today you will see huge piles of logs to your right, roughly 0.1 mile past the Bush Street Bridge and immediately after you pass by old bridge abutments next to the canal.

At 1.4 miles you will reach the Morgan Dry Dock Basin to your left, where repairs were made on canal boats. This was one of six turning basins that allowed long boats to turn and reverse direction. At 1.5 miles you will pass under the Murray Street Bridge (another access point to the canal).

Glens Falls (the waterfall) is off to your right at 1.8 miles, but cannot be seen from the canal.

At 1.9 miles you will paddle under Rte. 9 at Cooper's Cave Bridge, which spans the Hudson River between Glens Falls and South Glens Falls. Be prepared to duck your head as soon as you pass under the bridge to avoid a large, low-lying pipe that crosses over the canal immediately past the bridge. From here on you will notice that the canal walls change from limestone blocks to reinforced concrete.

Paddling through the Finch & Pruyn complex is like taking a trip back through time. Photograph 2009.

Coming up ahead is undoubtedly the most exciting and surreal part of the trip, as the canal takes you through the elaborate Finch Pruyn & Company complex, with industries to both your left and right. At one point you even go *under* one of the buildings. It is easy to feel that you have been transported back in time as you listen to the incessant rumble of machinery and the whistling of steam valves.

In 1865, brothers Jeremiah and Daniel Finch partnered up with Samuel Pruyn to purchase the Glens Falls Company sawmill at the front of Glen Street. The Finch Pruyn Paper Company developed from this partnership. In 1876 the company purchased the nearby Wing Sawmill to gain control of the waterpower by the fall.

At 2.7 miles you will go under the Shermantown Road bridge (another informal access site). To your right are the stone ruins of a lime kiln several hundred feet downstream from the bridge, but they cannot be seen unless you get out of your craft and walk along the towpath. This is the site of the 1832 Sherman Lime Company kilns. The kilns were called "perpetual kilns," for the fires burned without interruption in order to maintain the high temperatures needed. Back in the nineteenth century more than 83 such lime kilns lined the canal.[5] Today the Joint Galusha Company, formerly known as the Joint Lime Company, still operates nearby on Shermantown Road and is reputed to be the oldest surviving business in Glens Falls. It was formed in 1851 by John Keenan and Halsey R. Wing.[6] Black marble was also mined locally and is considered to be one of the purest carbonates in the world.

Shortly after the Shermantown Road bridge, you will pass by the Lehigh Cement Company as you float right past the front door of their office.

At 3.7 miles a large drainpipe carries the canal under Rte. 254. This is easily paddled through. For the next mile or so, the Feeder Canal leaves civilization behind, with only an occasional building passing by on your left. Along the right side of the canal, the towpath parallels the edge of a steep hill.

Once the canal alters direction from east to southeast, civilization begins to reappear. You will see numerous homes and other structures to your left.

At nearly 5.5 miles you will arrive at the Martindale Boat Basin in Hudson Falls. This is the exit point. If you continue farther south for another 0.4 mile, you will dead-end at the impassable Lock 13, next to Pearl Street. Since there is no way to climb out of the canal at Pearl Street, you will have to return to the Martindale Boat Basin to exit.

The historic Martindale Boat Basin is one of six boat basins that existed along the Feeder Canal. The original stone-lined basin was set back 200 feet and was able to accommodate up to 6 boats. These boats (or barges) were 90 feet long and 14 feet wide. During the 1800s an average of 80 to 100 boats passed through the canal each week. The last commercial boat to go through was in 1928.

The first Martindale Bridge was much larger, with its ends constructed of

▶ **Feeder Canal from Richardson Street Access (Glens Falls)**

massive limestone blocks. When the canal was abandoned, the bridge was dismantled and its large limestone blocks dumped into the water to help fill in the basin. The smaller bridge that you see today took its place. The three-tiered retaining wall used for accessing the canal at the southwest end of the bridge was constructed in 1990 by using some of the recovered stone blocks.[7] Martindale Boat Basin Park officially opened in 1994.

Although the current is never powerful enough to keep you from doing an easy 5.5-mile paddle back to the starting point, you may prefer to have two cars, one parked at each end of the canal, and make it a one-way trip.

You are not limited to just accessing the canal at its endpoints, however. Besides the Richardson Street Access and the Martindale Boat Basin, there are three other access points in between. The paddles are all easy to moderate.

Alternate Launch Site #1

Martindale Boat Basin Park (Hudson Falls)

- **Launch Site:** Martindale Boat Basin Park off of Martindale Avenue in Hudson Falls (Washington County); 15-foot carry to three-tiered wall leading to put-in
- **Delorme NYS Atlas & Gazetteer:** p. 81, B5; **Estimated GPS:** 43°18.36'N; 73°34.86'W
- **Destinations & Mileages:** *West*: to Shermantown Road Access—2.0 miles; to Murray Street Access—3.4 miles; to Bush Street Access—5.0 miles; to Richardson Street Access—5.5 miles.
- **Comments:** Read "Caution" beginning on page xxi and Hudson River Advisory on page 216.

Directions: From Glens Falls (junction of Rtes. 9 & 32 north of Cooper's Cave Bridge) head east on Rte. 32 for over 1.6 miles. When you come to a traffic light, continue straight ahead on Lower Warren Street as Rte. 32 goes left. In 0.2 mile a second traffic light is reached, with Rte. 254 entering from your left. Continue southeast, now following Rte. 254, for another 1.3 miles. At the roundabout in Hudson Falls, head northeast on Rte. 4 for 0.4 mile. Turn right onto Martindale Avenue.

From Hudson Falls (junction of Rtes. 254 & 4) head northeast on Rte. 4 for 0.4 mile and turn right onto Martindale Avenue.

From either direction, take Martindale Avenue for 0.1 mile and park to your left before crossing over the Feeder Canal.

Carry your watercraft a couple of hundred feet to the put-in, where a dock awaits at the bottom of several wide limestone steps.

The Martindale Boat Basin. Photograph 2009.

Alternate Launch Site #2

Bush Street (Glens Falls)

- ■ **Launch Site:** Off of Bush Street in Glens Falls (Warren County); 30-foot carry to informal put-in
- ■ **Delorme NYS Atlas & Gazetteer:** p. 81, B4–5; **GPS:** 43°17.56'N; 73°39.31'W
- ■ **Destinations & Mileages:** *West*: to Richardson Street Access—0.5 mile. *East*: to Murray Street Access—1.0 mile; to Shermantown Road Access—2.3 mile; to the Martindale Boat Basin—5.0 miles.
- ■ **Comments:** Read "Caution" beginning on page xxi and Hudson River Advisory on page 216.

Directions: From the Adirondack Northway (I-87) take Exit 18 for Glens Falls. Head west on Main Street for 1.1 miles. At the traffic light turn right onto Staples Street and proceed south for 0.4 mile. When you come to Knight Street,

▶ **Feeder Canal from Richardson Street Access (Glens Falls)**

turn left and go east for 100 feet, then turn right onto Bush Street and proceed south for 0.4 mile. As soon as you cross over the feeder canal, turn left into a small parking area.

Approaching from the north end of Cooper's Cave Bridge (junction of Rtes. 9 & 32), go west on Mohican Street for 0.4 mile. Turn right onto Murray Street and go north for less than 0.1 mile. Turn left onto South Street and go southwest for 0.4 mile. When you come to Knight Street, turn right, then turn left onto Bush Street after 0.1 mile and drive south for nearly 0.4 mile, turning left into a parking area right after you cross over the feeder canal.

Put in at the southeast end of the bridge.

If the road leading across the bridge is gated in the off season, park to the side (making sure not to block anyone's route) and carry your watercraft across the bridge and down to the informal put-in, a trek of no more than several hundred feet.

Alternate Launch Site #3

Murray Street (Glens Falls)

- **Launch Site:** Off Murray Street in Glens Falls (Warren County); 100-foot carry
- **Delorme NYS Atlas & Gazetteer:** p. 81, B4–5; **GPS:** parking—43°18.10'N; 73°38.64'W; launch—43°18.14'N; 73°38.64'W
- **Destinations & Mileages:** *West*: to Bush Road Access—1.0 mile; to Richardson Street Access—1.5 miles. *East*: to Shermantown Road Access—1.3 miles; to Martindale Boat Basin—4.0 miles.
- **Comments:** Read "Caution" beginning on page xxi and Hudson River Advisory on page 216.

Directions: From the Adirondack Northway (I-87) take Exit 18 for Glens Falls. Go east on Main Street for 1.4 miles and turn right onto Murray Street. Drive southeast for 0.5 mile. As soon as you cross over the feeder canal, turn left into a parking area.

Approaching from the north end of Cooper's Cave Bridge (junction of Rtes. 9 & 32), go southwest on Mohican Street for 0.4 mile, then turn left onto Murray Street and head southeast for 0.2 mile. Turn left into the parking area at the end of the bridge spanning the canal.

From the parking area follow the towpath northeast for 100 feet and turn left, walking down a short boardwalk that leads to the canal put-in.

Access to the Feeder Canal and Hudson River was created by Finch Pruyn & Company in conjunction with the City of Glens Falls. The railed walkways are wheelchair accessible and a testimony to the goodwill of Finch Pruyn & Company and city officials.

Alternate Launch Site #4

Shermantown Road (East Glens Falls)

■ **Launch Site:** Off Shermantown Road (Warren County); 50-foot carry to informal put-in
■ **Delorme NYS Atlas & Gazetteer:** p. 81, B4–5; **GPS:** 43°18.47'N; 73°37.58'W
■ **Destinations & Mileages:** *West*: to Murray Street Access—1.3 miles; to Bush Street Access—2.3 miles; to Richardson Street Access—2.8 miles. *East*: to Martindale Boat Basin—2.7 miles.
■ **Comments:** Read "Caution" beginning on page xxi and Hudson River Advisory on page 216.

Directions: From the north end of Cooper's Cave Bridge in Glens Falls (junction of Rtes. 9 & 32), head east on Rte. 32 (Oakland Avenue) for over 0.3 mile. At the traffic light turn right onto Warren Street, following Rte. 32 as it continues east. After another 0.4 mile turn right onto Shermantown Road and drive south for 0.1 mile.

Approaching from Hudson Falls (junction of Rtes. 4 & 254) proceed northwest on Rte. 254. At 1.3 miles Rte. 254 goes off to the right, becoming Quaker Road. Stay left, continuing straight on Lower Warren Street. At 1.5 miles you will come to a traffic light where Rte. 32 comes in on your right from Highland Avenue. Continue straight as Lower Warren Street now becomes Rte. 32. At 2.4 miles you will reach Shermantown Road, where you turn left and drive south for 0.1 mile.

From either direction park on either side of the road just before crossing the canal bridge. The put-in is near the northeast end of the bridge where a tiny dock is permanently affixed to the side wall. The dock's height makes this a challenging access depending upon the height of the water in the canal.

Additional Point of Interest: The *Five Combines* in *Feeder Canal Park* consist of five hammer-dressed limestone locks—#6–#10—which were constructed in 1845 to replace locks made of timber in the 1820s and 1830s. The locks served to connect the lower-level waters of the Champlain Canal with the higher-level waters of the Hudson River, surmounting a ridge that ran diagonally southeast of Hudson Falls. The old sluiceway, partially uncovered, can be seen next to and paralleling the locks.

To get to Feeder Canal Park from Hudson Falls (junction of Rtes. 254 & 4), drive south on Rte. 4 for 0.05 mile and turn left onto Pearl Street. Go east for 0.4 mile and turn right onto Pine Street. In 0.3 mile you will reach Burgoyne Ave. Turn left and you will be at Feeder Canal Park in less than 0.05 mile. Locks #6–#10 are to the right. Locks #11–#13 are to the left, upstream, stretching from the Burgoyne Avenue bridge to the Pearl Street Bridge.

The park is open daily from dawn to dusk. For further information: feedercanal.com.

▶ **Feeder Canal from Richardson Street Access (Glens Falls)**

Murray Street Access (Glens Falls)
Hudson River between Feeder Dam and Glens Falls Dam

51

- ■ **Launch Site:** Off Murray Road in Glens Falls (Warren County); 300-foot carry
- ■ **Delorme NYS Atlas & Gazetteer:** p. 81, B4–5 **GPS:** parking—43°18.10'N; 73°38.64'W; Launch—43°18.17'N; 73°38.64'W
- ■ **Destinations & Mileages:** *North and East*: to warning buoys above Glens Falls Dam—0.2 mile. *South and West*: to cove—0.7 mile; to Haviland Cove—1.0 mile; to Haviland Cove Beach—1.4 miles; to Feeder Dam—2.0 miles.
- ■ **Comments:** Read "Caution" beginning on page xxi and Hudson River Advisory on page 216.

    Stay a safe distance back from the Feeder Dam and Glens Falls Dam. Always check the current before heading out when a dam is in close proximity to the launch site.

Directions: From the Adirondack Northway (I-87) take Exit 18 for Glens Falls. Go east on Main Street (which becomes Broad Street) for 1.4 miles and turn right onto Murray Street. Drive southeast for 0.5 mile. As soon as you cross over the feeder canal, turn left into the designated parking area.

Approaching from the north end of Cooper's Cave Bridge (junction of Rtes. 9 & 32), go southwest on Mohican Street for 0.4 mile, then turn left onto Murray Street and head southeast for 0.2 mile. As soon as you cross over the Feeder Canal, turn left into the designated parking area at the end of the bridge.

From the parking area carry your watercraft northeast along the towpath for 100 feet and then turn right, walking down an elaborate gravel ramp that descends to the river in less than 100 feet.

The launch site was established by Finch Pruyn & Company.

The Paddle:

From the launch look nearly straight across the river and you will see the Boralex South Glens Falls Hydro Electric Project's canoe portage site (see alternate launch site #3, "South Glens Falls"). To its right (south) is the Betar Byway and Park. Farther downstream, to your left, is the Glens Falls Dam, the Rte. 9 bridge, and Finch Pruyn & Company industrial complex.

The Murray Street access to the Hudson River (which also contains a separate access to the Glens Falls Feeder Canal, on the opposite side of the canal towpath) was created by Finch Pruyn & Company in conjunction with the City of Glens Falls. The company was established in 1865 when brothers Jeremiah and Daniel Finch in partnership with Samuel Pruyn purchased the Glens Falls Company sawmill at the front of Glen Street. In 1876 the company purchased the nearby Wing Sawmill, thereby gaining full control of the waterpower by the falls.

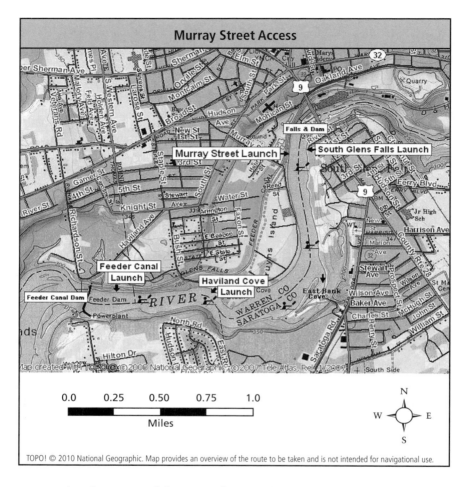

TOPO! © 2010 National Geographic. Map provides an overview of the route to be taken and is not intended for navigational use.

North and East—Head downriver for 0.2 mile until you reach a line of orange buoys that warn against approaching the Glens Falls Dam. Go no farther. The falls at Glens Falls were well known to Native Americans for centuries prior to European contact. They called the waterfall *Chepontuc*, meaning "difficult place to get around."[1] The first white man to view the falls is reputed to have been Father Isaac Jogues, the French priest whose zeal for converting natives to Christianity concluded with his martyrdom at Auriesville, New York.

Glens Falls is over 30 feet high and spans the river, but it is by no means straight across like a ruler's edge; rather, it is jagged and broken up into sections. The falls were first dammed by Abe Wing, who built a sawmill with 14 saws on the site currently occupied by Finch Pruyn & Company's visitor's parking lot on the opposite side of the river. At that time the falls were known as Wing's Falls.

South and West—Proceed upriver for 0.7 mile and you will pass by a cove on

▶ **Murray Street Access (Glens Falls)**

your left that can be explored inland for 0.2 mile. At 1.0 mile you will pass by Haviland Cove and then, at 1.4 miles, Haviland Cove Beach, both to your right. The ski slopes of West Mountain are visible in the distance. Keep in mind that you have been paralleling the east bank of Pruyns Island (to your right) since the start of the paddle. Pruyns Island lies between the Hudson River and the Glens Falls Feeder Canal.

The base of the Feeder Dam is reached in another 0.6 mile. You will see the power plant next to the south end of the dam.

Additional Point of Interest: Historic Cooper's Cave, located near the southwest end of Cooper's Cave Bridge (which links Glens Falls with South Glens Falls), is a must-see if you are in the area. The viewing platform for the cave can be accessed by turning west onto River Road at the south end of Cooper's Cave Bridge to reach a parking area in less than 0.1 mile. From there walk back on River Road for less than 0.05 mile and turn left at Cooper's Cave Drive. Head downhill for 0.05 mile, going under the massive bridge, to reach an observation platform overlooking the cave and falls. Cooper's Cave's viewing platform is open daily from Memorial Day to Columbus Day, 9 AM–8 PM.

Cooper's Cave became historically significant after being described in James Fenimore Cooper's classic novel *The Last of the Mohicans*. People clamored to visit the cave, even though it was actually a fairly undistinguished, wide fissure that had formed in the bedrock at the base of Glens Falls.[2] When the Viaduct Bridge was built in 1913, a long circular stairway was constructed from the bridge to the cave. Many thousands of people took advantage of this access to see the cave. By 1961 the stairway was deemed unsafe and was removed. When the present bridge was built, no attempt was made to recreate the descending stairway; rather, access to an overlook of Cooper's Cave was constructed under the south end of Cooper's Cave Bridge, with many historical plaques erected to recount the history of the cave and the fall.

Alternate Launch Site #1

Haviland Cove (Glens Falls)

■ **Launch Site:** Haviland Cove Beach & Recreation Area at end of Bush Road in Glens Falls (Warren County); 50-foot carry to slip-in
■ **Delorme NYS Atlas & Gazetteer:** p. 81, B4–5; **GPS:** 43°17.54'N; 73°39.21'W
■ **Destinations & Mileages:** *East*: to Murray Street access & South Glens Falls access—1.2 miles; to buoys above Glens Falls Dam—1.4 miles. *West*: to Feeder Dam—0.6 mile.
■ **Comments:** Read "Caution" beginning on page xxi and Hudson River Advisory on page 216.
    Stay a safe distance back from the Feeder Dam and the Glens Falls Dam.

Directions: From the Adirondack Northway (I-87) take Exit 18 for Glens Falls and head west on Main Street for 1.1 miles. Turn right onto Staples Street at the traffic light and proceed south for 0.4 mile. When you come to Knight Street, turn left and go east for 100 feet, then turn right onto Bush Street and go south for 0.4 mile into the entrance to Haviland Cove Beach & Recreation Area.

From the north end of Cooper's Cave Bridge (junction of Rtes. 9 & 32), go west on Mohican Street for 0.4 mile. Turn right onto Murray Street and go north for less than 0.1 mile. At South Street turn left and go southwest for 0.4 mile. When you come to Knight Street, turn right and go 0.1 mile, then turn left onto Bush Street and drive 0.4 mile into the entrance to Haviland Cove Beach & Recreation Area.

When you enter the Haviland Cove Beach & Recreation area, turn right into the parking area, facing the Hudson River. Carry your watercraft 30 feet across the lawn to slip-in at river's edge.

During the off season, the park is closed and entry is not possible.

Alternate Launch Site #2

Feeder Canal (Glens Falls)

- ■ **Launch Site:** Off of Feeder Canal in Glens Falls (Warren County); less than 0.1-mile carry
- ■ **Delorme NYS Atlas & Gazetteer:** p. 81, B4–5; **GPS:** parking—43°17.56'N; 73°39.93'W; launch—43°17.50'N; 73°39.80'W
- ■ **Destinations & Mileages:** *East:* to Haviland Cove Beach—0.6 mile; to buoys above Glens Falls—2.1 miles.
- ■ **Comments:** Read "Caution" beginning on page xxi and Hudson River Advisory on page 216.

    Stay back a safe distance from the Feeder Dam, just upstream, and the Glens Falls Dam, farther downstream.

Directions: From the Adirondack Northway (I-87) take Exit 18 for Glens Falls and head east on Main Street for over 0.5 mile. At the traffic light turn right onto Richardson Street and proceed south for 0.6 mile. When you come to the junction of Richardson Street and Haviland Avenue, turn right into a paved parking area overlooking the river and dam.

Approaching from the north end of Cooper's Cave Bridge (junction of Rtes. 9 & 32), go west on Mohican Street for 0.4 mile. Turn right onto Murray Street and drive north for less than 0.1 mile. When you come to South Street, turn left and drive southwest for 0.4 mile, then turn right onto Knight Street and go west for 0.2 mile. Turn left onto Haviland Street and drive southwest for over 0.5 mile. The paved parking area is directly to your left, facing the river and overlooking the dam.

▶ **Murray Street Access (Glens Falls)**

The falls at Glens Falls. Postcard ca. 1940.

From the parking area, carry your watercraft down the hill to the Feeder Canal and cross over to the other side via the footbridge. Follow the towpath east for less than 0.05 mile, just past park benches that line the towpath. A steep 8-foot-wide path to your right leads down in 50 feet to the river, where your canoe or kayak can be launched.

Alternate Launch Site #3

South Glens Falls (South Glens Falls)

- ■ **Launch Site:** Canoe Portage Access Point on Hudson River (Saratoga County); gravel put-in
- ■ **Delorme NYS Atlas & Gazetteer:** p. 81, B4–5; **Estimated GPS:** 43°18.19'N; 73°38.52'W
- ■ **Destinations & Mileages:** *West*: to east bank cove—0.7 mile; up cove—0.2 mile; to Haviland Cove—1.0 mile; to Haviland Cove Beach—1.4 miles; to Feeder Dam—2.0 miles.
- ■ **Comments:** Read "Caution" beginning on page xxi and Hudson River Advisory on page 216.
  Stay a safe distance back from the Glens Falls Dam and the Feeder Dam. Always check the current before heading out onto the river when a dam is in close proximity to the launch site.

Directions: From the north end of Cooper's Cave Bridge at Glens Falls (junction of Rtes. 9 & 32), drive south on Rte. 9 for over 0.2 mile, crossing over the Hudson River. At the south end of Cooper Cave's Bridge, turn right onto River Street and drive 0.1 mile west to the end of the road and the boat launch.

From South Glens Falls (junction of Rtes. 9 & 32 South) go northwest on Rte. 9 for 1.0 mile. When you come to the traffic light at the south end of Cooper's Cave Bridge, turn left onto River Street and drive west 0.1 mile to the end of the road and the boat launch.

The Canoe Portage Access Point was made available through the Boralex South Glens Falls Hydro Electric Project.

The launch is not far from Betar Park and its trail that parallels the east bank of the Hudson River for roughly 1.0 mile.

▶ **Murray Street Access (Glens Falls)**

Hudson River Park (Glens Falls)
Hudson River between Sherman Island Dam and Feeder Dam

52

- ■ **Launch Site:** Hudson River Park (Warren County); hard-surface ramp and floating dock; parking for 10 cars & trailers
- ■ **Delorme NYS Atlas & Gazetteer:** p. 81, BC4; **GPS:** 43°15.84'N; 73°40.45'W
- ■ **Destinations & Mileages:** *North and West*: to Adirondack Northway (I-87)—0.05 mile; to west bank cove—0.3 mile; up cove—0.3 mile; to Big Bay—1.5 miles; to Clendon Brook—2.1 miles; to Hudson Pointe Nature Preserve—2.5 miles; to Sherman Island Power Plant—3.0 miles. *East & North:* to south bank channel—0.3 mile; down south bank channel—0.6 mile; to Town of Moreau Boat Launch—0.8 mile; to river mounds—0.9 mile; to channel on west bank—1.0 mile; up channel—0.5 mile; to islands—2.0 miles; around islands—1.6 miles; to Feeder Dam & Richardson Street access—2.9 miles.
- ■ **Comments:** Read "Caution" beginning on page xxi and Hudson River Advisory on page 216.
    Stay a safe distance back from the Feeder Dam and Sherman Island Dam.

Directions: From the Adirondack Northway (I-87) take Exit 18 for Glens Falls. Drive east on Main Street for less than 0.05 mile and turn right onto Big Boom Road, heading south. In 0.4 mile you will come to a fork in the road where Twin Channels Road veers left. Stay to the right on Big Boom Road. At 2.1 miles you will reach the entrance to Hudson River Park, and at 2.6 miles the boat launch and parking area, located on a section of the river called Big Bend.

There are two river accesses to choose from—the main launch site (and dock) at the parking area, and a second site (which includes a dock) located several hundred feet east beyond the picnic tables at the end of a gravel walkway.

The Paddle:

The 44-acre Hudson River Park contains over 2,000 feet of shoreline.[1] The land encompassing the park was donated by Carl and Barbara DeSantis with the stipulation that it be used for recreation.[2]

The general area near the boat launch has been described in several colorful ways including Big Bay, Big Bend, and Big Boom. The origin of Big Bend's name is self-evident once you look at a topographic map, for the river bends dramatically by Hudson River Park, making a pronounced U-shaped turn. In the days before bridges, David Tillotson established a ferry service here. The name Big Bay refers to an area slightly northwest where the river widens temporarily, becoming bay-like. In 1812 the bay was called Oak Hollow.[3]

As for Big Boom, that was the name of a huge log boom chained across the river to intercept logs rushing downstream, constructed by the Hudson River Boom Association between 1849 and 1851. From Big Boom, logs would be

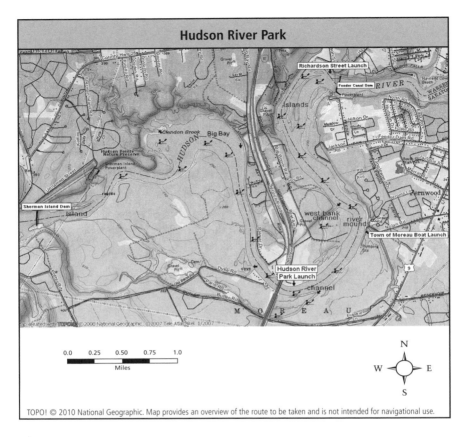

Hudson River Park

0.0   0.25   0.50   0.75   1.0
Miles

N
W — E
S

TOPO! © 2010 National Geographic. Map provides an overview of the route to be taken and is not intended for navigational use.

sorted according to brand marks etched into them and channeled farther down-river to one of over thirty mills and docks that flourished in the area.[4] The boom also prevented logs from racing downriver to be swept over Glens Falls and dashed into pieces below. Nothing was wasted. Even sawdust was sent downstate for use as insulation in icehouses.

Benson J. Lossing, who witnessed lumbermen at work firsthand, described the Big Boom as "made of heavy, hewn timbers, four of them, bolted together raft-wise. The ends of the groups were connected by chains, which worked over friction rollers, to allow the boom to accommodate itself to the motion of the water. Each end of the boom was secured to a heavy abutment by chains; and above it were strong triangular structures to break the ice, to serve as anchors for the boom, and to operate as shields to prevent the logs striking the boom with the full speed of this current."[5]

The only time the boom failed was during the great flood of 1913. The boom snapped under the relentless onslaught of the raging Hudson and half a million logs were sent down the river and scattered from Fort Edward to Troy.[6]

▶ Hudson River Park (Glens Falls)

North and West—Head upstream, passing under the Adirondack Northway (I-87) at 0.05 mile, and then by a series of seasonal camps on both sides of the river. At 0.3 mile you will come to a cove on your left. Paddling in, you can proceed either north or west. If you head north, you can explore an offshoot of the cove for about 0.1 mile. If you continue west you will quickly reach what appears to be the end of the cove, only to discover that a small island is hiding an opening that leads into a second cove. Here you can continue west for another 0.2 mile as the cove gradually narrows into a channel.

Back on the Hudson River heading upstream, you will notice that the shore to your left is wild (and posted), whereas the bank to your right is lined with homes (the result of Big Bay Road making this section of the river accessible to homeowners).

At 1.5 mile you will reach a part of the river called Big Bay, where the Hudson temporarily appears less like a river and more like a bay. To your right is Carman's Neck, the narrowest part of the peninsula formed by Big Bend. Carman's Neck was named after John Carman in 1789. Carman was an original proprietor under the Prindle Patent.[7] Near the upper, northwest, part of Big Bay is Clendon Brook (formerly called Trout Brook), which is passed by at 2.1 miles.

At 2.5 miles you will reach the Hudson Pointe Nature Preserve along the north bank to your right. You can put in your watercraft and hike the preserve's two miles of trails, including a boardwalk that crosses over a wetland area. There are many places along the shoreline where it is possible to land, including the "Observation Bridge" at the northwest side of the preserve. The bridge, however, is at water level and prevents kayakers from going farther into the interior of this section of the preserve without carrying over it. Several tiny islands are in close proximity to the Observation Bridge—one to the north, two to the east, and one (the largest) to the southeast.

The Hudson Pointe Nature Preserve consists of 83 acres of trails and riverfront views that were created by the Open Space Institute (OSI) in conjunction with the Town of Queensbury using land generously donated to OSI by the Niagara Mohawk Power Corporation. Funds for the planning and improvement of the land were furnished through the Lila Acheson & Dewitt Wallace Fund for the Hudson Highlands. (Lila Acheson and Dewitt Wallace were the founders of the Readers Digest Association, Inc.) Materials and labor were provided by Curtis Lumber, the Michaels Group, volunteers of the Hudson River Preservation Group, Southern Adirondack Audubon, and Queensbury Cub Scout Pack #16.[8]

Just ahead on the Hudson River past the Hudson Pointe Nature Preserve is Little Bay—a smaller version of Big Bay. The Sherman Island Power Plant is visible at the northwest end of the bay. When you reach the power plant, at 3.0 miles, and veer left, you will discover that rapids and shallows block the way after another 0.1 mile. This is a good place to turn around. Continuing farther upstream would involve portaging around the rapids in order to reach a slender island 0.1 mile downstream from the Sherman Island Dam.

North and East—Proceed downstream for 0.3 mile and you will come to a small passageway along the south bank at a point where the river begins to veer left. This passageway immediately opens up into a 50-foot-wide channel that goes west for 0.6 mile, coming to a dead end just before the Adirondack Northway is reached. On this side trek, at 0.4 mile, you will see an opening to your left that leads into a huge, marshy, pond area. Unfortunately, beavers have dammed the entranceway, which means that only a determined paddler is going to portage over this obstacle to see what lies beyond. Prior to the Adirondack Northway being constructed, the channel continued west for another 0.3 mile or more.

Back on the Hudson River, at 0.8 mile you will pass by the Town of Moreau Boat Launch and then, 0.1 mile beyond that, a series of tiny, square-shaped mounds that extend across the full width of the river. The mounds are relics left over from the river drives of logging days; river men would stand on the mounds while "herding" the logs.

In another 0.1 mile you will come to a west bank channel, on your left, which can be followed inland for up to 0.5 mile depending upon blowdown and other obstacles that can vary year by year. Because the channel is fairly deep, many of the trees that toppled into it now lie below the water's surface and can be skimmed over by a canoe or kayak.

Rock mounds remain as vestiges from the days of dangerous log drives on the river. Photograph 2010.

▶ **Hudson River Park (Glens Falls)**

Back on the river, at 2.0 miles you will reach a bay-like section that is broken up to the left by a series of islands. The main island is 0.6 mile long, with a fingerlike projection of land along its southeast side. Satellite islands can be seen near each side of its south end and near its north end. The islands can be circumnavigated in 1.6 miles.

At 2.9 miles, orange-colored buoys warn that you are approaching the Feeder Dam. Turn around here.

Should you need to make this a one-way trip, the Richardson Street canoe/kayak take-out is located on the north bank shoreline, to your left, by the orange buoys before the Feeder Canal and dam.

Alternate Launch Site #1

Richardson Street Access (Glens Falls)

▦ **Launch Site:** Off Richardson Street in Glens Falls (Warren County); car-top launch; 50-foot carry to slip-in
▦ **Delorme NYS Atlas & Gazetteer:** p. 81, B4–5; **GPS:** 43°17.54'N; 73°39.98'W
▦ **Destinations & Mileages:** *South:* to islands near put-in—0.1 mile; around island—1.6 miles; to west bank channel—2.0 miles; down west bank channel—0.5 mile; to river mounds—2.1 miles; to Town of Moreau Boat Launch—2.2 miles; to south bank channel—2.7 miles; down south bank channel—0.6 mile; to Hudson River Park—2.9 miles; to Adirondack Northway overpass—3.0 miles; to west bank cove—3.3 miles; up cove—0.3 mile; to Big Bay—4.5 miles; to Clendon Brook—5.1 miles; to Hudson Pointe Nature Preserve—5.5 miles; to Sherman Island Power Plant—6.0 miles.
▦ **Comments:** Read "Caution" beginning on page xxi and Hudson River Advisory on page 216.
    Stay a safe distance back from the Feeder Dam and Sherman Island Dam. Always check the current before heading out when a dam is in close proximity to the launch site.

Directions: From the Adirondack Northway (I-87) take Exit 18 for Glens Falls and head east on Main Street for over 0.5 mile. At a traffic light turn right onto Richardson Street and proceed south for nearly 0.6 mile. At 0.05 mile before reaching the junction of Richardson Street and Haviland Avenue, turn into a small pull-off on your right where a sign reads "Car top Boat Launch."

From the north end of Cooper's Cave Bridge (junction of Rtes. 9 & 32), go west on Mohican Street for 0.4 mile. Turn right onto Murray Street and drive north for less than 0.1 mile. When you come to South Street, turn left and drive southwest for 0.4 mile, then turn right onto Knight Street and go west for 0.2 mile. Turn left onto Haviland Street and drive southwest for over 0.5 mile to the junction of Haviland Street and Richardson Street, where the parking area for the

Feeder Canal is to your left. Continue west on Richardson Street for 0.05 mile to a pull-off on your left where a sign reads "Car top Boat Launch."

From the pull-off it is a 50-foot carry to the put-in on the Hudson River, directly next to a line of orange buoys spanning the river above the Feeder Dam.

Alternate Launch Site #2

Town of Moreau Boat Launch (Fernwood)

■ **Launch Site:** Town of Moreau Boat Launch (Saratoga County); beach slip-in
■ **Delorme NYS Atlas & Gazetteer:** p. 81, BC4–5; **GPS:** 43°16.26'N; 73°39.64'W
■ **Destinations & Mileages:** *North:* to river mounds—0.1 mile; to west bank channel—0.2 mile; up channel—0.5 mile; to downstream islands—1.1 miles; around downstream islands—1.6 miles; to Feeder Dam—2.0 miles. *West:* to south bank channel—0.7 mile; down south bank channel—0.6 mile; to Hudson River Park—0.9 mile; to Adirondack Northway (I-87)—1.0 mile; to west bank cove—1.3 miles; up cove—0.3 mile; to Big Bay—2.5 miles; to Clendon Brook—3.1 miles; to Hudson Pointe Nature Preserve—3.5 miles; to Sherman Island Power Plant—4.0 miles.
■ **Comments:** Read "Caution" beginning on page xxi and Hudson River Advisory on page 216.
    Stay a safe distance back from the Feeder Dam and Sherman Island Dam.

Directions: From the Adirondack Northway (I-87) take Exit 17N for South Glens Falls and head northeast on Rte. 9 for approximately 3.5 miles (or 1.9 miles past Rte. 9's junction with Rte. 197). Turn left onto Nolan Road and drive southwest for 0.6 mile to a large parking area next to the river. The sandy launch site allows you to slip in your watercraft without effort.

▶ **Hudson River Park (Glens Falls)**

Upper Hudson River Boat Launch (Lake Luzerne)
Accessing the Hudson River between a Waterfall and a Dam

53

- **Launch Site:** Upper Hudson River Boat Launch off of River Road (Warren County); hard-surface ramp; parking for 30 cars & trailers
- **Delorme NYS Atlas & Gazetteer:** p. 80, BC3; **Estimated GPS:** 43°17.25'N; 73°49.55'W
- **Destinations & Mileages:** *North*: to Rte. 9N bridge—1.7 miles; to mouth of Sacandaga River—2.5 miles; to Rockwell Falls—2.7 miles. *South*: to Sturdevant Creek—2.8 miles; to Densmore Memorial Bridge/River Road launch site— 2.9 miles.
- **Comments:** Read "Caution" beginning on page xxi and Hudson River Advisory on page 216.
  Stay a safe distance back from the Curtis Falls Dam and Rockwell Falls. The paddle to Rockwell Falls is best undertaken in summer when the river's water volume is lower.

Directions: From the center of Corinth (junction of Main Street & Maple Street where Rte. 9N does a right-angle turn), head north on Main Street/Rte. 9N for less than 0.1 mile. Turn right at a traffic light onto River Road (which soon becomes East River Road) and drive northeast for 3.0 miles. When you come to Boat Launch Drive, turn left and head west for 0.2 mile to the parking area for the boat launch.

From a traffic light just south of the village of Lake Luzerne (junction of Rtes. 9N & East River Road), turn onto East River Road and drive southeast for 2.0 miles. When you come to Boat Launch Drive, turn right and go 0.2 mile to the large parking area for the boat launch.

The Paddle:
The launch site is just north of Schaeffers Brook, a small stream that rises in the hills northeast of Corinth. The stream is essentially unnavigable for any length.

Heading in either direction on the Hudson River, you can only go slightly under 3.0 miles before encountering a waterfall (Rockwell Falls, going north) or a dam (Curtis Falls Dam, going south).

North—Heading upriver you will pass by 1,154-foot-high Twist Mountain to your right at 0.7 mile. On the opposite side of the river, 1.5 miles to the west, is 1,637-foot-high Mount Anthony.

At 1.3 miles the river becomes more serpentine, changing direction from north to west, and then, after another 0.7 mile, from west back to north. The Rte. 9N bridge is reached at 1.7 miles.

At 2.5 miles you will come to the confluence of the Hudson River with the Sacandaga River, where the Hudson becomes lakelike. Locals call it Phelps Bay. You will experience a significant increase in current as the two rivers

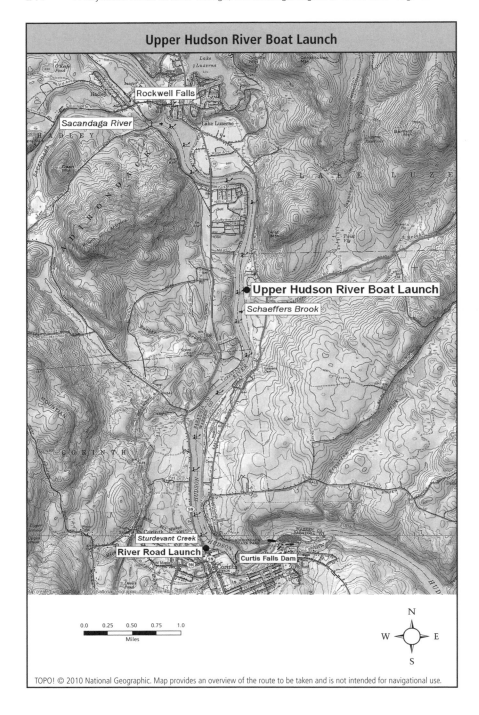

Upper Hudson River Boat Launch

TOPO! © 2010 National Geographic. Map provides an overview of the route to be taken and is not intended for navigational use.

▶ **Upper Hudson River Boat Launch (Lake Luzerne)**

combine their forces. Pronounced rapids and current make it tiresome to paddle up the Sacandaga River for any distance. Instead, continue pushing upriver on the Hudson River for another 0.2 mile, passing through a narrow, rocky gorge and under the towering Bridge of Hope. An earlier version of this bridge contained a pedestrian walkway below the main deck.[1] The gorge was described by Charles Farnham in 1880 when he wrote, with considerable hyperbole: "The gorge of the river here is very narrow, crooked, and walled in with precipitous rocks. The current is swift, tortuous, and turbulent. Just below the foot of the fall is a steep plunge or shoot, where the water almost falls over some rocks, and rolls up crested waves of quite formidable appearance. A few yards below this is a second plunge, rather rougher than the first. Elsewhere the current is deep, and safe enough if it does not dash you against the cavernous walls of rock."[2]

Just north of the Bridge of Hope is a tiny cascade/rapid where the gorge narrows appreciably. Most paddlers will be content to reach this point and then turn around. For those who persevere, a second small cascade/rapid is reached in another 50 feet. Beyond this is 12-foot-high Rockwell Falls, which is one of the Adirondack Park's most photogenic waterfalls. While the majority of visitors will be satisfied with just viewing it from the Bridge of Hope, paddlers have the opportunity of seeing it from the river at eye level. If you make it up to Rockwell Falls, be sure to stay a safe distance back from the fall because of severe hydraulics.

South—Proceeding downriver from the launch, you will immediately pass by Schaeffers Brook on your left, and then reach Sturdevant Creek, to your right, at 2.8 miles. Sturdevant Creek is a medium-sized stream that rises from the east shoulder of Spruce Mountain. As early as 1820 a gristmill had been established on the stream by a family named Boardman.[3] It is possible to follow Sturdevant Creek through the culvert under Rte. 9N and into a tiny swamp. The water is shallow, however, and Sturdevant Creek is unnavigable for any distance upstream.

The Irving H. Densmore Memorial Bridge & River Road launch site are reached at 2.9 miles. The bridge and River Road access are near the former site of Jessup's Ferry, named after Edward and Ebenezer Jessup, two brothers who were the region's first lumbermen. The ferry was the only means of crossing the Hudson River here until 1896, when an iron bridge was constructed between the present bridge and the Curtis Falls Dam.[4] The Irving H. Densmore Memorial Bridge connects Saratoga County with Warren County and was named after a former mayor who walked across the bridge daily as part of his exercise. The dedication ceremony took place in September 2000.[5]

Stay back from the Curtis Falls Dam (also called the Corinth Dam), a mere 0.2 mile downstream (south) from the River Road put-in. Curtis Falls is a dammed waterfall named after Warren Curtis, Jr., founder of the Corinth Electric Light Company.[6] The dam continues to be used for generating hydroelectric power.

Alternate Launch Site

River Road (Corinth)

- **Launch Site:** Hudson River access at northwest end of Densmore Memorial Bridge in Corinth (Saratoga County); hard-surface ramp
- **Delorme NYS Atlas & Gazetteer:** p. 80, BC3; **GPS:** 43°14.87'N; 73°49.99'W
- **Destinations & Mileages:** *North*: to Sturdevant Creek—0.1 mile; to Schaeffer Brook/Upper Hudson River Boat Launch—2.8 miles; to Rte. 9N bridge—4.6 miles; to confluence of Hudson & Sacandaga Rivers—5.4 miles; to Rockwell Falls— 5.6 miles.
- **Comments:** Read "Caution" beginning on page xxi and Hudson River Advisory on page 216.

  Stay a safe distance back from the Curtis Falls Dam and Rockwell Falls. Always check the current before heading out when a dam is in close proximity to the launch site.

Directions: From the traffic light at the center of Corinth (the intersection of Main Street & Maple Street where Rte. 9N does a right-angle turn), drive north on Main Street (Rte. 9N) for 0.1 mile until you reach the next traffic light. Turn right onto River Road and drive east for 100 feet. Just before crossing over the Densmore Memorial Bridge, turn left and then immediately right into a small parking lot where several parking spaces are designated for boaters.

Walk: You can take a short river walk between the Corinth Beach & Park and Curtis Park, following along a paved walkway that parallels the river as it goes under the Densmore Memorial Bridge.

Curtis Falls & dam. Postcard ca. 1940.

▶ **Upper Hudson River Boat Launch (Lake Luzerne)**

Hudson River Recreation Area (Fourth Lake)
Paddle along a Quiet, Fairly Remote Section of the Hudson River   54

■ **Launch Sites:** Hudson River Recreation Area & downriver access sites (Warren County); 50-foot to 0.3-mile-long carries to put-in depending upon access site chosen

■ **Delorme NYS Atlas & Gazetteer:** p. 80, AB2–3; **GPS:** Launch #1—43°25.10'N; 73°52.82'W; Launch #2—43°25.00'N; 73°52.63'W; Launch #3—43°24.87'N; 73°52.51'W; Launch #4—43°24.31'N; 73°52.92'W; Launch #5/Bear Slide—43°24.06'N; 73°52.85'W; Launch #6—43°23.93'N; 73°52.92'W; Launch #7/Thomas Road—43°22.96'N; 73°52.31'W; Launch #8/Pikes Beach—43°20.71'N; 73°51.50'W; Launch #9/Scofield Flats—43°20.53'N; 73°51.32'W; Launch #10—43°24.34'N; 73°52.88'W; Launch #11/Warren County Canoe Access—43°24.96'N; 73°52.58'W

■ **Destinations & Mileages (starting from Launch #1, one-way):** *South*—to island across from Launch #2—0.2 mile; to Launch #3—0.4 mile; to Stony Creek—0.7 mile; to Launch #4—1.0 mile; to Launch #5/Bear Slide—1.5 miles; to Launch #6—1.7 miles; to Launch #7/Thomas Road—3.0 miles; to Wolf Creek—5.2 miles; to Tank Brook—5.6 miles; to Launch #8/Pikes Beach—6.0 miles; to Launch #9/Scofield Flats—6.2 miles; to Launch #10—6.9 miles; to Launch #11/Warren County Canoe Access—7.6 miles; to Hadley Canoe Take-out (on opposite shoreline)—8.3 miles.

■ **Comments:** Read "Caution" beginning on page xxi and Hudson River Advisory on page 216.

Although the waters can be swift moving with occasional small rapids, this section of the river is essentially Class I-II Whitewater. The only significant obstacles are sandbars, which tend to appear when the river level goes down during the summer.

The small rapids and the shallows make this trek a one-way paddle. You will need two cars, one parked at your launch site, and the second parked at your planned take-out site.

Map 2 is a continuation south of Map 1.

Directions: *From Lake Luzerne*—From the center of the village of Lake Luzerne (junction of Main Street and Bridge Street), drive north on Main Street for 0.3 mile. Instead of turning right onto Mill Street, bear left onto River Road. The following mileages apply as you head north on River Road:

0.8 mile—*Launch #11/Warren County Canoe Access*. Turn into a parking area on your right. Carry your watercraft across the road and down the embankment for 50 feet to the river.

1.5 miles—*Launch #10*. Pull into an area of state land on your left. Carry your watercraft down a steep embankment for 50 feet to a gravel put-in.

2.2 miles—*Launch #9/Scofield Flats*. Look for a roadside barricade to your left. Pull into a small parking area just south of the barricade on the same side of

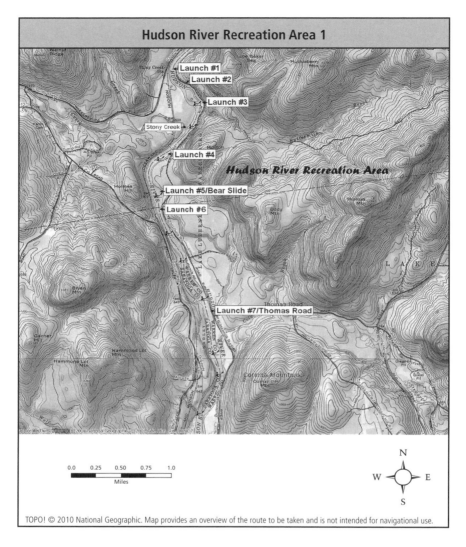

Hudson River Recreation Area 1

Launch #1
Launch #2
Launch #3
Stony Creek
Launch #4
Hudson River Recreation Area
Launch #5/Bear Slide
Launch #6
Launch #7/Thomas Road

0.0   0.25   0.50   0.75   1.0
Miles

N
W — E
S

TOPO! © 2010 National Geographic. Map provides an overview of the route to be taken and is not intended for navigational use.

the road. Walk past the barricade and follow the road downhill for 0.1 mile. The road quickly U-turns and leads to a lower parking area reserved for permitted drivers (CP-3) with disabilities. From the lower parking area, carry your watercraft another 100 feet down a well-groomed crushed-stone walk to the edge of the river for an easy slip-in.

2.4 miles—*Launch #8/Pikes Beach*. Look for a secondary gravel road to your left. Follow it for 100 feet to a sizeable parking area. From there walk past the barricade and follow a well-maintained secondary road for 0.3 mile to a lower parking area next to the river. A kayak carrier would be helpful to bridge this

▶ **Hudson River Recreation Area (Fourth Lake)**

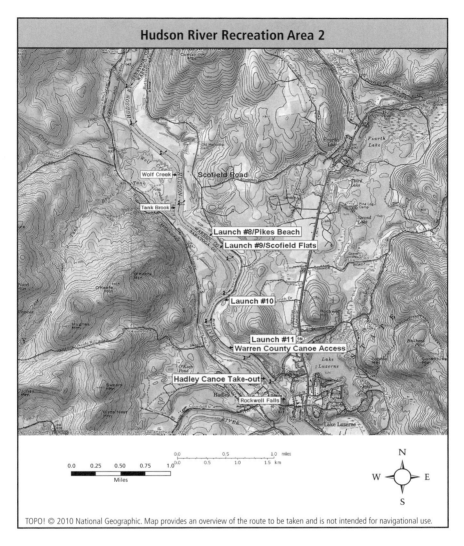

Hudson River Recreation Area 2

Wolf Creek
Scofield Road
Tank Brook
Launch #8/Pikes Beach
Launch #9/Scofield Flats
Launch #10
Launch #11
Warren County Canoe Access
Hadley Canoe Take-out
Rockwell Falls

N
W — E
S

0.0   0.25   0.50   0.75   1.0
Miles

0.0   0.5   1.0 miles
0.0
0.5   1.0   1.5 km

TOPO! © 2010 National Geographic. Map provides an overview of the route to be taken and is not intended for navigational use.

distance. Disabled drivers with permits (CP-3) are allowed to drive in. From the lower parking area, walk south across a wide-open expanse of bare earth for 100 feet, then follow a path to your left that leads immediately to a sandy beach where you can slip in your watercraft easily.

2.9 miles—Scofield Road (reference point).

5.6 miles—Thomas Road (reference point).

5.6 miles—*Launch #7/Thomas Road*. As soon as you pass by Thomas Road, which enters on your right, turn into a small pull-off on the left side of the road. A 50-foot carry leads to the edge of the river.

6.9 miles—*Launch #6*. Pull into the area on your right. This parking spot is the last one encountered before River Road narrows considerably and becomes more rutted, and it lies virtually on the Saratoga County/Warren County line. From the parking area, walk south back along River Road for 50 feet and then follow a 50-foot-long path that gradually descends to the edge of the river. Don't take the path directly across from the parking area—it is too steep.

7.1 miles—*Launch #5/Bear Slide*. Park in the large area to your right. Walk across the road and follow a barricaded secondary road where a sign states "Motor Vehicle Access Road—Permit only." The road, intended for drivers with disabilities who have an access permit (CP-3), leads in less than 0.1 mile to a small parking area and crushed-stone walkway to the river's edge, where a kayak or canoe can easily be launched. An island directly in front makes it difficult to see the launch site from the river.

7.4 miles—*Launch #4*. Park in pull-offs on either side of the road where a sign states, "Camping is now restricted along shoreline." This 200-foot carry takes you through an area of tall pine trees and picnic tables, where a moderately steep path leads quickly down to the edge of the river.

8.2 miles—*Launch #3*. Look for a small pull-off on your left where a series of large boulders have been placed. A moderately steep path leads down the embankment for 50 feet to the river's edge.

8.4 miles—*Launch #2*. You have reached the area where commercial outfitters customarily drop off clients. Be sure to park so that you will not obstruct large vehicles and buses. It is a 50-foot carry from the parking lot to a gravel launch area.

8.6 miles—*Launch #1*. You will come to a cul-de-sac with a large parking area at its end. (Take note that River Road still continues to your right before the cul-de-sac, but nothing is gained by taking it any farther.) Carry your watercraft along a 100-foot-long walkway of crushed stones that leads to the river's edge.

From the Adirondack Northway (I-87)—Take Exit 21 and proceed south on Rte. 9N for roughly 7.5 miles. Just before you reach Third Lake, turn right onto Gailey Hill Road and head northwest for 2.5 miles, then turn left onto Thomas Road and proceed west for 0.8 mile to River Road. From the junction of Thomas Road and River Road, you can either turn right to launch sites #1–7, or left to launch sites #8–11:

Mileages from Thomas Road, north on River Road:
    0.0 mile—Launch #7/Thomas Road
    1.3 miles—Launch #6
    1.5 miles—Launch #5/Bear Slide
    1.8 miles—Launch #4
    2.6 miles—Launch #3
    2.8 miles—Launch #2
    3.0 miles—Launch #1

▶ Hudson River Recreation Area (Fourth Lake)

Mileages from Thomas Road, south on River Road:
   3.2 miles—Launch #8/Pikes Beach
   3.4 miles—Launch #9/Scofield Flats
   4.1 miles—Launch #10
   4.8 miles—Launch #11/Warren County Canoe Access

All of these launch sites are located along the east bank of the Hudson River. An access site is also located on the west bank, just upstream from Hadley (see chapter "Hadley Canoe Take-Out"), that affords the last possible opportunity to exit the river before reaching the impassable Rockwell Falls.

The Paddle:
The Hudson River Recreation Area, also called the Buttermilk Area, is part of the Hudson River Special Management Area, which contains 5,500 acres of land between Lake Luzerne and Warrensburg that includes nearly seventeen miles of shoreline along the east bank of the Hudson River.[1] The recreation area is part of the 62,000-acre Lake George Wild Forest, which encompasses tracts of land on both the east and west sides of Lake George.[2] The recreation area also contains several miles of hiking trails, a natural waterslide called Buttermilk Falls, and opportunities for cross-country skiing.

The number and variety of launch sites allow paddlers to design treks of various length by putting in and taking out at different points. The reader should bear in mind that this particular section of the Hudson River is a "one-way river." While you may be able to pass over small rapids and shallows going downstream, those same obstacles will make paddling upstream difficult to nearly impossible unless you portage over the obstacles.

A much longer paddle can be taken by starting even farther upstream on the Hudson River (see chapter "Warren County Canoe Access") and using one of the access sites listed in this chapter as the take-out.

South—The paddle downstream takes you through a fairly natural-looking area of the Hudson as the river weaves its way between a number of mountains over 1,500 feet high. Paralleling the west side of the Hudson River are Stony Creek Road (Rte.1), a short section of Warrensburg Road, and the former Delaware & Hudson (D&H) Railroad. Fortunately, these roadways are generally far enough away from the river to be unobtrusive and thus not spoil the scenery. You will only see Warrensburg Road and a few houses on it briefly as you push off from Launch #1. River Road, which is not heavily traveled, follows along the east bank, remaining unnoticeable even though it stays fairly close to the river.

There are a couple of tiny islands along the trek, the largest one being the 0.2-mile-long island adjacent to Launch #2. Decisions will have to be made each time as to which side of the island to pass as you paddle downstream. Being able to read the river helps in these situations, since small rapids are often found close to the islands.

As you paddle downriver, most of the access sites listed in this chapter should be visible from the river, clearly identified by steeply cut paths leading down the embankment to the river's edge. Several of them, however, may require scouting ahead of time to familiarize yourself with how they look from the river.

Starting from Launch #1 at the cul-de-sac, head downriver for 0.2 mile to reach a 0.2-mile-long island. Stay to the left. You will immediately pass by Launch #2, where many of the commercial outfitters begin their trips.

Look for a steeply descending pathway at 0.4 mile that signifies Launch #3.

In 0.7 mile you will pass by the mouth of Stony Creek, which is aptly named. Like its cousin and namesake that enters the Sacandaga River slightly north of Northville, this Stony Creek is often a riverbed of stones. You may end up going right by Stony Creek without realizing it, for the mouth of the creek is partially concealed by a sandbar that runs parallel to the river. The shoulder of Morton Mountain (1,450') forms the east bank of the river near this point.

In another 0.3 mile you will pass by Launch #4, where a fairly steep path leads down the embankment to the river.

At 1.5 miles the river begins to widen. You will see two islands off to the left. The first one is typically bound to the mainland by a rocky shoal except at high water. As soon as you pass by the first island, bear left and paddle between the two islands. Launch #5/Bear Slide can be seen directly to your left behind the first island. Buttermilk Creek comes in nearly between the two islands here, but is generally unremarkable in appearance and therefore not likely to be readily noticed.

Launch #6 is reached in another 0.2 mile. This is the take-out point for many commercially led trips. You will see an orange-painted rock next to the bank, and a row of stones going out into the river for 15 feet that creates a tiny dam and safe landing port. A row of stand-alone pines will also be visible at the top of the 20-foot-high embankment.

At 3.0 miles you will come to Launch #7, where Thomas Road enters River Road. This is another favored take-out point for commercial outfitters. The shoulder of Bryans Mountain (1,598') forms the west bank of the river here.

Within another 0.6 mile the east bank of the river begins to close in as the shoulder of Coman Mountain (1,242') is passed. The land next to the river begins to flatten out 0.3 mile later. Although not visible, River Road momentarily pulls away at this point, eventually ending up as far as 0.4 mile away from the river.

At 5.2 miles you will come to Wolf Creek on your right, which rises to the west between lofty Roundtop Mountain (2,406') and Bear Mountain (1,984').

It is only another 0.4 mile to Tank Brook, which also enters on the right but is hardly noticeable as it pushes through a marshland. Tank Brook is an insubstantial creek that rises near the east shoulder of Pond Mountain (1,845').

At 6.0 miles you will pass by Launch #8, where a sandy beach area can be seen, particularly when the river level is low. This spot is known as Pikes Beach.

At 6.2 miles you will pass by Launch #9, known as Scofield Flats.

At 6.9 mile you will reach Launch #10, an informal point of entry and exit.

▶ Hudson River Recreation Area (Fourth Lake)

Undoubtedly it is used more by fishing enthusiasts than paddlers.

In another 0.7 mile (7.6 miles from Launch #1) you will come to the Warren County Canoe Access (Launch #11), which is the last take-out on the east bank of the river.

One final take-out remains, however, for those who may want a longer day on the river. At 8.3 miles you will reach the Hadley Canoe Takeout, located on the west (right) side of the river, 0.2 mile upstream from the 12-foot-high Rockwell Falls. Rockwell Falls is unrunnable and must be avoided. If you descend the river past the Warren County Canoe Access, make sure you go no farther south than the Hadley Canoe Takeout. From there you can see the rocky banks and hear the rumbling of the waterfall downstream in the distance.

A number of outfitters provide a shuttle service and kayak or inner-tube rentals for trips down this section of the Hudson River:

Adirondack Tubing Adventures
877 Lake Ave. (Rte. 9N), Lake Luzerne, NY 12846
(518) 696-6133

Beaver Brook Outfitters
PO Box 96, Wevertown, NY 12886 (main office)
1-888-454-8433

Tubby Tubes Company
1289 Lake Ave., Lake Luzerne, NY 12846
(518) 696-7222

One of the launch sites at the Hudson River Recreation Area. Photograph 2010.

55 Sherman Island Boat Launch (Corinth)
Between Two Large Dams Lies an Area of Unexpected Natural Beauty

- **Launch Site:** Sherman Island Boat Launch (Saratoga County); gravel ramp
- **Delorme NYS Atlas & Gazetteer:** p. 80, B4; **GPS:** 43°15.04'N; 73°44.30'W
- **Destinations & Mileages:** *Southwest*: to islands near launch site—0.2 mile; around islands—0.3 mile; to Spier Falls Dam—1.3 miles. *Northeast*: to island before Sherman Island Dam—1.6 miles; around island—0.5 mile; to Sherman Island Dam—2.0 miles.
- **Comments:** Read "Caution" beginning on page xxi Hudson River Advisory on page 216.
  Stay a safe distance back from the Spier Falls Dam and the Sherman Island Dam.

Directions: From near the center of Corinth (junction of Main Street & Palmer Street), proceed southeast on Palmer Ave. (which quickly becomes Rte. 24). Take note that Rte. 24 turns into Spier Falls Road along the way. At 7.7 miles, just as the road begins to turn right and head uphill, turn left onto a dirt road that leads to the parking area for the Sherman Island Boat Launch in less than 0.1 mile.

From the Adirondack Northway (I-87) take Exit 17 for South Glens Falls and proceed northeast for 0.7 mile. Turn left onto Spier Falls Road (Rte. 24) and head west for 3.4 miles. When the road begins to veer abruptly left, turn right onto a dirt road that leads to the parking area for the Sherman Island Boat Launch in less than 0.1 mile.

The Paddle:
The boat launch is in Moreau Lake State Park. It is part of a larger parcel of land, totaling 3,400 acres and including 14 miles of Hudson River shoreline along both sides of the river, that had been protected from development and then conveyed to the state by the Open Space Institute (OSI) in the year 2000.[1]

Southwest—Head upstream for less than 0.2 mile to reach three tiny, rocky islands that attract numerous paddlers because of their close proximity to the launch. The islands can be circumnavigated in 0.3 mile.

As you head farther upstream you will pass by another small rocky island to your left at 0.6 mile.

Roughly 0.3–0.4 mile before you reach Spier Falls Dam, you will encounter huge blocks of riprap shoring up the south shoreline. When a slight breeze is blowing the coolness emanating from the rocks can be felt.

At 1.3 miles you will be near the base of Spier Falls Dam. Stay a safe distance back, approaching no closer than the line of buoys. Look to your right toward the north shore and you will see a great expanse of bedrock below the dam where several short channels lead off and quickly dead-end. Pay attention to the warning signs and "no trespassing" signs posted by the power company.

▶ **Sherman Island Boat Launch (Corinth)**

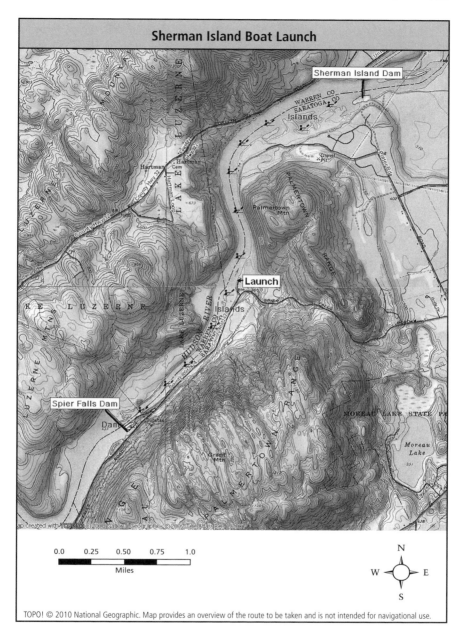

Sherman Island Boat Launch

TOPO! © 2010 National Geographic. Map provides an overview of the route to be taken and is not intended for navigational use.

During the summer only a smidgeon of water passes over the top of the dam, as the river is essentially diverted to the power plant for hydroelectric power generation. If you paddle to the center of the river and look back at the power plant, you will see a huge chute of falling water that is being exploited for its kinetic energy, after which the water is returned to the riverbed along the south shore.

Northeast—Paddling downstream you will quickly be in the shadow of Palmertown Mountain to your right—a 1,035-foot-high mountain that bends the river around it. Take note of how the right (south) bank of the river rises steeply in response to its close proximity to the mountain.

At 1.3 miles you will arrive at the beginning of a section of rocky peninsulas to your right. There are many coves, nooks, and crannies to explore over a 0.7-mile length of shoreline. The exposed bedrock around the base of these coves and peninsulas gives the area a look somewhat reminiscent of coastal Maine.

The large island 0.4 mile before reaching the Sherman Island Dam can leisurely be paddled around in 0.5 mile.

While it is possible to continue downstream for another 0.3 mile to the orange buoys in front of the Sherman Island Dam, there is no need to do so in order to see the dam, for it is clearly visible from afar. Take note of the feeder canal entrance located at the north end of the dam. The canal diverts water from the Hudson River to a power plant 0.6 mile farther downstream from the dam.

The Sherman Island industrial complex was built in 1923 by the International Paper Company.[2] The power plant has gone through a series of names—Hudson River Power, Eastern New York Power, and Niagara Mohawk Power—before settling on its present name, Sherman Island Power Plant.[3] The plant is one of seven hydroelectric dam impoundments on the Hudson River between Corinth and the Glens Falls area.[4]

Alternate Launch Sites: There are a number of informal accesses, primarily used by fishing enthusiasts, between the Spier Falls Dam and the Sherman Island Dam. Proceeding southwest along Spier Falls Road (Rte. 24) from the Sherman Island Boat Launch, you will encounter informal accesses on your right at 0.2 mile, 0.4 mile, 0.6 mile, 0.7 mile, 0.8 mile, 0.9 mile, and 1.0 mile. The Spier Falls Hydroelectric Plant is reached at 1.3 miles.

These access points only need to be used if the main access at the Sherman Island Boat Launch is overcrowded or if you simply want a more secluded launch site.

▶ Sherman Island Boat Launch (Corinth)

Spier Falls Boat Launch (Corinth)
The Hudson River between Palmer Falls Dam and Spier Falls Dam

56

▪ **Launch Site:** Boat launch at Spier Falls Park (Saratoga County); slip-in at hard-surface ramp; parking for 5–6 cars
▪ **Delorme NYS Atlas & Gazetteer:** p. 80, BC3–4; **GPS:** 43°13.25'N; 73°46.12'W
▪ **Destinations & Mileages:** *Northeast*: to Spier Falls Dam—1.0 mile. *Northwest*: up Beaver Creek Cove—0.1 mile; to Bennie Brook—1.6 miles; to Heath Brook—2.4 miles; up Heath Brook—0.2 mile; to Beaverdam Brook—2.8 miles; to Palmer Falls/International Paper Company Dam—3.5 miles. If returning to the launch site by paddling down the north side of the river, it is a round trip of 7.0 miles.
▪ **Comments:** Read "Caution" beginning on page xxi and Hudson River Advisory on page 216.
   Stay a safe distance back from the Spier Falls Dam and the Palmer Falls/International Paper Company Dam.

Directions: From near the center of Corinth (junction of Main Street & Palmer Street), proceed southeast on Palmer Ave. (which quickly becomes Rte. 24) for 5.0 miles. Along the way Spier Falls Road enters from the right and becomes part of Rte. 24. At 4.9 miles, at the bottom of a long hill, turn left into the Spier Falls Boat Launch. Look for a kiosk near roadside to mark where the turn is.

From the Adirondack Northway (I-87) take Exit 17 for South Glens Falls. Go northeast on Rte. 9 for 0.7 mile, then turn left onto Spier Falls Road (Rte. 24) and proceed west for roughly 6.1 miles until you reach the parking area for the Spier Falls Boat Launch on your right. Look carefully, for it is easy to drive right by the turn-in as you approach from this direction.

The Paddle:

Northeast—This is a short, but pretty, paddle. To your left (west and northwest) are the Luzerne Mountains, which are really more the height of large hills. To your right (east and northeast) is the Palmertown Range.

In less than 0.3 mile you will pass by an immense section of exposed bedrock along the south shoreline. Don't be surprised if you see people milling about on the rocky mantle, for the site can readily be accessed by foot from Spier Falls Road.

At 1.0 mile you will approach the top of the Spier Falls Dam looming directly ahead of you. Turn around before getting too close. The dam, 1,500 feet long and 90 feet high, was built between 1900 and 1903, and at that time was the fourth-largest in the world.[1] The waters backed up by the dam cover over the site of an 1850s toll bridge.[2] Spier Falls Dam was the brainchild of Eugene F. Ashley, a Glens Falls attorney, and was named after William E. Spier—a Glens Falls resident, major financial backer, and president of the Glens Falls

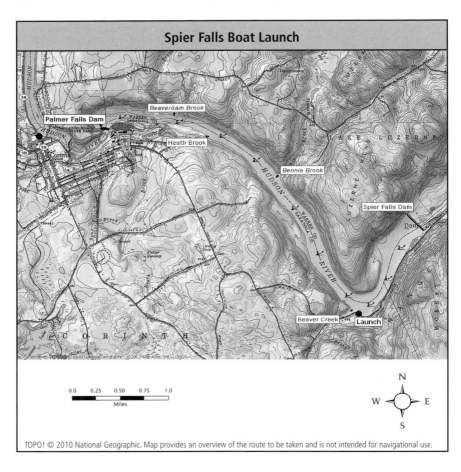

Spier Falls Boat Launch

TOPO! © 2010 National Geographic. Map provides an overview of the route to be taken and is not intended for navigational use.

Paper Company. Generating 24,000-kilowatts, the dam's power plant furnished electricity to customers as far south as Troy and Albany. Today the power plant is still vibrant and continues to provide hydroelectric power for the region.

Northwest—This is a very serene and scenic paddle for most of its length (the caveat being, as long as motorboats aren't about). For the first 2.4 miles you are following a wide section of the river with heavily forested banks rising up steeply along both sides. There are no camps or roads to be seen. This all changes after 2.5 miles, when camps start to appear along the north bank and factories along the south bank.

From the launch site, turn immediately left into a tiny cove created by Beaver Creek whose interior can be explored for 0.1 mile. Just west of the cove, paralleling Rte. 24 momentarily, is the area where Beaver Creek (draining Lake Bonita) and Stony Brook (draining the hills northeast of North Greenfield) enter the river together.

▶ **Spier Falls Boat Launch (Corinth)**

Continue following the south shore of the Hudson River upstream. On the way back you may wish to return along the north shore for variety.

In 1.6 miles you will pass by Bennie Brook, entering on your right, which drains a swampy area northeast of Danielstown. (On the return trip you can paddle for 150 feet into the tiny inlet created by the stream. Beyond that point, Bennie Brook rises above the waterline and becomes a streambed of rocks. While at the inlet, look for a trail off the southwest point of the cove that leads to a campsite. It may be the only public campsite on this section of the river. For those wishing to debark momentarily to stretch their legs, this affords an excellent opportunity to do so.)

In another 0.8 mile you will come to Heath Brook on your left, whose inlet can be explored southeast for up to 0.2 mile. Look for an enormous smokestack straight ahead in the distance, framed by tree lines on both banks of the inlet. The chimney is so lofty that a blinking light has been placed on top of it to warn low-flying aircraft.

Back on the Hudson River, continue upstream for another 0.4 mile. You will pass under a set of high-tension wires that span the river. To the right, just beyond the high-tension wires, is a tiny inlet produced by Beaverdam Brook that can be entered (on your return trip) for 50 feet before the stream rises above the waterline and becomes rocky.

Within another 0.3 mile you will hear the humming and clanking sound of factory machinery whose buildings now line the top of the south bank. Soon

Spier Falls Dam was once the fourth-largest dam in the world. Postcard ca. 1940.

you will pass by a green-colored sign announcing the presence of a NYS Permitted Discharge Site.

Around this time you will begin to notice that the current is gradually growing stronger. More factory buildings along the south bank are passed, including another NYS Permitted Discharge Site.

Just beyond this point, you will paddle out from behind the protective wall of the south bank and immediately feel the full sweep of the river's current. Paddle straight across the Hudson to the opposite shore. Palmer Falls and the International Paper Company Dam will come into view as you make your way across. It is not necessarily a pretty sight. The waterfall is a huge rise of bedrock with an enormous dam sitting on top of it. Don't approach the waterfall any closer than the line of buoys. Except when the Hudson River is running at full volume in the early spring, there is not a lot of water coming over the dam. Most of it is siphoned off by the factory at the base and the side of the fall, and returned to the river below. At this point you are roughly 3.5 miles from the launch site.

Paddle back downstream, this time following along the north side of the river, for a round trip of 7.0 miles.

Alternate Launch Sites: There are a number of informal accesses between the Spier Falls Boat Launch and Spier Falls Dam. Proceeding northwest along Spier Falls Road (Rte. 24) from the Spier Falls Boat Launch, you will encounter a parking area on your right at 0.2 mile (where a path from the opposite side of the road leads to the river in 0.05 mile), a pull-off on your left at 0.6 mile (with a short carry down the bank to the river's edge), and a tiny pull-off on your left at 1.0 mile.

▶ **Spier Falls Boat Launch (Corinth)**

Hadley Canoe Take-out (Hadley)
Last Chance to Get off the River before Rockwell Falls   **57**

■ **Launch Site:** Hadley Canoe Take-out (Saratoga County); ramp
■ **Delorme NYS Atlas & Gazetteer:** p. 80, B3; **GPS:** 43°19.18'N; 73°50.83'W
■ **Destination & Mileages:** *North*: upstream on the Hudson River, the mileage is variable depending upon conditions. *East*: to Mill Creek—0.1 mile.
■ **Comments:** Read "Caution" beginning on page xxi and Hudson River Advisory on page 216.

Stay away from Rockwell Falls, which is 0.2 mile downstream from the put-in. Always check the current before heading out when a waterfall is in close proximity to the launch site.

The historic Hadley River Trail follows along the bank of the river for 2,100 feet.

Directions: From Lake Luzerne (junction of Bridge Street/Rte. 4 & Main Street) cross over the Bridge of Hope spanning the Hudson River and drive west for over 0.2 mile. Turn right onto a road with a sign for "Woodard Avenue/Canoe Takeout" and head northwest for over 0.1 mile. Turn right at the sign for the "Hadley Canoe Takeout" and follow a dirt road that leads downhill in 100 feet to a large circular parking area. The slip-in ramp is only several hundred feet beyond this point.

The Paddle:

Northwest—Heading upriver, you can paddle for variable distances depending upon water level and current. In many ways this part of the Hudson River is more fun as a one-way paddle, launching from upriver sites along the east bank of the Hudson River (see chapter "Hudson River Recreation Area") and enjoying an easy drift downstream over shallow sections that might prove problematic if you try to force your way upstream. The Hadley Canoe Take-out then would be the downriver point of exit.

Stony Creek Road and the old D&H Railroad tracks follow along the west side of the river; River Road follows the Hudson along the east side.

Return downriver after exploring sections of the river upstream. The take-out site is clearly marked by a large yellow sign. A large boulder also sits in the river in front of the launch, making the exit point more easily identifiable.

Southeast—It is possible to paddle downstream diagonally across the river for 0.1 mile, keeping well away from the brink of Rockwell Falls, which is located 0.2 mile downriver from the put-in. The exposed bedrock around the falls is clearly visible. You will come to a stream called Mill Creek entering from the east bank. Mill Creek drains Lake Luzerne and the chain of smaller lakes above. The stream is too shallow to be followed for any distance.

Later, if you drive into the village of Lake Luzerne to where Main Street crosses over Mill Creek, you will see a 100-foot-high smokestack next to upper

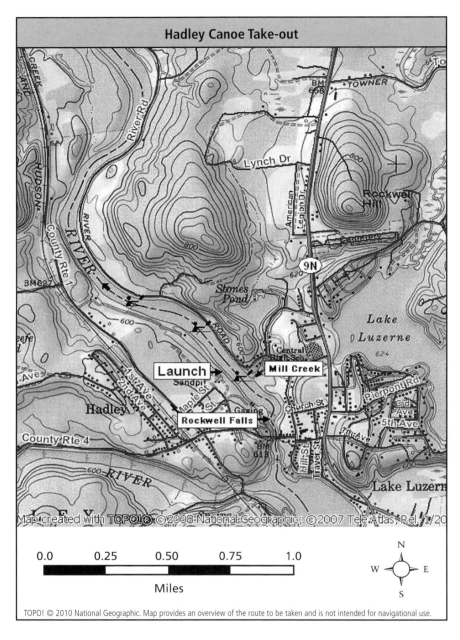

Hadley Canoe Take-out

TOPO! © 2010 National Geographic. Map provides an overview of the route to be taken and is not intended for navigational use.

Mill Creek—the remains of the Garnar Leatherworks owned by Thomas Garnar & Co. from 1868 to 1909. The business was engaged in bookbinding and leather tanning.[1]

▶ Hadley Canoe Take-out (Hadley)

Rockwell Falls is arguably the Adirondacks' most photographed waterfall. Photograph 1998.

Rockwell Falls, a 12-foot-high waterfall, is formed at the narrowest point on the navigable Hudson River and just upstream from the Hudson's confluence with the Sacandaga River. It is named after Jeremy Rockwell, who operated the first sawmill in the area, on the west side of the river by the fall. Previously the waterfall was called Jessup's Little Falls, to distinguish it from Jessup's Great Falls at Corinth. Its Native American name was *Ti-o-sa-ron-da*, an eminently sensible name meaning the "marriage of the two rivers" and denoting the convergence of the Hudson and the Sacandaga rivers downstream from the falls.[2]

The Walk: The historic Hadley River Trail can be followed along the river for 0.3 mile. Near the south end of the trail, approximately 0.2 mile upstream from Rockwell Falls, is a zip line that crosses the river. Hadley, uniquely situated next to the confluence of the Hudson and Sacandaga rivers, was founded in 1801 and became a popular resort area in the mid-1800s with the arrival of the Adirondack Railroad (later merging to become the D&H Railroad), which brought tourists into the region in droves. In more recent times, nearby Hadley Mountain has become a mecca for hikers with its fire tower and outstanding views of the northeastern part of Great Sacandaga Lake.

58

Warren County Canoe Access (Thurman Station)
Paddling an Unspoiled Section of the Hudson River

■ **Launch Site:** Warren County Canoe Access (Warren County); 50-foot carry down moderately steep embankment to slip-in at river's edge
■ **Delorme NYS Atlas & Gazetteer:** p. 80, A3; **GPS:** 43°28.33'N; 73°49.15'W
■ **Destinations & Mileages:** *South*: to railroad bridge—0.2 mile; to Number Nine Brook—1.7 miles; to Thousand Acres Ranch Resort—4.6 miles; to multiple take-outs along the Hudson River Recreation Area—starting at 6.0 miles (see chapter "Hudson River Recreation Area" for further details).
■ **Comments:** Read "Caution" beginning on page xxi and Hudson River Advisory on page 216.

Paddlers need to be aware that this is a one-way-only trek. Once you begin your journey, rapids will prevent you from returning to the launch site in your watercraft.

Beaver Brook Outfitters will provide shuttle service back from Thousand Acres Ranch Resort for a fee, and also rent you a kayak if you need one. For more information: Beaver Brook Outfitters, Rte. 418, Thurman Station, NY, (888) 454-8433, beaverbrook.net. (See "Directions: Shuttle Service" that follow in this chapter.)

Directions: *To put-in*: From the Adirondack Northway (I-87) take Exit 23 for Warrensburg & Diamond Point and drive 0.1 mile west to Rte. 9. Turn right onto Rte. 9 and proceed northwest for 0.8 mile, passing through part of the village of Warrensburg. Turn left onto Rte. 418 (Richards Avenue). You will immediately cross over a bridge spanning the Schroon River. At the end of the bridge, turn right onto River Street, continuing on Rte. 418 southwest for another 3.1 miles as it parallels the Schroon River. As soon as you cross over the Thurman Station Bridge spanning the Hudson River, turn left into the Warren County Canoe Access Site.

From the parking area carry your watercraft 50 feet down a moderately steep slope to a slip-in by the shoreline.

To take-outs at Hudson River Recreation Area: From the Adirondack Northway (I-87)—take Exit 21 and proceed south on Rte. 9N for roughly 7.5 miles. Just before you reach Third Lake, turn right onto Gailey Hill Road and head northwest for 2.5 miles. When you come to Thomas Road, turn left and proceed west for 0.8 mile until you arrive at River Road. There are multiple take-outs along this road, heading either left (south) or right (north). (See chapter "Hudson River Recreation Area" for further details.)

From Thurman Station and the Warren County Canoe Access—go north on Rte. 418 for 0.2 mile. Turn left onto Warrensburg Road and drive southwest for over 7.8 miles, then turn left onto Grist Mill Road and head south for 0.2 mile. Turn left again onto Stony Creek Road and drive south for 8.0 miles. When you

▶ **Warren County Canoe Access (Thurman Station)**

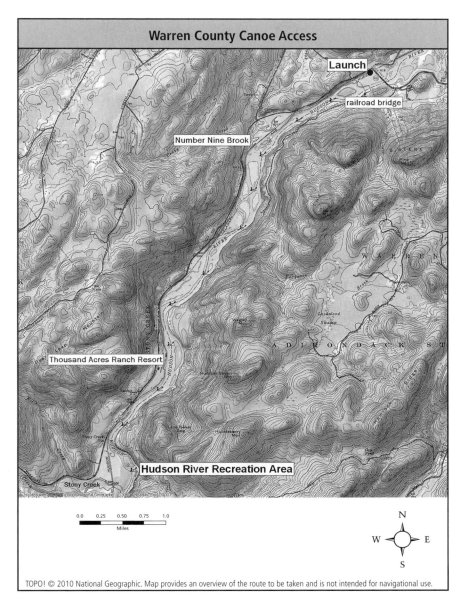

Warren County Canoe Access

Launch

railroad bridge

Number Nine Brook

Thousand Acres Ranch Resort

Hudson River Recreation Area

Stony Creek

0.0   0.25   0.50   0.75   1.0

Miles

N
W — E
S

TOPO! © 2010 National Geographic. Map provides an overview of the route to be taken and is not intended for navigational use.

come to the junction of Rtes. 4 & Stony Creek Road, turn left onto Rte. 4 and drive east for 0.4 mile. From the center of Lake Luzerne (junction of Main Street and Bridge Street), drive north on Main Street for 0.3 mile. Instead of turning right onto Mill Street, bear left onto River Road. See chapter "Hudson River Recreation Area" for the multitude of take-outs along this road.

Shuttle Service: Many paddlers will wish to take advantage of Beaver Brook Outfitters' shuttle service, which will pick you up at the Thousand Acres Ranch Resort and return you to the launch site near the Thurman Station Bridge for a modest fee.

The take-out at Thousand Acres Ranch Resort cannot be used unless you are a client of Beaver Brook Outfitters or staying at the resort.

To reach Beaver Brook Outfitters from the public canoe launch at Thurman Station, continue northwest on Rte. 418 for another 50 feet and turn left onto a dirt road. The parking area and outpost for Beaver Brook Outfitters is 0.05 mile from the road, only several hundred feet downstream from the public launch.

If you do the 4.6-mile paddle to Thousand Acres Ranch Resort and return via shuttle, the halfway point along the river is identified by a large yellow sign with the letter A to your left. It is nearly opposite the take-out on the right (west) side of the river that is used by tubers.

The Paddle:
This section of the Hudson River offers long tracts of nearly unspoiled wilderness as it leads you through a canyon of mountains rising above both sides of the river. To the east, in descending order of appearance, are Three Sisters Mountains (1,553'), Number Seven Mountain (1,750'), Huckleberry Mountain (1,730'), and Morton Mountain (1,050'). To the west, in descending order, are Sugarloaf Mountain (1,347'), Deer Leap Mountain (1,758', and Bear Mountain (1,968').

Look upstream to view the Thurman Station Bridge. You crossed over it initially to reach the launch site. This truss bridge was built in 1941.

Be aware that you will encounter numerous islands as you head downstream. Decisions will have to be made as to which side of the island to paddle past. As a general rule of thumb, stay to the left (east) side of the river. This is not a hard-and-fast rule, however, particularly if you want to enjoy different routes each time you paddle down the river. The *NYS Atlas & Gazetteer*, for instance, depicts the route careening from one side of the river to the other.

Expect that many sections of the river will be shallow as summer advances— just how shallow will depend upon how late in the season the trip is being undertaken and the amount of recent rainfall. You are likely to find more water flowing in late spring than in late summer.

Begin the downstream paddle by moving away from the shoreline into deeper water near the middle of the river. In less than 0.2 mile you will pass under an old railroad bridge that is part of the Upper Hudson River Railroad (formerly the North Creek Branch of the Delaware & Hudson Railroad). As you continue paddling downstream, the railroad line will closely parallel the Hudson River along the west bank.

▶ **Warren County Canoe Access (Thurman Station)**

In another 0.1 mile the first of many little rapids is encountered. Unless the water level is unusually low during midsummer, you should be able to progress without scraping along the bottom.

You will quickly encounter a 0.2-mile-long island—the first of many that have formed along this section of the river.

At 1.7 miles you will see to your right a rusted railroad bridge where Number Nine Brook, rising from Coon Pond, enters the Hudson. The tributary can be paddled upstream for only a short distance.

A substantial 0.3-mile-long island is reached at 1.8 miles. You are now on a section of the river containing four principal islands, all within 0.8 mile. Because of rapids and shallows, however, circumnavigating them would be very difficult.

At 2.6 miles the last of the four islands is left behind. Two smaller islands are encountered, one at 3.0 miles and the other at 3.2 miles. Look for a large golf course to your right, owned by Thousand Acres Ranch Resort. The golf course borders the west bank of the river for nearly a mile.

At 4.6 miles you will pass by the dock and private beach owned by the Thousand Acres Ranch Resort, a historic dude ranch. This is the take-out if you are using the shuttle service provided by Beaver Brook Outfitters, and you may land here only if you are using the shuttle or are a guest at the resort. The resort was started in 1942 by Jack and Ester Arehart and is still a family-run business. For more information, call (518) 606-2444 or visit 1000acres.com.

Two islands can be seen directly across from the resort's private beach; the larger one is nearly 0.4 mile long.

Many small rapids are encountered along the paddle. Photograph 2010.

Continuing down the Hudson River, you will pass by a variety of access sites along the east bank of the Hudson River beginning at 6.0 miles. Take out at the site you chose and scouted out earlier, where your downriver car awaits (see chapter "Hudson River Recreation Area" for a roster of take-out sites).

A take-out site at 7.6 miles is identified by an orange-painted rock on the left side of the river by the shore. You will also see a row of tall stand-alone pines at the top of a 30-foot-high embankment, and a tiny dam made of stones that extends into the river for 20 feet and provides a makeshift landing site. This may be the ideal place to exit the river in terms of length of paddle and availability of parking space. Take note that, after this site, the take-outs become less frequent.

▶ **Warren County Canoe Access (Thurman Station)**

Appendix A:
Paddling & Hiking Clubs

Adirondack Mountain Club
ADK Member Services Center
814 Goggins Road
Lake George, NY 12845
518-668-4447, (800) 395-8080
adkinfo@adk.org
adk.org

Adirondack Pirate Paddlers
adirondackpiratepaddlers.org

Albany Area Kayaking Meet-up Group
meetup.com/Albany-Area-Kayaking

Appalachian Mountain Club (AMC)
Mohawk-Hudson Chapter
5 Orchard Drive
Kinderhook, NY 12106
amcmohawkhudson.org

Greene County Canoe & Kayak Club
Coxsackie, NY
paddlegreene.com

L.L. Bean Albany Outing Group
meetup.com
L-L-Bean-Albany-Outing-Group

Monday Paddlers
No website presently listed

Saratoga Springs Nature/ Kayak Paddle Group
meetup.com/saratoga-springs-nature-kayak-group/members

Taconic Hiking Club
29 Campagna Drive
Albany, NY 12205
taconichikingclub.blogspot.com

Troy Motor Boat & Canoe Club
Troy, NY
(518) 235-9697
troyboatclub.com

Western Mass. Kayak and Outdoor Group
meetup.com/western-mass-kayakers

Appendix B: Recommended Reading

Hudson River, Champlain Canal, Lake Champlain,
and Adirondack Mountains

1. Adams, Arthur G. *The Hudson River Guidebook*, 2nd ed. New York: Fordham University Press, 1996.

2. Armstrong, Kathie, and Chet Harvey, eds. *Canoe and Kayak Guide: East-Central New York State.* Lake George, N.Y.: Adirondack Mountain Club, 2003.

3. Burmeister, Walter F. *Appalachian Waters 2: The Hudson River and its Tributaries.* Oakton, Va.: Appalachian Books, 1974.

4. Carpenter, Michael, and Roger Fulton. *25 Flatwater Kayak & Canoe Trips in the Lake George. NY Region.* Glens Falls, N.Y.: Glens Falls Publishing, 2006.

5. Carpenter, Michael, and Roger Fulton. *25 Kayak & Canoe Trips in the Saratoga Springs, NY Region.* Glens Falls, N.Y.: Glens Falls Publishing, 2011.

6. Cilley, Dave. *Adirondack Paddler's Guide: Finding Your Way by Canoe and Kayak in the Adirondacks.* Saranac Lake, N.Y.: Paddlesports Press, 2008.

7. Giddy, Ian H. *The Hudson River Water Trail Guide: A River Guide for Small Boats*, 6th ed. New York: Hudson River Watertrail Association, 2003.

8. Frank, Catherine, and Margaret Holden. *A Kayaker's Guide to Lake Champlain: Exploring the New York, Vermont & Quebec Shores.* Hensonville, N.Y.: Black Dome Press, 2009.

9. Hudson River Waterfront Map. Hudson Valley Tourism, 2001.

10. Jamieson, Paul, and Donald Morris. *Adirondack Canoe Waters: North Flow.* Glens Falls, N.Y.: The Adirondack Mountain Club, 1987.

11. McKibben, Alan, and Susan McKibben. *Cruising Guide to the Hudson River, Lake Champlain, and the St. Lawrence River: The Waterway from New York City to Montreal and Quebec City.* Burlington, Vt.: Lake Champlain Publishing Company, 2006.

12. McMartin, Barbara. *Fun on Flatwater: An Introduction to Adirondack Canoeing.* Utica, N.Y.: North Country Books, 1995.

13. New York State Canal Corporation. *The Cruising Guide to the New York State Canal System: Champlain, Erie, Oswego, Cayuga-Seneca*, 3rd ed. Albany, N.Y.: New York State Canal Corporation, 2006.

14. Padeni, Capt. Scott A. *Lake George Boaters Guide: Everything You Should Know for Fun, Safe and Responsible Boating on the Queen of American Lakes.* Ballston Spa, N.Y.: Quarterdeck Productions, 2011.

15. Proskine, Alec C. *Adirondack Canoe Waters: South and West Flow.* Glens Falls, N.Y.: Adirondack Mountain Club, 1986.

16. Wilkie, Richard W. *The Illustrated Hudson River Pilot: Being a Small-Craft Sailor's Pictorial Guide to the Tidewater Hudson, Albany to New York.* Albany, N.Y.: Three City Press, 1974.

Lower Hudson River
1. Aber, Shari. *A Kayaker's Guide to the Hudson River Valley: The Quieter Waters: Rivers, Creeks, Lakes, and Ponds.* Hensonville, N.Y.: Black Dome Press, 2007.

Mohawk River & Erie Canal (with other NYS canals)
1. *The Cruising Guide to the New York State Canal System,* 3rd ed. Albany, N.Y.: New York State Canal Corporation, 2006.

White-water Paddling
1. Squires, Dennis. *New York Exposed: The Whitewater State,* vol. 1. Margaretville, N.Y.: A White Water Outlaw Publishing, 2002.
2. ———. *New York Exposed: The Whitewater State,* vol. 2. Margaretville, N.Y.: A White Water Outlaw Publishing, 2003.

General
1. Burmeister, Walter F. *Appalachian Waters 2: The Hudson River and its Tributaries.* Oakton, Va.: Appalachian Books, 1974.
2. Downs, Jack. *A Trail Marker Books Guide to Kayak and Canoe Paddles in the New York Champlain Valley.* N.p.: Trail Marker Books, 2004.
3. Grinnell, Lawrence I. *Canoeable Waterways of New York State and Vicinity.* New York: Pageant Press, 1956. This book, over fifty years old, was superseded by Proskine's *No Two Rivers Alike* (see below).
5. Hayes, John, and Alex Wilson. *Quiet Water New York,* 2nd ed. Boston, Mass.: Appalachian Mountain Club, 2007.
6. Keesler, M. Paul. *Canoe-Fishing New York Rivers and Streams.* Prospect, N.Y.: New York Sportsman, 1995.
7. Proskine, Alec C. *No Two Rivers Alike: 56 Canoeable Rivers in New York State.* Fleischmanns, N.Y.: Purple Mountain Press, 1995.
7. Stiegelmaier, Kevin. *Canoeing & Kayaking New York.* Birmingham, Ala.: Menasha Ridge Press, 2009.

Appendix C: Regional Outfitters

Adirondack Canoes & Kayaks
96 Old Piercefield Road & Route 3
Tupper Lake, NY 12986
(518) 359-3968
capital.net/com/adkcanoe

Adirondack Lakes & Trails Outfitters
541 Lake Flower Avenue
Saranac Lake, NY 12983
(800) 491-0414
adirondackoutfitters.com

Adirondack Paddle 'n' Pole
2123 Central Avenue
Schenectady, NY 12304
(518) 346-3180
onewithwater.com

ADK Kayak Warehouse
4786 State Highway 30
Amsterdam, NY 12010
(518) 843-3232
adkkayakwarehouse.com

Beaverbrook Outfitters
PO Box 96
Wevertown, NY 12886
(888) 454-8433
beaverbrook.net

The Boat House
2855 Aqueduct Road
Schenectady, NY 12309
(518) 393-5711
boathousecanoeskayaks.com

Coxsackie Bike & Sport
369 Mansion St.
W. Coxsackie, NY 12192
(518) 731-9313

Dick's Sporting Goods
(dickssportinggoods.com)
Crossgates Mall
  1 Crossgates Mall
  Albany, NY 12203
  (518) 464-1948
Latham Farms
  579 Troy / Schenectady Road
  Latham, NY 12110
  (518) 783-0701
Wilton Mall
  3065 Route 50
  Saratoga Springs, NY 12866
  (518) 583-7218
Aviation Mall
  578 Aviation Road
  Queensbury, NY 12804
  (518) 743-8790

Eastern Mountain Sports (EMS)
(ems.com)
Stuyvesant Plaza
  1475 Western Avenue
  Albany, NY 12203
  (518) 482-0088
The Shoppes at Wilton
  3066 Route 50
  Saratoga Springs, NY 12866
  (518) 580-1505
Mohawk Commons
  412C Balltown Road
  Schenectady, NY 12304
  (518) 388-2700

Goldstock's Sporting Goods
98 Freemans Bridge Road
Scotia, NY 12302
(518) 382-2037
goldstockssportinggoods.com

Hornbeck Boats
131 Trout Brook Road
Olmstedville, NY 12857
(518) 251-2764
hornbeckboats.com

Kayak Shack
3999 Rte. 9
Plattsburgh, NY 12901
(518) 566-0505
kayakshack.com

Kenco
1000 Hurley Mountain Road
Kingston, NY 12401-7603
(845) 340-0552
atkenco.com

Lake George Kayak Company
Main Street
Bolton Landing, NY 12814
(518) 644-9366
lakegeorgekayak.com

L.L. Bean
131 Colonie Center, Suite 194
Albany, NY 12205
(518) 437-5460
llbean.com

Mountainman Outdoors Supply Company
Old Forge, NY
(315) 369-6672
mountainmanoutdoors.com

Pine Lake Stoves of Saratoga
747 Saratoga Road (Route 9)
Gansevoort, NY 12831
(518) 584-9070
pinelakestovesandspas.com

Placid Boatworks
263 Station Street
Lake Placid, NY 12946
(518) 524-2949
placidboats.com

Raquette River Outfitters
1754 State Route 30
Tupper Lake, NY 12986
(518) 359-3228
RaquetteRiverOutfitters.com

St. Regis Canoe Outfitters
73 Dorsey Street
Saranac Lake, NY 12983
(518) 891-1838
canoeoutfitters.com

Schenectady Canoe Sales
502 Summit Avenue
Schenectady, NY 12307
(518) 370-0367

Steiner's Sports
(steinerssports.com)
329 Glenmont Street
Glenmont, NY 12077
(518) 427-2406
301 Warren Street
Hudson, NY 12534
(518) 828-5063
3455 U.S. 9
Valatie, NY 12184
(518) 784-3663

The Towne Store
1089 Main Street
Schroon Lake, NY 12870
(518) 532-9954
townestore.com

Annual Expos

Adirondack Paddlefest
On-water canoe & kayak sale held annually in spring.
Mountainman Outdoor Supply Company
Old Forge, NY
(315) 369-6672
mountainmanoutdoors.com

Adirondack Sports & Fitness Summer Expo
Held annually in April at Saratoga Springs City Center
Saratoga Springs, NY
(518) 877-8788
adksports.com

Mid-Hudson ADK Paddle Fest
Held annually at Plum Point Park in New Windsor
P.O. Box 3674
Poughkeepsie, NY 12603
midhudsonadk.org/paddlefest.htm

Appendix D: Organizations: Government & Private

Erie Canalway National Heritage Corridor
PO Box 219
Waterford, NY 12188
Visitor Center phone: (518) 237-7000
nps.gov/erie

Feeder Canal Alliance
PO Box 2414
Glens Falls, NY 12801
(518) 792-5363
feedercanal.com

Friends of the Kayaderosseras
PO Box 223
Ballston Spa, NY 12020
kayaderosseras.org

Great Sacandaga Lake Association
Box 900
Northville, NY 12134
(518) 863-6848
gsla.org

Hudson River Maritime Museum
50 Rondout Landing
Kingston, NY 12401
(845) 338-0071
hrmm.org

Hudson River Watertrail Association
hrwa.org

Lake George Association, Inc.
PO Box 408
Lake George, NY 12845
(518) 668-3558
lakegeorgeassociation.org

Lake George Land Conservancy
4905 Lake Shore Drive
Bolton Landing, NY 12814
(518) 644-9673
lglc.org

Lake George Waterkeeper
PO Box 591
Lake George, NY 12845
(518) 668-5913
lakegeorgewaterkeeper.org

Lakes to Locks Passage
PO Box 65
Crown Point, NY 12908
(518) 597-9660
lakestolocks.org
info@lakestolocks.org

New York State Canal Corporation
200 Southern Blvd.
Albany, NY 12201
(518) 436-2700, (800) 422-6254
canals.state.ny.us

NYS Hudson River Valley Greenway
Capitol Building, Capital Station,
Room 254
Albany, NY 12224
(518) 473-3835
e-mail: hrvg@hudsongreenway.ny.gov
hudsongreenway.ny.gov

Hudson River Greenway Water Trail
hudsongreenway.state.ny.us/trailsand-
scenicbyways/watertrail.aspx

Open Space Institute (OSI)
1350 Broadway, Suite 201
New York, NY 10018
(212) 290-8200
osiny.org

Riverkeeper
828 South Broadway
Tarrytown, NY 10591
(800) 21-RIVER
info@riverkeeper.org
riverkeeper.org

Saratoga Lake Association
PO Box 2152
Ballston Spa, NY 12020
(518) 580-0656
saratogalake.org

Scenic Hudson, Inc.
One Civic Center Plaza, Suite 200
Poughkeepsie, NY 12601
(845) 473-4440
scenichudson.org

Schenectady County–Mohawk River Blueway Trail Plan
cityofschenectady.com/pdf/.../Blueway%20Trail%20Plan%202008.pdf

Annual Events

Great Hudson River Paddle
hudsongreenway.ny.gov
greathrpaddle.org

One Square Mile of Hope
Fourth Lake (Inlet, NY)
onesquaremileofhope.org

Paddling for a Cure
Mohawk River
alplaus.org

Notes

Caution: Safety Tips

1. Catherine Frank and Margaret Holden, *A Kayaker's Guide to Lake Champlain: Exploring the New York, Vermont and Quebec Shores* (Hensonville, N.Y.: Black Dome Press, 2009), 3.

2. Kenneth Kamler, *Surviving the Extremes: What happens to the body and mind at the limits of human endurance* (London: Penguin Books, 2005), 91.

3. Brochure PDF (enter.net/~skimmer/coldintro.html) © Charles Sutherland 3/23/2007, e-mail: Skimmer@enter.net.

Lake George Region
Introduction

1. Ray Stross and Barbara Rottier, "Protecting Water Clarity in Lake George," *The Conservationist* vol. 44, no. 2 (September/October 1989), 44–46.

2. William Preston Gates, *History of the Sagamore Hotel* (Queensbury, N.Y.: W. P. Gates Publishing Company, 2001), 9.

3. Russell P. Bellico, *Chronicles of Lake George: Journeys in War and Peace* (Fleischmanns, N.Y.: Purple Mountain Press, 1995), 292. From the 1842 travel accounts of Francis Parkman.

4. lakegeorgevillage.com/LAKE-GEORGE-HISTORY.htm.

5. Frank Leonbruno with Ginger Henry, *Lake George Reflections: Island History and Lore* (Fleischmanns, N.Y.: Purple Mountain Press, 1998), 29–31. Estimates do vary considerably. Some say 200 islands. See Mark Bowie, "Island Treasures," *2006 Outings Guide to the Adirondacks*, 42.

6. Bellico, op. cit., 391; Thomas Reeves Lord, *Stories of Lake George Fact and Fancy* (Pemberton, N.J.: Pinelands Press, 1987), 107.

7. fundforlakegeorge.org/index.asp?lg=1andw...r...

8. fundforlakegeorge.org/index.asp?lg=1andw...r...

Additional Reading

Stephen Jermanok, "Island Cruising: Exploring Lake George's nooks and narrows," *1998 Annual Guide to the Adirondacks*, 36–41.

Lake Avenue Park

1. fundforlakegeorge.org/index.asp?lg=1andw...r...

2. Wallace E. Lamb, *Lake George: Facts and Anecdotes* (Bolton Landing, N.Y.: n. p., 1934), 42; Russell P. Bellico, *Chronicles of Lake George: Journeys in War and Peace* (Fleischmanns, N.Y.: Purple Mountain Press, 1995), 257. In Theodore Dwight Jr.'s 1831 travel accounts, Tea Island is described as follows: "The little bay in which the boats land is remarkably retired and beautiful, and there is an old hut standing which affords something of a shelter."; Erica Henkel-

Karras, *Postcard History Series: Lake George* (Charleston, S.C.: Arcadia Publishing, 2005). A picture of Tea Island is shown on page 114.

3. Bellico, op. cit., 381.

4. Thomas Reeves Lord, *More Stories of Lake George Fact and Fancy* (Pemberton, N.J.: Pinelands Press, 1994), 43.

5. Frank Leonbruno with Ginger Henry, *Lake George Reflections: Island History and Lore* (Fleischmanns, N.Y.: Purple Mountain Press, 1998), 32–33.

6. Thomas Reeves Lord, *Still More Stories of Lake George Fact and Fancy* (Pemberton, N.J.: Pinelands Press, 1999), 49.

7. nynjctbotany.org/lgtofc/georgehist.html.

8. fundforlakegeorge.org/index.asp?lg=1andw...r...

9. Ibid.

10. Thomas Reeves Lord, *Stories of Lake George Fact and Fancy* (Pemberton, N.J.: Pinelands Press, 1987), 22.

11. Roadside historic marker.

12. lakegeorgeassociation.org/html/wetlands.htm.

13. Thomas Reeves Lord, op. cit., *More Stories of Lake George Fact and Fancy,* 27.

Additional Reading

Trip Sinnott, *Tea Island: A Perfect Little Gem* (Clinton Corners, N.Y.: The Attic Studio Press, 1993).

Hearthstone Point Campgrounds

1. Thomas Reeves Lord, *More Stories of Lake George Fact and Fancy* (Pemberton, N.J.: Pinelands Press, 1994). A postcard photo of the park can be seen on page 45.

2. Thomas Reeves Lord, *Stories of Lake George Fact and Fancy* (Pemberton, N.J.: Pinelands Press, 1987), 21.

3. Ibid., 40.

4. Ibid., 41.

5. Thomas Reeves Lord, *Still More Stories of Lake George Fact and Fancy* (Pemberton, N.J.: Pinelands Press, 1999), 64.

6. Lord, op. cit., *Stories of Lake George Fact and Fancy,* 42.

7. Ibid., 43.

8. Russell P. Bellico, *Chronicles of Lake George: Journeys in War and Peace* (Fleischmanns, N.Y.: Purple Mountain Press, 1995), 381; Wallace E. Lamb, *Lake George: Fact and Anecdotes* (Bolton Landing, N.Y.: n.p., 1934), 44.

9. Bellico, op. cit., 257. "Diamond Island is … famous for abounding in crystals of quartz, which are found in a loose rock by digging a little under the surface."

10. Trip Sinnott, *Tea Island: A Perfect Little Gem* (Clinton Corners, N.Y.: The Attic Studio Press, 1993), 15. The rocks sold were called "Lake George Diamonds."

11. Frank Leonbruno with Ginger Henry, *Lake George Reflections: Island History and Lore* (Fleischmanns, N.Y.: Purple Mountain Press, 1998), 34.

12. Ibid., 34. A photograph of the monument is on page 36.

Huddle Beach

1. Thomas Reeves Lord, *Stories of Lake George Fact and Fancy* (Pemberton, N.J.: Pinelands Press, 1987), 65.

2. Frank Leonbruno with Ginger Henry, *Lake George Reflections: Island History and Lore* (Fleischmanns, N.Y.: Purple Mountain Press, 1998), 56.

3. Thomas Reeves Lord, *Still More Stories of Lake George Fact and Fancy* (Pemberton, N.J.: Pinelands Press, 199), 95; lakegeorge.com/boltonlanding/mohican-point.cfm.

4. Lord, op. cit., *Stories of Lake George Fact and Fancy*, 53.

5. Thomas Reeves Lord, *More Stories of Lake George Fact and Fancy* (Pemberton, N.J.: Pinelands Press, 1994), 80.

6. Leonbruno, op. cit., 59.

7. Lord, op. cit., *More Stories of Lake George Fact and Fancy*, 78.

8. Lord, op. cit., *Stories of Lake George Fact and Fancy*, 53.

9. Leonbruno, op. cit., 53.

10. Russell P. Bellico, *Chronicles of Lake George: Journeys in War and Peace* (Fleischmanns, N.Y.: Purple Mountain Press, 1995), 259. Taken from the 1831 travel accounts of Theodore Dwight, Jr.

11. fundforlakegeorge.org/index.asp?lg=1andw...r...; Leonbruno, op. cit., 54.

12. Leonbruno, op. cit., 48. A photograph of the joined islands can also be seen on page 48; Trip Sinnott, *Tea Island: A Perfect Little Gem* (Clinton Corners, N.Y.: The Attic Studio Press, 1993), 16.

Additional Reading

Richard MacDonald, "Double-blade Runner: A Sea Kayaker's tour of Lake George," *1991 Adirondack Life Guide to the Adirondacks*. A paddle from Bolton Landing to Rogers Rock is described on pages 80–83.

Green Island

1. Frank Leonbruno with Ginger Henry, *Lake George Reflections: Island History and Lore* (Fleischmanns, N.Y.: Purple Mountain Press, 1998), 65.

2. William Preston Gates, *History of the Sagamore Hotel* (Queensbury, N.Y.: W. P. Gates Publishing Company, 2001), 9–115. A detailed history of the hotel is provided.

3. Thomas Reeves Lord, *Stories of Lake George Fact and Fancy* (Pemberton, N.J.: Pinelands Press, 1987), 67.

4. Thomas Reeves Lord, *Still More Stories of Lake George Fact and Fancy* (Pemberton, N.J.: Pinelands Press, 1999), 100; Wallace E. Lamb, *Lake George: Fact and Anecdotes* (Bolton Landing, N.Y.: n.p., 1934), 47.

5. William Preston Gates, *Millionaires' Row on Lake George New York* (Lake George, N.Y.: W. P. Gates Publishing Company, 2008), 108.

6. Lord, op. cit., *Stories of Lake George Fact and Fancy*, 68.

7. Thomas Reeves Lord, *More Stories of Lake George Fact and Fancy* (Pemberton, N.J.: Pinelands Press, 1994), 89.

Northwest Bay

1. fundforlakegeorge.org/index.asp?lg=1andw...r...

2. Elsa Kay Steinback, *Sweet Peas and a White Bridge on Lake George when Steam was King* (Sylvan Beach, N.Y.: North County Books, 1974), 117.

3. Thomas Reeves Lord, *Stories of Lake George Fact and Fancy* (Pemberton, N.J.: Pinelands Press, 1987), 73.

4. Steinback, op. cit., 117.

5. Lord, op. cit., 70.

Additional Reading

Kathie Armstrong and Chet Harvey, eds., *Canoe and Kayak Guide: East-Central New York State* (Lake George, N.Y.: Adirondack Mountain Club, 2003), 179–181.

Michael Carpenter and Roger Fulton, *25 Flatwater Kayak and Canoe Trips in the Lake George, N.Y. Region* (Glens Falls, N.Y.: Glens Falls Printing, 2006), 79; Alan Wechsler, "George's quieter side: Kayakers explore Northwest Bay, Tongue Mt." *Adirondack Explorer* vol. 12, no. 3 (May/June 2010), 24–25.

Hague Town Beach

1. townofhague.org/townofhague/Calendar/Park.htm.

2. Thomas Reeves Lord. *More Stories of Lake George Fact and Fancy* (Pemberton, N.J.: Pinelands Press, 1994), 165.

3. Edward R. Gazda, *Place Names in New York. Why are they so called?* (Schenectady, N.Y.: Gazda Associates, 1997), 34.

4. Thomas Reeves Lord. *Stories of Lake George Fact and Fancy* (Pemberton, N.J.: Pinelands Press, 1987), 156.

5. Ibid., 156.

6. Ibid., 157.

7. Ibid., 158.

8. Lord, op. cit., *More Stories of Lake George Fact and Fancy*, 171.

9. Lord, op. cit., *Stories of Lake George Fact and Fancy*, 158; Wallace E. Lamb, *Lake George: Fact and Anecdotes* (Bolton Landing, N.Y.: n. p., 1934), 150–151. Mention is made of the Friend's encounter.

10. Historic plaque at Visitor Center.

11. Lord, op. cit., *Stories of Lake George Fact and Fancy*, 146.

12. Lord op. cit., *More Stories of Lake George Fact and Fancy*, 164.

13. Lord, op. cit., *Stories of Lake George Fact and Fancy*, 144–145.

14. Russell P. Bellico, *Chronicles of Lake George: Journeys in War and Peace*

(Fleischmanns, N.Y.: Purple Mountain Press, 1995), 396; Lord, op. cit., *Stories of Lake George Fact and Fancy*, 143.

Additional Reading
Michael Carpenter and Roger Fulton, *25 Flatwater Kayak and Canoe Trips in the Lake George, N.Y. Region* (Glens Falls, N.Y.: Glens Falls Printing, 2006), 92–94.

Rogers Rock Campground
1. dec.ny.gov › ... › Camping › DEC Campgrounds.
2. dec.ny.gov › ... › Camping › DEC Campgrounds.
3. Thomas Reeves Lord, *Stories of Lake George Fact and Fancy* (Pemberton, N.J.: Pinelands Press, 1987), 168.
4. Ibid., 168.
5. Ibid. A photo of the Indian Kettles can be seen on page 159; Wallace E. Lamb, *Lake George: Fact and Anecdotes* (Bolton Landing, N.Y.: n.p., 1934), photo insert of Indian Kettles between pages 50 and 51.

Additional Reading
Michael Carpenter and Roger Fulton, *25 Flatwater Kayak and Canoe Trips in the Lake George, N.Y. Region* (Glens Falls, N.Y.: Glens Falls Printing, 2006), 83–86.

Mossy Point
1. On-site historic marker.
2. On-site stone marker. A full account of Henry Knox's epic struggle to transport sixty cannon from Fort Ticonderoga to Boston is recounted in John J. Dupont's "Henry Knox and the Guns of Ticonderoga," which appeared in the December 1975 issue of *The Conservationist*, 34–35.
3. historiclakegeorge.org/explore/Exploring.html.
4. William E. Lamb, *Lake George: Facts and Anecdotes* (Bolton Landing, N.Y.: n.p., 1934), 51.
5. Frank Leonbruno with Ginger Henry, *Lake George Reflections: Island History and Lore* (Fleischmanns, N.Y.: Purple Mountain Press, 1998), 139.
6. Russell P. Bellico, *Chronicles of Lake George: Journeys in War and Peace* (Fleischmanns, N.Y.: Purple Mountain Press, 1995), 323.
7. Thomas Reeves Lord, *More Stories of Lake George Fact and Fancy* (Pemberton, N.J.: Pinelands Press, 1994), 189.
8. Ibid., 187.

Washington County Beach
1. Betty Ahearn Buckell, *No Dull Days at Huletts with Reminiscences of Henry W. Buckell* (n.p., 1984), 4. Buckell's book also contains a mid-1870 photograph of the settlement and, on page 15, a chronology of Hulett's Landing.
2. Erica Henkel-Karras, *Postcard History Series: Lake George* (Charleston, S.C.:

Arcadia Publishing, 2005), 22.

3. Thomas Reeves Lord, *Stories of Lake George Fact and Fancy* (Pemberton, N.J.: Pinelands Press, 1987), 123.

4. Thomas Reeves Lord, *More Stories of Lake George Fact and Fancy* (Pemberton, N.J.: Pinelands Press, 1994), 140.

5. Ibid., 141.

6. Lord, op. cit., *Stories of Lake George Fact and Fancy*, 116.

7. Ibid., 116; Erica Henkel-Karras, op. cit. A picture of Nobles Island is shown on page 80.

8. Lord, op. cit., *More Stories of Lake George Fact and Fancy*, 134–135.

9. Frank Leonbruno with Ginger Henry, *Lake George Reflections: Island History and Lore* (Fleischmanns, N.Y.: Purple Mountain Press, 1998), 132; Wallace E. Lamb, *Lake George: Fact and Anecdotes* (Bolton Landing, N.Y.: n.p., 1934), 49; Lord, op. cit., *Stories of Lake George Fact and Fancy*, 113, claims island was named after Marcus Vicar, an old hermit.

10. Leonbruno, op. cit., 130.

11. Thomas Reeves Lord, *Still More Stories of Lake George Fact and Fancy* (Pemberton, N.J.: Pinelands Press, 1999), 155; Leonbruno, op. cit., 128.

12. Lord, op. cit., *Stories of Lake George Fact and Fancy*, 109.

13. Ibid., 109.

14. Ibid., 108.

15. Ibid., 106; Lord, op. cit., *More Stories of Lake George Fact and Fancy*, 122.

16. Lord, op. cit., *Stories of Lake George Fact and Fancy*, 106.

17. Lord, op. cit., *More Stories of Lake George Fact and Fancy*, 122.

18. Lord, op. cit., *Stories of Lake George Fact and Fancy*, 108.

19. Ibid., 107; Elsa Kay Steinback, *Sweet Peas and a White Bridge on Lake George when Steam was King* (Sylvan Beach, N.Y.: North County Books, 1974), 89.

20. Lord, op. cit., *Stories of Lake George Fact and Fancy*, 106.

21. Lord, op. cit., *Still More Stories of Lake George Fact and Fancy*, 145.

Additional Reading

Alan Mapes, "A Paddle from Huletts Landing," *Adirondack Sports and Fitness* (June 2009).

Warner Bay

1. Thomas Reeves Lord, *More Stories of Lake George Fact and Fancy* (Pemberton, N.J.: Pinelands Press, 1994), 62.

2. Thomas Reeves Lord, *Stories of Lake George Fact and Fancy* (Pemberton, N.J.: Pinelands Press, 1987), 36.

3. Thomas Reeves Lord, *Still More Stories of Lake George Fact and Fancy* (Pemberton, N.J.: Pinelands Press, 1999), 76.

4. Lord, op. cit., *Stories of Lake George Fact and Fancy*, 35.

5. Lord, op. cit., *Still More Stories of Lake George Fact and Fancy*, 80.

6. Lord, op. cit., *Stories of Lake George Fact and Fancy*, 37.

7. Frank Leonbruno with Ginger Henry, *Lake George Reflections: Island History and Lore* (Fleischmanns, N.Y.: Purple Mountain Press, 1998), 41.

8. Wallace E. Lamb, *Lake George: Facts and Anecdotes* (Bolton Landing, N.Y.: n.p., 1934), 44.

9. Leonbruno, op. cit., 40.

10. Lord, op. cit., *Still More Stories of Lake George Fact and Fancy*, 70.

11. Lamb, op. cit., 44.

12. Leonbruno, op. cit., 44.

13. Lord, op. cit., *Stories of Lake George Fact and Fancy*, 33.

14. Ibid., 34; Lamb, op. cit., 39.

15. lakegeorgeassociation.org/.../lake_saving_projects_descriptions.htm.

16. Lord, op. cit., *More Stories of Lake George Fact and Fancy*, 60.

Dunham Bay

1. Wallace E. Lamb, *Lake George: Facts and Anecdotes* (Bolton Landing, N.Y.: n.p., 1934), 39; Thomas Reeves Lord, *More Stories of Lake George Fact and Fancy* (Pemberton, N.J.: Pinelands Press, 1994), 52.

2. fundforlakegeorge.org/index.asp?lg=1andw...r...

3. "Dunham Bay," *Adirondack Life* vol. 4, no. 4 (Fall 1973), 51. A great photo of the bay can be seen on page 50.

4. Thomas Reeves Lord, *Stories of Lake George Fact and Fancy* (Pemberton, N.J.: Pinelands Press, 1987), 33.

5. Ibid, 27.

Additional Reading

Michael Carpenter and Roger Fulton, *25 Flatwater Kayak and Canoe Trips in the Lake George, N.Y. Region* (Glens Falls, N.Y.: Glens Falls Printing, 2006), 35–37.

Glen Lake

1. recreation.queensbury.net/index.php?option...glen-lake...

2. Robert L. Eddy, *Queensbury's Heritage: Notes and Quotes on Queensbury's History and Picturesque and Historic Homes of Queensbury* (n.p., 1986), 12. Eddy cites Dr. A. W. Holden as his source.

3. ny-glenlake.org.

4. Ibid.

5. Ibid.

Fourth Lake Campgrounds

1. dec.ny.gov/outdoor/24480.html.

2. Russell Dunn, *Adventures around the Great Sacandaga Lake* (Utica, N.Y.: Nicholas K. Burns, 2002), 90; firstwilderness.com/lake/Luzerne.

Halfway Creek
  1. On-site historical marker.
  2. On-site historical marker.
  3. Wallace E. Lamb, *Lake George: Facts and Anecdotes* (Bolton Landing, N.Y.: n.p., 1934), 37.
  4. On-site historical marker.

Saratoga Region
Saratoga Lake
  1. Richard MacDonald, "Paddling Saratoga Lake and Environs," *Adirondack Sports and Fitness* (May 2002).
  2. Frank Oppel, ed., "Saratoga Springs (1876)," *New York: Tales of the Empire State* (Secaucus, N.J.: Castle, 1988), 140.
  3. brownbeach.com.
  4. Chris Carola, Beverly Mastrianni, and Michael L. Noonan, *George S. Bolster's Saratoga Springs* (Saratoga Springs, N.Y.: The Historical Society of Saratoga Springs, 1990), 144.
  5. agilitynut.com/carousels/ny2.html.
  6. Evelyn Barrett Britten, *Chronicles of Saratoga* (Saratoga Springs, N.Y.: Evelyn Barrett Britten, 1959), 154.
  7. Edward R. Gazda, *Place Names in New York* (Schenectady, N.Y.: Gazda Associates, 1997), 70.
  8. Nathaniel Bartlett Sylvester, *History of Saratoga County New York with Illustrations and Biographical Sketches of some of its Prominent Men and Pioneers* (Philadelphia: Everts and Ensign, 1878), 15.
  9. Carola, op. cit., 149.
  10. Ibid, 146, 148, 149.
  11. R. F. Dearborn, *Saratoga Illustrated: A complete Description of the American Watering Place* (Troy, N.Y.: The Northern News Company, 1872), 108.
  12. Britten, op. cit., 158.
  13. Ibid., 158.
  14. Oppel, op. cit., 140.
  15. brownsbeach.com.
  16. Britten, op. cit., 161.
  17. Carola, op. cit., 145.
  18. agilitynut.com/carousels/ny2.html.

Lake Lonely
  1. William L. Stone, *Reminiscences of Saratoga and Ballston* (New York: Virtue and Vorston, 1875), 155.
  2. *Saratoga Illustrated: The Visitor's Guide to Saratoga Springs* (New York: Taintor Bros, Merrill and Co., 1876), 93.
  3. saratogaplan.org/np-ramsdillpark.html.

Moreau Lake

1. Claire K. Schmitt and Judith Wolk, *Natural Areas of Saratoga County, New York* (Niskayuna, N.Y.: The Environmental Clearinghouse of Schenectady, 1998), 71; Bill Bailey, *New York State Parks: A Guide to New York State Parks* (Saginaw, Mich.: Glovebox Guidebooks of America, 1997), 286.

2. Bailey, op. cit., 291.

3. Michael Carpenter and Roger Fulton, *25 Flatwater Kayak and Canoe Trips in the Lake George, N.Y. Region* (Glens Falls, N.Y.: Glens Falls Printing, 2006), 1.

4. Violet B. Dunn, ed., *Saratoga County Heritage* (Saratoga County, N.Y.: Saratoga County, 1974), 436; Edward R. Gazda, *Place Names in New York: Why are they so called?* (Schenectady, N.Y.: Gazda Associations, 1998), 53.

Lake Desolation

1. wikimapia.org/1998360/Lake-Desolation.

2. Ron Feulner, local historian and author.

3. lakedesolation.com/_wsn/page11.html.

Round Lake

1. James H. Stoller, *Geological Excursions: A Guide to Localities in the Region of Schenectady and the Mohawk Valley and the Vicinity of Saratoga Springs* (Schenectady, N.Y.: Union Book Co., 1932), 39.

2. Alan Mapes, "Three Quiet Lakes: Paddling Small Waters in the Capital Region," *Adirondack Sports and Fitness* (Sept.–Oct. 2008), 11.

3. Mary Hesson, David J. Rogowski, and Marianne Comfort, *Round Lake: Little Village in the Grove* (Round Lake, N.Y.: Round Lake Publications, 1998), 90.

4. rootsweb.com.

5. Violet B. Dunn, ed., *Saratoga County Heritage* (Saratoga County, N.Y.: Saratoga County, 1974), 417.

6. Hesson, op. cit., 9–12.

7. Ibid, 84.

8. Ibid, 90–91.

9. Ibid, 90.

10. Ibid, 84.

11. Mary Hesson, "The History of the Village of Round Lake," *Town of Malta Bicentennial Booklet: 1802–2002* (Malta, N.Y.: Town of Malta, 2002), pages unnumbered.

Ballston Lake

1. James H. Stoller, *Geological Excursions: A Guide to Localities in the Region of Schenectady and the Mohawk Valley and the Vicinity of Saratoga Springs* (Schenectady, N.Y.: Union Book Co., 1932), 35.

2. johnnymilleradventures.com.

3. johnnymilleradventures.com.

4. Stoller, op. cit., 38 and 39.

5. Katherine Q. Briaddy, *Images of America: Around Ballston Lake* (Dover, N.H.: Arcadia Publishing, 1997), 19; Larry Hart, *Schenectady's Golden Era (Between 1880–1930)* 3rd ed. (Scotia, N.Y.: Old Dorp Books, 1974). A photograph of the Comanche is shown on page 62, along with a second picture showing the entrance to Forest Park.

6. John L. Scherer, *Images of America: Clifton Park* (Dover, N.H.: Arcadia Publishing, 1996), 97; William R. Washington and Patricia S. Smith, *Crossroads and Canals: The History of Clifton Park, Saratoga County, New York* (1975; reprint, Albany, N.Y.: Fort Orange Press, 1985), 108.

7. Briaddy, op. cit., 89.

8. Larry Hart, *Tales of Old Schenectady. Vol. II. The Changing Scene* (Scotia, N.Y.: Old Dorp Books, 1977), 54; Scherer, op. cit., 118.

9. Briaddy, op. cit., 69.

10. Ibid., 18.

11. Violet B. Dunn, ed., *Saratoga County Heritage* (Saratoga, N.Y.: Saratoga County, 1974), 220; Edward F. Grose, *Centennial History of the Village of Ballston Spa, including the towns of Ballston and Milton* (New York: The Ballston Journal, 1907). On page 12 can be seen a line drawing of the McDonald homestead.

12. johnnymilleradventures.com.

13. Dunn, op. cit., 220.

14. en.wikipedia.org/wiki/Ballston.

Kayaderosseras Creek: Upper Section

1. Mrs. J. B. VanDerwerker, *Early Days in Eastern Saratoga County* (Interlaken, N.Y.: Empire State Books, 1994), 42.

2. Kayaderosseras Creek Canoe and Kayak Trail, saratogaplan.org/trail_kayaderosseras.html.

3. Evelyn Barrett Britten, *Chronicles of Saratoga* (Saratoga Springs, N.Y.: Evelyn Barrett Britten, 1959), 264.

Kayaderosseras Creek: Lower Section

1. Kiosk.

Fish Creek: Saratoga Lake to Grangerville Dam

1. Mrs. J. B. VanDerwerker, *Early Days in Eastern Saratoga County* (Interlaken, N.Y.: Empire State Books, 1994), 30.

2. Walter F. Burmeister, *Appalachian Waters 2: The Hudson River and its Tributaries* (Oakton, Va.: Appalachian Books, 1974), 114.

3. Violet Dunn, ed., *Saratoga County Heritage* (Saratoga, N.Y.: Saratoga County, 1974), 479.

Additional Reading

Kathie Armstrong and Chet Harvey, eds., *Canoe and Kayak Guide: East-Central New York State* (Lake George, N.Y.: Adirondack Mountain Club, 2003), 134–139.

Cossayuna Lake

1. lakelubbers.com/cossayuna-lake-893.

2. Washington County Planning Department for the Washington County Planning Board, *An Introduction to Historic Resources in Washington County, N.Y.* (Utica, N.Y.: Dodge-Graphic Press, 1976), 64.

3. greenwichny.org/history/index.cfm.

4. cossayuna.com/history.htm.

Carter's Pond State Wildlife Management Area

1. dec.ny.gov/outdoor/24402.html; ny.audubon.org/advocate/2003winter/page4.pdf; dec.ny.gov/enb2002/20021002/not0.html; *Birding New York's Hudson-Mohawk Region* (Delmar, N.Y.: Hudson-Mohawk Bird Club, 1996). On pages 271–277 the authors mention the variety of birds that can be seen by paddlers setting out into the marshlands.

Great Sacandaga Lake and Environs
Introduction

1. Phil Brown, *Longstreet Highroad Guide to the New York Adirondacks* (Atlanta, Ga.: Highstreet Press, 1999), 164.

DEC North Broadalbin State Boat Launch

1. *The Great Sacandaga Lake: 1991* (n.p., 1991), 44. A collection of historic markers around the Great Sacandaga Lake, including one about Frenchman's Creek, is reproduced in this book.

2. Russell Dunn, *Adventures around the Great Sacandaga Lake* (Utica, N.Y.: Nicholas K. Burns Publishing, 2002), 3; Roadside historic marker near Hans Creek on Rte. 110.

3. Larry Hart, *The Sacandaga Story: A Valley of Yesteryear* (Schenectady, N.Y.: n.p., 1967), 24.

DEC Northampton Beach Campground

1. Kenneth B. Shaw, *Northampton, Then and Now: A Pictorial History* (Northampton, N.Y.: Northville-Northampton Historical Society, 1975), 90.

2. Larry Hart, *The Sacandaga Story: A Valley of Yesteryear* (Schenectady, N.Y.: n.p., 1967), 29.

DEC Northville State Boat Launch

1. Larry Hart, *The Sacandaga Story: A Valley of Yesteryear* (Schenectady, N.Y.: n.p., 1967), 75.

2. Ibid., 73.

DEC Saratoga County State Boat Launch

1. Russell Dunn, *Adventures around the Great Sacandaga Lake* (Utica, N.Y.: Nicholas K. Burns Publishing, 2002), 28–29; Larry Hart, *The Sacandaga Story: A Valley of Yesteryear* (Schenectady, N.Y.: n.p., 1967), 6.

Conklingville Dam

1. Nancy S. Morris, *In Days Past: The History of the Town of Day, Saratoga County, New York* (Hadley, N.Y.: Greenfield Press, 1995), 16.

2. Russell Dunn, *Adventures around the Great Sacandaga Lake* (Utica, N.Y.: Nicholas K. Burns Publishing, 2002), 83; Larry Hart, *The Sacandaga Story: A Valley of Yesteryear* (Schenectady, N.Y.: n.p., 1967), 6.

Northville Lake

1. Charlotte D. Russell, *Northampton: Times Past, Times Present* (Northampton, N.Y.: n.p., 1976), 56.

2. northvilleny.com/html/village.html.

Lake Luzerne

1. townoflakeluzerne.com.

2. Lester St. John Thomas, with Evelyn Cirino Donohue and Anita Beaudette Ranado, *Timber, Tannery and Tourists: Lake Luzerne, Warren County, New York* (Lake Luzerne, N.Y.: Committee on Publication of Local History, 1979), 143.

3. townoflakeluzerne.com.

4. Historic roadside marker.

5. Thomas, op. cit., 107.

Sacandaga River: From Stewart Bridge Dam to Hudson River

1. Russell Dunn, "10,000 Years Ago," *Adventures around the Great Sacandaga Lake* (Utica, N.Y.: Nicholas K. Burns Publishing, 2002), 21–22.

2. Mabel Pitkin Shorey, *The Early History of Corinth, Once Known as Jessup's Landing* (Ballston Spa, N.Y.: The Journal Press, 1959), 37–38.

3. greenfieldpress.com/BowBridge.html.

4. Russell Dunn, "The Buoys of Summer," *Adirondack Life Annual Guide 1995*, 82–87. An earlier article entitled "Tubing the Sacandaga" by Philip C. Johnson appeared in the July/August 1982 issue of *Adirondack Life*, 44–45.

Additional Reading

Kathie Armstrong and Chet Harvey, eds., *Canoe and Kayak Guide: East-Central New York State* (Lake George, N.Y.: Adirondack Mountain Club, 2003), 106–111.

Dennis Squires, *New York Exposed: The Whitewater State. Volume 2* (Margaretville, N.Y.: A White Water Outlaw Publishing, 2003), 185. Squires describes a paddle down the lower, final portion of the Sacandaga River from the perspective of a white-water kayaker.

Mal Provost, "Surf's up!", *Adirondack Explorer* vol. 12, no. 2 (March/April 2010), 18–19.

Champlain Canal & Environs:
From Stillwater to Fort Edward
Introduction
1. New York State Canal Water Trail brochure.

East Shore: Hudson River & Champlain Canal
Champlain Canal Lock C-4
1. The Saratogian, *Saratoga County, New York: Our County and its People* (Boston: The Boston History Company, 1890), 351.

2. Violet B. Dunn, ed., *Saratoga County Heritage* (Saratoga, N.Y.: Saratoga County, 1974), 488.

3. en.wikipedia.org/wicki/Hoosic_River.

4. orionline.org/pages/ogn/vieworg.cfm?action+oneandogn_org_ID=619 andviewby=name.

5. Francis P. Kimball, *The Capital Region of New York State: Crossroads of Empire* vol. 2 (New York: Lewis Historical Publishing Company, 1942), 316.

6. Arthur G. Adams, *The Hudson River Guidebook* 2nd ed. (New York: Fordham University Press, 1996), 285.

7. Claire K. Schmitt, Norton G. Miller, Warren F. Broderick, John T. Keenan and William D. Niemi, *Natural Areas of Rensselaer County, New York* 2nd ed. (Schenectady/Troy, N.Y.: The Rensselaer-Taconic Land Conservancy and Environmental Clearinghouse of Schenectady, 2002), 32.

8. dmna.state.ny.us/forts/fortsQ_S/Stillwaterblockhouse.htm; on-site historic marker.

Clarks Mills Lower Dam, Access #1
1. greenwichny.org/history/index.cfm.

2. Washington County Planning Department for the Washington County Planning Board, *An Introduction to Historic Resources in Washington County, N.Y.* (Utica, N.Y.: Dodge-Graphic Press, 1976), 65.

3. Raymond C. Houghton, *A Revolutionary Week along the Historic Champlain Canal* (Delmar, N.Y.: Cyber Haus, 2003), 39.

Champlain Canal above Lock C-6
1. Washington County Planning Department for the Washington County Planning Board, *An Introduction to Historic Resources in Washington County, N.Y.* (Utica, N.Y.: Dodge-Graphic Press, 1976), 50.

2. Historic marker near Fort Miller Road.

Moses Kill
    1. tug44.org/canal.history/moses-kill-aqueduct.
    2. Ibid.

Fort Edward Public Dock
    1. Raymond C. Houghton, *A Revolutionary Week along the Historic Champlain Canal* (Delmar, N.Y.: Cyber Haus, 2003), 47.
    2. Washington County Planning Department for the Washington County Planning Board, *An Introduction to Historic Resources in Washington County, N.Y.* (Utica, N.Y.: Dodge-Graphic Press, 1976), 93.

West Shore: Hudson River and Champlain Canal
Stillwater Bridge
    1. Stillwater.org>History.
    2. Stillwater.org>village-government.
    3. history.rays-place.com/ny/stillwater-ny.htm, from *History of Stillwater, N.Y.* (1899).

River Road Access
    1. Tom Delaney and Nora Delaney, Dutch scholars.
    2. *History of Washington County, N.Y.: Some Chapters in the History of the Town of Easton, N.Y.* (Washington County, N.Y.: Washington County Historical Society, 1959), 15.
    3. Wallace E. Lamb, *Lake Champlain and Lake George* (New York: The American Historical Company, 1940), 272.

Fishing Access Site #1
    1. Arthur G. Adams, *The Hudson River Guidebook* 2nd ed. (New York: Fordham University Press, 1996), 286; Benson J. Lossing, *The Hudson: From the Wilderness to the Sea* (1866; reprint, Hensonville, N.Y.: Black Dome Press, 2000), 96.
    2. Violet B. Dunn, ed., *Saratoga County Heritage* (Saratoga County, N.Y.: Saratoga County, 1974), 477.
    3. darrp.noaa.gov/northeast/hudson/habitats.html.

Schuylerville Boat Launch
    1. villageofschuylerville.org/Areas-of.../Schuyler-House.asp.
    2. Peter Lourie, *River of Mountains: A Canoe Journey down the Hudson* (Syracuse, N.Y.: Syracuse University Press, 1995), 212.
    3. U.S. Army Corps of Engineers in Vermont, *Water Resources Development: New England Division* (Waltham, Mass.: Department of Army New England Division, Corps of Engineers, 1979), 39.
    4. dec.state.ny.us.
    5. Schuylerville Yacht Basin brochure.

6. Ibid.

7. Ibid.

8. Thomas X. Grasso, *Champlain Canal: Watervliet to Whitehall. Field Trip, Saturday, October 5, 1985* (Rochester, N.Y.: Canal Society of New York State, 1985), 11.

Champlain Canal Lock C-5, Upriver

1. villageofschuylerville.org/Areas-of-Interest/Parks-and-Recreation.asp.

2. Raymond C. Houghton, *A Revolutionary Week along the Historic Champlain Canal* (Delmar, N.Y.: Cyber Haus, 2003), 38.

Former West Shore Marina

1. epa.gov/hudson/sed_sampling_fs07_04.htm.

Hudson River: From Fort Edward to Thurman Station
Rogers Island

1. Arthur G. Adams, *The Hudson River Guidebook* 2nd ed. (New York.: Fordham University Press, 1996), 292.

2. Washington County Planning Department for the Washington County Planning Board, *An Introduction to Historic Resources in Washington County, N.Y.* (Utica, N.Y.: Dodge-Graphic Press, 1976), 92.

3. Ibid., 48.

4. Raymond C. Houghton, *A Revolutionary Week along the Historic Champlain Canal* (Delmar, N.Y.: Cyber Haus, 2003), 44.

5. Washington County Planning Department for the Washington County Planning Board, op. cit., 48.

6. Stephen P. Stanne, Roger G. Panetta and Brian E. Forist, *The Hudson: An Illustrated Guide to the Living River* (New Brunswick, N.J.: Rutgers University Press, 1996), 171.

Additional Reading

David R. Starbuck, *Rangers and Redcoats on the Hudson: Exploring the Past on Rogers Island, the Birthplace of the U.S. Army Rangers* (Lebanon, N.H.: University Press of New England, 2004).

Glens Falls Feeder Canal: Introduction

1. Katie Armstrong and Chet Harvey, eds., *Canoe and Kayak Guide: East-Central New York State* (Lake George, N.Y.: Adirondack Mountain Club, 2003), 192, 194.

2. Thomas X. Grasso, *Champlain Canal: Watervliet to Whitehall. Field Trip, Saturday, October 5, 1985* (Rochester, N.Y.: Canal Society of New York State, 1985), 15.

3. Betty Lou Bailey, "The Amazing Hudson-Sacandaga Settlement," *Adirondac* vol. 64, no. 6 (Nov./Dec. 2000), 22.

Additional Reading

Barbara McMartin, "Canal Zones: Two man-made waterways offering diverting canoe trips," *Adirondack Life* vol. 27, no. 2 (March/April 1996), 40–43. A trip down the Feeder Canal is nicely described, with superb visuals.

Barbara McMartin, *Fun on Flatwater: An Introduction to Adirondack Canoeing* (Utica, N.Y.: North Country Books, 1995).

Michael LaCross, "The Glens Falls Feeder Canal: Historical Past, Recreational Future," *Adirondac* vol. 54, no. 5 (June 1990), 7. The writer talks about the Glens Falls Feeder Canal Alliance and the work they have done to bring the canal back to life.

Feeder Canal from Richardson Street Access

1. aarch.org/archives/pastnews/Vol.12-2win03-04.pdf.
2. On-site historic marker.
3. adirondack.net/orgs/feedercanal/index.html.
4. Gwen Palmer, Bob Boyle, and Stan Malecki, *Images of America: Glens Falls* (Charleston, S.C.: Arcadia Publishing, 2004). On page 11 is a photograph of stacks of lumber next to the canal.
5. feedercanal.com/FeederCanalAlliance3.htm.
6. Wayne Wright, ed., *"Listening In" Memories of Glens Falls 1755–1931* (Glens Falls, N.Y.: Adirondack Press, 2009), 262.
7. On-site historic plaque.

Murray Street Access

1. Walter F. Burmeister, *Appalachian Waters 2: The Hudson River and its Tributaries* (Oakton, Va.: Appalachian Books, 1974), 49; Russell Dunn, *Hudson Valley Waterfall Guide: From Saratoga and the Capital Region to the Highlands and Palisades* (Hensonville, N.Y.: Black Dome Press, 2005), 49.
2. Gwen Palmer, Bob Boyle, and Stan Malecki, *Images of America: Glens Falls* (Charleston, S.C.: Arcadia Publishing, 2004). Turn-of-the-century photographs of Cooper's Cave can be seen on pages 14 & 15.

Hudson River Park

1. Michael Carpenter and Roger Fulton, *25 Flatwater Kayak and Canoe Trips in the Lake George, N.Y. Region* (Glens Falls, N.Y.: Glens Falls Printing, 2006), 22.
2. queensbury.net/Recreation/HudsonRiverPrk.htm.
3. Robert L. Eddy, *Queensbury's Heritage: Notes and Quotes on Queensbury's History and Picturesque and Historic Homes of Queensbury* (n.p., 1986), 10.
4. Kathie Armstrong and Chet Harvey, eds., *Canoe and Kayak Guide: East-Central New York State* (Lake George, N.Y.: Adirondack Mountain Club, 2003), 45.
5. Benson Lossing, *The Hudson: from the Wilderness to the Sea* (1866; reprint, Hensonville, N.Y.: Black Dome Press, 2000), 65–66.
6. Thomas Reeves Lord, *Still More Stories of Lake George Fact and Fancy*

(Pemberton, N.J.: Pinelands Press, 1999), 29.

    7. Eddy, op. cit., 10.

    8. Kiosk at Hudson Pointe Nature Preserve. Approaching by land, the preserve can be reached by taking exit 18 of the Adirondack Northway (I-87), heading west on Corinth Road for 2.0 miles, turning left onto Hudson Pointe Blvd., and proceeding 0.8 mile. The parking area for the preserve is on the left and is clearly marked.

Upper Hudson River Boat Launch

    1. Sue Wilder, Director, Adirondack Folk School.

    2. Roland Van Zandt, *Chronicles of the Hudson: Three Centuries of Travel and Adventure* (1971; reprint, Hensonville, N.Y.: Black Dome Press, 1992), 261. A description of Rockwell Falls (also called Hadley Falls) and the gorge below the falls is provided by Charles Farnham in his 1880 account, "Running the Rapids of the Upper Hudson."

    3. firstwilderness.com/corinth.

    4. On-site historic markers.

    5. Roadside marker.

    6. Mabel Pitkin Shorey, *The Early History of Corinth, Once Known as Jessup's Landing* (Ballston Spa, N.Y.: The Journal Press, 1959), 65; Russell Dunn, *Hudson Valley Waterfall Guide: From Saratoga and the Capital Region to the Highlands and Palisades* (Hensonville, N.Y.: Black Dome Press, 2005), 45.

Hudson River Recreation Area

    1. Phil Brown, *Longstreet Highroad Guide to the New York Adirondacks* (Atlanta, Ga.: Highstreet Press, 1999), 185.

    2. placewiki.com/viewplace_detail.php?placeID=255.

Sherman Island Boat Launch

    1. osiny.org/site/PageServer?pagename...Spier_Falls.

    2. William H. Brown, ed., *History of Warren County, New York* (Glens Falls, N.Y.: Board of Supervisors of Warren County, 1963), 97.

    3. sunyacc.edu/.../interview_geraldine_dowden_holmquist.htm.

    4. On-site kiosk.

Spier Falls Boat Launch

    1. On-site kiosk; William H. Brown, ed., *History of Warren County, New York* (Glens Falls, N.Y.: Board of Supervisors of Warren County, 1963), 93–96, provides additional information on the dam. Other figures have been given for the size of the dam. In Ann Breen Metcalfe's *The Schroon River: A History of an Adirondack Valley and its People* (Lake George, N.Y.: Warren County Historical Society, 2000), 42, the dam is described as 157 feet high, 115 feet thick at its base, 22 feet thick at its top, and 1,570 feet long.

2. Violet B. Dunn, ed., *Saratoga County Heritage* (Saratoga County, N.Y.: Saratoga County, 1974), 307.

Hadley Canoe Take-out

1. Historic roadside marker.

2. Russell Dunn, *Adventures around the Great Sacandaga Lake* (Utica, N.Y.: Nicholas K. Burns Publishing, 2002), 105; Mabel Pitkin Shorey, *The Early History of Corinth, Once Known as Jessup's Landing* (Ballston Spa, N.Y.: The Journal Press, 1959). There are different spellings to Native American words. Shorey spells the marriage of the two rivers *Tio-sa-yoh-do*.

Bibliography

Adams, Arthur G. *The Hudson River Guidebook*. 2nd ed. New York: Fordham University Press, 1996.

Allen, R. L. *Hand-book of Saratoga, and Strangers' Guide*. New York: Arthur & Co., 1859.

Armstrong, Kathie, and Chet Harvey, eds. *Canoe and Kayak Guide: East-Central New York State*. Lake George, N.Y.: Adirondack Mountain Club, 2003.

Bailey, Betty Lou. "The Amazing Hudson-Sacandaga Settlement." *Adirondac*, vol. 64, no. 6 (Nov/Dec 2000).

Bailey, Bill. *New York State Parks: A Guide*. Saginaw, Mich.: Glovebox Guidebooks of America, 1997.

Bellico, Russell P. *Chronicles of Lake George: Journeys in War and Peace*. Fleischmanns, N.Y.: Purple Mountain Press, 1995.

Bowie, Mark. "Island Treasures." *2006 Outings Guide to the Adirondacks*. Jay, N.Y.: Adirondack Life Magazine, 2006.

Briaddy, Katherine Q. *Images of America: Around Ballston Lake*. Dover, N.H.: Arcadia Publishing, 1997.

———. *Images of America: Around Burnt Hills*. Charleston, S.C.: Arcadia Publishing, 1998.

Britten, Evelyn Bassett. *Chronicles of Saratoga*. Saratoga Springs, N.Y.: Evelyn Basset Britten, 1959.

Brown, Phil. *Longstreet Highroad Guide to the New York Adirondacks*. Atlanta, Ga.: Highstreet Press, 1999.

Brown, William H., ed. *History of Warren County, New York*. Glens Falls, N.Y.: Board of Supervisors of Warren County, 1963.

Buckell, Betty Ahearn. *No Dull Days at Huletts with Reminiscences of Henry W. Buckell*. N.p., 1984.

Burmeister, Walter F. *Appalachian Waters 2: The Hudson River and its Tributaries*. Oakton, Va.: Appalachian Books, 1974.

Capossela, Jim. *Fishing in the Catskills: From the Waters of the Capital District to the Delaware River* 2nd ed. Woodstock, Vt.: Backcountry Publications, 1992.

Carola, Chris, Beverly Mastrianni, and Michael L. Noonan. *George S. Bolster's Saratoga Springs*. Saratoga Springs, N.Y.: The Historical Society of Saratoga Springs, 1990.

Carpenter, Michael, and Roger Fulton. *25 Flatwater Kayak & Canoe Trips in the Lake George, NY Region*. Glens Falls, N.Y.: Glens Falls Printing, 2006.

Citizens Sesquicentennial Committee. *Pathways of Time: Schenectady 1798–1984*. Schenectady, N.Y.: City of Schenectady, 1948.

Cullen, Jim, John Mylroie, and Art Palmer. *Karst Hydrogeology and Geomorphology of Eastern New York*. N.p., 1979.

Dearborn, R. F. *Saratoga Illustrated. A complete Description of the American Watering*

Place. Troy, N.Y.: The Northern News Company, 1872.

"Dunham Bay." *Adirondack Life,* vol. 4, no. 4 (fall 1973).

Dunn, Russell. *Adventures around the Great Sacandaga Lake.* Utica, N.Y.: Nicholas K. Burns Publishing, 2002.

———. "The Buoys of Summer," *Adirondack Life Annual Guide 1995.*

———. *Hudson Valley Waterfall Guide: From Saratoga and the Capital Region to the Highlands and Palisades.* Hensonville, N.Y.: Black Dome Press, 2005.

———. *Mohawk Region Waterfall Guide: From the Capital District to Cooperstown & Syracuse.* Hensonville, N.Y.: Black Dome Press, 2007.

———. "Walk on the Water," *Adirondack Life,* vol. 25, no. 5 (July/August, 1994).

———. "Workhorses of the Industrial Revolution: Hudson River Waterfalls." *New York State Conservationist,* vol. 64, no. 5 (April 2010).

Dunn, Russell, and Barbara Delaney. *Trails with Tales: History Hikes through the Capital Region, Saratoga, Berkshires, Catskills & Hudson Valley.* Hensonville, N.Y.: Black Dome Press, 2006.

Dunn, Violet B., ed. *Saratoga County Heritage.* Saratoga County, N.Y.: Saratoga County, 1974.

Eddy, Robert L. *Queensbury's Heritage: Notes & Quotes on Queensbury's History and Picturesque and Historic Homes of Queensbury.* N.p, 1986.

Gates, William Preston. *Millionaires' Row on Lake George, New York.* Lake George, N.Y.: W. P. Gates Publishing Company, 2008.

Gazda, Edward R. *Place Names in New York: Why are they so called?* Schenectady, N.Y.: Gazda Associates, 1997.

Godfrey, Fred G. *The Champlain Canal: Mules to Tugboats.* Monroe, N.Y.: LRA Inc., 1994.

Grasso, Thomas X. *Champlain Canal: Watervliet to Whitehall. Field Trip, Saturday, October 5, 1985.* Rochester, N.Y.: Canal Society of New York State, 1985.

The Great Sacandaga Lake: 1991. Booklet.

Grose, Edward F., and John C. Booth. *Centennial History of the Village of Ballston Spa, including the towns of Ballston and Milton.* New York: The Ballston Journal, 1907.

Hart, Larry. *The Sacandaga Story: A Valley of Yesteryear.* Schenectady, N.Y.: n.p., 1967.

———. *Schenectady's Golden Era (Between 1880–1930).* 3rd ed. Scotia, N.Y.: Old Dorp Books, 1974.

———.*Tales of Old Schenectady.* Vol. II. The Changing Scene. Scotia, N.Y.: Old Dorp Books, 1977.

Henkel-Karras, Erica. *Postcard History Series: Lake George.* Charleston, S.C.: Arcadia Publishing, 2005.

Hesson, Mary. "The History of the Village of Round Lake." *Town of Malta Bicentennial Booklet: 1802–2002.* Malta, N.Y.: Town of Malta, 2002.

Hesson, Mary, David J. Rogowski, and Marianne Comfort. *Round Lake: Little Village in the Grove.* Round Lake, N.Y.: Round Lake Publications, 1998.

Higgins, Dan. "Round Lake Bypass project progressing," *Times Union*. January 27, 2008.

Hine, C. G. *Albany to Tappen: The West Bank of the Hudson River*. 1906. Reprint, Astoria, N.Y.: J. C. & A. L. Fawcett, n.d.

History of Washington County, NY: Some Chapters in the History of the Town of Easton, NY. Washington County, N.Y.: Washington County Historical Society, 1959.

Houghton, Raymond C. *A Revolutionary Week along the Historic Champlain Canal*. Delmar, N.Y.: Cyber Haus, 2003.

Hyde, Louis Fiske. *History of Glens Falls, New York, and its Settlements*. Glens Falls, N.Y.: n.p., 1936.

Jermanok, Stephen. "Island Cruising: Exploring Lake George's nooks and narrows." *1998 Adirondack Life Annual Guide to the Adirondacks*.

Johnson, Philip C. "Tubing the Sacandaga." *Adirondack Life*, vol.13, no. 4 (July/August 1982).

Joki, Robert. *Saratoga Lost: Images of Victorian America*. Hensonville, N.Y.: Black Dome Press, 1998.

Kamler, Kenneth. *Surviving the Extremes: What happens to the body and mind at the limits of human endurance*. London: Penguin Books, 2005.

Kimball, Francis P. *The Capital Region of New York State: Crossroads of Empire*, vol. 2. New York: Lewis Historical Publishing Company, 1942.

LaCross, Michael. "The Glens Falls Feeder Canal: Historical Past, Recreational Future." *Adirondac*, vol. 54. no. 5 (June 1990).

Lamb, Wallace E. *Lake Champlain and Lake George*. New York: The American Historical Company, 1940.

Loding, Paul R. *Images of America: Kingsbury and Hudson Falls*. Charleston, S.C.: Arcadia Publishing, 2001.

Lord, Thomas Reeves. *More Stories of Lake George Fact and Fancy*. Pemberton, N.J.: Pinelands Press, 1994.

———. *Still More Stories of Lake George Fact and Fancy*. Pemberton, N.J.: Pinelands Press, 1999.

———. *Stories of Lake George Fact and Fancy*. Pemberton, N.J.: Pinelands Press, 1987.

Lossing, Benson J. *The Hudson: From the Wilderness to the Sea*. 1866. Reprint, Hensonville, N.Y.: Black Dome Press, 2000.

Lourie, Peter. *Rivers of Mountains: A Canoe Journey down the Hudson*. Syracuse, N.Y.: Syracuse University Press, 1995.

MacDonald, Richard. "Double-blade Runner: A Sea Kayaker's tour of Lake George." *1991 Adirondack Life Guide to the Adirondacks*.

———. "Paddling Saratoga Lake & Environs." *Adirondack Sports & Fitness* (May 2002).

Mapes, Alan. "Paddling for Exercise." *Adirondack Sports & Fitness* (July 2010).

———. "Three Quiet Lakes: Paddling Small Waters in the Capital Region."

Adirondack Sports & Fitness (September/October 2008).

McMartin, Barbara. "Canal Zones: Two man-made waterways offering diverting canoe trips." *Adirondack Life*, vol. 27, no. 2 (March/April 1996).

———. *Fun on Flatwater: An Introduction to Adirondack Canoeing.* Utica, N.Y.: North Country Books, 1995.

Metcalfe, Ann Breen. *The Schroon River: A History of an Adirondack Valley and its People.* Lake George, N.Y.: Warren County Historical Society, 2000.

Morris, Nancy S. *In Days Past: The History of the Town of Day, Saratoga County, New York.* Hadley, N.Y.: Greenfield Press, 1995.

Nature Trail: Weare C. Little Memorial Preserve. Brochure. Education Committee, 1999.

Oppel, Frank, ed. "Saratoga Springs (1876)." *New York: Tales of the Empire State.* Secaucus, N.J.: Castle, 1988.

Our Heritage: Town of Berne, Albany County, New York. Berne, N.Y.: Town of Berne, 1977.

Palmer, Gwen, Bob Boyle, and Stan Malecki. *Images of America: Glens Falls.* Charleston, S.C.: Arcadia Publishing, 2004.

Podskoch, Marty. *Adirondack Stories: Historical Sketches.* Colchester, Ct.: Podskoch Press, 2007.

Provost, Mal. "Surf's up!" *Adirondack Explorer*, vol. 12, no. 2 (March/April 2010).

Russell, Charlotte D. *Northampton: Times Past, Times Present.* 1976. Reprint, Northampton, N.Y.: 1997.

Saratoga Illustrated: The Visitor's Guide to Saratoga Springs. New York: Taintor Bros., Merrill & Co., 1876.

The Saratogian. *Saratoga County New York: Our County and its People.* Boston: The Boston History Company, 1890.

Scherer, John L. *Images of America: Clifton Park.* Dover, N.H.: Arcadia Publishing, 1996.

Schmitt, Claire K., and Judith Wolk. *Natural Areas of Saratoga County, New York.* Niskayuna, N.Y.: The Environmental Clearinghouse of Schenectady, 1998.

Schmitt, Claire K., Norton G. Miller, Warren F. Broderick, John T. Keenan, and William D. Niemi. *Natural Areas of Rensselaer County, New York.* 2nd ed. Schenectady/Troy, N.Y.: The Rensselaer-Taconic Land Conservancy & Environmental Clearinghouse of Schenectady, 2002.

Schneider, Paul. *The Adirondacks: A History of America's First Wilderness.* New York: Henry Holt and Company, 1997.

Schueller, Gretel H. "Savoir of the islands: Caretaker rescues lake's heritage." *Adirondack Explorer*, vol. 5, no. 1 (Sept/Oct 2002).

Shaw, Kenneth B. *Northampton, Then and Now: A Pictorial History.* Northampton, N.Y.: Northville-Northampton Historical Society, 1975.

Shorey, Mabel Pitkin. *The Early History of Corinth, Once Known as Jessup's Landing.* Ballston Spa, N.Y.: The Journal Press, 1959.

Smith, H. P., ed. *History of Warren County with Illustrations and Biographical*

Sketches of some of its Prominent Men and Pioneers. Syracuse, N.Y.: D. Mason & Co., 1885.

Squires, Dennis. *New York Exposed: The Whitewater State*, vol. 2. Margaretville, N.Y.: A White Water Outlaw Publishing, 2003.

Stanne, Stephen P., Roger G. Panetta, and Brian E. Forist. *The Hudson: An Illustrated Guide to the Living River*. New Brunswick, N.J.: Rutgers University Press, 1996.

Starbuck, David R. *Rangers and Redcoats on the Hudson: Exploring the past on Rogers Island, the Birthplace of the U.S. Army Rangers*. Lebanon, N.H.: University Press of New England, 2004.

Steinback, Elsa Kay. *Sweet Peas and a White Bridge on Lake George when Steam was King*. Sylvan Beach, N.Y.: North County Books, 1974.

Stoller, James H. *Geological Excursions: A Guide to Localities in the Region of Schenectady and the Mohawk Valley and the Vicinity of Saratoga Springs*. Schenectady, N.Y.: Union Book Co., 1932.

Stone, William L. *Reminiscences of Saratoga and Ballston*. New York: Virtue & Vorston, 1875.

Thomas, Lester St. John. *Timber, Tannery and Tourists: Lake Luzerne, Warren County, New York*. Lake Luzerne, N.Y.: Committee on Publication of Local History, 1979.

Sylvester, Nathaniel Bartlett. *History of Saratoga County New York with Illustrations and Biographical Sketches of some of its Prominent Men and Pioneers*. Philadelphia: Everts & Ensign, 1878.

Township of Kingsbury. Glens Falls, N.Y.: Bicentennial Committee of the Town of Kingsbury and the Village of Hudson Falls, 1984.

"Troy: Hub of Industry." *Schenectady & Upstate New York*, vol. II, no. 3 (Fall 1989).

U.S. Army Corps of Engineers in Vermont. *Water Resources Development: New England Division*. Waltham, Mass.: Department of Army New England Division, Corps of Engineers, 1979.

VanDerwerker, J. B. *Early Days in Eastern Saratoga County*. Interlaken, N.Y.: Empire State Books, 1994.

Van Zandt, Roland. *Chronicles of the Hudson: Three Centuries of Travel and Adventure*. 1971. Reprint, Hensonville, N.Y.: Black Dome Press, 1992.

Warpaths, Wildcats and Waterfalls: A view of early times in the village of Sandy Hill and the Township of Kingsbury. Glens Falls, N.Y.: Bicentennial Committee of the Town of Kingsbury and the Village of Hudson Falls, 1984.

Washington County Planning Department. *An Introduction to Historic Resources in Washington County, N.Y.* Utica, N.Y.: Washington County Planning Board, 1976.

Wright, Wayne, ed. *"Listening In" Memories of Glens Falls 1755–1931*. Glens Falls, N.Y.: n.p., 2009.

Websites

aarch.org/archives/pastnews/Vol.12-2win03-04.pdf
adirondack.net/orgs/feedercanal/index.html
agilitynut.com/carousels/ny2.html
brownbeach.com
bulk.resource.org/gpo.gov/record/2001/2001_E00217.pdf
cossayuna.com/history.htm
darrp.noaa.gov/northeast/Hudson/habitats.html
dec.ny.gov/docs/fish_marine_pdf/annleepdmap.pdf
dec.ny.gov/docs/lands_forests_pdf/helderbergsump.pdf
dec.ny.gov/enb2002/20021002/not0.html
dec.state.ny.us
en.wikipedia.org/wiki/Ballston
epa.gov/Hudson/sed_sampling_fs07_04.htm
feedercanal.com/FeederCanalAlliance3.htm
firstwilderness.com/corinth
greenwichny.org/history/index.cfm
history.rays-place.com/ny/stillwater-ny.htm
johnnymilleradventures.com
lakedesolation.com/_wsn/page11.html
lakegeorgevillage.com/LAKE-GEORGE-HISTORY.htm
lakelubbers.com/cossayuna-lake-893
ny.audubon.org/advocate/2003winter/paged.pdf
ny-glenlake.org
nysparks.state.ny.us/parks/info.asp?parkid=116
orionline.org/pages/ogn/vieworg
osiny.org/site/PageServer?pagename...Spier_Falls
placewiki.com/viewplace_detail.php?placeID=255
queensbury.net/Recreation/HudsonRiverPrk.htm
reserveamerica.com
saratogaplan.org/np-ramsdillpark.html
stainlessrebar.com/bowbridge.html
sunyacc.edu/.../interview_geraldine_dowden_holmquist.htm
townoflakeluzerne.com
villageofschuylerville.org/Areas-of-Interest/Parks-and-Recreation.asp
villageofschuylerville.org/Areas-of.../Schuyler-House.asp
wikimapia.org/1998360/Lake-Desolation

About the Author

Russell Dunn is author of *A Kayaker's Guide to New York's Capital Region: The Hudson & Mohawk Rivers from Catskill & Hudson to Mechanicville & Cohoes to Amsterdam* (Black Dome Press, 2010)—the first in a series of guidebooks on paddling the Hudson River Valley/Capital Region/Mohawk Valley/Saratoga Springs/Lake George regions.

Dunn has written five guidebooks to the waterfalls of eastern New York State and western Massachusetts: *Adirondack Waterfall Guide: New York's Cool Cascades* (Black Dome Press, 2003); *Catskill Region Waterfall Guide: Cool Cascades of the Catskills & Shawangunks* (Black Dome Press, 2004); *Hudson Valley Waterfall Guide: From Saratoga and the Capital Region to the Highlands and Palisades* (Black Dome Press, 2005); *Mohawk Region Waterfall Guide: From the Capital District to Cooperstown and Syracuse* (Black Dome Press, 2007); and *Berkshire Region Waterfall Guide: Cool Cascades of the Berkshires & Taconics* (Black Dome Press, 2008).

Dunn is also author of *Adventures around the Great Sacandaga Lake* (Nicholas K. Burns Publishing, 2002), and coauthor with his wife, Barbara Delaney, of *Trails with Tales: History Hikes through the Capital Region, Saratoga, Berkshires, Catskills and Hudson Valley* (Black Dome Press, 2006) and *Adirondack Trails with Tales: History Hikes through the Adirondack Park and the Lake George, Lake Champlain & Mohawk Valley Regions* (2009).

Dunn has had numerous articles published in regional magazines and newspapers including *Adirondack Life, Adirondac, Hudson Valley, New York State Conservationist, Kaatskill Life, Adirondack Sports & Fitness, Adirondack Explorer, Catskill Mountain Region Guide, Glens Falls Chronicle, Northeastern Caver, Voice of the Valley, Sacandaga Times, Edinburg Newsletter,* and *Shawangunk Mountain Guide.*

Russell Dunn is a New York State-licensed guide. Together with Barbara Delaney (also a NYS-licensed guide), he leads hikes to waterfalls in the Adirondacks, Catskills, and Hudson Valley, as well as to other sites of exceptional beauty and historical uniqueness, always with the emphasis placed on history.

Dunn and Delaney have given numerous lecture & slideshow presentations to regional historical societies, libraries, museums, civic groups, organizations, and hiking clubs on a wide variety of subjects, ranging from waterfalls to natural areas of historic interest.

Dunn can be reached at rdunnwaterfalls@yahoo.com.

Index